UNITED NATIONS

UNITED NATIONS

❧ *The First Fifty Years* ❧

STANLEY MEISLER

THE ATLANTIC MONTHLY PRESS
NEW YORK

Published simultaneously in Canada
Printed in the United States of America

FIRST EDITION

Library of Congress Cataloging-in-Publication Data
Meisler, Stanley.
United Nations: the first fifty years / Stanley Meisler. — 1st ed.
Includes bibliographical references and index.
ISBN 0-87113-616-3
1. United Nations — History.   2. United Nations — Anniversaries,
etc.   I. Title.
JX1977.M442   1995   641.23 — dc20   95-30563

DESIGN BY LAURA HAMMOND HOUGH

The Atlantic Monthly Press
841 Broadway
New York, NY 10003

10 9 8 7 6 5 4 3 2 1

TO THE MEMORY OF

MY FATHER AND MOTHER

AND SARAH

Contents

A Note from the Author

As a sophomore at James Monroe High School, I was one of those, armed with a blanket, who took a bus across the Bronx one evening in 1946 to sleep outside Hunter College for a chance to see the United Nations Security Council in action. It was not a sleepless, backbreaking night. After a couple of hours, a burly but kindly New York City policeman handed us little numbered tickets and told us to go home. When we returned the next morning, we were placed into the front of the line according to our numbers.

I cannot remember much about the gymnasium that served as the site or about the discussions onstage. But I do remember some of the dignitaries that I recognized from photographs in the *New York Times* and the newspaper *PM*: a well-groomed Edward R. Stettinius Jr. with elegant white hair, an overstuffed and serious Trygve Lie, a dour, enigmatic Andrey Gromyko. The topic of the day has long escaped me. Perhaps it was Iran. But I was impressed by the interpreters who stood up after every speech to render versions in English, French, and Russian. Simultaneous interpretation had not yet arrived. At one point, Gromyko interrupted the English interpreter to correct him. I remember wondering why Gromyko bothered to speak in Russian if he knew enough English to correct the interpreter. All in all, it was a wondrous day, for we sensed that these great figures were playing history in front of us.

As a foreign correspondent many years later, I never boasted to my colleagues that I was once willing to sleep all night on the ground outside Hunter College for a glimpse of the Security Council in action. I would have been stamped as hopelessly naïve. The U.N. fell into bad repute during my two decades as a foreign correspondent from the late 1960s to the late 1980s. Reporters did not expect much from the U.N. or cover it very thoroughly. They did not go around proclaiming ties to it. The U.N., in fact, was a hypocritical irritant, especially in Africa, where I began my work. The U.N. blathered on day after day about the terrible injustice of South Africa but closed its eyes to horrors like the enervating civil war and the legions of bloated Biafran babies in Nigeria, the blatant genocide of the Hutus in Burundi, and the unabashed evil of a cunning and cruel Idi Amin in Uganda. These blights were at least as terrible as that of South Africa and, in fact, depressed me even more, for I had expected so much better of newly independent Africa.

In 1991, during the Persian Gulf War, the *Los Angeles Times* assigned me to cover the United Nations. There was a new mood. With the Cold War over, the United States and the Soviet Union (soon to split into Russia and others) could now cooperate and perhaps order the world the way some of the founders of the U.N. intended. The Security Council realized its relevance now, and the corridors rustled with confidence and tension. This mood would dissipate in a few years, but diplomats and bureaucrats would still hold on to a sense that their U.N. mattered.

There is a hoary notion, common among journalists who do not work there, that the U.N. must be a boring place. That notion comes from the stupefying image of hordes of delegates (there are now 185) droning on in interminable, insignificant speeches for home consumption. But the most important work of the U.N. takes place within the Security Council, which has fifteen members who waste little of their time speechifying. The work of the council gets done behind closed doors in many hours of wrangling, cajoling, pleading, arguing, and threatening. For better or worse, the final decisions affect the course of events in troubled zones throughout the world from Haiti to Bosnia to Somalia to El Salvador. The closed-door sessions are far from boring, and a reporter soon uncovers the tension and conflict through later conversations with the ambassadors. It is not cops-and-robbers stuff, but it is diplomatic reporting of a high order.

I suppose those who look on the U.N. as a boring talk shop have no time for its history as well. Yet that is even more of a foolish notion. The history of the United Nations bristles with excitement, for the U.N. involved itself with some of the momentous events of the last half-century: the end of World War II, the birth of Israel, the Korean War, the Congo, the Suez crisis, the Cuban missile crisis, the invasion of Cyprus, the Six-Day War, the Persian Gulf War, Somalia, Bosnia.

There has been great drama as well in the story of the U.N. as an institution. It has lurched up and down since its beginnings like a well-plotted movie. The U.N. was created amid fancy hopes and great expectations that were quickly snuffed by the Cold War. But it nevertheless found itself a niche dealing with those troubles like Israel (in the early days) and Cyprus and the Congo and Suez that were only on the fringes of Cold War rivalry. But the fortunes of the U.N. plummeted in the late 1970s when the Third World engulfed it and, with Soviet acquiescence, turned the U.N. into a screeching storm of anti-Western and anti-American invective. Those were the days of Kurt Waldheim and the "Zionism Is Racism" resolution—the nadir of U.N. history. Fortunes and hopes then rose just as fast as they once plummeted as the Berlin Wall collapsed, the Cold War ended, and the United States induced the Soviet Union and the rest of the Security Council to help turn back Saddam Hussein after his invasion of Kuwait. But the enervating frustrations of Somalia and Bosnia dashed many of the hopes, and, on the eve of its fiftieth anniversary, a mature and chastened U.N. wrestled with the nature of its role in the post–Cold War era.

I have tried here to set down the drama, excitements, and significance of the first fifty years of the United Nations. And I have also tried to depict some of the figures like Dag Hammarskjöld and Ralph

Bunche and Adlai Stevenson who personified the organization over the years and set its mood. This is not a history of resolutions and speeches. In the words of the American poet and playwright Archibald MacLeish, who wrote the preamble to the U.N. Charter, the United Nations was created "to save succeeding generations from the scourge of war," and I have written mainly about how it has tried and often failed to do just that.

For my coverage of the U.N., I have talked with scores of diplomats, international civil servants, analysts, and journalists, and their ideas clarified my understanding of the organization. I am therefore indebted to many people. But anyone who knows the U.N. will see the special debt I have to former Undersecretary-General Brian Urquhart. No history of the U.N. can be written without consulting his memoirs, his biographies of Hammarskjöld and Bunche, and his many articles and pamphlets. Urquhart has also subjected himself generously over the years to my interviews and phone calls whenever I needed clarification or analysis while covering a story at the U.N.

Secretary-General Boutros Boutros-Ghali put time aside during hectic days to reply to my questions about the U.N. and his policies. He often slipped back into his old role of a professor during these sessions, creating a university atmosphere that benefited me greatly.

My stay at the U.N. has happily coincided with the assignment there of my good friend Angel Viñas, the distinguished Spanish historian who represents the European Union as its ambassador. Angel, an astute observer and subtle analyst, has brushed aside innumerable U.N. thickets with his analyses to make me see things more clearly. I was also lucky to have Diego Arria, the former Venezuelan ambassador, on the Security Council during my watch. Ambassador Arria believed that the world would be better served if journalists like myself understood the politics of the Security Council deliberations behind closed doors.

Many other U.N. diplomats offered me a good deal of their time and analysis. They included Ambassador Thomas R. Pickering, Ambassador Madeleine K. Albright, Ambassador Karel Kovanda, Ambassador Jean-Bernard Mérimée, Ambassador Juan Antonio Yáñez-Barnuevo, Ambassador Muhamed Sacirbey, Pierre Henri Guignard, Philip Arnold, and James P. Rubin.

U.N. civil servants have always struck me as models of efficiency and generosity, far different from the caricature cited by U.N. bashers who insist that U.N. bureaucrats do little work for exorbitant pay. Shashi Tharoor, the brilliant Indian novelist who analyzes and crafts peacekeeping policy for Bosnia and the rest of the former Yugoslavia, is surely unmatched in clarity of analysis and ease of expression; I have benefited from many conversations with him. Many other U.N. officials contributed to my understanding of the organization. They included Kofi Annan, Joe Sills, Ahmad Fawzi, Fred Eckhard, Taye B. Zerihoun, Fayza Aboulnaga, and Juan Carlos Brandt. Many U.N. correspondents shared their extensive knowledge with me, including Trevor Rowe, Julia Preston, Josh Friedman, Genevieve Ast, Evelyn Leopold, and Gianna Pontecorboli. Among the outside experts always kind enough to discuss U.N. issues, I found Edward Luck and Herbert Okun most helpful.

The book would not have been written without the encouragement of Joan Bingham, the executive editor of Atlantic Monthly Press. I had given up the idea of writing a history of the U.N. after a proposal ran into a stone wall of publishers several years ago. A phone call from Bingham suggesting such a book quickly revived a dormant idea. At the *Los Angeles Times*, I am in debt to those responsible through assignments for my understanding of foreign countries and the U.N.: Robert W. Gibson, Alvin Shuster, Norman Miller, Jack Nelson, and Simon Li. And I am even in more debt to two of my predecessors as *Los Angeles Times* correspondents at the U.N.: Louis Fleming and Don Shannon, who left me their copious files and shared their astute observations with me. I also was lucky enough to work for five years in Paris alongside Don Cook, a foreign correspondent in the grand tradition. He taught me how to understand the machinations of international institutions and the subtleties of multilateral diplomacy. To my sorrowful regret, he left us before I could show him this book.

I used three libraries extensively: the small but remarkable Little Falls branch of the Montgomery County library in Maryland; the Dag Hammarskjöld Memorial Library at the U.N., where librarians were kind enough to let me dip into the Yale University–U.N. Oral History transcripts; and the *Los Angeles Times* Washington bureau library. The last is a treasure trove guarded by two diligent, over-worked, and generous librarians: Caleb Gessesse and Pat Welch.

Finally, I am indebted to the support of a family that put up with an ill-tempered writer for many, many months: at home, my wife and Gabriel and Jenaro encouraged the work in good spirit; from afar, Sam, Josh, Mike, and Michèle cheered me on. As an added bonus, my wife, Dr. Elizabeth Fox, shared her scholarly understanding of UNESCO and the New World Information and Communication Order and other insights with me.

❦ 1 ❦

The Beginnings:
From Dumbarton Oaks to San Francisco

At 7:09 P.M., the twelfth of April, 1945, two and a half hours after the death of Franklin D. Roosevelt, Harry S Truman held a Gideons' Bible in his left hand and took the oath of office as thirty-third president of the United States. About two dozen onlookers—cabinet members, congressional leaders, Roosevelt aides, Bess Truman, their daughter, Margaret—had assembled in the cabinet room of the White House for the swift ceremony. Chief Justice Harlan Stone administered the oath to Truman while both stood near a marble mantelpiece beneath a portrait of Woodrow Wilson, a symbolic witness. Wilson had galvanized the allies to victory in World War I but had fumbled the peace, failing to win Senate approval for even a toothless League of Nations. As World War II rushed through its final months, Roosevelt—and now Truman— knew that a wartime president had to avoid the pitfalls of Wilson in peacetime yet build on what he had attempted.

After the ceremony, Truman asked the members of Roosevelt's cabinet to remain behind so that he could formally request them to stay on the job as he coped with the awesome mantle dropped on him so suddenly. Before he could address them, Steve Early, Roosevelt's press secretary, interrupted and whispered that the White House newspapermen wanted to know if the San Francisco conference on the United Nations would take place as scheduled in less than two weeks. "I said it most certainly was," Truman recalled later. "I said it was what Roosevelt had wanted, and it had to take place if we were going to keep the peace. And that's the first decision I made as President of the United States."

It was a fitting first move. In the short years between the climactic months of World War II and the onset of the Cold War, Americans had high hopes for a future United Nations. Although there were some suspicions, Americans brimmed with admiration for the bitter and furious defenders of Moscow and Leningrad and Stalingrad and for the relentless Soviet counteroffensives that followed. Americans could envision the Soviet Union joining the United States in policing the peace in the brighter new world that would arise from the carnage. There were dissenters. Some were isolationists who still abhorred entangling alliances. But pragmatic intellectuals like Walter Lippmann also joined the naysayers. "We cannot repeat the error of counting upon a world organization to establish peace," he warned. "The responsibility for order rests upon the victorious governments. They cannot delegate this responsibility to a world society which does not yet exist or has just barely been organized." But, for most Americans, hopes drove out doubts.

꧁꧂

The United Nations was forged in a pair of extraordinary conferences—at Dumbarton Oaks from late August to early October 1944 and at San Francisco from late April to late June 1945. The Dumbarton Oaks conference was limited in numbers but not power. Only Britain, Russia, the United States, and China took part. At San Francisco, however, fifty governments, almost all anti-Axis belligerents, met to ratify a U.N. charter, accepting somewhat grudgingly what the Big Four had imposed. The noisiest disagreements—pitting the Soviet Union against its English-speaking partners—had to be settled through compromise outside the conferences, requiring a good deal of cajoling by Roosevelt in person at Yalta and by Truman through emissaries in Moscow.

The United Nations was mainly an American idea, and its structure today closely follows the plans prepared by American diplomats during World War II. Even before the United States entered the war, President Roosevelt had asked Secretary of State Cordell Hull to set up a State Department team of planners for peace. Roosevelt himself talked often of the need for "Four Policemen"—the United States, the Soviet Union, Britain, and China—to order the postwar world. The policemen would operate out of a station house run by an international organization, but it would be the strength and unity of the policemen that gave that organization its vitality. He did not mind fitting his scheme into the framework of some kind of League of Nations, but he envisioned a league of awesome power. When the Dumbarton Oaks conference was announced, Roosevelt, meeting reporters in his shirtsleeves on a warm day, explained what he had in mind: If some aggressor "started to run amok and seeks to grab territory or invade its neighbors," the new organization would "stop them before they got started."

Winston Churchill, fearful of the postwar machinations of Joseph Stalin, was more concerned with molding a West European–American alliance to balance the power of the Soviet Union. He derided the Americans for setting off on the wrong track. He also suspected the American visionaries of plotting the dismemberment of the British Empire. Undersecretary of State Sumner Welles, after all, had told a Memorial Day audience in 1942, "The age of imperialism is ended." Churchill did not see the point of the early American planning. He had his hands full with a war. In 1942, he told Foreign Secretary Anthony Eden that postwar studies should be assigned "mainly to those on whose hands time hangs heavy" and that all the planners should "not overlook Mrs. Glass's Cookery Book recipe for jugged hare—first catch your hare." But Churchill did not intend to antagonize Roosevelt. While Churchill looked on the early American planning as naïve and premature, he and his diplomats went along, humoring the Americans they needed so desperately as allies.

Stalin's postwar vision was closer to that of Churchill than Roosevelt. He intended to conquer an Eastern European buffer belt that would protect the Soviet Union from any future German or other European aggression. Since Roosevelt's vision of Four Policemen leading a universal peacekeeping organization did not seem to clash with his postwar plans, Stalin accepted it. "I think Stalin, with all his nastiness, scheming and beastliness with regard to his own people," says Russian historian Henry A. Trofimenko, "was serious about that. . . . He was quite prepared to police the world together with the United States, conveniently picking up in the process some neglected chunks of land." Stalin just wanted to make sure this new organization did not isolate him.

Throughout the war there were hints of what was to come. As early as August 1941, four months before Pearl Harbor, Roosevelt and Churchill included a call for the postwar "establishment of a wider and permanent system of general security" in the Atlantic Charter that they signed aboard the British battleship *Prince of Wales* off Newfoundland. The hint might have been stronger. Churchill was ready to slip a reference to an "effective international organization" into this declaration of principles by the leaders of the two most powerful English-speaking democracies. But isolationist sentiment still ran strong in prewar America, and the president did not want to provoke the American public and Senate with reminders of the scorned League of Nations. He rejected any wording that promised anything so specific as an international organization.

Roosevelt's objection would soon have a familiar ring to the British and, later, the Russians. Throughout the arguments at Dumbarton Oaks, San Francisco, Yalta, and Moscow, American diplomats liked to justify their stubbornness by invoking the nightmare of the Senate rejection and humiliation of Woodrow Wilson and his League of Nations after World War I: if they yielded on this or that point, the Americans would argue, the same dismal fate would await the U.N. It was both a haunt and a convenient club for bargaining.

☙ ❧

Washington in August rivals West Africa for muggy heat, and Eden asked the State Department to find a cooler site for the first conference in 1944. But American officials looked on the conference as too vital to allow American delegates too far from headquarters. Alger Hiss, a young State Department officer who would be imprisoned six years later for perjury in a controversial espionage case that skyrocketed the anti-Communist career of young Congressman Richard Nixon, suggested Dumbarton Oaks, a secluded mansion with acres of sculpted garden on high land above Georgetown in northwest Washington. Harvard University, which had received the mansion as a gift from Ambassador Robert Woods Bliss and his wife in 1940, agreed to loan the estate to the U.S. government for the rest of the summer. An enormous horseshoe-shaped table was assembled to replace the pianos and antique furniture of the mansion's ornate Music Room, and the Dumbarton Oaks conference opened on August 21, 1944.

The Americans, in an ebullient mood, catered to the needs and sensibilities of their guests. Hiss provided a member of the British delegation with the schedule of remaining home games for "the Washington American League club, also known as the Senators." To avoid offending the Soviet delegation, an accommodating official removed a portrait of the late Polish pianist-statesman Ignacy Jan Paderewski from a wall in the Music Room; Paderewski was too closely identified with the government that Stalin and Hitler overthrew in their joint invasion of Poland in 1939.

On the first Friday, Undersecretary of State Edward R. Stettinius, the head of the American delegation, arranged for a U.S. Army plane to fly the delegates to New York for a weekend on the town. They gaped at seminude showgirls in Billie Rose's Diamond Horseshoe after midnight and hobnobbed backstage with the Rockettes after a movie and stage show at Radio City Music Hall the next day. Andrey Gromyko, the Soviet ambassador to Washington and chief of his delegation, refused to go. Sir Alexander Cadogan, the British permanent undersecretary for foreign affairs and chief of his delegation, described Billie Rose's nightclub as an "astonishing scene" and wrote his wife that Americans were "extraordinary people" who were "in some respects rather like ourselves but (as you can see) so utterly different." When asked by reporters a few days later if it were true that the delegates had attended a nightclub floor show in New York on the past weekend, Stettinius denied it.

☙ ❧

Three very different men dominated the conference. Stettinius, forty-three, the Lend-Lease administrator and former chairman of U.S. Steel, had only recently replaced Sumner Welles as undersecretary after a well-publicized spat between Welles and his boss, Secretary of State Cordell Hull. Stettinius, a man with a toothy grin, bushy black eyebrows, and prematurely white hair, had secured a reputation in Washington as an efficient administrator with a flair for public relations. Cadogan recorded in his diary that Stettinius reminded him of "a dignified and more monumental Charlie Chaplin." Few contemporary chroniclers were that kind in their descriptions of the amiable lightweight who would replace Hull within a year. Dean Acheson remarked that Stettinius had "gone far with comparatively modest equipment." Ralph Bunche called him "a complete dud, whatever the press may say about him. He is simply in a job for which he has utterly no qualifications and about which he knows nothing."

Gromyko, thirty-five, even younger than Stettinius, was not well known even though he had been stationed in Washington for five years. Rarely seen at diplomatic parties and rarely in a joking mood when he did show up, he was once described as "the oldest young man in Washington." Stalin had promoted him to take the place of Maksim Litvinov as ambassador only a year before the Dumbarton Oaks conference. Litvinov, a former foreign minister fluent in English, had enjoyed spirited popularity in Washington, and there were some rumors that he had been replaced by Stalin to show displeasure with the delay in launching an invasion of western Europe. In Moscow, a story, probably apocryphal, spread that some Americans, jealous of Litvinov's access to Roosevelt, had lobbied against him, prompting an angry Stalin to scold them, "Well, you seem not to like a smart and brainy guy from Moscow—so I'll treat you with Gromyko." Cadogan described Gromyko as "a very nice and sensible fellow," although, by the end of the conference, he began to regard the Russian delegates on the whole as "slow and sticky and rather stupid." Gladwyn Jebb, Cadogan's deputy, found Gromyko "imperturbable, sardonic, scrupulous, humorless and formidably exact."

Cadogan, a far more experienced diplomat than the other two, headed the League of Nations section of the foreign office before World War II and, as permanent undersecretary, now held the highest bureaucratic rank in his ministry. Stettinius admired him as "calm, intelligent . . . very quick on the trigger." The conference wore down the nerves of the sharp-witted Cadogan. After a month, he attended an embassy cocktail party and looked on it as "a foretaste of hell." "A million people in a small, hot room," he wrote, "and a noise in which one couldn't hear oneself scream."

The makeup of the conference raised eyebrows. Roosevelt insisted that China be included as the Fourth Policeman because he wanted it to replace Japan someday as the power of Asia in the postwar world. The idea of China developing into a world power struck Churchill as ludicrous. He would have preferred France at Dumbarton Oaks, for he looked on a rejuvenated France as the vital balance in Western Europe against any westward moves by the Soviet Union. But Roosevelt, though he finally accepted the principle of France as Fifth Policeman, disliked General Charles de Gaulle enough to veto his movement's participation at Dumbarton Oaks, hoping that someone else could rise up and supplant him as the knight of a free France. Churchill called China a "faggot vote"—casting its ballot slavishly with the United States—and referred to Chinese diplomats as "pigtails." Despite this grumbling, he did not oppose Roosevelt's decision to make China one of the Big Four.

But the Soviet Union, since it had not yet declared war on Japan, refused to share the table with China during the conference, forcing the delegations to meet in cumbersome phases. The Big Three first ironed out the main features of a future United Nations. Then the British and American delegations presented the agreements to the Chinese in the second phase. There was little that delegation chief V. K. Wellington Koo, the Chinese ambassador to London, could do but acquiesce.

꧁꧂

Stettinius and the other delegation chiefs decided to keep all proceedings of the conference secret, doling out worthless press releases that set down the schedule of sessions but little more. But they were undercut by James Reston, on his first major assignment for the Washington bureau of the *New York Times*. Reston had run into young Chen Yi, a member of the Chinese delegation who had once worked as an apprentice at the *Times*. While talking over those days, Reston discovered that Chen had copies of all the position papers tabled by the four delegations. Reston persuaded Chen that "it would be a pity not to share these wonderful proposals and suggestions with the peoples who had suffered so much." Chen opened up his bulging briefcase and handed Reston all the papers. "I ran, literally ran, all the way to the office and turned them over to Arthur Krock," Reston recalled in his memoirs. Krock, the bureau chief, "looked like a guy who had just won the Kentucky Derby." The main competition for the *Times* in those days was the *New York Herald-Tribune*, and Krock decided to give "them the Chinese torture treatment by publishing the U.S. text one day, the Soviet the next, and so on."

The publication of the papers infuriated the delegation chiefs. Gromyko called on Krock and accused the *Times* of taking part in a conspiracy to divide the wartime allies. Stettinius called on British Ambassador Lord Halifax and wrongly accused the British delegation of "this outrageous breach of security." Stettinius then rushed to New York and warned publisher Arthur Hays Sulzberger that the conference might collapse if the *Times* continued to publish the papers. Reston wrote a letter to Stettinius assuring him that the British were not his source. Lord Halifax told Reston that, while he accepted this assurance as true, he would never again have anything to do "with a man implicated in this affair." The *Times* continued to publish the papers.

The other correspondents, suspecting that the State Department was feeding Reston while shunning them, angrily confronted Stettinius and demanded more news. Stettinius, Gromyko, and Cadogan agreed to meet the press a little more than a week after the conference opened. Two hundred correspondents assembled for a news conference in the Music Room. But the three negotiators, as Cadogan put it, intended only to "tell them that we weren't going to tell them anything." The *Detroit Free Press* said that Stettinius's replies to questions "could have been written on a postal card a year ago." Stettinius tried to hold a news conference of his own in September, but, despite his cheery attempt to call reporters by their first names, proved as ill at ease and uninformative as before. The Dumbarton Oaks conference shattered Stettinius's reputation as a master of public relations and enabled Reston to win the 1945 Pulitzer prize for national reporting.

≈≈

Although Russian intransigence is often blamed for almost scuttling the United Nations at birth, Gromyko, in fact, accommodated the Americans on almost all issues at Dumbarton Oaks. The Americans proposed that five permanent members with a veto and a few other rotating delegates make up a security council with the authority to maintain international peace and security. Unlike the League of Nations, which had the power only to impose sanctions by unanimous vote, this Security Council could use "any means necessary," including military force, to thwart aggression. This key proposal aroused no objection from Gromyko. The Soviet ambassador, in fact, was even stronger than the others in pleading for a security council with teeth.

At the request of Roosevelt, who was hoping to fashion a new Latin American champion just like China in Asia, Stettinius suggested that Brazil join the Security Council as the Sixth Policeman. But Cadogan and Gromyko objected, and the matter was dropped. Roosevelt, however, told Stettinius that Brazil was still a card up his sleeve. But few cards were necessary at Dumbarton Oaks. The remarkable unanimity continued as Stettinius, Cadogan, and Gromyko agreed on establishment of a general assembly comprising all members that would debate issues and approve budgets but have no enforcement power, a secretariat of international civil servants and an international court of justice.

There was some disagreement over a name. Roosevelt wanted to carry the name of the United Nations wartime alliance into the postwar crusade for permanent peace. Gromyko objected that it was not wise to adopt a bellicose name for peacetime and proposed International Security Organization or World Union instead. Cadogan

surprised Stettinius by announcing that his government did not like
the name United Nations either. When Stettinius refused to give in,
Gromyko did not press the matter. Nor did Cadogan. The British
said they were "reluctant to take the initiative in producing another
wrangle in the conference."

The conference came close to foundering on two issues that
seem trivial today but filled the British and American delegates with
gloom then. The issues were exacerbated at Dumbarton Oaks and
later at San Francisco by a growing Anglo-American suspicion of
Russian intentions as the war wound down and by a growing Soviet
fear that the Americans and British could use the United Nations
against them in the uncertain postwar world. Gromyko proposed that
all sixteen republics of the Soviet Union have a seat in the General
Assembly. Stettinius called the proposal "the bombshell." Roosevelt
ordered Stettinius to inform Gromyko "privately and personally and
immediately" that the proposal was totally unacceptable; it "might
ruin the chance of getting an international organization accepted in
this country." If the Soviet Union had sixteen votes, the United States
ought to have forty-eight, Roosevelt said.

Stettinius delivered the message from Roosevelt while walking
with Gromyko in the gardens of Dumbarton Oaks. Secretary of State
Hull also warned Gromyko that the proposal might "blow off the
roof" of the U.N. But Gromyko was adamant, for the Soviet Union
feared that it would be hopelessly outvoted in a general assembly
dominated by both the bloc of Britain and its dominions and the bloc
of the United States and its Latin American allies. The negotiators
decided to let the disagreement rest for future solution. But Stettinius
feared that news of the Soviet attempt to vote sixteen times on every
General Assembly issue would infuriate the American public and
turn it against the U.N. He clamped such secrecy over the proposal
that most members of the American delegation did not find out
about it until the conference ended. Stettinius referred to the unresolved issue in his working papers only as the "X-matter."

The second contentious issue—which would persist until it almost broke up the San Francisco conference—centered on the veto
in the Security Council. The Americans, the British, and the Soviets
all agreed that a veto was essential. There could be no peace in the

postwar world if the United States and the Soviet Union did not agree. But the delegates differed on just how extensive that veto would be.

Gromyko believed that the Americans supported the Soviet view that the veto would be absolute—that it could be invoked by any of the Big Five on any issue, no matter how trivial. Most important, the veto, in the Soviet view, could be used to prevent the Security Council from even discussing a dispute. This seemed to be Secretary Hull's position as well, for he feared that Americans would not support the U.N. if they believed that the United States could be outvoted there. The British dissented at first. But, as the Dumbarton Oaks conference progressed, the Americans, who seemed rather confused and divided, turned away from the Soviet position while the British turned toward it.

Secretary Hull changed his mind and told the American delegates in August that he now supported the British view that a member of the Big Five should not be able to veto a resolution if it were a party to the dispute. When this was relayed to the conference, Cadogan said, the new American position "was in the nature of a shock to the Soviet delegation." Gromyko took up the matter with Stettinius privately in the gardens. The Soviet ambassador said he was very discouraged by the change in the American position and was sure this would cause serious difficulties in Moscow; he implored Stettinius to reconsider. But the undersecretary of state said that President Roosevelt had told him only the night before that the American people would never accept the right of veto by a government involved in a dispute. Yet Roosevelt did not devote much time to this problem, and Stettinius found, in later discussions with him, that the president "seemed confused on the issue."

He was not the only one confused. "From some of the things he said," Cadogan wrote in his diary, "it became clear that he [Gromyko] didn't understand the point himself, so can't have put the arguments properly to Moscow." Stettinius hoped that his "biggest and last remaining gun" might be able to drive the American position home to Gromyko. On September 7, at 9:30 A.M., Stettinius escorted Gromyko into the bedroom of President Roosevelt in the White House. Trying to charm the Soviet ambassador, the president, in a cheerful mood, conjured up a homey but rather irrelevant image. He said that spatting husbands and wives in America traditionally leave it to outsiders to arbitrate their troubles. They didn't vote on their own cases, and it ought to be the same within the family of nations. He also said that the notion of fair play stemmed from the days of the Founding Fathers and that any break with fair play would surely endanger a U.N. treaty in the Senate. This story touched the emotions of Stettinius, but it did not seem to affect Gromyko.

Roosevelt decided to put the same argument in a message sent out that day to Stalin. The metaphor about disputing husbands and wives, however, disappeared in the drafting. The cable didn't seem to make much of an impact on Stalin. A week later, Gromyko informed the steering committee of the conference that he had received his instructions from Moscow: The Soviet position on the veto was "final and unalterable"; the veto would have to be absolute. Stettinius called this a "great blow" and said it might make it impossible to call a conference of nations to establish the United Nations. "We cannot tell whether we will be able to work it out to a successful conclusion," Stettinius wrote in his diary, "or whether the conference will blow up." The undersecretary of state also warned delegates that there must be "no whisper" of this impasse. The world must not yet learn that the United States and the Soviet Union could not agree on the vital issue of the veto.

There were various attempts at compromise formulas. Some American delegates urged Stettinius to accept the Soviet position, which, after all, was the original American position. But neither Stettinius nor Gromyko would budge. As the conference neared its close, Churchill began to take more interest in what was going on and to waver about the veto. He forwarded a telegram that he had received from South African Prime Minister Jan Christiaan Smuts, who tried to explain Soviet stubbornness over the veto. Smuts said that the Kremlin fretted over the Soviet Union's "honor and standing . . . amongst her allies" and wondered whether "she is trusted and treated as an equal or is still an outlaw and pariah." Churchill said he had changed his mind and now agreed with Smuts that no action should be taken in the Security Council without the unanimity of the great powers. Churchill told Roosevelt that he regretfully had "come to this conclusion contrary to my first thought."

But this came too late to alter the course of the Dumbarton Oaks conference. The seven-week conference ended on October 7 with the vital issue of the veto left open. The final draft of the Dumbarton Oaks proposals for the United Nations, released two days later, stated that "the question of voting procedure in the Security Council is still under consideration." Stettinius professed not to be discouraged by the failure to win a 100 percent victory at Dumbarton Oaks; he wrote in his diary that 75 percent was good enough. But most delegates knew that, unless their governments solved the problem of the veto, they would not have three-quarters of a United Nations organization but none at all.

꽃꽃

Two days after his inauguration for a fourth term as president in January 1945, Roosevelt embarked on a long journey by sea and air to Yalta in the Soviet Crimea, joining Churchill and Stalin in hopes of smoothing the last few squabbles during the closing months of war. More than 80 percent of Americans supported the Dumbarton Oaks blueprint for the United Nations. But Roosevelt knew that the blueprint was worthless without an agreement on the veto. Both Roosevelt and his closest adviser, Harry Hopkins, were seriously ill. Hopkins remained in bed except for official sessions. Roosevelt did not always follow the discussions. Churchill's physician, Lord Moran, wrote, "To a doctor's eye, the President appears a very sick man. . . . I give him only a few months to live." Yet the Americans appeared to win the veto issue at Yalta.

Stettinius, now secretary of state, presented the new American proposal with British support. The Big Five would have the right of veto on all but procedural issues before the Security Council. In the case of a peaceful dispute, however, a member of the council would abstain from voting if it were a party to that dispute. This formula, as the Americans understood it, meant that none of the Big Five could prevent an issue from coming before the council, though they could veto any decision to take action on this issue. The single exception to the rule—peaceful disputes involving the Big Five—did not seem significant since the Security Council's crucial assignment was the halt and punishment of aggression, not the arbitration of peaceful arguments.

Without much debate, Soviet Foreign Minister V. M. Molotov accepted the formula. On the second unresolved issue of Dumbarton Oaks, he said that the Soviet Union no longer demanded a vote for all sixteen of its republics in the General Assembly but would be satisfied with four. To the dismay of his delegation, Roosevelt reluctantly offered three—votes for the Soviet Union, the Ukraine, and White Russia—and also requested that the United States have three votes as well. The compromise was accepted—though the quest for three American votes at the U.N. seemed so ludicrous back in Washington that the United States soon abandoned the idea and contented itself with one vote. Roosevelt, Stalin, and Churchill also agreed that a conference of nations would be convened in San Francisco in a few months to adopt the charter of the United Nations.

Since Roosevelt and Churchill failed to budge Stalin on allowing a democratic government in Poland, which was the main issue of Yalta, Charles Bohlen, the American adviser, interpreter, and note taker at the conference, called the settlement of the veto "the one solid and lasting decision of the Yalta Conference." Without it, he said, "there would hardly have been a United Nations."

꽃꽃

Internationalists looked on the San Francisco conference, which opened on April 25, 1945, as a grand and gala beginning—the launching by fifty countries of a brave, new organization that would keep the peace after the horrors of World War II. The crucial decisions had been made at Dumbarton Oaks and Yalta, but the conference had the vital—though far less controversial—task of writing the charter that would put the grand ideas into soaring yet practical rhetoric. The conference, however, faltered often over snares and traps, and it came close to failing.

The Soviet Union shocked Washington weeks before the conference by announcing that Foreign Minister Molotov would not head the Soviet delegation because of the press of business in wartime Moscow. This struck Washington as a deliberate downgrading of the conference. Churchill called it "a grimace" that "leaves a bad impression on me."

Shortly after the death of Roosevelt on April 12, Stalin called U.S. Ambassador Averell Harriman to the Kremlin. He wondered what he ought to do—as a gesture to the memory of Roosevelt—to assure the American people of his desire for continued cooperation with the United States. Harriman replied that "the thing the American people would appreciate most would be to send Molotov to the San Francisco Conference." Molotov, who was present, repeated his reluctance. But Stalin announced to both Harriman and Molotov that Molotov would lead the Soviet delegation in San Francisco. And he, of course, did.

Roosevelt appointed a bipartisan delegation: Secretary Stettinius, two members of the House of Representatives, the dean of Barnard College, Chairman Tom Connally (a Texas Democrat) of the Senate Foreign Relations Committee, Senator Arthur Vandenberg (a Michigan Republican), and former Republican Governor Harold Stassen of Minnesota, now on duty in the navy. The delegation included Cordell Hull, the retired secretary of state, as well, but he was too ill to attend. The key member of the delegation was probably Senator Vandenberg, for he was only a recent convert from isolationism. He had been so vehemently against foreign entanglements that he had even voted against the Lend-Lease Act of 1941 that supplied war matériel to Britain, confessing, in his diary, that "I had the feeling that I was witnessing the suicide of the Republic." The delegation had numerous advisers, like Ambassador Harriman and Republican international lawyer John Foster Dulles. Upon his return from Yalta, Roosevelt informed the delegates of his acceptance of three Soviet votes. They were stunned. "This will raise hell," Vandenberg wrote in his diary. ". . . It looks like a bad business to me."

When Connally and Vandenberg took leave of the Senate to head to San Francisco, there was, as Vandenberg noted, "a sudden stirring of emotions such as the staid old chamber had seldom witnessed." Democrats and Republicans rose, clapped their hands lustily, rushed toward Connally and Vandenberg, shook hands, hugged them, and wished them well. "America was going to San Francisco—the second great international effort to establish lasting peace in the world—in a manner far removed from the lonely pilgrimage of Woodrow Wilson to Paris hardly a generation before," Vandenberg wrote.

San Francisco, one of the most cosmopolitan of American cities, had to deal with an enormous influx of peoples from fifty countries: 1,726 delegates and their assistants, a secretariat of 1,058 international civil servants, 2,636 newspaper and radio reporters, and a support staff of almost 4,500, including telephone and telegraph operators and volunteers from the Boy Scouts and Red Cross.

The conference opened in unpleasant controversy. Other countries grumbled about the two extra Soviet seats. The Latin American delegates would not vote for the Ukraine and White Russia unless the United States supported a seat for Argentina. This was a sore point. The fascistlike Argentine régime had traded with Nazi Germany throughout the war and did not declare war on the Axis until two months before the San Francisco conference. The Soviets rightly regarded American support of Argentina's participation in the conference as reneging on a promise. But the Americans felt that the Soviet Union should understand that there was no other way to get wide support for the seating of the two extra Soviet republics. Molotov stormed that it was incomprehensible for the conference to seat Argentina while refusing to support the Communist-dominated Lublin government of Poland. Moscow had recognized the Lublin government despite the Yalta agreement on free elections for Poland. But the conference, while voting to seat the Ukraine, White Russia, and Argentina, put off a decision on Poland.

Walter Lippmann, the influential columnist, believed that the United States was deliberately and dangerously humiliating the Soviet Union. The American delegates, Lippmann believed, had fallen under the sway of the hard line anti-Soviet views of Ambassador Harriman. When Harriman told a news conference in San Francisco that "our objectives and the Kremlin's objectives are irreconcilable," Lippmann walked out. He was disturbed by the way the United States had marshaled the votes of nineteen Latin American delegations, almost half the countries at the conference, to win a seat for Argentina. "If we were going to use that kind of majority to dominate things," Lippmann said, "we were going to run into iron resistance to anything else from the Russians." He was afraid that some American officials looked on the future U.N. as a means of policing the Soviet Union. "We cannot police the Soviet Union," he wrote, "and we must not flirt with the idea of attempting it."

But the real issue of the San Francisco conference was the same that plagued Dumbarton Oaks—the veto of the Big Five. Although the Soviet Union had agreed to the American formula at Yalta, Molotov now insisted that the formula meant that any of the Big Five could veto even the discussion of a dispute: a public debate over a dispute was too significant to be regarded as a procedural matter not subject to veto. When the Soviets resisted all efforts to change this view, Senator Vandenberg wrote in his diary, "We all knew that we had reached the 'zero hour' of this great adventure. With what seemed to be finality, the Soviet said they could not accept our proposal for 'free discussion.' We all knew that none of the rest of us can accept the Soviet view. Did it mean the immediate breakup of the conference? Did it mean going on to a charter without Russia?"

In mid-May, the conference seemed doomed. Molotov and Eden returned home. Harriman and Bohlen flew to Washington, according to playwright and Hopkins biographer Robert E. Sherwood, "with a sense of despair in their hearts." Bohlen suggested that Truman might ask Harry Hopkins to undertake a new mission to Moscow to negotiate with Stalin. Although this would, in a sense, usurp Harriman's role as ambassador to Moscow, Harriman embraced the suggestion and took it to Hopkins.

Hopkins had served Roosevelt as secretary of commerce, head of the Works Progress Administration (the New Deal jobs program during the 1930s Depression), administrator of Lend-Lease, and confidential adviser. He was so close to Roosevelt that he lived in the White House. It was often easier for critics to attack Hopkins as an éminence grise than to take on the extraordinarily popular Roosevelt, and Hopkins often felt unfairly vilified during his years of faithful service. His fading health forced him to retire from the government soon after Roosevelt died. But, when Harriman and Bohlen made their proposal, according to Sherwood, "the mere intimation of a flight to Moscow converted him into the traditional old fire horse at the sound of the alarm." Truman approved the plan and instructed Hopkins to "make it clear to Uncle Joe Stalin that I knew what I wanted—and that I intend to get—peace for the world for at least 90 years." Hopkins set off to Moscow as the president's personal envoy, accompanied by Harriman and Bohlen.

When Hopkins met Molotov in the Kremlin during the evening of May 25, he asked if the Soviet foreign minister "had recovered from the battle of San Francisco." Molotov replied that he did not "recall any battles but merely arguments at San Francisco." Several evenings were devoted to discussions of Poland, the Argentine vote, and Soviet-American relations in general. The veto was not discussed until the sixth and final meeting on June 6. Hopkins and Molotov debated their two positions before Stalin. Stalin then discussed the issue with Molotov in Russian. It became clear to the Americans that Stalin was seeking clarification of a problem that he had not understood before. Stalin remarked to Molotov that it struck him as "an insignificant matter." He said that they should accept the American position allowing discussion of any conflict but providing the Big Five with a veto over any decision.

While informing Hopkins that he accepted the American position, Stalin warned the United States to beware of little nations that like to exploit the differences among big powers. "It was a mistake to believe that just because a nation was small it was necessarily innocent," Stalin said. That was something he would say not only in secret but was "quite prepared to tell the little nations . . . to their faces." After all, he went on, "two world wars had begun over small nations." Hopkins cabled Truman immediately with the news that the San Francisco conference had been saved.

At San Francisco, the smaller nations began to chafe under the prospect of a U.N. dominated by five nations with a veto. Australia led a drive to add more limits to the use of the veto. Senator Connally, an old-fashioned, flamboyant speaker, told the other delegates,

"You may go home from San Francisco, if you wish, and report that you have defeated the veto. . . . But you can also say, 'We tore up the charter.' " Whereupon the senator picked up his copy of a draft of the charter, tore it into shreds, and flung the scraps upon the negotiating table. The histrionic threat that the choice lay between a strong veto and no U.N. at all carried the day. By a vote of twenty to ten (with fifteen abstaining and five absent), the conference decided to keep the Yalta veto formula.

On June 25, exactly two months after the opening ceremony, the San Francisco conference unanimously approved the new U.N. Charter. "At this point," recounted the official minutes, "the delegates and the entire audience rose and cheered." A slow signing processing ensued; each delegation signed five copies. The American delegates signed just before the closing ceremonial session at the San Francisco Opera House the next day. President Truman witnessed the signing and addressed the delegates. It was the president's first public appearance since assuming office. Chopping the air with his hands to emphasize his words, Truman said that the new U.N. must keep the world "free from the fear of war." Less than a week later, he personally delivered the charter to the Senate. "The choice before the Senate . . . is not between this Charter and something else," he said. "It is between this Charter and no charter at all."

❧❧

There was little serious objection to the charter at Senate hearings. Socialist leader Norman Thomas supported it. John Foster Dulles told the senators that it was approved by Governor Thomas E. Dewey of New York, the defeated Republican candidate for president. A variety of fringe groups insisted that the charter had gone too far or not far enough. One witness condemned the charter as the handiwork of a British-Israel world federation intent on creating a world state with the duke of Windsor as king. On July 28, the Senate ratified the charter by a vote of eighty-nine to two. Senator Theodore Bilbo, a Mississippi Democrat, better known as a hard-core segregationist than an advocate of internationalism, hailed the charter as "a great document which we believe will usher in the millennial dawn." Five senators were absent. The only senators voting against ratification were Republican Senators William Langer of North Dakota and Henrik Shipstead of Minnesota, who denounced the U.N. as an unlawful superstate. Langer was the best known of the two holdouts, a windy speaker who liked to pound his fist so hard to make a point that he once split a desk on the Senate floor. Their lack of support would hardly undermine the U.N.

❧ ❦

The United States served as the repository for the formal instruments of ratification. The first country to officially deposit the formal documents with the United States was the United States itself on August 8. The charter would "come into force," according to Article 110, when all of the Big Five and a majority of the rest deposited their ratifications. That happened on October 24, 1945, when the Soviet Union, the Ukraine, White Russia, and Poland (finally admitted to the U.N.) handed their ratifications to the United States at the same time. James F. Byrnes, the new secretary of state, certified that all the requirements of Article 110 had been satisfied. "The United Nations Charter is now a part of the law of nations," he said. October 24 would be celebrated each year as the U.N.'s birthday.

The postwar world that took shape after 1945 fit more closely the visions of Churchill and Stalin than of Roosevelt. A balance of power—between the American-led North Atlantic Treaty Organization and the Soviet-led Warsaw Pact—would order the world. Roosevelt's Five Policemen could not police the world because a bitter enmity had sundered the friendship of the two strongest policemen, and it had done so while both possessed the most terrifying weapons of mass destruction ever known. The United Nations would thus play a secondary—though still significant—role during its first four decades. In the fifth decade, it would start to realize its potential, though still falling short of those wondrous dreams in the closing months of World War II.

❧ 2 ❧

Trygve Lie and Iran:
Off to a Bad Start

On January 29, 1946, the eleven-member Security Council, meeting in London, unanimously selected Trygve Lie, the forty-nine-year-old foreign minister of Norway, as the first secretary-general of the United Nations, a choice swiftly ratified by the General Assembly. The Americans would have preferred Lester B. Pearson, the Canadian ambassador to Washington, a distinguished and admired diplomat who would become prime minister of Canada and a Nobel prize laureate. But the Soviet Union did not want a secretary-general from a country so allied to the United States and Britain.

In those early days, long before the influx of scores of infant states from Africa and Asia, the U.N. counted only the United States, China, Latin America, the victors of Europe, the British dominions, and a few Middle Eastern countries as members. In this mix, Scandinavia came closest to neutral in any squabbling between the Soviet Union and the United States, and Lie looked like a safe though little-known compromise. When Edward R. Stettinius Jr., the first American ambassador to the U.N., prepared to rise in the General

Assembly to hail the virtues and achievements of the Security Council's candidate for secretary-general, U.N. official Brian Urquhart had to point out Lie for him. Stettinius mispronounced the Norwegian's name, calling him "Lye," not "Lee."

For Lie, the election as secretary-general was a kind of consolation prize. The potential of power inherent in that post was not understood, and Lie would have preferred election as president of the General Assembly. He had been led to believe that he was the American candidate for that job and would win with near-universal support. A skier carried an urgent telegram to him high in the mountains of Norway on Christmas Day 1945. The telegram from the foreign ministry in Oslo informed him that Adlai Stevenson, acting head of the American delegation to the U.N. preparatory meetings, needed to know as soon as possible if Lie would run for the presidency. "If Foreign Minister Lie is willing," Stevenson had told the ministry, "the Americans intend to suggest him." Lie sent the skier back to the telegraph office with his acceptance.

When the General Assembly convened in London for the first time a few weeks later and took up the matter, however, Lie found the Americans in irritating retreat and confusion. The British and Latin Americans were pushing Paul-Henri Spaak, the Belgian foreign minister, and the Americans had decided to go along. But the Russians, who looked on Spaak as too West European, then cornered the Americans and, pleading the cause of big power unity, persuaded them to shift back to Lie.

The Americans and British had expected a quiet and secret ballot without any nominating speeches. But Soviet Ambassador Andrey Gromyko surprised them by suddenly demanding recognition in the General Assembly. Extolling the wartime record of Norway in florid prose, Gromyko broke the understanding and formally nominated Lie. The Ukrainian delegate then leaped up and called for approval of Lie by acclamation. But this attempt to seize the moment for Lie failed, and the General Assembly decided to go through with the secret ballot as scheduled. Secretary of State James F. Byrnes, who headed the American delegation, said nothing, making Lie look like an exclusively Moscow candidate. The United States reportedly voted for Lie in the secret ballot, but the final count was twenty-eight to twenty-three in favor of Spaak. "My candidacy was Washington's idea," Lie wrote with some bitterness years later, "but Mr. Byrnes had not made a move."

A little more than two weeks later, however, Lie, a burly former labor lawyer, was elected secretary-general. Lie had lived in London most of the war as the foreign minister of the Norwegian government in exile and was best known for ordering the Norwegian merchant fleet to steam into British ports in 1940 and thus escape Nazi hands. His seven years as secretary-general were hectic, bristling with controversy, and, of course, precedent-setting. But, all in all, it was probably an unhappy performance. Soviet officials derided him in the end as a lackey of the West, yet Secretary of State Dean Acheson sometimes belittled him as an appeaser of Communism.

His personal assistant, Brian Urquhart, was harsh in his overall appraisal. "As Secretary-General of the new world organization," Urquhart wrote, "he was out of his depth. Lie was an unsophisticated man who relied more on peasant shrewdness and what he called his 'political nose' than on intellectual effort or hard diplomatic work. He was, in public life at any rate, a naturally suspicious man with a hair-trigger temper. . . .

"Lie had the massive physique of an athlete who had run to seed in middle age," Urquhart went on. ". . . He was apt to go dark red in the face with rage and to utter, jowls quivering, complex and ominous Norwegian oaths. . . . Rightly or wrongly, I felt that he was confused, temperamental, and insecure in his new and demanding job and was often carried away by the emotions of the moment."

Lie won notice for indulging his taste in exquisite cuisine and excellent wine and, at the same time, fretting continually over the propriety of his position and the respect it demanded. His U.N. staff discovered him making a reservation at a nightclub in Geneva one evening under the assumed name of Rodney Witherspoon.

Perhaps it did not matter that Trygve Lie was a clumsy and confused diplomat. The United Nations would have been off to a bad start no matter who served as secretary-general. Its first days coincided with the advent of the Cold War, and it was soon evident that the

U.N. would not fit the visions of Dumbarton Oaks and San Francisco. The postwar rhetoric was turning barbed and mean, and acrimony would soon take center stage at the U.N.

≈≈

On February 9, ten days after the election of Lie as secretary-general, Stalin, laying down his new Five-Year Plan, announced that armament would still take precedence over consumer consumption in the postwar Soviet Union. The Soviet Union, Stalin said, had to defend itself against "all kinds of eventualities" because "no peaceful international order is possible" between the Communists and the capitalist-imperialist world. Washington was shocked. Supreme Court Justice William O. Douglas called the speech "the declaration of World War III."

On February 22, two weeks after the Stalin speech, an eight-thousand-word "long telegram" arrived at the State Department from George F. Kennan, the American chargé d'affaires in Moscow. Secretary of the Navy James Forrestal, regarding it as a cry of alarm that must be sounded again and again, reproduced and dispatched scores of copies throughout the U.S. capital. The telegram made the rounds of official Washington as if it were the latest Hemingway novel. Kennan, a foreign service officer and scholar of Soviet affairs, was trying to explain and assess the reality of Soviet thinking for U.S. officialdom. His analysis soon hardened the Truman administration's attitudes against the Soviet Union, squelching those who believed that compromise could seduce Stalin into cooperation.

Kennan described a Soviet Union so fearful and insecure that it could not negotiate in confidence. He said that Soviet leaders "are driven by necessities of their own past and present position to put forward a dogma which pictures the outside world as evil, hostile and menacing." "We have here," he went on, "a political force committed fanatically to the belief that with the US there can be no permanent *modus vivendi*, that it is desirable and necessary that the internal harmony of our society be disrupted, our traditional way of life be destroyed, the international authority of our state be broken, if Soviet power is to be secure." Kennan said that the Soviet Union would continually push forward at various dangerous pressure points, and "strong resistance" was necessary to stop them. Soviet power usually backed off when resisted, he said. The American Cold War policy of containment—active resistance to Soviet and Soviet client aggression and pressure wherever possible—was founded on the Kennan telegram.

On March 5, two weeks after the long telegram reached Washington, Winston Churchill, no longer in office, made his renowned "iron curtain" speech at Westminster College in Fulton, Missouri. Truman accompanied Churchill to his home state by train and read the speech before its delivery. He told Churchill it "would do nothing but good though it would make a stir." Churchill, Truman, and the president's staff played poker throughout the night. Westminster had bedecked itself in British and American flags. When he introduced Churchill, wearing the scarlet academic robe and plush black cap of Oxford University, Truman told the audience, "I know that he will have something constructive to say to the world."

"From Stettin in the Baltic to Trieste in the Adriatic," Churchill said, "an iron curtain has descended across the continent. Behind that line lie all the capitals of the ancient states of central and eastern Europe. Warsaw, Berlin, Prague, Vienna, Budapest, Belgrade, Bucharest and Sofia, all these famous cities and their populations around them lie in what I might call the Soviet sphere, and are all subject, in one form or another, not only to Soviet influence but to a very high and in some cases increasing measure of control from Moscow." He called for a "fraternal association of the English-speaking peoples" to halt Soviet expansion. Like Kennan, he did not believe war was necessary to stop them. "I am convinced," he said, "that there is nothing they admire so much as strength, and there is nothing for which they have less respect than for weakness, especially military weakness."

Stalin told *Pravda*, "Mr. Churchill is now in the position of a firebrand of war. And Mr. Churchill is not alone here." The American public had not read Kennan's "long telegram" and were not prepared for the Churchillian battle cry against the Soviet Union. Even newspaper columnist Walter Lippmann railed against the rhetoric. He warned his readers that British interests were not always the same as American interests, and he described the speech in private as an "almost catastrophic blunder." The popular distaste for the speech prompted Truman to lie that he had not read it before delivery. He told Secretary of Commerce Henry Wallace, the former vice president and the leader of the leftist Democrats, that Churchill had "put me on the spot," and he offered Stalin an invitation, declined by Stalin, to speak at the University of Missouri. Despite these protestations, the Kennan and Churchill analyses had made a profound impression on the Truman administration, hardening its resistance, most noticeably at the U.N., to what it believed was Soviet aggressive behavior.

❧❦

The U.N. also had more mundane matters to deal with. Most important of these, a site had to be chosen. After the San Francisco conference, a preparatory commission set up shop in London to get the new organization started. Stettinius headed the American delegation to the commission but was absent so often because of illness that his deputy, Adlai Stevenson, a young Illinois lawyer and a grandson of a U.S. vice president, did most of the work. Reporters knew Stevenson well, for he had served as the American delegation's private briefer of the press during the San Francisco conference. Ralph Bunche, a black Howard University professor with a thorough background in African colonial politics, also was a member of the American team in London. Bunche, who had studied in London before the war, described it in late 1945 as "a badly battered city . . . grey and somber, like the weather." "There is no gaiety," he said. "The great hordes of people look grim and weary."

London would host the U.N. for the first few weeks of 1946, simply because the preparatory commission was already there, but no one intended to keep the world organization in the British capital. The European delegates to the commission, especially Philip Noel-Baker, the British minister of state, argued steadfastly for Geneva, the home of the League of Nations. Noel-Baker, however, had to cope with the feeling by many that Geneva was haunted by failure.

Andrey Gromyko, the Soviet ambassador, argued just as forcefully for the United States. "The United States is located conveniently between Asia and Europe," he said. "The Old World had it once, and it is time for the New World to have it." Stevenson took himself out of the debate, pronouncing the United States neutral, but there was no doubt that many Americans hoped that the brainchild of Franklin Delano Roosevelt would reside in the land of Roosevelt. Stevenson, in fact, privately gave advice to a group of Chicagoans trying to bring the U.N. there. Geneva lost even more support when the traditionally neutral Swiss government informed delegates that any Security Council decision to use force would have to be taken outside Swiss soil.

In the end, the commission selected the United States, and a special site subcommittee later proposed a tract of land covering parts of New York's Westchester County and Connecticut's Fairfield County. This was ratified in early 1946 by the General Assembly, which also decided to transfer the new U.N. to New York City while a permanent site was readied.

On March 21, 1946, the Security Council moved into its new temporary home in the gymnasium on the Bronx campus of Hunter College, a women's school run by the city of New York. The campus had been used to train naval officers during World War II, and the city leased it to the U.N. for $9,333 a month until the next fall, when classes for women would resume. Workmen transformed the gym into a Security Council chamber, embellishing the windows and walls with rose pink and buff draperies and providing seats for six hundred spectators.

For most Americans, the history of the U.N. began with its first meetings on American soil. Americans could take notice. The few with television sets could even watch the white-haired Stettinius and the dour Gromyko on grainy black-and-white screens. Newsreels featured them in the movie houses. Newspapers covered their doings as if the U.N. were a local, not a universal, story. There were eight hundred reporters at the opening sessions. Young people even bundled down in blankets all night outside the gates of Hunter College so they would be assured of tickets to enter the Security Council in the morning. Washington may have been disillusioned and apprehensive, but many Americans still had euphoric hope that this new orga-

nization—the revered Roosevelt's organization—would somehow
ensure the Four Freedoms that he had proclaimed in 1941—freedom
of speech and religion, freedom from want and fear—and prevent
the horrors of a world war from recurring. It did not take long, however, for the most casual newspaper reader to sense things falling
apart.

※※

The Iran crisis of the 1940s seems rather tame in retrospect. But
it quickly became the first East-West battleground of the U.N. The
troubles erupted, in fact, even before the Security Council moved to
New York. The background was simple: The allied forces had occupied Iran during World War II to ensure a southern supply route for
the neighboring Soviet Union. Soviet troops moved into the north of
Iran while British and American troops took the south. At the time,
they signed an agreement pledging to leave six months after the end
of hostilities. The deadline was March 2, 1946. By January, the British
and Americans had left, but there was no sign that the Soviet troops
intended to go. Moreover, the soviets were stirring up secessionist
sentiment among the Azerbaijanis in northern Iran. In applying pressure to Iran, the Soviet Union, according to Dean Acheson, then
undersecretary of state, was following "the route of invasion by bar-
barians against classical Greece and Rome and later of the czars to
warm water."

On January 19, two days after the inaugural session of the Security Council, Iranian Ambassador Hussein Ala, clearly egged on by
the United States, accused the Soviet Union of internal interference
and demanded a full U.N. investigation. Soviet Ambassador Andrey
Vyshinsky, assuring everyone that his government would negotiate
the matter with the Iranians, proposed that the Security Council do
no more than endorse the negotiations. But the council, at American
insistence, decided to keep the Iranian complaint on the agenda. An
angry Vyshinsky countered by formally complaining about the continued occupation of Indonesia by British troops and of Syria by
French and British troops.

This led to a vote that cracked the image of the U.N. During the

protracted and confusing debates over the veto a year before, almost
no one anticipated that any of the Big Five would exercise its veto
often and even frivolously. Yet, when Stettinius introduced a resolution on February 16 authorizing negotiations for the immediate withdrawal of British and French troops from Syria, Vyshinsky vetoed the
resolution because it struck him as too weak. It was the first veto ever
cast in the Security Council. "Why was this first veto cast?" Lie wrote
in his memoirs. "Not because Mr. Vyshinsky opposed the substance
of the resolution, but because its language was not strong enough to
please him." Lie was troubled by "this first, almost lighthearted use of
the veto that I hoped would rarely be exercised." Fifty more Soviet
vetoes would follow during Lie's seven years in office.

In March—after the Kennan telegram had stirred up Washington and hardened feelings about Stalin—reports reached the State
Department of Soviet troop movements en route to Teheran. Kennan cabled that he believed Moscow was intent on intimidating Iran
into installing a pro-Soviet régime. President Truman told Averell
Harriman, the new ambassador to Britain, "There is a very dangerous
situation in Iran. The Russians are refusing to take their troops out
. . . and this may lead to war."

Iran asked the Security Council to take up its complaint in a
formal session scheduled for March 25. Gromyko called for a post-
ponement in view of the ongoing negotiations, certainly not an out-
landish request, but Truman and Secretary of State James F. Byrnes
ordered Stettinius to refuse. The Americans simply did not trust the
Russians anymore. Truman instructed Walter Bedell Smith, en route
to Moscow as the new American ambassador, "to tell Stalin I had
always held him to be a man to keep his word" but the troops in Iran
"upset that theory."

The debate was regarded as so important that Secretary Byrnes
arrived in New York to take Stettinius's place at the table in the
Hunter College gymnasium. Truman predicted to Assistant Secretary of State Adolf A. Berle that the Russians "would carry on local
aggression unless world opinion stopped them." Truman hoped to
galvanize the U.N. into serving as the arena for stopping them. On
March 25, the day the Security Council debate on Iran began, Tass
announced that the Soviet Union was close to an agreement with

Iran and that all Soviet troops would leave the country within six weeks. Gromyko asked that the Security Council therefore postpone the Iranian question until April 10. But Truman and Byrnes would not accept Soviet assurances. Gromyko warned that unless the Security Council postponed discussion, he could not take part in the council's business.

Trygve Lie tried to talk him out of this position. He met with Gromyko privately and urged him not to carry out the threat. "I made it clear then, as I was to state publicly and repeatedly later, that I did not believe in the boycott as a weapon for dealing with political differences," Lie wrote. "But Mr. Gromyko had his instructions, and of course he stuck to them."

Two days later, on March 27, Gromyko moved that the council postpone its discussion until April 10. The vote was overwhelmingly against him. Gromyko arose, as usual speaking in Russian despite his excellent English, and said, "For reasons which I explained clearly enough in our meeting of yesterday and in today's meeting, Mr. Chairman, I, as representative of the Soviet Union, am not able to participate further in the discussions of the Security Council because my proposal has not been accepted by the council, nor am I able to be present at the meeting of the council. I am, therefore, leaving the meeting." Gromyko gathered up all his papers and walked slowly from the room. A Soviet general followed behind.

Photographers rushed to the bottom of the stairs to catch him walking down and out of the building. But, just before his descent, Frank Begley, the U.N. chief of security, grabbed Gromyko and whispered to him. The Russian ambassador's fly was open. The grim-faced Gromyko flashed a rare grin and turned away from the photographers. Once the problem was repaired, he descended the staircase and faced the cameras.

But it was not a comic moment. The shock was enormous. The Security Council had met in the United States for barely a week, and the message resounded clearly: The Soviet Union was prepared to turn its back on the U.N. when things did not go its way. "Russia has served notice on the United Nations Organization," a *New York Times* editorial said, "that unless she gets her way she will paralyze it even at the risk of wrecking it."

The Iranian crisis petered out. The Soviet troops did leave Iran within a few weeks, as promised, and the Azerbaijanis did not try to secede from Iran. As a matter of Soviet pride, Gromyko, who returned to the Security Council, again asked that the issue be expunged from the agenda. This, he insisted, would prove that it had been "incorrect and illegal" for the Security Council to take it up in the first place. Trygve Lie agreed with him somewhat—there was no point in keeping it on the agenda—and decided to say so in a memorandum. But, even after the crisis ended, the Security Council, under American pressure, intended to keep it on the agenda. "The delegate of the United States," said Gromyko, glaring at Stettinius, "sacrifices logic in order to prolong and inflate the so-called Iranian question."

For the future of the U.N., Trygve Lie's memorandum may have been more important than Gromyko's antics. It angered some ambassadors, in fact, as much as the walkout. Lie fretted continually about the proper role of the secretary-general. He did not intend to follow the model of Sir Eric Drummond, the first secretary-general of the League of Nations. Sir Eric never said a word in public and made not the slightest effort to be looked on as the symbol or personification of the league. In the true tradition of the British civil service that produced him, he was silent and invisible.

But Lie was not sure how loud and visible the secretary-general of the United Nations ought to be. Article 99 of the U.N. Charter said, in its entirety, "The Secretary-General may bring to the attention of the Security Council any matter which in his opinion may threaten the maintenance of international peace and security." That implied that the secretary-general was an independent actor on the international scene who could make his own judgments about the problems of the world and attempt to galvanize the Security Council into acting on them. Sir Eric never had that kind of authority with the League of Nations. All Lie's successors have founded their authority on Article 99—one of the most significant and oft-quoted articles in the charter—but it has never been clear just how much power can be derived from those few words.

Some advocates hoped that the secretary-general could become a bold international figure who symbolized the United Nations as a whole and wielded the authority and moral standing to call rogue nations to order and thunder governments into action. Lie, however, refused to think of himself that way. He believed his position generated significant influence, but "it was a moral power, not a physical one, and moral power in this world is not conclusive." In his memoirs, he mused, "The Secretary-General, it was said, should be more the general than the secretary—but where were his divisions?" Conscious of these limitations, Lie described himself as "a force for peace" but a pragmatic one, without illusions.

So it is not surprising that Lie's first bold venture should seem rather tepid in the light of a half-century of U.N. history. But it set a vital precedent. Lie had attended the first meetings of the Security Council as silent and invisible as Sir Eric Drummond. But the Security Council's imminent dismissal of Gromyko's plea to take Iran off the agenda troubled him. "The United Nations, I felt, should aim to settle disputes, not to inflame them," he recalled later. "If both Iran and the U.S.S.R. agreed that their quarrel had been resolved, the Security Council should not indicate the contrary."

Lie and his counsel, Abraham Feller, an American, prepared a memorandum arguing that Gromyko was right; from a legal point of view, there was no justification for keeping the Iran issue on the agenda. In the preamble to the memorandum, addressed to that month's president of the Security Council, Lie said, "I submit the views herein expressed to you for such use as you may care to make of them."

As Ambassador Quo Tai-chi of China, president that month under the rotating system of the Security Council, entered the meeting room on April 16, Lie tried to hand him the memorandum. Quo looked puzzled and annoyed and refused to take it. A persistent Lie then sent the memorandum to a Quo aide, asking that it be read at the meeting. Quo assigned an interpreter to read the Lie memorandum aloud at the start of the session and then ordered it submitted to consideration by a so-called Committee of Experts. With utter contempt for what these experts would decide, Quo gaveled the Security Council to prepare to vote on Gromyko's motion to expunge the issue from the agenda. Gromyko and Ambassador Oscar Lange of Poland protested that it was unfair to vote without hearing the assessment by the experts of Lie's memorandum. "The Secretary-General is an important official of the United Nations, invested by the Charter with special and important powers," Lange argued, "and . . . we cannot vote now as if his opinion did not count or exist." Quo acknowledged his mistake, reversed his position, and postponed the vote pending the report of the experts.

"My memorandum fell like a bombshell," Lie wrote to an old colleague in the Norwegian foreign ministry. It was headline news worldwide. Stettinius accosted him in the delegates' lounge, complaining that Lie had failed to consult him in advance. Secretary of State Byrnes told a news conference in Washington that Lie had exceeded his powers by submitting the memorandum. Gossips in Washington derided Lie as "Moscow's man."

The Committee of Experts was hardly an independent body but a group of eleven specialists, each representing a government on the Security Council. Usually the legal counsels of their missions, they voted the dictates of their employers, not the logic of their expertise. In this case, they voted eight to three that Gromyko and Lie were wrong: it was legal to keep the Iran issue on the agenda. The three dissenters came from the Soviet Union, Poland, and France. The Security Council, when it received the report from its experts, voted the same way, with the same three dissenters. The question of Soviet troops in Iran never came before the Security Council again, yet it remained on the agenda for thirty years.

But the committee had a second issue to deal with: the propriety of Lie's memorandum. Did he trespass by submitting it? If not, just how far should he be allowed to go? Australian Foreign Minister Herbert Evatt instructed his expert to insist that the secretary-general's right to intervene was "absolute and not limited." But the American expert, Joseph E. Johnson, under the orders of the Truman administration, argued that the United States was "not at all sure that the Charter can be construed as authorizing the Secretary-General to make comments on political and substantive matters." Some delegates said that the secretary-general could speak only when invited to do so. In the end, the Soviet-Australian view prevailed, and the committee decided unanimously that "the Secretary-General, or his deputy acting on his behalf, may make either oral or written statements

to the Security Council concerning any question under consideration by it."

Trygve Lie did not inundate the Security Council with
speeches and statements. "The concept of a spokesman for the world
interest is in many ways far ahead of our times . . . ," he wrote in his
memoirs. "To have gone too far, too fast, might have lost everything.
I believe that the influence of the office of Secretary-General must be
developed slowly and steadily over the years." He was pleased and
proud that "these rights were secured at an early stage in the organization's history."

⚜⚜

Perhaps due to the walkout, the veto, the acrimony, the sense of
disappointment over the beginnings, some Americans began to wonder whether they really wanted the U.N. as a neighbor. In Westchester County, New York, protest groups merged into a United
Westchester Citizens Committee to Save Our Homes. In Connecticut, the city of Greenwich voted 5,505 to 2,019 against the use of their
area as a site for the U.N. The General Assembly reopened the whole
question of where in America the U.N. would stay.

In the meantime, Lie had to scurry about for temporary hous-
ing. Once the school year resumed, the Security Council moved
from Hunter College to the Sperry Gyroscope plant at Lake Success
on Long Island. The plant, geared up for war production just a few
years ago, was now the property of the federal government's War Assets Administration. New York City donated the New York municipal
auditorium on the site of the 1939 World's Fair in Flushing Meadow
for the annual meetings of the General Assembly. It had been used as
a skating rink since the close of the World's Fair.

There was some sentiment in the General Assembly to locate
the U.N. permanently in Philadelphia or San Francisco. President
Truman offered use of the old Spanish fortress known as the Presidio
in San Francisco without cost. But the Russians and British rejected
San Francisco as too far from Europe. Trygve Lie favored New York
and appealed to Mayor William O'Dwyer and Robert Moses, New
York's urban planner and overseer of construction, to come up with

an offer. Moses suggested the Turtle Bay area, six blocks of slaughter-houses and slums alongside the East River in central Manhattan. The cost was too high for the U.N., but Moses began soliciting donations.

On December 11, 1946, U.N. Ambassador Warren Austin, the former senator from Vermont who succeeded Stettinius, informed the U.N. that John D. Rockefeller Jr. had offered it $8.5 million to buy the Turtle Bay slum area. The General Assembly accepted the offer by a vote of forty-six to seven. The U.N. complex, including the thirty-nine-story Secretariat Building, the General Assembly Hall, and the Conference Building for the Security Council on eighteen acres of land, was designed mainly by Wallace K. Harrison, the architect for Rockefeller Center. With the work completed in less than six years, the U.N. settled into its own complex in 1952.

In these early years, the pattern was set for most of the next four decades. At a cocktail party in May 1946, Senator Tom Connally of Texas, a member of the U.S. delegation to the General Assembly, asked Soviet Foreign Minister V. M. Molotov sarcastically if he knew how to say "yes" in any language. Molotov burst into laughter and shook his head. Unless one side was napping, like the Russians at the start of the Korean War, the U.N. could do very little in crises involving either the United States or the Soviet Union. It would thus play a secondary role in the Cold War. But there were other terrible crises in the world, some independent of the Cold War or only tangential to it. U.N. leaders of vision and wisdom would find ways to deal with them.

✤ 3 ✤

Ralph Bunche
and the Infant State
of Israel

Ralph Bunche never rose to the higher ranks of American officialdom because he was black and never rose to the highest position in the United Nations because he was American. Yet there is little doubt that he deserves acclaim as one of the great civil servants of the twentieth century, a man who helped infuse the United Nations for its first two decades with integrity, intelligence, and sensitive diplomatic skill.

He was born in Detroit on August 7, 1903, the son of a barber often out of work and of a beautiful, sickly mother. The family moved from Detroit to Cleveland to Knoxville to Toledo to Detroit to Albuquerque before his mother died of tuberculosis in 1917 and his father dropped out of sight. Bunche was thirteen. He and his sister were then brought up by their maternal grandparents in Los Angeles.

His grandmother, whom he called Nana, was surely the single most important influence on his life. She was so light-skinned that she could easily have denied her culture but refused to do so. "Nana was fiercely proud of her origin and her race, and everyone in our 'clan' got the race-pride message very early in life," Bunche once wrote. "It has stuck with me." When Ralph graduated from Jefferson High School in Los Angeles as the valedictorian in 1922, the principal told Nana that her grandson was such a good student that the teachers and staff had never thought of him as a Negro. "You are wrong to say that," replied Nana angrily. "It is an insult to Ralph, to me, to his parents and his whole race. Why haven't you thought of him as a Negro? He is a Negro and he is proud of it. So am I."

Brian Urquhart, his colleague and biographer, who had access to Bunche's private files after his death, cites numerous instances of Bunche's need to prove himself in a society that classified him first and foremost as a black. Harvard historian Benjamin Fielding Wright, recommending Bunche for a government position, described him in 1941 as "one of the few—perhaps the only—Negro graduate student . . . at Harvard . . . able to compete for fellowships on equal terms with the better white students."

His wife, Ruth, in a complaining letter, once wrote to him, "I know you think you are the Miracle Negro with the whites, but I am sure you are just a novelty and whom they can get two men's work out of . . . though it may be killing you and hurting your family." Bunche replied with some exasperation at her complaint that "much of my conduct in the presence of whites is not at all the result of any special feeling about them, but a calculated and deliberate intent to prove to them that I am, despite my race, their equal if not their superior in intellect, ability, knowledge and general savoir-faire." He attended the opening session of the San Francisco conference as an adviser to the American delegation and wrote Ruth, "I did feel a bit proud this afternoon at being the only Negro who sat on the first floor."

He graduated from UCLA (then known as the University of California, Southern Branch) with highest honors in political science in 1927. He was valedictorian, president of the debating society, a star of the basketball team, and a writer for the *Daily Bruin*, the college newspaper. He won a fellowship at Harvard University, completed his master's degree, and then accepted an appointment to Howard University in Washington. Howard wanted him to reorganize its political science department. This was Bunche's first experience at living in a segregated city, and he did not like it. "Living in the nation's capital is like serving out a sentence," he said. "It's extremely difficult for a Negro to maintain even a semblance of human dignity in Washington."

In the 1930s, Bunche married Ruth, a student at Howard, taught at Howard, completed his doctorate at Harvard, and won several grants that allowed him to study and conduct research in Europe and Africa. He wrote his dissertation on "French Administration in Togoland and Dahomey." He was not a sophisticated traveler. "French food is terrible," he wrote Ruth after a few days in Paris. "I've had indigestion and dysentery ever since I've been here." He also studied at the London School of Economics, attending the weekly cultural studies class of anthropologist Bronislaw Malinowski. His most flamboyant classmate was Jomo Kenyatta, the future president of Kenya, who championed female circumcision and posed for his book *Facing Mount Kenya* wearing skins and brandishing a spear. By the beginning of World War II, Bunche was one of the few specialists on Africa in the United States.

Bunche, however, did not neglect studies on the role of the black in American society. In 1940, he was a close associate of the Swedish sociologist Gunnar Myrdal, who published the monumental study *An American Dilemma: The Negro Problem in Modern Democracy* in 1944. Bunche wrote four monographs for Myrdal's study, including a 1,660-page analysis, *The Political Status of the Negro*. Myrdal's *An American Dilemma* held its place as the premier examination of the place of the black in America for more than a generation.

During World War II, Bunche worked for the OSS (the Office of Strategic Services), the forerunner of the CIA, mainly preparing analyses of African politics. In 1944, however, the State Department asked him to join its team preparing proposals for a future international organization. The team needed a specialist who knew a good deal about colonialism and mandates: the former German and Turkish colonies that had been parceled out to the World War I victors under the supervision of the League of Nations; the U.N. would continue the system, change the name of mandates to trusteeships, and prepare them for independence.

In the role of a specialist advising the U.S. delegations on colonialism and trusteeships, Bunche took part in the Dumbarton Oaks, San Francisco, and London preparatory conferences. After the establishment of the U.N., he worked for the Secretariat for a few months. Trygve Lie then asked the State Department if it would object to the permanent appointment of Bunche to the U.N. Secretariat as director of the trusteeship division. The United States agreed, and Bunche took up his new post at the end of 1946. Since the San Francisco conference, he had been hoping for a new U.N. career that would take him away from Washington. "In many ways it would be great for all of us and especially the children," he had written Ruth, "—a new life, new surroundings, good schools, no ghettoes and no jim crow." In his new position, he would soon have to deal with the most knotty and dangerous mandate of all—the British mandate of Palestine.

❧❦

"The long-range fate of Palestine," President Truman told his aides, "was the kind of problem we had the U.N. for." At the beginning, in fact, Palestine seemed like the only kind of problem that the U.N. could tackle. Free of Soviet-American bickering and tension, the Palestine conflict was powered by the enmity of three weaker antagonists: the Jews, the Arabs, and an imperial Great Britain in decline. The U.N. was midwife at the birth of Israel, and the hatreds and machinations of the Arab-Israeli conflict would occupy much of the time of both the Security Council and the General Assembly for most of the first half-century. The good intentions of the U.N., however, would become suspect, especially to the Israelis, and when the Israeli government finally reached an accord with Yasser Arafat and his Palestine Liberation Organization in 1993, the U.N. would be no more than a distant observer. But the Jews and Arabs could not chase the U.N. out of their history.

During World War I, the British inspired and financed an Arab revolt against the Ottoman Empire and occupied Palestine and other Arab lands in a Middle East campaign designed to tie up enemy Turkish troops. Colonel T. E. Lawrence ("Lawrence of Arabia") became the hero of this derring-do, and his popular books stamped the image of the romantic Arab on the minds of the British. But the British government also courted its own Jewish citizens as well. Since early in the century, Zionists led by the Vienna journalist Theodore Herzl had sought a Jewish state in the biblical lands of Palestine. In a letter to Lord Rothschild, the president of the British Zionist Organization, on November 2, 1917, Foreign Secretary Arthur J. Balfour promised that "His Majesty's Government view with favor the establishment in Palestine of a national home for the Jewish people, and will use their best endeavors to facilitate the achievement of this objective"; the sentence, however, did not end there. Balfour added a subordinate clause as caveat: "it being clearly understood that nothing shall be done which may prejudice the civil and religious rights of existing non-Jewish communities in Palestine. . . ." Fulfilling both the promise and the subordinate clause would prove difficult and delicate, if not impossible.

After World War I, the British kept control of Palestine as a League of Nations mandate. The wording of the Balfour Declaration was endorsed by the league in the 1922 resolution creating the mandate. The British tried to keep hatreds in check but failed after World War II. The attempted genocide of that war made the conflict irreconcilable. The Jews believed that Britain could no longer justify failing to fulfill its promise of a homeland. In the eyes of the Arabs, however, that would amount to Christians giving the Jews Arab land to assuage European guilt. The Arabs thus looked on the Jews as European colonial oppressors.

The Nazi Holocaust—on top of killing six million Jews in Europe—had displaced hundreds of thousands of other Jews and left them destitute and desperate for a new home. Zionists wanted the British to open Palestine to these refugees of Nazism. Many Americans and Europeans—out of sympathy, horror, and perhaps a sense of guilt over the Holocaust—supported the Jewish campaign to open Palestine. But the Palestinian Arabs feared they would be swamped by massive Jewish immigration. Arab governments insisted that the British must block Jewish immigration. The British acquiesced and severely limited acceptance of Jewish refugees into the mandate. In the most-publicized incident the British turned back the ship *Exodus* at the port of Haifa in 1947, forcing it to return to Europe with forty-five hundred displaced Jews.

The frustrated British grew weary of Jewish terror and the financial drain on its strapped budget. In July 1946, the underground Irgun, led by Menachem Begin, the future prime minister, blew up the wing of the King David Hotel in Jerusalem used by the British for their military headquarters, killing ninety-one people. In July 1947, the Irgun hung two British sergeants in retaliation for the execution of Jewish terrorists and left the bodies booby-trapped. "We repaid our enemy in kind," said Begin. The Stern Gang, whose leadership included Yitzhak Shamir, another future prime minister, was regarded as even more notorious. The British decided to drop the whole issue of immigration and the future of Palestine on the United Nations.

In May 1947, the General Assembly named a Special Committee on Palestine of eleven ambassadors to study the issue and make recommendations. Secretary-General Trygve Lie appointed Assistant Secretary-General Victor Hoo of China as his representative to the committee and Ralph Bunche as Hoo's special assistant. Bunche was impressed neither by Hoo nor by the ambassadors. He described them as petty, vain, and "not infrequently either vicious or stupid." They were "just about the worst group I have ever had to work with," Bunche said. "If they do a good job it will be a real miracle." The problem was so complex and the frustrations so inevitable that he told a friend, "I am now a Near East expert, completely befuddled."

The Special Committee presented its report to the General Assembly three months later. A majority of seven ambassadors (representing Canada, Czechoslovakia, Guatemala, the Netherlands, Peru, Sweden, and Uruguay) proposed that "Palestine within its present borders, following a transitional period of two years from 1 September 1947, shall be constituted into an independent Arab state, an independent Jewish state, and the (international) City of Jerusalem." The three political entities would remain within an economic union. In a minority report, three ambassadors (representing India, Iran, and Yugoslavia) instead proposed a single federal state. The Australian ambassador would not sign either report.

Bunche was cynical about the motivation of the majority. He described most of them as anti-Semites looking for "a means of dumping world Jewry on the Arabs." Yet their conclusions paralleled the views of the governments of the world's two most powerful countries. Both the United States and the Soviet Union supported the creation of a Jewish state through partition. The Soviet Union, in fact, hoped that the Socialist leaders of the Jewish state might serve as a kind of opening wedge for Marxism in the Middle East. President Truman often endorsed the idea of a Jewish state and resented the condescending memorandums from the State Department that warned him about the adverse reaction from Arab governments if the United States ever recognized one.

Despite the Balfour Declaration, the British, with their imperial ties to the Arab lands of the Middle East, were worried about the consequences of a Jewish state and resented Truman's endorsements, accusing him of pandering for votes. "There's no Arab vote in America," wrote Prime Minister Clement Attlee later, "but there's a very heavy Jewish vote and the Americans are always having elections." British Foreign Secretary Ernest Bevin even adopted Bunche's cynicism about the motives of those who wanted masses of Jews to settle in Palestine. "I hope it will not be misunderstood in America," he told a Labour Party meeting in 1946, "if I say, with the purest of motives, that [U.S. policy toward Jewish immigration into Palestine] was because they did not want too many of them in New York."

In November 1947, the General Assembly, by a vote of thirty-three to thirteen (with ten abstentions), approved the majority report, thus accepting partition and a Jewish state. American lobbying assured the Jewish victory. The Jewish state would have 498,000 Jews and 468,000 Arabs on fifty-five hundred square miles of land while the Arab state would have 800,000 Arabs and 10,000 Jews on forty-five hundred square miles. Unlimited Jewish immigration, of course, would dramatically increase the proportion of Jews in the Jewish state. The vote was the legal foundation for the creation of the state of Israel. When the vote was announced in the General Assembly in Flushing Meadow, Zionists in the lobby were jubilant. "This is the day the Lord hath made," a rabbi shouted. Abba Eban, a witness who later became an Israeli foreign minister, wrote, "There were Jews in tears, and non-Jews moved by the nobility of the occasion. Nobody who ever lived that moment will ever lose its memory from his heart."

But Arab governments decried the General Assembly vote and refused to accept the carving of a Jewish state out of what they insisted was their land. They vowed war if partition took place. Secretary of the Navy James Forrestal warned the White House that, if war broke out, the Arabs would "push the Jews into the sea." The British government announced that it would relinquish the mandate on May 14, 1948, but would play no part in trying to force partition upon the Arabs. That decision prompted some second thoughts. If the Arabs rejected partition and the British refused to impose it, how could it be carried out, short of war? Some American diplomats felt it was time to back off.

⚜⚜

Much now depended on the steadfastness of President Truman. For the next six months, he was buffeted by American Jews who pressured him to support the establishment of a Jewish state and State Department diplomats—he called them "the striped-pants boys"— who warned him against antagonizing the Arabs. He resented the tone of the diplomats who were "in effect telling me to watch my step, that I didn't really understand what was going on over there and that I ought to leave it to the *experts.*" And he resented just as much the tone and persistence of the American Zionists. One Jewish leader pounded on Truman's desk in the Oval Office and shouted at him. "Jesus Christ couldn't please them when he was on earth," Truman told the cabinet, "so how could anyone expect that I would have any luck."

The issue split the State Department and the White House staff. The White House suspected that the diplomats were anti-Semitic, while the diplomats suspected that the men around Truman cared only about the Jewish vote. The State Department feared a Middle East war and a rupture with the Arab world that would endanger the supply of oil. A secret paper from George Kennan's policy planning staff even raised the specter of increased anti-Semitism in America if the U.N. went ahead with partition. Memos from State Department headquarters in Foggy Bottom, reflecting the views of Kennan's staff, proposed that the United States support a temporary U.N. trusteeship for Palestine as a way of buying time for partition. Truman, while cruising near the Virgin Islands, agreed in principle, though he did not seem to understand that trusteeship would be viewed by the Jews as an abandonment of partition and a Jewish state. Truman, however, did ask to see an advance copy of any American speech at the U.N. that announced a major change in policy.

While this battle roared on behind the closed doors in Washington, Eddie Jacobson, Truman's old army buddy and Kansas City haberdashery store partner, came to see the president. Jacobson, an ardent Zionist, wanted Truman to meet Chaim Weizmann, the British scientist who had become the world leader of Zionism and would go on to become the first president of Israel. Jacobson obviously hoped to cement Truman's support of partition. But Truman was sick of hearing from Zionist leaders and refused. Jacobson suddenly found himself thinking "that my dear friend, the President of the United States, was at that moment as close to being an anti-Semite as a man could possibly be." While pointing to an equestrian statue of Andrew Jackson on a table, Jacobson then made an impassioned speech proclaiming that Weizmann was his hero just the way Jackson was the hero of Truman. Comparing Weizmann to Andrew Jackson was a long stretch of imagination, but it worked with Truman. "You win, you baldheaded son of a bitch," Truman said. "I will see him."

Weizmann slipped into the White House secretly on the evening of March 18, 1948. They met for forty-five minutes, and Truman assured Weizmann of his support for partition and a Jewish state. On the very next day, however, Truman's ambassador to the United Nations, former Republican Senator Warren Austin of Vermont, astounded the General Assembly by announcing that the U.S. government no longer supported immediate partition and proposed instead to turn Palestine into a U.N. trusteeship. Austin spoke under orders from Secretary of State George C. Marshall, who assumed the new policy had the approval of Truman. The speech created a sensation, but Truman did not find out about it until he read the newspapers the next morning.

"How could this have happened?" Truman said to his aide Clark Clifford. "I assured Chaim Weizmann that we were for partition and would stick to it. He must think I'm a shitass." On his calendar, the president wrote, "The State Dept. pulled the rug from under me today. . . . This morning I find that the State Dept. has reversed my Palestine policy. The first I know about it is what I see in the papers! Isn't that hell? I'm now in the position of a liar and a double-crosser. I never felt so in my life." Although Truman suspected a conspiracy by some of the striped-pants boys who "have always wanted to cut my throat," the foreign policy debacle was based mostly on misunderstanding and confusion. Truman clearly had failed to realize the enormity of the policy change that he had approved. And the State Department had failed to understand that the Austin speech was so sensational, it needed clearance from the White House.

At the United Nations, Trygve Lie interpreted the American abandonment of partition as a slap in the face of the U.N. and of himself. Since the General Assembly had approved partition by majority vote, he reasoned, the United States should have supported it. "The American reversal was a blow to the United Nations and showed a profoundly disheartening disregard for its effectiveness and standing," Lie wrote in his memoirs. "I could not help asking myself what the future of the United Nations would be, if this was the measure of support it could expect from the United States."

Lie called on Ambassador Austin at his luxurious apartment in the Waldorf-Astoria towers and proposed that the two of them resign. The secretary-general said that Austin should resign in protest against his instructions from Washington and that he himself would resign "as a means of arousing popular opinion to the realization of the danger in which the whole structure of the United Nations has been placed." Austin replied—without sarcasm—"Trygve, I didn't know you were so sensitive." But he rejected the idea of resigning and advised Lie to give it up as well.

The secretary-general also called on Russian Ambassador Andrey Gromyko and informed him that he intended to resign in protest at the American shift of position. "I have never found Ambassador Gromyko more friendly," Lie wrote later. "His melancholy features lit up with sympathy." Gromyko, like Austin, personally advised against any resignation but cabled Moscow for an official reaction. Moscow, too, saw no need for a resignation. Lie decided to remain on the job.

The American turnabout, according to Lie, had caused depression at the U.N., jubilation among Arabs, despair among Zionists, and self-righteousness among the British. Protests poured into the White House and State Department. Congressman Emanuel Celler of New York said that no more shameful decision in international politics had ever been made. He called it an "under-handed turnabout." The American Jewish Congress, in an emergency meeting, accused the State Department of "thoroughly dishonorable" conduct. Friends deluged Eddie Jacobson with protest calls, sending him to a sickbed for the weekend. "Oh, how could you stoop so low?" a Carnegie Tech professor wrote the White House. ". . . This revolting move must and should be the death of the United Nations." Mrs. Eleanor Roosevelt submitted her resignation as a member of the American delegation to the General Assembly, but Truman refused to accept it.

Despite his annoyance, the president did not try to clear things up in public. Ambassador Austin, in fact, moved ahead and persuaded the Security Council to call a special session of the General Assembly beginning in mid-April to consider a trusteeship for Palestine. The American idea did not evoke much enthusiasm. Jewish leaders, however, did not intend to wait for the outcome of the special session. They planned to declare an independent Jewish state as soon as the British departed on May 14. Truman felt the pressure to recognize it, but Secretary Marshall adamantly opposed recognition.

On May 12, just two days before the fateful day, State Department and White House aides met in Truman's office to iron out Palestine policy. Truman asked Clark Clifford to make the case for recognition, but Secretary Marshall objected even to Clifford's presence. "This is not a political meeting," he said. Truman overruled Marshall, noting he had personally invited Clifford to take part. Undersecretary of State Robert A. Lovett argued for trusteeship and against recognition; Clifford argued that recognition would be an act of humanity—"everything this country should represent." Lovett read from intelligence reports that warned of a conspiracy by the Soviet Union to send Soviet Jews and Communist agents to Palestine. In any event, he insisted, it was foolish to recognize a Jewish state before it was clear it could exist. Premature recognition would be disastrous to American prestige at the U.N., Lovett said, and would look like a transparent attempt to win the Jewish vote. Secretary Marshall broke in and told Truman somberly that "if the President were to follow Mr. Clifford's advice and if in the [1948 presidential] elections I were to vote, I would vote against the President." Clifford believed that Truman had never received a sharper rebuke. The meeting ended immediately. Truman had made up his mind to endure the wrath of his revered secretary of state.

☙❧

On the Sabbath eve of May 14, 1948 — the fifth day of Iyar, 5708, in the Jewish calendar — the Provisional State Council in Tel Aviv issued the proclamation declaring "the establishment of the Jewish State in Palestine, to be called Medinath Yisrael [the State of Israel]." It was midnight, Tel Aviv time; 6 P.M., Washington time. By then, tempestuous Palestine had been abandoned by the British; Sir Alan Gordon Cunningham, the British high commissioner, accompanied by the last British soldiers and colonial officers, had sailed out of Haifa on a Royal Navy cruiser a half hour earlier. At eleven minutes after six, White House Press Secretary Charlie Ross announced that the United States had recognized the state of Israel, the first country in the world to do so. Recognition by the Soviet Union followed swiftly.

In retrospect the Truman decision does not seem so surprising. "Three years after the full disclosures about the gas furnaces," wrote his biographer Robert J. Donovan, "it is inconceivable that any president of the United States in office in May 1948 would have done essentially other than that which Truman did." Trygve Lie, who believed that all members of the U.N. were duty bound to support the original decision for partition, hailed the establishment of Israel as "one of the epic events of history, coming at the end not merely of thirty years, but of two thousand years of accumulated sorrows, bitterness and conflict."

Shortly before the announcement of the American recognition, Clifford called Dean Rusk, the assistant secretary of state in charge of U.N. affairs, and asked him to notify Austin. "But this cuts across what our delegation has been trying to accomplish in the General Assembly," Rusk said. Nevertheless, Clifford told him, he must do what the president wanted. The news reached the U.N. while delegates were discussing a French-American proposal for temporary international rule of Jerusalem. Ambassador Austin, who had left the floor to take the phone call from Rusk, was so upset that he left by limousine for the Waldorf-Astoria without telling anyone else in the delegation.

When they heard the rumors, some American delegates burst out laughing, for it seemed so absurd. When the truth sank in, Trygve Lie reported, "the mortification of the American representatives was understandably acute." They had been arguing for weeks in favor of trusteeship. But now their own president, by recognizing the new Jewish state, had rendered their arguments for trusteeship ludicrous. Philip Jessup, an American delegate, reached the rostrum and confirmed the rumor, reading an Associated Press dispatch to the General Assembly. Ambassador Guillermo Belt of Cuba, who had pushed the trusteeship resolution through a committee at American insistence, was so angry that he told diplomats he was marching to the podium to announce that Cuba would withdraw from the United Nations and never again take part in an organization with such duplicitous members. American press officer Porter McKeever sat down on Belt and stopped him from going up. Mahmoud Bey Fawzi of Egypt denounced the special session as a "fake." Gromyko accused the United States of "unprincipled conduct." "For four weeks we were dupes," said Charles Malik of Lebanon, "and the whole thing was a show and a game." Secretary Marshall ordered Rusk to New York to talk the American delegates out of resigning.

When the Security Council met the next day, it found a cable from the Egyptian minister of foreign affairs. The cable announced, "Egyptian armed forces have started to enter Palestine to establish security and order." Although it did no more than carry out the threat made so often by the Arab world, Trygve Lie described the cable as brazen and an open defiance of the United Nations. Other Arab armies entered Palestine as well. The first Arab-Israeli war had officially begun.

🌿

Bloody battling had ravaged Palestine long before then. In January 1948, the Arab Liberation Army—a makeshift force of five thousand irregulars from Syria, Iraq, and Lebanon organized, trained, and armed by Syria—had made their way into the territory. The Liberation Army had few Palestinian Arabs. This force quickly put the Jewish army known as the Haganah on the defensive. But the Haganah, bolstered by a shipment of arms from Communist Czechoslovakia, took the offensive in March, captured the port of Haifa by late April, and wrested control of Jaffa and most of eastern Galilee by Independence Day in May. As the Jews advanced, Arab civilians fled, leaving behind empty towns and villages.

There were numerous terrorist attacks by both sides. An explosion on Yehuda Street in Jerusalem in late February left 52 dead, most of them Jews. The most sensational and horrifying act of terrorism came at dawn on April 10 when the Irgun of Begin and the Stern Gang of Shamir attacked the sleeping Arab village of Deir Yassin on a hill on the outskirts of Jerusalem. The terrorists had not expected resistance, but when the Arabs fought back the Jews rushed from one flat-topped stone house to another, throwing bags of dynamite inside. The Jews murdered 240 men, women, and children. The Haganah condemned the attack but never punished those responsible. The attack was part of a campaign to capture all those areas allotted to the Jewish state under partition and clear them as much as possible of Arabs. The Arabs retaliated four days later, ambushing a convoy of Jewish doctors and nurses en route to the Hadassah Hospital on Mount Scopus outside Jerusalem. The death toll was 77.

🌿

The Security Council, soon after the declaration of Israeli independence, appointed Count Folke Bernadotte, the former president of the Swedish Red Cross, as the U.N. mediator for the conflict. Tall and slender with a deeply lined face, Count Bernadotte liked to walk about in his white bemedaled Red Cross uniform. He was energetic, enthusiastic, and incapable of sitting still for any length of time. Trygve Lie asked Bunche to go along with Bernadotte as the secretary-general's own special representative in Palestine.

The Arabs had moved swiftly. The Arab Legion of Jordan, led by a British officer, John Bagot Glubb, better known as Glubb Pasha, with Iraqi troops alongside, occupied Judea and Samaria, the West Bank area that had been allotted to the Arabs under partition. The Arab Legion's artillery pounded the Jewish areas of Jerusalem. Lebanese troops marched into Arab Galilee. The Egyptians took over Gaza and Beersheba and laid siege to Jewish settlements in the Negev. Syrian troops massed on their border with Palestine. The new state of Israel was battling or threatened on all sides.

When Count Bernadotte arrived in Jerusalem, Jews crowded the streets to cheer him. Using a white-painted DC-3 with both U.N. and Red Cross insignia, he and Bunche rushed from capital to capital in the Mideast. In Amman, Glubb Pasha urged Bunche to impose a deadline on both sides to avert interminable haggling. Bernadotte did so and, by threatening to throw the whole matter to the Security Council by June 9, managed to persuade both sides to reluctantly accept a month-long truce in mid-June. Unarmed U.N. observers arrived, wearing U.N. armbands and carrying U.N. flags. It was the first military observer group in U.N. history. When the Arabs in July stubbornly refused to sign an extension of the truce, Count Bernadotte and Bunche flew to New York and persuaded the Security Council to impose one.

As the peace mediation continued, Bunche found it difficult to deal with the Arabs. "My patience with Arabs wearing thin," he wrote. "They refuse to face realities and peddle myths." In late June, Count Bernadotte unveiled preliminary proposals for a new partition and peace plan, largely drafted by Bunche: Lines would be redrawn to give all of the Negev in the south to the Arabs and all of the Galilee in the north to Israel. The two states might be united in some kind of economic union. Most controversial, Jerusalem would be an Arab city with an autonomous Jewish community. The Israeli outcry was instant. Bernadotte had betrayed them. He would take away not only hallowed Jerusalem but also land that they had won in battle. Some hysterical commentators in the Israeli press, probably allied to the Stern Gang, even accused him of Nazi sympathies and of acting as a British agent. In the face of this rage, Bernadotte modified his plan during the next few months and settled on the original idea of designating Jerusalem an international city under U.N. control. This did not allay Israeli anger. The Arabs condemned the Bernadotte plan as well, for they still refused to accept any Jewish state at all. Bernadotte knew that the plan was not acceptable to either side but hoped the U.N. would impose it on the belligerents.

On September 16, the Stern Gang assassinated Count Bernadotte in Jerusalem. The plot had been approved by Shamir and others in the hierarchy of the gang. A group of men in khakis blocked the path of the mediator's three-car convoy with their jeep. One sauntered over to the last car as if he were a guard checking identification and then aimed an automatic pistol at the backseat and fired at Bernadotte. Bernadotte and a French observer died in the fusillade. The killer—Yehoshua Cohen—and his accomplices disabled the cars in the convoy by blasting the engines and tires and then escaped in the jeep. Bunche would have been in the car with Bernadotte, but mechanical repairs had delayed his flight. The worldwide outcry prompted the Israelis to disband the Stern Gang and arrest more than two hundred people in their investigation of the killing, but no one was brought to trial. The Swedish foreign ministry accused the Israeli investigators of "astonishing negligence." Prime Minister David Ben-Gurion, in fact, retired years later to a kibbutz with Yehoshua Cohen. When Ralph Bunche visited Ben-Gurion at that kibbutz in 1959, Ben-Gurion said that he regretted the murder of Count Bernadotte, but "remember what Count Bernadotte did to us."

※ ※

Full-scale fighting erupted again after the assassination. The battling pitted forty thousand Arab troops against more than sixty-five thousand Israeli troops (if the home guard is counted). Bunche was named to succeed Count Bernadotte as acting mediator and then as mediator. By the end of 1948, the Arab armies were badly beaten. The Haganah controlled the Negev, and an Egyptian brigade was trapped at Faluja near Gaza. But the Israelis had lost six thousand people during the war, almost 1 percent of the new state's population. Perhaps seven hundred thousand Palestinian Arabs were now refugees, having fled or been driven from their homes, a legacy of the 1948 war as significant for the Middle East as the creation of Israel.

Bunche lobbied the General Assembly to accept and impose the Bernadotte peace plan but failed. He then put all his energy into the only other avenue toward peace: pushing the belligerents toward a negotiated agreement. He managed to mediate face-saving armistices in tortuous negotiations on the Greek island of Rhodes. At the end, Israel was a fifth larger than the Jewish state that had been envisioned in the original U.N. Palestine resolution. These armistice borders held until the Six-Day War of 1967.

For the Israelis, the Bunche mediation talks in the Hôtel des Roses on Rhodes were always a model of what the U.N. ought to be doing. Direct talks were sometimes minimal but still direct. After agreeing to a cease-fire, the Israeli and Egyptian delegations arrived on January 13, 1949. Bunche and his staff lived in one wing of the hotel, the Israeli and Egyptian delegates lived in the other, on separate floors. When all assembled in Bunche's sitting room, the Egyptians tried to talk to Bunche rather than to the Israelis, but this awkwardness broke down often. The Jews and Arabs would argue with each other in English and French. Bunche even organized billiards games between the two sides. He ordered ceramic plates from a Rhodes manufacturer inscribed with the legend RHODES ARMISTICE TALKS 1949. Opening a chest of drawers in his room, he pointed to the plates and told the delegates, "If you reach agreement, each of you will get one to take home. If you don't, I'll break them over your heads!"

The chain-smoking Bunche had to persuade the Egyptians to accept the reality of defeat in the Negev and to persuade the Israelis to allow the Egyptians to save face by holding on to the Gaza Strip and withdrawing their trapped troops from Faluja with honor. The Israelis would give up some territory seized in war but would have peace and a viable independent state. Acceptance of this bargain required of Bunche hours of cajoling, bouts of toughness, interminable rewriting of draft agreements, a deft understanding of bruised sensitivities, good humor, and incredible patience. As he continually drafted compromises, Bunche wrote, "Neither side anxious to meet the other, but both want me to persuade the other. What a life!" Israeli negotiator Walter Eytan said that Bunche was so good at drafting proposals that "sooner or later he was able to contrive a formula to defeat almost any problem." Bunche was helped by support from the Truman administration. In early February, U.S. Secretary of State Dean Acheson urged Israeli Prime Minister David Ben-Gurion to accept Bunche's proposals. A few weeks later, Secretary-General Trygve Lie applied the same kind of pressure to Egyptian Foreign Minister Mahmoud Fawzi Bey, meeting him three days in a row.

The armistice was signed February 24, 1949, celebrated by a party at the hotel in the evening. The festivities even featured Israelis and Egyptians in Ping-Pong matches. One of the Israeli delegates, Yitzhak Rabin, a future prime minister, refused to attend in protest at the compromise allowing the Gaza Strip to go to Egypt. Eytan, the chief Israeli delegate, tried to mollify him. "An armistice with Egypt is worth the Gaza area," Eytan said. But an angry Rabin flew back to Israel ahead of his colleagues. Eytan later described Bunche to *Time* magazine as "superhuman."

In the next few months, Bunche and his U.N. staff mediated armistices as well between Israel and Jordan, Lebanon, and Syria. These talkfests and arguments were just as trying as the first set. "You can't imagine what it takes to hold these monkeys together long enough to squeeze agreement out of them," he wrote his wife. ". . . I swear by all that's holy, I will never come anywhere near the Palestine problem once I liberate myself from this trap." His work done, Bunche decided to stop in Stockholm on his way home so he could lay a wreath on the grave of Count Bernadotte.

Bunche and Israel had hoped the armistices would lead to peace agreements within six months, but they did not. The Bunche-mediated negotiations marked the last time Israel felt sanguine about the United Nations. Disenchantment and bitterness followed in a few years. Israel soon felt that U.N. mediation always meant a loss of territory won in battle and an alibi for Arabs refusing to negotiate directly with the Israelis. U.N. peacekeepers would later be scorned by Israelis for failing to stop Arab infiltrators and terrorists from slipping into Israeli territory. When the mushrooming numbers of Third World governments took control of the General Assembly, the United Nations—in Israeli eyes—turned into a seething cauldron of anti-Semitism.

The Israelis also remembered that neither the U.N. nor any of its members had sent troops to defend the new state of Israel when it was invaded by the Arabs in 1948. In fact, in the view of the Israelis, the U.N. did not even try to stop the fighting until it was clear the Israelis would win. Yet Israel could not ignore the U.N. The Arab-Israeli conflict would monopolize the attention of the young United Nations, only three years older than Israel itself, many times in its history, and Israel often had to bend to its will.

❧❦

Ralph Bunche returned to New York an international hero. Newspapers throughout the world credited him with bringing peace to the Middle East. Secretary of State Dean Acheson offered him the post of assistant secretary for Near Eastern, South Asian, and African affairs. "In the most courteous manner he declined the invitation," Acheson wrote in his memoirs. "All too much of his present duty, he said, had been taken up with these seemingly unsolvable problems. His most heartfelt wish was for relief from them, not deeper involvement." When pressed by President Truman, Bunche acknowledged the true reason: He did not intend to live again in a segregated city like Washington.

Bunche was lunching in the U.N. delegates' dining room overlooking the East River on September 22, 1950, when his secretary informed him that he had been awarded the Nobel peace prize. Bunche toyed with the idea of refusing on the grounds that U.N. peacemaking was not undertaken for prizes, but Trygve Lie talked him out of it. He was the first black American to win a Nobel prize. In his Nobel lecture, delivered in the great hall of Oslo University, Bunche said that "the United Nations exists not merely to preserve the peace but also to make change—even radical change—possible without violent upheaval." By then, he was surely the best known U.N. face in America. He even flew to Los Angeles in 1951 to hand out Oscars on Academy Awards night.

❧ 4 ❧

The Korean War:
No More Manchurias

Secretary-General Trygve Lie heard the phone ring around midnight Saturday, June 24, 1950. A radio newscast a few minutes earlier had reported skirmishing along the border separating North and South Korea, but the report had been too vague to fret over. The late-night caller was John Hickerson, assistant secretary of state for U.N. affairs, and he had more solid, more depressing news. He informed Lie that North Korean troops had invaded South Korea. "My God, Jack," said Lie, "that's war against the United Nations." "Trygve you're telling me," Hickerson replied.

Lie said he was ready to convene the Security Council in an emergency meeting. The secretary-general then phoned his aides and instructed them to get full information from the U.N. Commission and its observers stationed on the thirty-eighth parallel that served as the artificial border. He also asked his aides to tell Ambassador Benegal Rau of India, president of the council for the month of June, to prepare for an emergency meeting. Lie tried to go back to sleep but was wakened repeatedly by Ernest A. Gross, the deputy American ambassador, who wanted to discuss the crisis. Former Senator Warren Austin, the ambassador, was ill and at home in Burlington, Vermont. In one of the calls, at 3 A.M., Gross formally requested an emergency meeting. Lie agreed to convene one at two o'clock that Sunday afternoon.

A half hour before Hickerson phoned the secretary-general, Secretary of State Dean Acheson had called President Harry S Truman in Independence, Missouri. The president had arrived in his hometown that afternoon for a visit of a couple of days. "Mr. President, I have very serious news," said Acheson. "The North Koreans have invaded South Korea." Truman, fearing this could mean the start of World War III, wanted to return to Washington immediately. But Acheson counseled him to try to get a good night's sleep. State Department officials were asking for an emergency session of the Security Council. "Everything is being done that can be," the secretary of state said. There was no point in alarming the nation with a sudden night flight to Washington.

❧ ❧

Korea was divided for the sake of convenience at the end of World War II. In August 1945, when it really didn't matter much anymore, the Soviet Union finally fulfilled its promise to enter the battle against Japan. Stalin declared war against Japan two days after the United States dropped the atomic bomb on Hiroshima, and he sent troops into northern Korea just three days before the Japanese surrender ended the war. When American troops landed in Korea a month later, the United States proposed that Japanese troops north of the thirty-eighth parallel turn themselves over to the Russians while those south of the parallel do so to the Americans. The dividing line was picked by Colonel Dean Rusk and another young officer in the Pentagon only because it was so easy to make out on a map. This proposal, accepted by the Russians and dutifully followed by the defeated Japanese, eventually transformed the parallel into a border between two hostile countries.

The allies had agreed during the war that Korea, annexed by Japan in 1910, would regain its independence after the defeat of the Japanese. But the occupiers could not agree on a way of uniting the country. The Americans, refusing to accept the Russian demand that the less populous North share power equally with the South in any united government, took the impasse to the U.N. in 1947.

At the urging of the United States, the General Assembly passed a resolution providing for separate U.N.-supervised elections in the two zones for a united national assembly. The more populous South would have more seats there than the North. The General Assembly created a U.N. commission to supervise the elections, but the commission swiftly ran into the refusal of the North to hold any. Despite this, the commission, bowing to American pressure, allowed the South to go ahead with elections that would select a government for the South alone.

These elections gave power in 1948 to a conservative government led by Syngman Rhee while the Russians installed a Communist government in the North headed by Kim Il Sung. Although each government claimed to represent a united Korea, there were now two Koreas. Both the United States and the Soviet Union withdrew their troops. But, worried about conflict between two hostile governments, the U.N. Commission remained, stationing observers in a series of posts along the thirty-eighth parallel. Peace and unity in Korea were clearly a U.N. matter when the North Koreans launched their attack upon the South.

※❧

Trygve Lie did not look on himself as some kind of neutral mediator trying to end a conflict between two antagonists. It was clear in his eyes that the U.N. had to stand up and beat back aggression; it had to shake off the shadows of impotence that still lingered from the League of Nations. The sudden North Korean thrusts had "all the elements of surprise which reminded me of the Nazi invasion of Norway." Korea was the first true test of the U.N., and he intended to show its mettle. The Security Council had a clear duty to defend South Korea, and he prepared to demand that it fulfill its duty. "I consider my stand on Korea the best justified act of seven years in the service of peace," he wrote in his memoirs. Before the emergency meeting opened, he persuaded Ambassador Rau and Egyptian Ambassador Mahmoud Fawzi Bey to vote for the American resolution even though neither had yet received instructions from his capital.

Americans looked at the problem a little differently than Lie did. They felt certain that the invasion was choreographed by the Soviet Union, and they therefore regarded it as a Russian thrust intended to test American resolve or find it napping. This thrust must be contained, they insisted, or there would be no way of halting the spread of Communism. They believed in a strong United Nations and intended to act with U.N. approval and under a U.N. umbrella. They would invoke the name of the U.N. on every step they took in Korea in the next three years—even when that step actually shunted the U.N. aside. It is not fair to proclaim that the United States did no more than use the U.N. throughout the war. But it is clear that the Truman administration would have sent troops to beat back the North Koreans even if the U.N. had refused its blessing. Asked years later if this were true, Truman replied, "No question about it."

Use of the U.N. was eased by the absence of the Soviet Union from the Security Council. For six months, Jacob Malik, the usually genial, joking Soviet ambassador, had been boycotting council sessions because China's seat was occupied by the Nationalist government of Chiang Kai-shek that had escaped to the island of Formosa and not by the Communist government of Mao Tse-tung that controlled the land mass of China. Despite the obvious crisis over Korea, Malik maintained the boycott and thus gave up his veto. "If he had appeared," Acheson said later, "we would immediately have adjusted ourselves to that and taken some other action, either through the General Assembly or unilaterally." But Acheson sounds almost cavalier in his discounting of the significance of a Malik veto. The U.N. was so involved in Korean affairs that a Security Council refusal to stem or even denounce aggression there might have demeaned the organization as spineless and useless. And, despite Acheson's planned use of it, General Assembly action in the face of Security Council inaction would have left a legal cloud over the key U.N. resolutions that committed the United States to war.

When the emergency meeting of the eleven-member Security Council opened, Ambassador Rau called on Trygve Lie to make the first statement. Lie said that reports from U.N. monitors and other sources in Korea "make it plain that military actions have been un-

dertaken by Northern Korean forces." He said these actions violated both General Assembly resolutions and the principles of the U.N. Charter. "The present situation is a serious one and is a threat to international peace," he said. "The Security Council is, in my opinion, the competent organ to deal with it. I consider it the clear duty of the Security Council to take steps necessary to reestablish peace in that area." Lie had clearly by now won his battle over the right of a secretary-general to speak his mind to the Security Council. But he also had offended his old Soviet champions, for they did not view this council as legally competent to deal with the issue. The Security Council lacked legitimacy, they insisted, because they were absent and because the Chinese seat had been usurped by a representative of the defeated Chiang Kai-shek.

The American resolution was adopted just before 6 P.M. by a vote of nine to nothing, with the Soviet Union absent and Yugoslavia abstaining. The resolution branded North Korea as guilty of a breach of peace, demanded an "immediate cessation of hostilities," ordered North Korea to withdraw its forces north of the thirty-eighth parallel, called on all members to help the U.N. carry out the resolution, and asked everyone to refrain from assisting the North Korean government. By that time, however, North Korea, claiming it had been invaded by Syngman Rhee's forces, had declared war on South Korea.

※ ❧

Truman's plane, the *Independence*, landed at Washington's National Airport a little more than an hour after the Security Council vote. Before departing Missouri, he had told his secretary of state by phone, "Dean, we've got to stop the sons of bitches no matter what." He was met at the airport by Acheson, Secretary of Defense Louis A. Johnson, and other officials. On the drive into the city, he said, "By God, I am going to let them have it." He had called his key advisers to Blair House for dinner and a conference. (Blair House was used as the president's temporary residence while the White House across the street was under repair.) Soon after arriving at Blair House, he was heard muttering, "We can't let the U.N. down."

After the table was cleared, Truman asked his diplomatic and

military advisers for their counsel. A cable from the U.S. embassy in Moscow earlier in the day had described the North Korean aggression as a "clear-cut Soviet challenge which in our considered opinion US should answer firmly and swiftly as it constitutes direct threat our leadership of free world against Soviet Communist imperialism." Historians like Walter LaFeber now believe that Truman was facing a civil war between Rhee and Kim rather than an aggression by Joseph Stalin. Moreover, there is some evidence that the North Korean onslaught was conceived not by Stalin but by Kim Il Sung alone, though Stalin acquiesced. But no one at Blair House in those frantic hours disputed the conclusions of the American embassy in Moscow.

Acheson spoke first. Six months earlier, the secretary of state had made a speech to the National Press Club that would later prove controversial. Acheson had described America's line of defense against Communism in the Pacific as a string of islands stretching from the Aleutians to Japan to the Ryukyus to the Philippines. General Douglas A. MacArthur said much the same in a newspaper interview. During the Korean War, Republican critics would accuse Acheson of inviting the invasion by excluding Korea from the American line of defense. But Acheson had also said that, as a practical matter, a country outside the line could still count on help from "the commitments of the entire civilized world under the Charter of the United Nations." Moreover, both Acheson and MacArthur, when outlining the line of defense, were thinking of a war against the Soviet Union not against a small Communist surrogate. In any case, neither Acheson nor MacArthur had any doubts now that South Korea must be defended. Acheson's Blair House plea for action was quickly embraced by the president.

Truman decided to order the navy and air force to take all action needed to protect Seoul and its airport and seaport during the evacuation of American dependents and to authorize General MacArthur, the commander of American forces in Japan, to send military supplies to the South Koreans. The president's dispatch to MacArthur advised that "further high level decisions may be expected as military and political situations develop."

After the meeting, Truman told Assistant Secretary of State Hickerson, "Jack, in the final analysis I did this for the United Na-

tions. I believed in the League of Nations. It failed. Lots of people thought it failed because we weren't in it to back it up. Okay, now we started the United Nations. It was our idea, and in this first big test we just couldn't let them down. If a collective system under the U.N. can work, it must be made to work, and now is the time to call their bluff." Not all of Truman's aides, however, shared his feelings about the U.N. Although Secretary of State Dean Acheson often invoked the image of the U.N. while discussing Korea, he never had, according to Deputy Ambassador Gross, "a very high interest in or regard for the U.N." When Gross first asked for a transfer to New York and the U.N., Acheson "rather thought that I was a little bit silly."

꽃

By Monday, June 26, the South Korean forces were fleeing in a rout. Rhee left Seoul and transferred his government to a port near Pusan on the southeast corner of the peninsula. "South Korean units unable to resist determined Northern offensive," MacArthur cabled Washington. ". . . Our est[imate] is that complete collapse is imminent." Truman called for another Blair House conference at 9 P.M., the second night meeting in a row. At Acheson's recommendation, Truman decided to commit full American air and sea support to South Korea, station the Seventh Fleet between mainland China and Formosa to prevent an invasion by either, and submit a resolution to the Security Council that would call on all members of the U.N. to come to the military aid of South Korea.

In a public statement issued the next day, Truman justified his actions by telling the American people, "The attack upon Korea makes it plain beyond all doubt that Communism has passed beyond the use of subversion to conquer independent nations and will now use armed invasion and war."

On that day, Tuesday, June 27, a Soviet official of the U.N. Secretariat hosted a luncheon at the Stockholm Restaurant in Syosset, Long Island, for Jacob Malik, who was returning to the Soviet Union that week. Deputy American Ambassador Gross, sitting between Malik and Lie, was shocked to hear the secretary-general invite the Russian ambassador to drive back with him to Lake Success that afternoon and resume his seat in the Security Council as it took up the latest American resolution on Korea.

"Won't you join us?" Lie asked Malik. "The interests of your country would seem to me to call for your presence." Gross recalled years later, "I think that Trygve felt this would be a great thing for the organization and might be a step toward a resumption of peace. I don't know what was in his mind, but it made me very unhappy, and I kept glaring at Trygve." He need not have worried so. Malik replied to Lie, "No, I will not go there." As Gross and Lie walked back to the secretary-general's car, the American diplomat admonished his friend, somewhat petulantly, "Think what would have happened if he had accepted your invitation." "Yes," Lie replied, "it would have been difficult. We would have had to fight it out and move on to the General Assembly."

At Lake Success that night, the Security Council adopted the American resolution calling on all U.N. members to "furnish such assistance to the Republic of Korea as may be necessary to repel the armed attack and to restore international peace and security in the area." The resolution received only seven votes in favor—the bare majority needed for Security Council approval. The Soviet Union, of course, was absent, while Yugoslavia, India, and Egypt abstained. Ambassadors Rau of India and Fawzi Bey of Egypt abstained only because they were still waiting for their instructions. When these arrived too late, it turned out that Fawzi Bey had guessed correctly: Cairo wanted him to abstain. But New Delhi wanted Rau to vote in favor of the resolution. This resolution gave Truman the legal authority to commit American troops to defend South Korea.

Despite continual bombing by American planes, North Korean troops surged forward and captured Seoul the very next day. Before dawn of Friday, June 30, a fateful cable from MacArthur reached the Pentagon. "If the enemy advance continues much further, it will seriously threaten the fall of the Republic," he said. ". . . The only assurance for the holding of the present line, and the ability to regain later the lost ground, is through the introduction of U.S. ground combat forces into the Korean battle area." Truman quickly made up his mind. At a morning meeting of his key diplomatic and military advisers, he announced that he would grant MacArthur the authority to use all four divisions now under his command. In the early afternoon, the Joint Chiefs of Staff dispatched a new order to MacArthur in Tokyo: "Restrictions on the use of Army Forces . . . are hereby removed and authority granted to utilize Army Forces available to you as proposed." The authority to use American ground troops came less than a week after the invasion.

A week later, on July 7, the Security Council passed a resolution setting up a unified U.N. command in Korea under American leadership. The vote was seven to nothing, with Yugoslavia, India, and Egypt abstaining. President Truman announced the next day that he had appointed General MacArthur as U.N. commander. Trygve Lie quickly ordered an old U.N. flag sent to MacArthur. It was the same flag that Ralph Bunche had flown when he was the Arab-Israeli mediator on the island of Rhodes.

Throughout the war, which lasted three years, American diplomats tried hard to persuade members of the United Nations to supply troops and matériel, but the response was always limited. Truman told the nation that the unified U.N. command represented a "landmark in mankind's long search for a rule of law among nations." But, despite such rhetoric and the unfurling of the U.N. flag, the war remained mainly an American crusade against Communist aggression. Trygve Lie believed that the Americans hurt their appeals for help by rejecting his proposal at the beginning to create a U.N. committee that would coordinate offers of military assistance and monitor the pace of the fighting. For the Pentagon, the proposal smacked too much of U.N. meddling. In practice, the American disdain for any responsibility to the U.N. was so great that General MacArthur's reports to the Security Council were released to the press in Tokyo before they showed up in New York.

❧

In his history of the war, Max Hastings, the British editor and historian, concludes that Washington's determination to justify the war as an anti-Communist crusade only made allies skittish about taking part in an adventure that could lead to world war with the Soviet Union. To make matters worse, General MacArthur's defiance of Washington with bellicose pronouncements about the need to take the war to China made officials wary of putting their troops under his command. It was also hard to rally worldwide democratic support for the dictatorial Syngman Rhee and his repressive government and corrupt army.

Fifteen countries joined the United States in sending ground troops or air support to Korea. The most significant units came from the British Commonwealth: Britain, Canada, Australia, and New Zealand. They were strong enough to form a Commonwealth Division that fought with distinction. Troops also came from some non-British members of NATO: Turkey, Greece, Belgium, Luxembourg, and the Netherlands. The Turks with more than six thousand men earned a reputation for relentless courage. Token forces came from Colombia, the only contributor in Latin America. The Pacific nations of the Philippines and Thailand contributed contingents somewhat smaller than that of Turkey. Emperor Haile Selassie sent the only African ground forces—a thousand troops; white-ruled South Africa, while not dispatching any troops, did send a fighter squadron.

❧❦

The fortunes of war changed like a roller coaster. The first American troops simply joined the demoralized South Koreans in retreat, unable to stop the larger North Korean army with its heavy Russian T-34 tanks. The soldiers fell back under pounding rain on one-hundred-degree days, finally moving into a pocket around the southern port of Pusan. By the end of July, the North Koreans controlled the entire peninsula except this Pusan perimeter.

In mid-September, MacArthur unleashed a bold military strike far behind North Korean lines, landing a force of seventy thousand American troops at Inchon, the port for Seoul. Many military strategists had opposed the plan as too risky. MacArthur himself said it had no more than a 5,000-to-1 chance of success. General Omar Bradley, the chairman of the Joint Chiefs of Staff, called it "the wildest kind" of plan and feared that "a failure could be a national or even international catastrophe." But the attack stunned and routed the North Koreans, who gave up Seoul in a little more than a week. The American troops in the Pusan perimeter broke out and stormed north, joining the new American troops in the west in a maneuver that cut off half the North Korean army. By October 1, 1950, two weeks after the Inchon landing, the U.N. forces controlled all of South Korea and massed at the thirty-eighth parallel. At the U.N., according to Trygve Lie, there was "a feeling of elation and high and successful purpose." "This was Korea, not Manchuria," Lie wrote in his memoirs. "This was the United Nations, not the League of Nations."

Even before then, the Soviets had begun to chafe under their own boycott. At the end of July, Malik had informed Secretary-General Lie that he would return to his seat on the council on August 1. He would also take over as council president, for it was the Soviet Union's turn for that month-long duty. He used the presidency and the veto to thwart any more Security Council resolutions condemning North Korea. Once the American forces had turned their near-defeat into a rout of the North Koreans, Secretary of State Dean Acheson decided it was time to circumvent the veto-paralyzed Security Council.

Acheson proposed—and the General Assembly adopted by a vote of fifty-two to five, with two abstentions—his "Uniting for Peace" plan: Seven members of the council or a majority of the members of the U.N. could call an emergency meeting of the General Assembly whenever a veto blocked action by the Security Council. Under the U.N. Charter, a General Assembly resolution, unlike a Security Council resolution, is not legally binding on all U.N. members. But this did not trouble the Americans during the Korean War. The United States still controlled a two-thirds majority of the General Assembly (the vote needed to pass a resolution there), and, as the main military power in Korea, it would carry out General Assembly recommendations, even though they were not mandatory.

The North Korean army was so badly cut up that it was too tempting for the Americans to stop at the thirty-eighth parallel. Public opinion demanded that the victorious troops cross the line and put an end to the Communist régime in the north. Korea would be united just the way the United States had promised during World War II. As Robert J. Donovan, Truman's biographer put it, "To proceed was to seize a rare opportunity victoriously to roll back the Communist orbit in Asia to the borders of China and the Soviet Union, realizing the grandest dream of containment." Washington and its allies felt a sense of euphoria. To stop at the thirty-eighth parallel seemed to make no sense. "It hardly seemed sensible to repel the attack and then abandon the country," said Acheson.

But MacArthur awoke nightmarish Chinese memories as he prepared to take the same route through northern Korea that the Japanese had in conquering Manchuria in the 1930s. Chinese Foreign Minister Chou En-lai asked diplomats to warn Washington that China would send troops to defend North Korea if U.N. forces crossed the parallel into North Korea. If the Americans approached the border, he told Indian diplomats, China would not "sit back with folded hands." Indian Foreign Minister Girja S. Bajpai delivered the message to the American ambassador in New Delhi. Similar reports and messages reached Washington through other channels. But U.S. officials dismissed these admonitions as a bluff. The Truman administration changed its war aims: The U.N. would not just repel an invasion but would destroy the North Korean army and unite the country.

Secretary of State Acheson told the General Assembly that "the aggressors' forces should not be permitted to have refuge behind an imaginary line, because that would recreate a threat to the peace of Korea and of the world." By a vote of forty-five to five, with seven abstentions, the General Assembly approved a British-sponsored resolution recommending that "appropriate steps be taken to ensure conditions of stability throughout Korea." That was tantamount to authority to cross the line. MacArthur sent his troops across the thirty-eighth parallel on October 9, and President Truman flew to Wake Island a week later to discuss war plans with him. At this brief meeting, the general assured the president that victory had been achieved in Korea and that the Chinese would either refrain from battle or send in a token force at most. Truman gave MacArthur permission to bomb the bridges on the Yalu River between China and North Korea but refused to permit bombing of any bases north of the Yalu in China. Truman later felt he was taken in at Wake Island. "He was just like a little puppy at that meeting," Truman said. "I don't know which was worse, the way he acted in public or the way he kissed my ass at that meeting."

MacArthur proved to have blinded himself to Chinese determination. On November 24, he launched his "end-the-war" offensive to drive north toward the Chinese border, boasting so war correspondents could overhear, "I hope we can get the boys home for Christmas." The reckless offensive would bring American troops closer to the Yalu River than the Joint Chiefs of Staff had authorized, but such nuances did not bother MacArthur. Four days after the offensive began, General Bradley telephoned President Truman with a "terrible message" from General MacArthur: The Chinese had crossed the Yalu River with 260,000 troops and MacArthur was now retreating. Chou En-lai had not been bluffing. "The Chinese have come in with both feet," Truman told his staff. ". . . This is the worst situation we have had yet." MacArthur demanded heavy reinforcements, including Chinese Nationalist troops from Formosa, and authority to bomb China and blockade its coast. "We face an entirely new war," he said. But Truman and his closest advisers decided that they could not expand the Korean war into an all-out conflict with China and, possibly, the Soviet Union. The U.N. troops retreated toward the thirty-eighth parallel.

Acheson described the mood at the U.N. as "a virtual state of panic." Sending troops to Korea allowed a government to have some voice in Washington, and the British government, the largest contributor, took advantage of this situation. A foolish news-conference remark by Truman had implied the possible use of atomic weapons in Korea. This evident threat had frightened people throughout the world. A Saudi Arabian diplomat warned Mrs. Eleanor Roosevelt at the U.N., "The people of the whole Asiatic continent . . . would never forget that the atomic bomb was first used against the Japanese and later against the Chinese but never against any white peoples." There was so much fear and anger in the House of Commons that British Prime Minister Clement Attlee felt he had to fly to Washington to confer with the president. Truman assured him that he would not use the bomb without consulting the British. Even more important, the two agreed that there was no other recourse for the U.N. command but to seek an armistice that would split Korea once more at the thirty-eighth parallel. Truman had faced the implications of the Chinese intervention. The United States and its closest ally in Korea agreed that the war must not be widened against China.

But General MacArthur wanted the war widened against China and bombarded Washington with scores of dispatches and pleas describing the woeful state of his armies and demanding the right to take the war to the heartland of the enemy. His propaganda campaign was not confined to private channels. He spoke his mind in a succession of interviews and speeches and public statements. British Foreign Secretary Ernest Bevin cabled the British ambassador in Washington, "Our principal difficulty is General MacArthur. His policy is different from the policy of the U.N. He seems to want a war with China. We do not."

MacArthur's most shocking insubordination came in March 1951. As it became clear that the Korean battlefront was now in stalemate more or less along the thirty-eighth parallel, with 365,000 U.N. troops facing 486,000 Chinese and North Korean troops, President Truman decided to make a public appeal for an end to the war. The Joint Chiefs of Staff and the State Department prepared a draft for a declaration noting that, since the "aggressors have been driven back . . . to the general vicinity from which the unlawful attack was first launched," the U.N. was ready to enter negotiations for a settlement that could include withdrawal of all foreign troops from Korea. The draft was circulated to the other troop contributors for their approval and to key players including General MacArthur for their perusal.

MacArthur preempted the declaration by issuing one of his own. Instead of seeking negotiations, MacArthur issued what amounted to an ultimatum to the Chinese: "The enemy . . . must by now be painfully aware that a decision of the United Nations to depart from its tolerant effort to contain the war to the area of Korea through expansion of our military operations to his coastal areas and interior bases would doom Red China to the risk of imminent military collapse." He said he was ready to meet with the commander in chief of the enemy forces "to find any military means whereby the realization of the political objectives of the United Nations in Korea . . . might be accomplished without further bloodshed." In short, he was threatening, China was doomed to defeat unless it met MacArthur and sued for peace.

MacArthur's ultimatum had torpedoed Truman's plan, and the draft declaration was abandoned. Secretary of Defense George Marshall would testify later to Congress that MacArthur's statement had lost "whatever chance there may have been at that time to negoti- ate a settlement of the Korean conflict." It took another two years for the war to end. Yet, the political power of MacArthur—a hero of the Republican right wing—was so great that President Truman still hesitated to fire him. The final straw came a few weeks later when House Republican leader Joseph W. Martin read a MacAr- thur letter to Congress advocating the use of Chiang Kai-shek's troops in Korea and insisting that if the U.N. failed to defeat Com- munism in all-out war in Asia, "the fall of Europe is inevitable." On April 10, Truman finally dismissed MacArthur, relieving him of all commands. The president acted, according to his statement, under "the specific responsibilities imposed upon me by the Con- stitution and the added responsibility which has been entrusted to me by the United Nations."

The dismissal infuriated the Republican Party, but it pleased many of America's U.N. allies. The British ambassador to Japan ca- bled London, "To me personally, MacArthur's departure was a tre- mendous relief as it is, I think, to nearly all my colleagues." In Paris, Premier Robert Schuman expressed his "heartfelt thankfulness" at the dismissal, for he feared that the Truman administration "had al- most lost control of the situation." Truman said years later, "I fired him because he wouldn't respect the authority of the President. . . . I didn't fire him because he was a dumb son of a bitch, although he was, but that's not against the law for generals."

❧

General Matthew B. Ridgway took over from MacArthur and proved a shrewder and more dynamic commander in what all now agreed would be a limited war. His job was to hold the line near the thirty-eighth parallel while inflicting heavy casualties on the Chinese as they rammed again and again at the U.N. forces in fruitless offen- sives. The quest for a peaceful end, however, proved long and bitter and bloody. The problem was exacerbated by American domestic politics that made it difficult for a Democratic president to look soft on Chinese Communism. By the middle of 1951, however, the United States was ready to negotiate a way out of the stalemate.

The first contacts between military officers took place at Kaesong in Communist-held territory in early July and then moved to Panmunjom in no-man's-land three months later. It took until February 1952, however, before agreement was reached on all issues: a cease-fire; a two-mile demilitarized zone along the battlelines near the thirty-eighth parallel; an exchange of prisoners; and a vague promise for eventual talks about withdrawal of foreign troops and a permanent peace settlement. The prisoner exchange, however, paralyzed the agreement. The Americans insisted that no prisoner should be forced to return to Communism against his will. The prison camps had become pits of terror with ideologues and zealots from both sides coercing prisoners to their cause. Almost half the 130,000 Chinese and North Korean prisoners said they did not want to go back. This was too humiliating for China and North Korea to accept.

The continued battling and killing wore down both sides. In the United States, the same frustration and delusion set in that would afflict the nation during the Vietnam War fifteen years later. Dwight D. Eisenhower capitalized on this by promising "I shall go to Korea" during his successful presidential campaign of 1952. His trip only confirmed what everyone knew: Both sides wanted and needed a cease-fire. The Communist mood for compromise may have been heightened by the new Republican administration's glib threats about using atomic weapons.

A compromise on prisoners was finally reached, creating a neutral international commission to supervise repatriation. The commission would have the authority to allow prisoners to return to civilian status on the spot, thus giving them freedom to go wherever they wanted. Syngman Rhee, his hopes for ruling a united country crushed, defied the compromise by suddenly releasing 25,000 North Korean prisoners who disappeared before the commission could question them. The United States then forced Rhee to sign a statement that he would no longer obstruct implementation of an agreement, and the armistice was finally signed on July 27, 1953, three years after the North Koreans invaded, two years after peace talks began. General Mark Clark, who had succeeded General Ridgway as commander, signed the agreement for the United Nations. "I cannot find it in me to exult in this hour," he said. Later, in his memoirs, he described himself as "the first U.S. Army commander in history to sign an armistice without victory."

The casualties of the war were heavy, almost half coming after negotiations began, after both sides had accepted that neither could win, that the war would end with two Koreas. The South Koreans had 415,000 soldiers killed and 429,000 wounded. The Americans recorded 33,629 dead and 105,785 wounded. British Foreign Secretary Anthony Eden, noting the heavy loss of American life, wrote later, "No just man will question the spirit of that sacrifice which bore no selfish taint." The British Commonwealth had 1,263 killed and 4,817 wounded. The rest of the U.N. forces suffered 1,800 deaths and 8,000 wounded. It has been estimated that between 500,000 and 1.5 million Chinese and North Koreans died in the fighting.

꽃꽃

Trygve Lie was another casualty of the Korean War. He had been a favorite of the Soviet Union. In late 1949, Soviet Foreign Minister Andrey Vyshinsky had announced at a dinner for ambassadors that Lie was the only candidate he could imagine his country supporting at the next election of a secretary-general. All this changed when Lie took his stand against the North Korean invasion in June 1950. Moscow denounced him as "the abettor of American aggression . . . humbly aiding Truman and Acheson to wreck the United Nations." The Soviet Union was now intent on preventing his reelection, by veto if necessary; the United States was just as intent on keeping him in office. Lie contemplated refusing to run for a second term but, as he wrote a friend in Norway, "Had I said 'no,' I would have given the Russians the smoothest sailing they had ever enjoyed in a political conflict."

In the first round of voting, the Soviet candidate, Polish Foreign Minister Zygmunt Moedzelewski, won only the Soviet vote; four of the others voted against him and six abstained. On the next ballot, Lie won nine votes, with China abstaining and Russia voting no. The Russian vote, however, was a veto, and the Security Council, by a vote of ten to one, decided to inform the General Assembly that it had failed to agree on a candidate. Before it did so, however, Soviet Ambassador Jacob Malik prevailed on the council to try again. Ambassador Warren Austin informed him in private consultations that the United States, which had never used the veto before, would wield it against any candidate other than Lie. As it turned out, no veto was necessary, for none of the other Soviet candidates could muster more than four votes. In the end, the issue was turned over to the General Assembly despite a warning from Malik that "if the appointment of Mr. Lie is imposed, the U.S.S.R. will not take Mr. Lie into account and will not consider him as Secretary-General of the United Nations."

In the General Assembly debate, Canadian Ambassador Lester Pearson reminded the delegates that the Soviets had only recently been extolling Lie as the only possible candidate for the job. "Indeed, so highly praised was he by these people that extremists on the other side attacked him as a Red," said Pearson. But the Soviet bloc was not praising him now. Ukrainian Ambassador Anatoli M. Baranovsky accused him of "two-faced double dealing." Soviet Foreign Minister Vyshinsky even insulted his girth, describing him in a complicated metaphor as "big enough to enter through the door and perhaps too big to enter through the window." By a vote of forty-six to five, with eight abstentions, the General Assembly voted to extend Lie's term for three more years. Under the charter, the Security Council must recommend a candidate for the assembly's approval. The Russian veto had prevented such a recommendation for a new term. But the Americans and other sponsors of the resolution took the position that the extension satisfied the legal requirements because the assembly was not voting for a new term of office but simply adding to the original term that was recommended by the Security Council in 1945. British historian Evan Luard has called this successful maneuver on behalf of Lie "a typical example of a gross abuse by the ruling majority of its voting strength."

It was not a happy extension for Lie. The Soviets carried out their threat and refused to deal with him. The rules of procedure, for example, required all General Assembly delegates to submit their credentials to the secretary-general, but the Communist delegates ignored the rule and submitted nothing so long as Lie was in office. The Communists would not even invite Lie and his wife to their receptions and dinners, sometimes notifying the press that the secretary-general had been excluded. "I did not mind missing a few receptions and dinners, for international relations would be far better were there fewer of them," Lie wrote, "but I resented such uncivil behavior toward a man and his family." Lie and his staff, of course, dutifully invited the Soviets and their satellites to all U.N. social functions. The Communists neither showed up nor called to decline. Lie was disappointed in the lack of an outcry from other countries. "Delegates and others made no protest against this total political and social boycott—overlooking its implications for the prestige of the office of Secretary-General," he said.

Lie began to look on the situation as hopeless. "In a world organization where all sides were represented, my hands were tied with respect to governments which controlled or influenced one-third of the population of the world," he wrote in his memoirs. ". . . The influence of the United Nations for peace was weakened when its Secretary-General could not exercise the full influence of his office as the universally recognized spokesman of the whole organization."

On November 10, 1953, Lie shocked his chief aides with advance word of the news and then announced to the General Assembly that he was resigning as secretary-general and would remain in office only until the Security Council selected a successor. Radio Moscow did not hide its pleasure. "Trygve Lie's resignation was a revelation of his complete political bankruptcy," it broadcast. "His efforts to help the United States to hide with the United Nations' flag the American aggression in Korea gave rise to waves of indignation throughout the world." In a debate later in the General Assembly, Lie sarcastically thanked Soviet Foreign Minister Vyshinsky, who had continually branded various acts of the U.N. as illegal, for refraining from "declaring illegal and a gross violation of the Charter my resignation as Secretary-General." Vyshinsky could not hide a rare smile. When Lie met his successor, Dag Hammarskjöld, for the first time, he warned him, "The task of the Secretary-General is the most impossible job on earth."

❧❦

The armistice in Korea and the resignation of Trygve Lie signaled the impending end of an era for the young United Nations. The United States and its Commonwealth and Western European allies dominated the U.N. during the Korean War and used it as a kind of western satrapy. When the Soviet Union obstructed Western actions with its vetoes, the United States simply moved to the General Assembly and marshaled the votes that would drive the handful of Communist states into a corner. The allies then treated the victorious resolution as the statement of all mankind. The awful starkness of the North Korean invasion contributed to this atmosphere. Repelled by this aggression, the secretary-general, who began his term as a gentle and prodding arbiter in the Cold War, ended as an activist champion of the West. He refused to be neutral. "Neutrality implies political abstinence, not political action," he said.

Western domination, however, would slip away in the next decade. The age of decolonization in the late 1950s and early 1960s greatly inflated the size of the General Assembly with numerous new and poor African and Asian nations who would soon control a majority of the seats. The United States could not invoke Dean Acheson's "Uniting for Peace" plan in a General Assembly dominated by Third World countries that often voted with the Communist bloc.

The Trygve Lie era fostered a dangerous attitude in the United States about the United Nations. Americans believed that the U.N. was strongest and most dynamic and most significant when it did America's bidding. This attitude has persisted throughout the U.N.'s history and became most apparent again during the Persian Gulf War. In the give-and-take of diplomacy at the U.N., the Americans have never felt much like giving. Oddly, many other countries shared the same attitude: they, too, felt better about the U.N. when the United States took charge. Rather than resent American leadership and dominance, they longed for it. This atmosphere surely strengthened the U.N. whenever the United States managed to exert leadership. But, when they found themselves unable to lead because of Soviet vetoes and Third World intransigence, Americans tended to develop a contempt for the U.N. or even an indifference toward it. That moodiness would eventually hurt the United Nations badly.

❧ 5 ❧

Dag Hammarskjöld

In 1960 and 1961, when the terrible Congo crisis was most intense, Dag Hammarskjöld, Trygve Lie's successor as U.N. secretary-general, completed the Swedish translation of American avant-garde writer Djuna Barnes's play *Antiphon* for a performance by the Swedish Royal Democratic Theater; successfully lobbied fellow members of the Swedish Academy to award the Nobel prize in literature to Saint-John Perse (the nom de plume of the French poet Alexis Léger, whose writing he had translated); started work on the translation of Israeli philosopher Martin Buber's *Ich und Du*; and still found time for his own mystic poetry.

"Roused from my idle dream," he began one poem,

> *Freed from all my fetters,*
> *Anointed, accoutred,*
> *I stand ready.*
>
> *Asked if I have courage*
> *To go on to the end,*
> *I answer Yes without*
> *A second thought.*

The gate opens: dazzled,
I see the arena,
Then I walk out naked
To meet my death. . . .

Dag Hammarskjöld, who would die in service to the United Nations, was an international civil servant of such rare sensibility and catholic interests, of such stubborn principle and exquisite tact, of such determined mysticism and wise pragmatism that he seems to belong far more in a Herman Melville novel than in an account of the travails of an international organization. Yet, for a few short years, he not only led the United Nations but personified it. He seemed to restore the soul that had somehow slipped away in the U.N.'s first few years. The influence of his demeanor and leadership and philosophy was so great that believers in the U.N., no matter how disheartened later by weak performance and lackluster leadership, have managed to sustain some of their hopes ever since.

Hammarskjöld, only forty-seven when elected secretary-general in April 1953, was as much a compromise candidate as Trygve Lie had been and far less well known. When the Security Council met in March, American Ambassador Henry Cabot Lodge proposed Brigadier General Carlos Romulo of the Philippines, who had served as president of the General Assembly in 1949. But the Eisenhower administration did not have all the Western governments on its side. Danish Ambassador William Borberg, supported by Britain and France, instead proposed Canadian Foreign Minister Lester B. Pearson, the current president of the General Assembly. Pearson had irritated the State Department somewhat by his overtures to the Chinese Communists in the quest for a settlement of the Korean War, but the Americans still intended to vote for him if Romulo failed. Soviet Ambassador Valerian A. Zorin proposed Polish Foreign Minister Stanislaw Skrzeszewski. Stalin had died several days earlier, and the vote was the first chance to gauge whether Soviet intransigence would lessen.

The vote on Romulo was five to two, with four abstentions, two short of the seven needed to win. Skrzeszewski fared worse with a vote of one to three, with seven abstentions. Pearson did best, at least on the surface, with a vote of nine to one, with one abstention. But the one negative vote came from the Soviet Union, a veto. Moscow did not intend to accept anyone from a country allied to the United States. With the council deadlocked, Trygve Lie hinted he might reconsider his resignation. Ambassador Lodge liked the idea but found no other enthusiast.

To break the deadlock, French Ambassador Henri Hoppenot recommended that the Western allies submit a group of names to Zorin to see if any might escape a Soviet veto. At the suggestion of British Ambassador Gladwyn Jebb, Hammarskjöld's name was added to a list of three others. He had impressed the British while leading his country's delegation to the consultations on the Marshall Plan. Zorin rejected the others on the list but had no objection to Hammarskjöld. Ambassador Lodge did not know him but accepted the advice of a high-ranking State Department official who did: "If you can get him, grab him." The Security Council then officially nominated Hammarskjöld, incorrectly identifying him as "the Director-General of the Swedish Foreign Ministry"; he was actually a minister without portfolio in the Swedish cabinet. It was not unanimous; Nationalist China abstained in protest against Swedish recognition of Communist China.

Hammarskjöld had heard about the possibility of his nomination only a day before and did not take the report seriously. When the Associated Press correspondent in Stockholm phoned him on March 31 with the news that the Security Council had selected him as secretary-general earlier that day, Hammarskjöld scolded the correspondent that his watch must be fast—it was still a few hours short of April Fools' Day. His official acceptance was somewhat self-deprecating. "With a strong feeling of personal insufficiency, I hesitate to accept candidature," he cabled the president of the Security Council, "but I do not feel that I could refuse the task imposed upon me should the Assembly follow the recommendation of the Security Council by which I feel deeply honored." "God has a use for you," he wrote in his diary, "even though what He asks doesn't happen to suit you at the moment." The General Assembly confirmed the nomination in a week.

The Secretariat would now be headed by a civil servant rather than a politician. U.N. diplomats believed he would be far less willing to assert himself than Lie. The French newspaper *Le Monde*, describing his intellect and his lack of political experience, predicted that the United Nations would now be run by "the most charming oyster in the world." But Hammarskjöld was no ordinary civil servant. He was the son of Hjalmar Hammarskjöld, the prime minister who helped keep Sweden neutral during World War I. The young Hammarskjöld had made his mark as a government economist during the 1930s. He had served as permanent undersecretary—the top civil service position—in the Ministry of Finance, charged with transforming Sweden into a welfare state under the policies of the Social-Democratic government. In 1941, he took on the post of chairman of the board of the National Bank of Sweden as well. After World War II, he moved into key positions in the Swedish foreign ministry and finally was appointed to the cabinet as minister without portfolio—more or less the deputy foreign minister—even though he was not a member of parliament or even of a political party. He had a reputation as a skilled administrator but did not have much of a public image in or out of Sweden.

Hammarskjöld's father was descended from a medieval knight and nourished a strong sense of public service in his family. "From generations of soldiers and government officials on my father's side," the secretary-general told an American audience on radio, "I inherited a belief that no life was more satisfactory than one of selfless service to your country—or humanity." Dag Hammarskjöld was the youngest of four sons, and two of them joined him in government service. The father's term as prime minister was not happy, for he lost popularity when Allied blockades led to severe food shortages toward the end of World War I. Mean-spirited critics jeered at him as "Hungerskjöld." "A box on the ear taught the boy / That father's name / Was odious to them," Dag Hammarskjöld wrote in a poem. His mother, who brought a sense of poetry to enhance the sense of service instilled by his father, possessed, according to Hammarskjöld, "an antirationalism with warm undercurrents of feeling."

Dag Hammarskjöld never married, and rumors hovered for years that he was homosexual, a state of life that might have brought him down if proven and publicized in those days. Brian Urquhart, his biographer and a junior member of the Hammarskjöld U.N. team, denied the rumors emphatically and accused Trygve Lie of spreading them. Hammarskjöld, who sometimes identified himself as a unicorn in his poetry and liked to work in the Japanese three-line, seventeen-syllable verse form known as the haiku, wrote one about himself in 1959: "Because it never found a mate / Men called / The unicorn abnormal." In his own memoirs, Urquhart wrote, "I would guess that he was asexual. . . . He was certainly a determined loner in his personal life. . . . There is nothing particularly novel or unusual about homosexuality, but the rumors about Hammarskjöld have always struck me as vulgar, and sometimes self-serving, attempts to demean and diminish an exceptional and unusual person."

Most associates did not know Hammarskjöld well enough to feel they understood him. They often found him cold. He was understood better and perhaps admired even more after death and the publication of the diary, or notebook, he had left behind under the title *Markings*. The entries portrayed Hammarskjöld as a lonely mystic. Some readers were troubled by the hints of messianic sacrifice, but the book proved a remarkable worldwide success. By 1994, publisher Alfred A. Knopf had reprinted the English edition, translated by the Nobel prize–winning poet W. H. Auden and Leif Sjoberg, thirty-eight times.

"Below even the sunniest and most secure human relationship," he wrote in the year of his election as secretary-general, "the abyss lies waiting." "The light died in the low clouds," he noted in 1955. "Falling snow drank in the dusk. Shrouded in silence, the branches wrapped me in their peace. When the boundaries were erased, once again the wonder: that *I* exist." "Alone beside the moorland spring," he mused in the same year, "once again you are aware of your loneliness—as it is and always has been. As it always has been—even when, at times, the friendship of others veiled its nakedness." At the end of the year of the Suez Canal crisis, in which he played a significant and successful role, he wrote, "Rejoice if you feel that what you did was 'necessary,' but remember, even so, that you were simply the instrument by means of which He added one tiny grain to the Universe He has created for His own purposes."

Death and God obsessed him as he grew older. "As an element

in the sacrifice," he wrote in 1957, "death is a fulfillment, but more often it is a degradation, and it is never an elevation." A year later, he wrote: "Apart from any value it may have for others, my life is worse than death. Therefore, in my great loneliness, serve others. Therefore: how incredibly great is what I have been given, and how meaningless what I have to 'sacrifice.'" He produced this haiku the next year: "He gave his life / For the happiness of others, / But wished them evil." His entry for Whitsunday (or Pentecost) in 1961 begins: "I don't know Who—or what—put the question, I don't know when it was put. I don't even remember answering. But at some moment I did answer Yes to Someone—or Something—and from that hour I was certain that existence is meaningful and that, therefore, my life, in self-surrender, had a goal."

Excerpts from two poems make clear how the poetry brimmed with mysticism and death in his last year:

What have I to fear?
If their arrows hit,
If their arrows kill,
What is there in that
To cry about?

Do I fear a compulsion in me
To be so destroyed?
Or is there someone
In the depths of my being,
Waiting for permission
To pull the trigger?

Whatever he felt in front of his notebook in the loneliness of his East Seventy-third Street apartment, Hammarskjöld presented a different persona in public. Despite a shy aloofness, his news conferences were engaging, exciting events where correspondents took the measure of a subtle, supple, thoughtful, and dynamic mind. The secretary-general refused to share the secrets of his diplomacy but felt the need to explain his motives and goals, though he sometimes did so in cautiously opaque language. Hammarskjöld believed that a secretary-general faced "a public relations problem of a delicate and difficult nature." He was not a salesman or a propagandist but, as he told the American Political Science Association, "he has to try and reach the minds and hearts of people so as to get the United Nations' efforts firmly based in public reaction." He experimented with formats. He did not like private interviews. He found that he spoke as freely on the record as off. Although he did not like cameras and floodlights, he settled on the formal press conference as most suited to his need to educate the public about himself and the U.N., and he tried to hold one every two weeks.

Reporters obviously liked him even if they sometimes found him difficult to understand. Even his very first New York news conference in May 1953 reflected this ease of exchange. In reply to a question, Hammarskjöld tried to describe the extent of initiative he had as secretary-general to intervene in international crises. Reporters probably did not understand it at the time, but his thoughtful and complex reply laid down his creed—the rationale of his stewardship—for the succession of international crises that would torment him in the years ahead:

Q. How much initiative do you think the Secretary-General has under the Charter with respect to critical situations involving peace? . . .
A. May I broaden the question in order to make it more difficult?

Q. By all means.
A. . . . Under the Charter the Secretary-General has a fairly well defined right of initiative, and I feel deeply that in a situation of the kind you are describing he should use that right of initiative.

But when I say that I wanted to broaden the reply, it is for this reason: I think that the right of initiative in a certain sense, informally, of the Secretary-General goes far beyond what is described in the Charter, provided that he observes the proper forms, chooses his approaches with tact, and avoids acting in such a way as, so to say, counteract his own purpose. . . . That is to say I recognize the responsibility going even beyond the Charter, but obviously subject to very many reservations.

As secretary-general, Hammarskjöld soon found himself dealing with the anti-Communism hysteria of the McCarthy era in the United States. His handling of this situation became the first test of his leadership for the bureaucrats in New York. The troubles had begun during Trygve Lie's administration when fanciful witnesses and professional informers testified to Senate subcommittees about a Communist-dominated U.N. Secretariat hiding hundreds of agents engaged in subversive activities. A federal grand jury, without naming anyone, concluded in 1952 that the U.N. was infiltrated by "an overwhelmingly large group of disloyal U.S. citizens." Despite all the contrary evidence—only one staff member, a Russian, had ever been caught in espionage, taking his cache of files not from the U.N. but from his paramour, Judith Coplon, a Justice Department lawyer in Washington—the image of the U.N. as a nest of spies persisted in extremist circles for years. As late as the 1960s, car bumper stickers would warn, YOU CAN'T SPELL COMMUNISM WITHOUT U.N.

Trygve Lie derided the whole idea. "There was nothing to spy on in the United Nations," he said. "Governments did not give it secret information they wished to withhold. Its meetings and documents were public property." But it was not easy to defy the mood set in the country by the anti-Communist invective spewing from Republican Senator Joseph McCarthy of Wisconsin and his cohorts. Lie agreed with Washington that no American Communist had a right to work at the U.N. Since American laws classified the Communist Party as a subversive organization dedicated to the overthrow of the United States by force and violence, he wrote, "it was plain common sense not to want any American Communists in the Secretariat."

Lie cooperated with the U.S. International Organizations Employees Loyalty Board and its investigation of two thousand American employees of the U.N. and even allowed FBI agents into the U.N. compound to question and fingerprint the Americans. He was troubled, however, by the fact that he could find only one precedent for a government punishing suspect citizens for working for an international organization—Fascist Italy when it prohibited enemies of Mussolini from working for the League of Nations. When twenty American members of the U.N. staff invoked the Fifth Amendment protection against self-incrimination and refused to testify before the Senate Internal Security Subcommittee in October 1952, Lie fired them all, his decision buttressed by a panel of three prominent jurists that he had appointed. Those taking the Fifth Amendment "had not conducted themselves as international civil servants should," he said.

The U.N. Administrative Tribunal, however, ruled differently, handing down its controversial decision after Hammarskjöld took office. The tribunal approved the dismissal of nine temporary employees but overturned the dismissals of the eleven others because their use of the Fifth Amendment did not constitute "serious misconduct"—the only grounds for dismissal of a permanent employee of the U.N. Secretariat. The tribunal ruled that compensation must be paid to seven who wanted to leave anyway and that four others must get their jobs back. Hammarskjöld refused reinstatement but offered compensation instead. The total came to $189,370 for the eleven employees.

In the atmosphere of the times, Hammarskjöld's stand, though it disappointed many staff members, took some resolve because he had to deal with a Republican Congress vehemently opposing any payment and an Eisenhower administration hesitant about taking on its most rabid anti-Communist supporters. In the end, Congress passed a law decreeing that no American funds could be used to pay the compensation. Hammarskjöld sidestepped this by paying the compensation through an assessment on staff salaries. He also ordered the FBI agents out of U.N. headquarters and announced that the U.S. loyalty board's findings on employees would be only advisory, not binding. He even managed to persuade the Eisenhower administration to accept this notion about what the loyalty board ought to do.

The tentacles of McCarthyism even stretched toward Nobel peace prize laureate Ralph Bunche. He had attended meetings in the 1930s of radical organizations lik~ the National Negro Congress that later were dominated by Communists. Bunche was first called to testify in private before the Senate Internal Security Subcommittee in March 1953. The senators asked him if he had ever been a Communist Party member. Bunche denied this but later wrote to the subcommittee that he had thought it "would have been taken for granted that my long record of service to my country and my public utterances . . . were more than adequate testimonial to my unqualified loyalty to my country and to my unwavering devotion to the American way of life."

This did not satisfy the International Organizations Employees

Loyalty Board, which claimed it had derogatory information in its files and needed to investigate him. President Dwight D. Eisenhower was appalled. He told Maxwell Rabb, the White House assistant in charge of relations with minorities, "Bunche is a superior man, a credit to our country. I can't just stand by and permit a man like that to be chopped to pieces because of McCarthy feeling." But Eisenhower, though he invited Bunche to the White House for dinner during the investigation, did not speak out. Bunche faced the charges without help from the White House. Hammarskjöld, however, gave him full support and instructed his counsel, Ernest Gross, to help Bunche in the proceedings. The support from Hammarskjöld was especially important because Bunche had felt uncertain about his relationship with the shy and cautious new secretary-general.

One of Bunche's accusers had told the board that Communists were in a position to control him. Bunche likened the charges to an accusation that "Ralph Bunche is a Communist because he is one." He protested to the board, "This isn't an allegation—it is a combination of Gertrude Stein and loaded dice. It does seem to me that if someone were to make an allegation, unsupported by evidence, that I am 'Stalin's aunt,' I should not be called upon to disprove it." The six-member board finally announced on May 28, 1954, that it had "unanimously reached the conclusion that there is no doubt as to the loyalty of Dr. Bunche to the United States government."

An official statement came quickly from Hammarskjöld, "I am gratified to learn of the quick decision reached by the board concerning Dr. Bunche, who has always had my unreserved confidence as a man of outstanding integrity. He is an honor to the organization which he serves." Extremists would continue to smear Bunche for years. But Hammarskjöld appointed Bunche an undersecretary-general of the United Nations within three months. Hammarskjöld's stand against McCarthyism did not strike the staff as wholly courageous—many felt he should have accepted the tribunal's recommendation to reinstate four of the employees dismissed by Lie—but, all in all, he was far less acquiescent to the witch-hunters than Lie, and the contrast buoyed the spirits of the Secretariat somewhat.

U.N. officials and diplomats first sensed the true power of Hammarskjöld's imagination and independence and diplomacy in early 1955 when he took up the crisis of the American air force prisoners in Chinese Communist hands. This adventure underscored the import of his claim in the first New York news conference that his right of initiative extended beyond what the U.N. Charter had set down.

On November 23, 1954, Peking Radio announced that a military court had convicted eleven U.S. Air Force crewmen and two American civilians of espionage and sentenced them to prison terms ranging from four years to life. The air force crew had been shot down in their B-29 bomber and the two civilians, presumably CIA agents, in their C-47 transport while flying over Manchuria during the Korean War. The CIA operatives were evidently attempting to drop Chinese Nationalist agents into Communist China, but the air force plane was on a routine mission spreading leaflets. The U.S. government denied all the espionage charges, and the Chinese audacity infuriated the American public and politicians.

"The Chinese Communists should understand," said Ambassador Henry Cabot Lodge, "that just as they cannot shoot their way into the United Nations, they cannot blackmail their way in by holding innocent prisoners as hostages in a game of political warfare." Senate Republican leader William Knowland of California demanded a naval blockade of China, an act of war, until the men were released. President Eisenhower, who felt "the same resentments, anger and frustration as anyone else," refused the demand. "The hard way is to have the courage to be patient," he admonished Knowland. Since the men had flown over China under U.N. command during the war, Eisenhower said, the U.N. now had a responsibility to try to free them. "How the U.N. can possibly disabuse itself of a feeling of responsibility in this matter and retain its self-respect, I wouldn't know," he told a news conference.

Although the case of the imprisoned fliers would soon engross the U.N. and Hammarskjöld, it was only one element in an escalating Chinese-American conflict that threatened several times to rush into war. The Chinese Communists had started shelling Quemoy Island just off the Chinese coast in early September. This tiny island, the similar island of Matsu, and a handful of others were in the hands of Chiang Kai-shek, who had retreated to the large island of Formosa (or Taiwan) with his defeated Nationalist army. Quemoy and Matsu, though barricaded by Chiang's troops, had no strategic value in the defense of Formosa. The U.S. Seventh Fleet patrolled the Formosa Strait, prepared to destroy any Communist armada attempting to seize Formosa and capture Chiang. As British Prime Minister Winston Churchill, fearful of World War III, wrote President Eisenhower, the Americans could easily "drown any would-be Chinese invaders of Formosa" and therefore had no need to defend Quemoy and Matsu. The only military value of the offshore islands lay in their possible use as stepping-stones should Chiang, under protection of the U.S. Navy, attempt to invade the mainland. Since few analysts thought he had any realistic hopes of reconquest, Chiang's occupation of the islands had only symbolic value, encouraging the myth that all China would soon be Nationalist again.

For the Eisenhower administration, in those hate-drenched McCarthy era days, symbolic value mattered. The Republicans, after accusing the Democrats incessantly of "losing" China, had no intention of exacerbating that loss by giving up any more territory, no matter how worthless. The Americans still looked on Communism as monolithic and the Chinese as brainwashed figurines managed by the evil machinations of the post-Stalin Svengalis in the Kremlin. Few Americans accepted the Chinese grievances as real. They discounted Chinese anger over the U.N.'s refusal under American pressure to admit them. And Americans professed not to understand Chinese anger over the humiliating Nationalist occupation of islands that were really an integral part of China. Washington bristled with war talk. Secretary of State John Foster Dulles, echoing some of the feelings of Joint Chiefs Chairman Arthur Radford, told Eisenhower, "If we defend Quemoy and Matsu, we'll have to use atomic weapons. They alone will be effective against the mainland airfields."

The president, while willing to take that step if necessary, also knew his lieutenants were "talking about going to the threshold of World War III." Eisenhower tried to cool down tempers and opted for an ambiguous American policy that pledged the United States to defend Quemoy and Matsu if he determined that an attack was prelude to a future invasion of Formosa. To make sure the Chinese understood his determination, Eisenhower also told a news conference that he was prepared, if necessary, to use tactical atomic weapons against military targets in Asia.

Hammarskjöld's arduous campaign to free the American fliers played against this noisy background. In early December, the General Assembly, by a vote of forty-seven to five, with seven abstentions, passed a resolution that condemned Communist China for trying the fliers as spies instead of releasing them as prisoners of war and asked Hammarskjöld to seek their release. Ambassador Lodge, who introduced the resolution, did not demand freedom for the two presumed CIA agents (who were not released until the U.S. government admitted they were CIA agents in 1973). He did, however, demand—over the objection of some West European allies—that the resolution include the condemnation of the Chinese Communists. At Hammarskjöld's request, the resolution included two phrases that enhanced his independence. The resolution asked the secretary-general to act "in the name of the United Nations" and to use "the means most appropriate in his judgment" for persuading the Chinese to release the fliers. Despite these phrases, most outsiders thought that the General Assembly had handed Hammarskjöld a "mission impossible," since everyone believed that the Chinese would never comply with a U.N. resolution that carried a condemnation against them.

Hammarskjöld decided that his only chance for success lay in a dramatic flight to Peking (now Beijing) to see Chinese Prime Minister Chou En-lai personally. Lodge said later that Hammarskjöld had "put his life's reputation as a diplomat on the chopping block" by deciding to go to Peking. Hammarskjöld knew that the Chinese Communists would never receive him unless he distanced himself from the resolution and its condemnation. According to Andrew W. Cordier and Wilder Foote, two members of his staff who edited the public papers of Hammarskjöld as secretary-general, he had decided to act "on the basis of those independent responsibilities as Secretary-General which derived either explicitly from the Charter or from its philosophy rather than from the resolution itself." Within minutes of the passage of the resolution, Hammarskjöld sent a commercial cable to Chou En-lai asking for an audience.

Without even mentioning the resolution, Hammarskjöld simply informed Chou En-lai that the General Assembly had asked him to seek the release of the captured U.N. fliers (by then, the Chinese had announced that they held four more airmen, all captured fighter pilots, bringing the total to fifteen). He made it clear that this had now become his personal mission. "Taking into account all facts and circumstances the Secretary-General must, in this case, take on himself a special responsibility," Hammarskjöld said. "In the light of the concern I feel about the issue, I would appreciate an opportunity to take this matter up with you personally." Hammarskjöld proposed a meeting in Peking. His nuanced diplomacy worked. Within a week, the Chinese prime minister accepted. "We welcome you to China," Chou cabled.

A couple of weeks before leaving for China, Hammarskjöld flew to Stockholm to take the place of his late father in the Swedish Academy. Discussing his chances for success in China, he cited a line from the Danish philosopher Søren Kierkegaard that "to succeed is to realize what is possible." Asked if he was carrying any suggestions to China, he replied, "I don't think anybody has suggestions which he can carry with him. We're living in a fluid world, history is fluid, and to have preconceived ideas in any direction I think is just to sacrifice that flexibility which is a matter of course in diplomacy generally. So my reply to your question would be, for that very platitudinous reason, a flat no."

Hammarskjöld flew into Peking on the afternoon of January 5, 1955. Chou En-lai offered a reception in the Palace of the Purple Light and then invited Hammarskjöld to dine alone with him and the vice minister of foreign affairs. During the five days there, Hammarskjöld attended the Chinese opera and visited the Forbidden City, the Summer Palace, and the tombs of the Ming emperors. But there was not much time for sight-seeing. Hammarskjöld and Chou met in four working sessions of three to five hours' length in a room of the prime minister's offices in the Hall of Western Flowers. Each man had aides present but did not call on them to speak. The sessions amounted to a long dialogue between two of the world's most active political intellectuals. Hammarskjöld would say later that "Chou En-lai to me appears as the most superior brain I have so far met in the field of foreign politics."

Throughout the talks, according to the summaries of Cordier and Foote and to the secretary-general's notes published in Brian Urquhart's biography, Hammarskjöld made it clear that, although he had been asked to seek the release of the fliers by the General Assembly, he also had the independent right to do so, based on the principles of the U.N. Charter that imbued the secretary-general with the duty to reduce tensions and seek peace. By talking with him, the Chinese were thus not acknowledging a resolution that condemned them.

Hammarskjöld argued that the eleven B-29 airmen and four fighter pilots were not spies but prisoners of war. Hammarskjöld likened the enmity between the Chinese and the Americans to "the situation in that little Peking opera which we saw yesterday night where two men were fighting each other in the dark, each of them believing that he had been threatened by the other man." He dismissed one piece of espionage evidence cited by the Chinese—a portable radio and survival equipment found inside the bomber—because he said all bombers of that size carried this kind of equipment. Hammarskjöld also told Chou En-lai that a majority of members of the General Assembly had voted for the resolution not because they wanted to harm China but because they genuinely believed, as he did, that it was unjust to convict these U.N. fliers as spies. "This case is one of those which history suddenly lifts up to key significance," Hammarskjöld said, "as is evidenced by the sheer fact that, against all odds, it has brought me around the world in order to put before you . . . my deep concern both as Secretary-General and as a man."

Chou En-lai stuck to his contention that the fliers were spies but, as the sessions continued, indicated that the Chinese might show some leniency. He accused the U.N. of bowing to the domination of the United States and committing gross injustice against China, especially by barring its entry into the organization. But he provided photos and motion pictures of the captured fliers and invited their families to visit them in China. He asked Hammarskjöld to explain China's position on Taiwan to the U.N., and he expressed faith in the secretary-general's "will and ability to promote peace." But he warned that there would be no change in the status of the fliers if the United States continued to make bellicose statements over the case. In short, as Cordier and Foote summarized the end of the talks, "the prospect seemed to favor release of the fliers by unilateral Chinese action at some later date—perhaps in stages—provided that the United States government abstained from pressures and threats over the case."

When Hammarskjöld arrived at the Idlewild International Airport in New York on January 13, he described his visit to Peking as "a first stage" and promised "the door that has been opened can be kept open, given restraint on all sides." When he held a news conference the next day, the U.N. correspondents applauded him. Asked if he regarded his talks as a success, he replied, "If, by successful, you mean that I brought the fliers back in the plane, you know they were not successful. If, by successful, you mean that I achieved what I had hoped to achieve, they were successful."

A few days later, however, Senator Knowland pronounced the mission a "failure by any standard or yardstick." Secretary Dulles invited Hammarskjöld to meet with him in Washington. The secretary-general had already briefed Ambassador Lodge, but Dulles told a news conference that he wanted "a direct first-hand report from him as to just what took place." Dulles also said that he intended to explain to Hammarskjöld that it was difficult for the United States to maintain "a position of standing aside, to let the United Nations try to work this problem out." "I don't think that can go on forever," he added. Dulles gave Hammarskjöld only a few minutes to deliver a brief account of the trip and did not listen at all to what the secretary-general believed should be done next. Hammarskjöld felt that an opportunity for peace was vanishing in American bluster. "I am afraid that their emotions have run away with their political wisdom," he said.

On January 21, Peking Radio announced that Chou En-lai had invited the parents of the captured airmen to visit their children. Hammarskjöld, who confirmed this announcement, hoped that the offer would lead to the release of the airmen. But it was swiftly rejected by a State Department spokesman who denounced China for presenting the families with "a harrowing dilemma." The U.S. government went further, announcing that it could not in good conscience recommend a visit to China where "the normal protection of an American passport cannot be offered." This angered Hammarskjöld, who issued a statement saying he had "no doubt about the safety of those members of the families wishing to visit China to see their men." Just a few days later, Dulles decided to refuse all travel by the families to China. He wrote the parents that he was doing so because of "the increasingly belligerent attitudes and actions of the Chinese Communists." Hammarskjöld believed this action a great error for he had left Peking convinced that the parental visits would lead to the release of the prisoners.

As the rhetoric and shelling intensified in the Far East, Hammarskjöld removed himself from active negotiation. "When one prepares a soup," he told a news conference in April, "it is sometimes part of that preparation to take the soup off the fire. That may also be the case in this special kind of field. There are times when one furthers the purpose of negotiation by not sitting at the table all the time." Hammarskjöld kept up his private contacts with the Chinese ambassador in Stockholm and waited hopefully for some kind of breakthrough.

At the Bandung conference of Asian and African states that month, Chou En-lai indicated that he was ready to take part in talks with the United States. The State Department reacted negatively at first, but, in a few days, Secretary Dulles hinted that there might be some hope for talks. At the end of May, Chou En-lai announced the release of the four fighter pilots. Indian Foreign Minister V. K. Krishna Menon, who had visited Peking a few weeks earlier, promptly accepted credit for the delivery.

Diplomatic contacts between Hammarskjöld and Chou En-lai continued. On August 1, Peking finally announced the release of the eleven remaining American airmen. The announcement came two days after Hammarskjöld's fiftieth birthday, and the message from Chou to Hammarskjöld, via the Swedish ambassador to China, ended with birthday greetings. The secretary-general received the news while resting at his retreat in the Swedish fishing village of Hagestad. But Chou was not releasing the Americans as a birthday gift to Hammarskjöld. The United States had announced its willingness a few days earlier to hold talks with China in Geneva at the level of ambassador. Chou En-lai was clearly making a goodwill gesture to Washington in exchange.

Krishna Menon again claimed credit for the release of Americans. At a news conference almost two weeks later, a reporter asked Hammarskjöld about "the competing kidnappers who are trying to take the credit away from the United Nations." "I object very strongly to the language in various details, if you will excuse my saying so," Hammarskjöld replied. But he went on to say, "In a complex story of this type, all sorts of factors do influence the outcome and all sorts of personalities necessarily come into the picture. I think it is very premature to try and evaluate the significance of any single personality or any single action. That really belongs to history."

But his philosophical assessment did not stop there. "Many things have happened during my time here as Secretary-General for which I have great reason to be grateful," he said. "However, with the present perspective, I would say that no event or anything which I have been permitted to do ranks higher on that list of causes for gratitude than my trip to Peking."

There is little doubt that Hammarskjöld's personal entreaties influenced Chou En-lai when he had to choose a goodwill gesture. After Peking announced the freeing of the airmen, President Eisenhower thanked all who contributed to their release, "particularly . . . the United Nations and its Secretary-General, who actively sought this result." Colonel John K. Arnold, commander of the downed B-29, came to the U.N. a month later and thanked Hammarskjöld for his "personal role and the role of the United Nations in securing our release from China and return home." In 1956, during another crisis, Ambassador Lodge lavished more praise. "Last year, we saw Secretary-General Hammarskjöld going to Peking, and, as a result, our 15 U.S. aviators were released from the prisons of Communist China. . . . We can all be grateful, I think, that the position of the Secretary-General of the United Nations exists, and that it is filled by such a capable individual as Mr. Hammarskjöld."

For most American officials, however, the role of the secretary-general did not really loom large in a crisis that had powered emotions to foolish threats of nuclear war. The Americans saw their own steadfastness and aggressivity as far more important factors in the release of the airmen than any pleadings by Hammarskjöld. In his memoirs, Eisenhower neglected to even mention Hammarskjöld in the chapter about the crisis with China over the offshore islands. Perhaps the Americans were right. But, for U.N. diplomats and officials, the dramatic trip to Peking and the release of the airmen had tested the mettle of Hammarskjöld and their own respect and admiration for him, and they now felt very good about their secretary-general.

❧ 6 ❧

Suez:
The Empires Strike Out

On October 30, 1956, around mid-day, the ambassadors of the Security Council suddenly sensed the depth of the perfidy of the British and French. Israeli troops had stormed across the Sinai peninsula the day before to join their paratroopers dropping near Suez while other Israeli troops headed northward toward Ismailia on the Suez Canal and southward toward the outpost of Sharm al-Sheikh that blocked Israeli shipping through the Gulf of Aqaba. American Ambassador Henry Cabot Lodge introduced a resolution demanding that the Israelis withdraw behind the armistice lines that had been accepted under Ralph Bunche's mediation seven years earlier. But British Ambassador Pierson Dixon informed Lodge in advance that he could not support the resolution. "We were astonished," President Eisenhower chided his old friend Anthony Eden, the British prime minister, in a cable signed "Ike E." During the Security Council debate, Soviet Ambassador Arkady Sobolev interrupted to read the ambassadors an Associated Press news dispatch from London. The dispatch made it clear that the British and French had embarked on a strange imperial adventure.

Prime Minister Eden, according to the dispatch, had informed the House of Commons that he and French Premier Guy Mollet had issued an ultimatum to both Israel and Egypt to halt their fighting or face a British-French seizure of the Suez Canal. The ultimatum was worded in such a way that Egyptian President Gamal Abdel Nasser could never accept it. The British and French pronouncements were less an ultimatum than a prelude to armed attack. Many critics soon suspected that the Israelis had acted in collusion with the British and French and that the Israeli aggression was no more than a pretext for the impending British and French air strikes and ground assaults. The suspicions would prove well founded.

The Suez Canal crisis was a defining moment in the twentieth century—much like the fall of the Berlin Wall more than thirty years later—and it defined the end of traditional imperialism. The crisis exposed the British and French, masters of the two greatest empires in the world, as impotent blusterers, unable to face up to the condemnation of the United Nations, the United States, and indignant citizens at home. Although the British and French would manage to hold on to many of their African and Asian colonies for at least a half-dozen years or so, their empires actually died at Suez. The Suez crisis also enhanced the reputation of Dag Hammarskjöld, who worked incessantly to carve out a peaceful exit for the thrashed colonial powers and to create the first U.N. peacekeeping force. And the crisis demonstrated that the United Nations, no matter how imperfect a body, possessed a moral force of its own, steeled with surprising strength.

Britain had long been the ultimate power in Egypt, declaring the country a protectorate during World War I and keeping it that way into the 1920s. But British power and influence waned with the military coup that overthrew King Farouk in 1951. Lieutenant Colonel Gamal Abdel Nasser emerged as prime minister in 1954, and the last British troops left their base in the Suez Canal Zone early in 1956. The canal was vital to Britain and others in Western Europe, for it was the main link between the Middle East and the Mediterranean. That's how Britain obtained its oil. In tonnage, British ships led all others using the canal; the United States was second. The Suez Canal, with twice as much business as the Panama Canal, was profitable, benefiting the British government, for it was the largest shareholder in the Suez Canal company. French shareholders, however, were in the majority. One of their national heroes, Ferdinand de Lesseps, had constructed the canal, completing the job with great ceremony in 1869.

※ ✿

Aside from Hammarskjöld, there were three other main actors in the 1956 crisis, and they were as different as three characters could possibly be: Nasser, the relentless, defiant fiery nationalist who was prepared to play off the Soviets against the West; Eden, the debonair, handsome diplomat who had served for more than a generation as Winston Churchill's heir apparent; and John Foster Dulles, the strict, Calvinist, often disagreeable international lawyer who dominated American foreign policy as President Eisenhower's secretary of state.

The thirty-eight-year-old Nasser looked on himself as a pan-Arabist. In a slim book setting down his philosophy, he cited the 1920 Luigi Pirandello play *Six Characters in Search of an Author* and, varying the image somewhat, argued, "For some reason it seems to me that within the Arab circle there is a role wandering aimlessly in search of a hero. And I do not know why it seems to me that this role, exhausted by its wanderings, has at last settled down, tired and weary, near the borders of our country and is beckoning us to move, to take up its lines, to put on its costume since no one else is qualified to play it." In his exhaustive study of the Suez crisis, British journalist Keith Kyle describes this not as an egomaniacal boast but "a poetic restatement of a proposition often made . . . that Egypt was the natural metropolis of the Arab world." Yet Nasser clearly envisioned himself as the force that would help unite the Arab world under Egyptian leadership. Although a British diplomat described him as a politician who "thinks with his head rather than his heart," Nasser's drumbeat of anti-British and anti-Western rhetoric infuriated many Western statesmen, including Eden and Dulles, and persuaded them that the Middle East would be safer and quieter without him at the helm of Egypt.

Nasser, then a major, had been among the four thousand Egyptian troops trapped at Faluja in the 1948 wars and released only after Bunche persuaded the Israelis that allowing the Egyptians to march away with honor was a small price to pay for the possibility of an eventual peace settlement. Perhaps that experience explained why Israel obsessed Nasser. When French Foreign Minister Christian Pineau first met Nasser in Cairo in 1956, the Egyptian leader, who would soon assume the presidency, received him for a two-hour morning discussion that explored at length French ideas on the future of the underdeveloped world. The Egyptian nationalist struck the French Socialist as amiable and understanding. After lunch, however, the subject turned to Israel, and the mood changed. The reasonableness of Nasser vanished. "One of my goals," he said, shocking the French foreign minister, "is to destroy Israel."

The fifty-nine-year-old Eden had stood in waiting as Churchill's foreign secretary since the midst of World War II. He had first flashed across front pages worldwide in 1938 when he resigned as Prime Minister Neville Chamberlain's foreign secretary in protest against the government's appeasement of Fascism. The impeccably suited English statesman with his homburg, trim mustache, and youthful looks was a familiar international figure. He finally replaced a feeble eighty-year-old Churchill as prime minister in April 1955 and immediately won a resounding election that swelled the majority of his Conservative Party. No British prime minister seemed better prepared for the job in this century, certainly not in the area of foreign affairs. He was regarded universally as a wise and careful diplomat.

But this public image hid some fault lines. Eden was prone to attacks of fever and jaundice from a series of unsuccessful gallbladder operations and subject to fits of rages against his staff that belied his outward demeanor of charm and calm. He also had contempt for Nasser. "I have never thought Nasser a Hitler, he has no warlike people behind him, but the parallel with Mussolini is close," he wrote Eisenhower. As foreign secretary, he had approved the withdrawal of British troops from the Suez Canal Zone and now felt betrayed by the bellicose anti-Israel, anti-British propaganda spewing from Cairo. Almost thirty-five years later, Guy Millard, his private secretary, told an interviewer, "I think that he saw Nasser in very much the same terms as perhaps President Bush sees Saddam Hussein now, namely as a threat to world order, a threat to western interests in general and to British interests in particular."

The sixty-eight-year-old Dulles—an international lawyer, an adviser to Senator Vandenberg at the San Francisco conference, an inflexible warrior against what he regarded as monolithic Communism, and a fervent advocate of Christian ideals in foreign policy— dominated the play of foreign affairs so much during the Eisenhower administration that outsiders like Eden and French Premier Mollet were convinced that he rather than the president made the final decisions. This led them to misread American policy and assume that Dulles's hawkish distaste for Nasser would eventually put Eisenhower on their side or, at least, on the sidelines. Dulles was a gruff and dour man, and both American and foreign diplomats found it difficult to deal with him. State Department aides, in fact, liked to call him, behind his back, "Old Sourbelch."

A gulf of understanding, a gulf of culture, separated him from British and French leaders. His talk of "massive retaliation," his threats of punishing the Chinese Communists with atomic weapons, struck them as unreasonable and implacable. "There was a hatred, an almost religious hatred within Dulles against the Soviet Union," French Foreign Minister Pineau recalled later. Pineau said that he once found Dulles very despondent at a private dinner. "What's the matter?" Pineau asked. "You haven't spoken at all this evening." Dulles replied, "You know, I am very disappointed, very unhappy." Pineau asked him why. Dulles, the son of a Presbyterian minister, told Pineau, "My son has become a Jesuit priest." "But that does not sound so serious," the French foreign minister said. "That's easy for you to say," Dulles countered. "You are an atheist." "But," Pineau protested, "I am not an atheist. I believe in God." Dulles threw his arms up, Pineau recalled, and asked in astonishment, "You are a socialist and believe in God?"

"Dulles was highly ingenious," Donald Logan, one of the aides to British Foreign Secretary Selwyn Lloyd, recalled years later, "in thinking up new ideas which often, from our point of view, seemed to have little connection with his previous ideas. And so when working on one of his ideas you suddenly found that he'd gone off to Duke

Island and come up with a very different one. It was difficult to keep up with him."

※ ※

The vision of the Aswân Dam opened the drama. Nasser wanted to build an enormous dam near the Sudanese border that would regulate the flow of the Nile, irrigating huge tracts of land while supplying power to Cairo. Designed by a Greek engineer, the dam would stand 365 feet high and three miles across and would spawn a large new lake that would force seventy thousand people, mostly Sudanese, to settle elsewhere and would require the movement of some of Egypt's grandest monuments to drier ground. Eugene Black, president of the World Bank, pronounced the project feasible and sound, and both Britain and the United States offered grants to help finance the construction. Dulles saw this at first as insurance that Nasser would not slip into the Soviet camp.

But Dulles and his allies soon grew weary of Nasser and his Aswân Dam. Nasser deepened his dependence on the Soviet Union for arms. He continually objected to conditions put on the American and British grants and the World Bank loan as Western attempts to control his economy, and he kept flirting with Soviet offers to finance the project instead. Anti-Western propaganda continued to spew from Radio Cairo, and the French accused the Egyptians of helping to finance the rebellious nationalists in Algeria. Nasser's poorly timed decision to recognize Communist China and visit Peking crossed the Americans. Congress began to snipe at the Aswân deal, troubled by the idea of providing so much largess to an anti-Israeli, pro-Communist country that competed with the states of the American South in cotton production. Some critics complained that the Eisenhower administration was building a huge dam in Egypt while refusing to fund similar projects in the American West. Dulles concluded that it might not be a bad idea to let the Russians saddle themselves with such an expensive gift.

On July 19, 1956, Egyptian Ambassador Ahmed Hussein arrived in the State Department office of Dulles, pleased that he had finally persuaded Nasser to reject the Soviet offer and accept the Western loans and grants with all their conditions. But Dulles began a long discourse in which he set down all the concerns that the United States now had about the project. Moreover, he told Hussein, no foreign aid project was more unpopular in the United States than Nasser's Aswân Dam. A distraught Hussein asked Dulles if he was telling him that the Western offer had been withdrawn. Dulles replied that Hussein understood him correctly. According to Dulles biographer Townsend Hoopes, Hussein, in an act of desperation, warned Dulles that his country would now turn to the Soviets. That kind of threat only angered Dulles. He told the Egyptian ambassador contemptuously to go to Moscow. Dulles, according to Kyle, was pleased with his shock treatment of the Egyptians. The secretary of state called it "as big a chess move as U.S. diplomacy has made in a long time" and gloated that Nasser was "in a hell of a spot and no matter what he does can be used to American advantage."

The British, who agreed that the offer had to be withdrawn, believed that Dulles's manner and style had exacerbated the Egyptian humiliation. In his memoirs, Eden complained that the Eisenhower administration had informed him earlier that the deal was off but had not consulted him about it. "We were sorry that the matter was carried through so abruptly," he wrote, "because it gave our two countries no chance to concert either timing or methods, though these were quite as important as the substance." Guy Millard, Eden's private secretary, said later, "We felt that we had been rushed. . . . To some extent, I think that Eden and [Foreign Secretary] Selwyn Lloyd and the government in general attributed Nasser's violent reaction partly to the way in which this was done."

A week later, on July 23, the fourth anniversary of the revolution, a furious Nasser delivered his battle cry at the West, "Let them choke in their fury." But he did not disclose the form of his revenge. Three days later, the fourth anniversary of the abdication of King Farouk, Nasser addressed a massive crowd in Liberation Square (formerly Manshiya Square) in Alexandria. During his long and rambling speech, he brought up the name of the builder of the canal, Ferdinand de Lesseps. That was the code word for Egyptian troops, listening to the speech on radio, to take over the offices of the canal. Nasser then told the exultant Alexandria crowds and his nationwide radio audience, "Citizens, today the Suez Canal has been nationalized and this decision published in the Official Journal. . . . Now, even while I address you, some of your brothers, children of Egypt, are preparing to administer the canal company. At this instant they are taking charge of the canal, the Egyptian canal, not the foreign canal—that canal that is on Egyptian territory, that crosses Egyptian territory, that is a part of Egypt and that is now the property of Egypt." Neither Dulles nor his British and French allies had expected Nasser to go this far. He shocked the West with his defiance.

The seizure of the canal provoked Eden into almost desperate determination. A man like Nasser must not be allowed "to have his thumb on our windpipe," the prime minister said. "I had no doubt how Nasser's deed would be read, from Agadir to Karachi," he wrote in his memoirs. "This was a seizure of western property in reply to the action of the United States government. On its outcome would depend whose authority would prevail." In a telegram to President Eisenhower, he wrote that the West should exert the maximum political and economic pressure on Egypt. But, he went on, "my colleagues and I are convinced that we must be ready, in the last resort, to use force to bring Nasser to his senses." If he could have moved British forces swiftly enough, Eden might have tried a bold strike at Egypt immediately. "Eden has gone bananas," the chief of the air staff told an official of the air ministry. "We may have to mount some invasion of the Canal Zone." But the British forces no longer had the capability of swift attack in an emergency, and Eden knew that any military action would have to be planned carefully during the long crisis that awaited him. Within a week he decided that intervention was inevitable.

President Eisenhower, however, took the Suez Canal seizure in stride. In his view, Eden had panicked; the French were even worse. Unlike Eden, French Premier Guy Mollet looked on Nasser as a Hitler, not a Mussolini. Eisenhower did not agree that Nasser's act was illegal. All countries had the right to take over property on their territory so long as they compensated the owners. He also rejected the British and French contention that Egyptians were incapable of running the waterway. Eisenhower argued that resorting to force "at such a stage . . . would automatically weaken, perhaps even destroy, the United Nations." They were obligated to deal with the problem first through the peaceful resources of the U.N. He admonished Eden, "The step you contemplate should not be undertaken until every peaceful means of protecting the rights and the livelihood of great portions of the world had been thoroughly explored and exhausted." The president was not ruling out an armed intervention but advising its use only as a last resort. That, of course, misled the British and French about Eisenhower's determination to end the crisis without military action. In their eyes, force already was the last resort.

Three months of feverish diplomatic activity followed in which President Eisenhower, oblivious to his own administration's confusing signals, sought a peaceful solution to the crisis while Eden and Mollet, not quite sure what to do, mainly sought a pretext for a military solution. The British and French were reluctant at first to take the issue to the United Nations, and the main diplomatic fields were two conferences in London of the nations whose ships used the Suez Canal. These conferences, dominated by Dulles but boycotted and unheeded by Nasser, tried to set up some kind of international supervision of the canal; a users' association would collect tolls, defray expenses, and then turn the profits over to Egypt. Nasser rejected all this outside meddling, and Eden, continually writing to Eisenhower, accused Nasser of intending to hold the West for ransom. Drawing a parallel with his own stand against fascism in the 1930s, Eden wrote, "We have many times led Europe in the fight for freedom. It would be an ignoble end to our long history if we tamely accepted to perish by degrees."

Eden took heart from the hawkish rhetoric of Dulles. At the first London conference in August, Dulles said that "a way had to be found to make Nasser disgorge what he is attempting to swallow." Eden said the words "rang in my ears for months." In late September, according to Keith Kyle, Dulles told Harold Macmillan, then British chancellor of the exchequer, that, whether or not force was actually used, the threat of British force was vital to keep Nasser worried. On his return to London from Washington, Macmillan told his cabinet colleagues bent on intervention not to worry about any interference from Eisenhower. "I know Ike," he said. "He will lie doggo."

A charade followed at U.N. headquarters in New York. The British and French called for a meeting of the Security Council in early October. "What was the true purpose of the French and British in going to the United Nations?" Eisenhower wrote in his memoirs. "Was it, we wondered, a sincere desire to negotiate a satisfactory peaceful settlement (as the British insisted) or was this merely a setting of the stage for eventual use of force in Suez? We were apprehensive." Eisenhower had cause for his apprehension. The British and French wanted to prepare for armed intervention by putting their case to a world forum and exposing the intransigence of Nasser and his new champion, the Soviet Union.

Until then, Hammarskjöld had kept to the sidelines in the crisis. He seemed to chafe about this a bit. In his annual report to the U.N. General Assembly, written in early October, he noted his almost wistful belief that negotiations in a crisis "gain by being conducted against the background of the purposes and principles of the Charter and that the results can usefully be brought within the framework of the United Nations." Alluding to the movement of colonies toward independence, he said that "the emergence of a new nationalism . . . must arouse deep emotions on all sides." In this situation, he went on, "I am convinced that . . . the United Nations could be a source of greater assistance to governments than it has so far been." The U.N. had been the scene of important public debate, he said, but "its resources for reconciliation" had been overlooked. "The tensions of our time are too severe to permit us to neglect these resources," he said.

The issue was looked on as so critical that seven foreign ministers sat around the table when the debate opened in the Security Council on October 5. They included Dulles, British Foreign Secretary Selwyn Lloyd, French Foreign Minister Christian Pineau, and Egyptian Foreign Minister Mahmoud Fawzi. The British and French introduced a resolution that condemned Egypt and endorsed the proposals of the London conferences providing for international supervision of the canal. Since this was obviously headed for a Soviet veto, Hammarskjöld stepped in and proposed private meetings of British Foreign Secretary Lloyd, French Foreign Minister Pineau, and Egyptian Foreign Minister Fawzi in his office on the thirty-eighth floor.

With Hammarskjöld summing up points of convergence, proposing compromises, and nudging them, the antagonists reached agreement during six sessions on what became known as the "six principles." The principles, relayed to the Security Council by Hammarskjöld, promised free transit through the canal, respect for the sovereignty of Egypt, insulation of canal operations from the politics of any country, setting of tolls through bargaining between Egypt and the users, putting aside a proportion of profits for development of the canal, and the settlement of disputes by arbitration. Lloyd evidently looked on the principles as a significant achievement. "That's the one thing he wanted to do—to avoid the use of force which he could see coming closer and closer in Eden's timetable," his aide Donald Logan recalled later. "He believed at the end of the talks that he got just sufficient out of Fawzi for him to be able to succeed in that." The agreement seemed to go a long way toward satisfying the demands of Britain and France. "I have got the best announcement that I could possibly make to America tonight," Eisenhower told the nation through television. ". . . Egypt, Britain and France have met through their foreign ministers and agreed to a set of principles on which to negotiate, and it looks like here is a very great crisis that is behind us."

But, when the Security Council met, the British and French, while submitting one resolution endorsing the six principles, introduced a twin resolution endorsing the proposals of the London conferences as well. Eisenhower chided them for adding this "note of belligerence" but instructed Ambassador Lodge to vote for both resolutions. The first, endorsing the principles, was passed unanimously; the second was vetoed by the Soviet Union. Nevertheless, Hammarskjöld said that approval of the first resolution was enough to allow the British-French-Egyptian talks to continue in private. Lloyd agreed to stay on for these talks but was suddenly summoned back to London by Eden. The time had come for action.

꧁꧂

The collusion of Britain, France, and Israel was officially sealed in a series of secret meetings at a villa in the Parisian suburb of Sèvres for three days from October 22 to October 24. Prime Minister David Ben-Gurion and Army Chief of Staff Moshe Dayan flew in from Israel aboard a French military plane. Premier Mollet and Foreign Minister Pineau received them. Foreign Secretary Selwyn Lloyd, uneasy about abandoning a negotiated settlement for a scheme of collusion, represented Britain for a day and then returned to London, his place taken by Patrick Dean, the chairman of the British Joint Intelligence Committee.

The French and Israelis had concocted a plan that awaited and received British approval. British Prime Minister Eden, apprised by Mollet, had accepted the idea in principle; the meetings in Sèvres set down the details and finalized the agreement. The meetings themselves represented a heady moment for Israeli diplomacy—Ben-Gurion was treated as a vital player by the two most powerful countries in Europe. Ben-Gurion, Pineau, and Dean signed a secret protocol on October 24. The proceedings were so secret that Eden was upset when he heard that an actual document had been signed. He wanted all copies destroyed, but the French and Israelis refused. The Israelis especially wanted historical proof that they were acting in concert with the French and British.

The Protocol of Sèvres provided that in five days Israeli troops would launch "a large scale attack on the Egyptian forces with the aim of reaching the Canal zone the following day." The British and French would then issue separate "appeals"—amounting to ultimatums—to Egypt and Israel. The Egyptians would be required to stop fighting, withdraw troops ten miles from the canal, and accept temporary occupation of the canal by Anglo-French troops who would guarantee freedom of passage. The Israelis would be required to stop fighting and withdraw, not to Israel, but only ten miles east of the canal, and they would be required to do this only in the unlikely event that Egypt accepted the ultimatum. If it did not, the protocol said, "the Anglo-French forces will launch military operations against the Egyptian forces in the early hours of the morning of 31 October."

The operation began on schedule. Israel attacked, vowing to destroy terrorist bases in Egypt as an act of self-defense; this gave Britain and France their pretext. As planned, the two European governments issued their ultimatum the next day, proclaiming their concern for the security of the canal. Israel and Egypt would have to stop fighting within twelve hours, withdraw ten miles from each side of the canal (leaving Israelis on Egyptian territory), and allow Anglo-French occupation of the canal. When Nasser as expected rejected the ultimatum, the British and French ordered their forces forward. They might have pulled off their duplicitous scheme if they had moved swiftly, seizing the canal and toppling Nasser in bold strikes. Eisenhower, in fact, assumed that the British and French would seize the canal the day after the rejection of their ultimatums. But, trapped by the logic of their charade, the British and French did not set off from their base on Malta in the western Mediterranean until the ultimatum had been rejected. The Israelis, on the other hand, moved with dispatch, taking the Gaza Strip and almost all the Sinai peninsula, capturing five thousand prisoners. The British and French had started to bomb Egypt immediately; with the help of the Israelis, they put the Egyptian air force out of commission. But it took a week for their paratroopers and soldiers to reach the canal, enough time for an outcry, coming from afar and within, to mount steadily against Britain and France.

President Eisenhower was furious, for he was not even informed by his allies before they embarked on their rash adventure. "The United States," he said in a televised speech, "was not consulted in any way about any phase of these actions. Nor were we informed of them in advance. . . . We believe these actions have been taken in error, for we do not accept the use of force as a wise or proper instrument for the settlement of international disputes." Premier Mollet admitted to Eisenhower later that the American government was not consulted because of "our fear that if we had consulted it, it would have prevented us from acting."

The timing could not have been worse, for the Suez intervention diverted attention and energy from the brutal Soviet repression of Hungary. A propaganda coup for the West in Hungary was obscured by a propaganda debacle in Egypt. The Suez problem also diverted Eisenhower from his reelection campaign. Some American officials, in fact, suspected that Britain, France and Israel had timed their invasion so that it coincided with the campaign, hoping in vain that the President would be too busy to confront them. But Eisenhower was determined to stop the foolish Suez escapade, by opposing it vigorously at the United Nations and, even more important, by refusing to help Britain shore up its foreign exchange as investors lost faith in a troubled, adventurous government. The lack of American support for sterling shocked Macmillan, the chancellor of the exchequer, for he had counted on a bailout because of his old friendship with Eisenhower and the traditional alliance between Britain and France.

Eden did not anticipate the fury of the opposition at home, an opposition emboldened by condemnations at the United Nations and elsewhere. In an editorial, the *Sunday Observer* said, "We had not realized that our government was capable of such folly and such crookedness." The editorial concluded that "Sir Anthony Eden must go." Labour Members of Parliament shouted down government ministers with calls to resign. In a television address, Prime Minister Eden defended himself by imploring, "I've been a League of Nations man and a United Nations man and I'm still the same man with the same convictions. I couldn't be other even if I wished. But I'm utterly convinced that the action we have taken is right." But, in a televised reply, Hugh Gaitskell, the leader of the opposition, said, "We are doing all this alone, except for France, opposed by the world, in defiance of the world. It is not a police action, there is no law behind it—we have taken the law into our own hands." The British public appeared to agree with Gaitskell.

☙❧

As soon as the Israelis invaded Egypt, the United States decided to take the crisis to the U.N. Security Council. "We plan to get to the United Nations the first thing in the morning—when the doors open—before the U.S.S.R. gets there," Eisenhower told the British chargé d'affaires in Washington. The Security Council met at eleven the next morning. From that moment on, Dag Hammarskjöld became the main international player in blunting the Anglo-French intervention and reining the crisis. Hammarskjöld was shocked by the escapade. "He found it hard to believe," said Brian Urquhart, his biographer, "that . . . the two Western European countries which he most admired and which he believed to represent the best traditions of European civilization, could be guilty of so shoddy a deception or of so disastrous a course of action." The Suez crisis would prove Hammarskjöld's finest hour. When the crisis sputtered to its end, Urquhart wrote, "his reputation, except in France, Britain, and Israel, had never stood higher."

Hammarskjöld could not have managed the crisis without the full support of Eisenhower. The aggressive stance of the Americans embittered Anthony Eden. Only three years earlier, when the American Central Intelligence Agency had engineered the overthrow of the Guatemalan government, Britain had kept to the sidelines and abstained, allowing American Ambassador Lodge to prevail with an outrageous motion that the matter was none of the Security Council's business. "We could not help contrasting the American attitude now with our own attitude at the time of the Guatemala campaign," Eden wrote in his memoirs. ". . . We had understood her action and done what we could not to hamper her in the Security Council. The United States was now behaving in a precisely contrary manner towards us. When this point was put to the United States officials, they had no answer. . . . The attitude was rather that the President has been slighted because the allies had acted without permission. The allies must pay for it, and pay they did."

In the Security Council, the British and French vetoed resolutions by the United States and the Soviet Union demanding that Israel withdraw and others stay out of Egypt. It was the first time that Britain had ever used the veto. In a supreme irony, Yugoslavia then invoked the "Uniting for Peace" plan that Dean Acheson had devised to bypass Soviet vetoes. Since the Security Council was paralyzed, the issue would be sent to the General Assembly.

On the next day, Hammarskjöld read a statement of principles to the council, clearly aimed at the British and French. "The principles of the Charter are, by far, greater than the Organization in which they are embodied, and the aims which they are to safeguard are holier than the policies of any single nation or people," Hammarskjöld said. ". . . A Secretary-General cannot serve on any other assumption than that—within the necessary limits of human frailty and honest differences of opinion—all member nations honor their pledge to observe all articles of the Charter. . . . Were the members to consider that another view of the duties of the Secretary-General than the one here stated would better serve the interests of the Organization, it is their obvious right to act accordingly." This was a clear request for a vote of confidence, and every ambassador expressed one that day, including French Ambassador Louis de Guiringaud and British Ambassador Pierson Dixon. With this avowed support behind him, Hammarskjöld now had the moral authority to step forward and take charge of the crisis.

The opening debate of the emergency session of the General Assembly began on November 1 and lasted until four-twenty the next morning. "I doubt that any representative ever spoke from this rostrum with as heavy a heart as I have brought here tonight," said Secretary of State John Foster Dulles. "We speak on a matter of vital importance where the United States finds itself unable to agree with three nations with which it has ties of deep friendship, and two of which constitute our oldest and most trusted and reliable allies." He then painted the crisis in dark and moral terms. "The first thing is to stop the fighting as rapidly as possible lest it become a conflagration which would endanger us all," he said. ". . . What has been called a police action may develop into something which is far more grave." Dulles insisted that the United Nations would be rendered impotent if nations followed the lead of Britain, France, and Israel and took "into their own hands the remedying of what they believe to be their injustices." Dulles then introduced the American resolution demanding a withdrawal of all forces. It was Dulles's last major public contribution to the Suez crisis. He was stricken with pain and rushed the next day to a hospital for an emergency cancer operation. But he continued to advise Eisenhower from Walter Reed Hospital.

The anticolonialist stand of the United States excited the new

Asian countries like Pakistan and small Latin American countries like Colombia. Hammarskjöld passed a note to American Ambassador Lodge that said, "This is one of the darkest days in postwar times. Thank God you have played the way you have. This will win you many friends." But the harshness of Dulles's rhetoric pierced the British. Harold Macmillan wrote later that "Dulles had all along regarded himself as the legal adviser in the Suez case. . . . Now his clients had taken the matter out of his hands and acted on their own. This was an insult, almost a betrayal. Consequently, Dulles showed in the vital period a degree of hostility amounting almost to a frenzy." The clients, of course, also felt that their legal adviser had misled them.

Eden was astounded that the United States would put the principle of anticolonialism above the unity of the North Atlantic alliance. Nor could he understand why Dulles, who had deluded the British into regarding him as an implacable foe of Nasser, would not seize the moment to slap down the sneering Egyptian leader. "There was no suggestion of going to the root of the matter," wrote Eden. ". . . There was no attempt to snatch opportunity out of trouble which is the stamp of statesmanship." The American resolution passed by a vote of sixty-four to five, with six abstentions. Only Australia and New Zealand joined Britain, France, and Israel in voting against the resolution. "For the first time in history," said Vice President Richard M. Nixon, "we have shown independence of Anglo-French policies towards Asia and Africa which seemed to us to reflect the colonial tradition. This declaration of independence has had an electrifying effect throughout the world."

During the debate, Lester Pearson, the Canadian minister of external affairs, who abstained on the vote for the American resolution, proposed a U.N. military force to take over positions from the British, French, and Israelis. Hammarskjöld had serious doubts at first about the wisdom or effectiveness of such a move. But it would soon become the centerpiece of his drive to turn the British, French, and Israelis back. On November 4, the General Assembly instructed Hammarskjöld to submit a plan within forty-eight hours for the setting up of "an emergency international United Nations force to secure and supervise the cessation of hostilities."

In London, Eden, buffeted on all sides, grew fatigued and ill. The U.N. had enough moral standing in Britain for its condemnation to matter to the British public, and it was clear that his government and career were in grave danger. The U.N. force seemed to give Eden a chance to extricate himself somehow and salvage something from the crisis. He told Hammarskjöld that Britain would accept a U.N. force so long as the British and French paratroopers and marines would be regarded as a vanguard for the U.N. troops. But that was not acceptable to the secretary-general. The U.N. would have to supplant the British and French, not become an accessory to their adventure. Nevertheless, Eden's grudging acceptance of the principle of a U.N. force opened the way for Hammarskjöld to cajole all sides into a U.N. solution.

The British and French paratroopers and marines landed in Egypt while Hammarskjöld prepared his report for the General Assembly, but they moved at a slow and torpid pace down the canal zone. The Israelis, who had accomplished their end of the mission and felt the sting of Eisenhower's wrath, said they were ready to abide by a cease-fire. Canadian Prime Minister Louis Saint Laurent pressured Eden to give in. Chancellor of the Exchequer Harold Macmillan, once the hawk of the cabinet, now told Eden that the loss of sterling reserves was so great that the time had come to stop the adventure. The state of Eden's invasion was so ineffectual and his health so precarious that he seemed to have little choice; he succumbed and announced a cease-fire. With the retreat of the British colonial will, Premier Mollet would not go on alone. On November 7, the General Assembly, accepting Hammarskjöld's report, instructed him to proceed with the establishment of the U.N. Emergency Force, the first U.N. peacekeeping operation in history.

❧

The crisis would not end until Hammarskjöld organized the U.N. force and persuaded Nasser to accept it on Egyptian territory and persuaded the others to leave as soon as possible. The U.N. had never put together a military force before. Every step became a precedent. According to Urquhart, the secretary-general turned to Ralph

Bunche and said, "Now, corporal, go and get me a force." Hammarskjöld named Lieutenant General E. L. M. (Tommy) Burns of Canada, chief of staff for the U.N. observers assigned to Israeli-Arab borders, as commander while Bunche, assisted by Urquhart, an officer with the British army airborne forces during World War II, solicited offers of troops and transport. Colombian Ambassador Francisco Urrutia persuaded his president to dispatch troops by insisting, "If this was 1902 and the U.N. had existed and could have put in a peace force, Colombia would not have lost the Panama Canal."

The idea caught on, and Bunche soon found he had more offers of troops than he needed. "This is the most popular army in history— an army which everyone fights to get into," he said. The force, supplied by Brazil, Canada, Colombia, Denmark, Finland, India, Indonesia, Norway, Sweden, and Yugoslavia, would number six thousand. At Bunche's suggestion, troops were ferried to Italy so they would be ready to move into Egypt quickly. The U.N. soldiers, while wearing their own uniforms, would have distinctive headgear. Blue berets were chosen, but not enough could be produced in time. The United States offered surplus helmets, which were quickly painted blue and passed to the troops.

In a remarkable feat of management and energy, Hammarskjöld and Bunche put together the U.N.'s first peacekeeping force in a week. The first "Blue Helmets"—Danish troops—arrived in Egypt on November 15. The first Colombians arrived a day later, accompanied by Hammarskjöld who would spend three days in Egypt negotiating the conditions for the stay of the troops with Nasser and Foreign Minister Fawzi. They agreed that the U.N. force, though it would replace the British and French in the Suez Canal area, would have nothing to do with the canal zone after the European powers left. The rest of its mission was not clearly stated: In the end, the U.N. troops supervised the gradual withdrawal of the Israelis and then monitored the border between Egypt and Israel. In short, although the U.N. peacekeepers would serve as the pretext for the British and French to pull out, they would not fulfill the mission of the British and French troops by occupying the Suez Canal. The British and French withdrew their troops from the canal by the end of 1956; the Israelis left Egypt a few months later. Although Hammarskjöld's tact had supplied Britain and France with a fig leaf of honor to cover their withdrawal, their humiliation in history would be near absolute.

※☙

Eden's health could not withstand the tension and turmoil of the crisis, and, following the advice of his doctors, he resigned in early 1957. Despite his ill health, he survived another two decades, writing his best-selling memoirs. Receiving the title of earl of Avon in 1961, he did not waver in his view that he had been right to try to seize the canal and oust Nasser and that he had been betrayed by Dulles and his old friend Ike. He died in his eightieth year.

The Suez crisis ended triumphantly for Gamal Abdel Nasser. He had stood up to Israeli and imperialist aggression and was now the unrivaled hero of the Arab masses throughout North Africa and the Middle East. His troops had fared dismally; only the United States and the United Nations had saved him. But these nuances were lost in the general exultation of a victorious Egypt. His countrymen would manage the Suez Canal, and he would personally oversee the construction of the Aswân High Dam with Soviet funding. But he would never unite the Arabs under his leadership and would be humiliated by the Israelis in the 1967 Six-Day War that he provoked. Despite his youth, he would be worn down by diabetes, circulatory ailments, and heart failure, dying in 1970 at the age of fifty-two.

The maneuvering of Dulles during the Suez crisis should have raised questions about his judgment and his penchant for cataclysmic rhetoric on both sides of an issue. But Eisenhower did not waver in his confidence. Dulles continued as the prime architect of foreign policy during the Eisenhower administration until the recurrence of cancer forced him to retire in April 1959, a month short of his death at the age of seventy-one.

Hammarskjöld, who also supervised the clearing of ships sunk in the canal by the Egyptians when the Israelis invaded, received so much adulation and admiration for his work during the crisis that Ambassador Pierson Dixon, according to Keith Kyle, warned his British colleagues that "we may find it inconvenient to have to deal with a Secretary-General who will be elevated to the status of a Pope with temporal as well as spiritual powers." "Thank God we have Dag Hammarskjöld as Secretary-General," said Lester Pearson. "He has really done magnificent work under conditions of almost unbelievable pressure." President Eisenhower told a news conference in mid-November, "The last thing we must do is to disturb any of the delicate negotiations now going on under the leadership of Secretary-General Dag Hammarskjöld. . . . The man's abilities have not only been proven, but a physical stamina that is almost remarkable, almost unique in the world, has also been demonstrated by a man who night after night has gone with one or two hours sleep, working all day and, I must say, working intelligently and devotedly."

❧

Settlement of the Suez crisis was one of the most spectacular single achievements of the U.N. during its first fifty years. Unlike the Korean and Persian Gulf Wars, the U.N. did not serve as a mere cloak for American action. Moral condemnation by the United Nations proved a powerful force. The U.N., of course, might have proven impotent if Eisenhower and Dulles had decided to ignore the British and French escapade rather than block it. Nevertheless, a key factor in the dénouement was the attitude of many ordinary British and French citizens toward the U.N.—they believed in the U.N. and refused to accept the defiance of their governments.

But the Suez crisis played against the background of Hungary, and Hungary mocked the power of the U.N. The Soviet Union suppressed the Hungarian uprising in the fall of 1956 and executed Imre Nagy, the government's reformist leader. World public opinion was just as aroused by Hungary as Suez. The General Assembly condemned the Soviet Union, but the Soviet Union ignored the condemnation. Hammarskjöld came up with no dramatic gestures to put himself into the conflict. At the height of the Cold War, the U.N. was powerless to bend any of the two superpowers to its will. But, in the twilight of colonialism, the U.N. was strong enough, at least with American backing, to bend and almost break two tired old imperialist powers.

🌿 7 🌿

The Battles of Katanga and the Crash of Hammarskjöld

In July 1960, the United Nations dispatched the first contingents of its Blue Helmets to the former Belgian Congo (now Zaire) to restore law and order out of bloody chaos and replace the Belgian troops who no longer had any rightful place in an independent black country. The U.N. had not mounted such a large and audacious military force before. At Suez, the troops were performing what would become known as classic peacekeeping tasks—the impartial patrolling of cease-fire lines between belligerents who were content, for the time being, to avoid conflict; the Blue Helmets in Suez fired their arms only to protect themselves. The Congo operation would take the U.N. onto more dangerous ground.

When the U.N. withdrew its troops after four years, an era of chaos and murderous oppression still lay ahead in the Congo. But, amid much bitter controversy, the U.N. had managed to suppress the secession of Moise Tshombe's Katanga province with his mercenary-led army. It was a grand victory of sorts. But the U.N. would avoid mounting anything like it again for more than thirty years.

❧❧

President John F. Kennedy soon became the main supporter of Dag Hammarskjöld in the crisis, and American newspaper readers suddenly found Africa on their minds. Before then, hardly anyone but missionaries, big-game hunters, and a handful of obscure diplomats knew anything about the place that Hollywood and other mythmakers called "the dark continent." With the Congo crisis, Africa not only thrust itself upon Americans in a few quick months but did so, troubled and shrieking.

The United Nations intervention came during some of the most tense years of the Cold War. In a few months, Soviet leader Nikita Khrushchev would pound a shoe on his table at the General Assembly to protest the policies of Secretary-General Dag Hammarskjöld, the United States, and the West. In a little more than two years, Khrushchev and President Kennedy would confront each other's steel in the critical Cuban missile crisis. But there was far more than an East versus West conflict at stake in the Congo.

The Congo had jarred the mood of optimism about emerging Africa. Many intellectuals and political liberals, though they knew little about it, fervently wanted black Africa to succeed and blamed adverse news like the Congo chaos on the dark hand of colonialism. They supported the United Nations intervention and its suppression of Katanga and assumed that only neocolonialists would favor the independence of Katanga. In the eyes of those who sympathized with the Third World, the Katanga lobby was made up of reactionaries who wanted to dismember and weaken black Africa. Differences over the new Africa did not fit the East versus West conflict at all. The British, for example, counted themselves the staunchest ally of the United States in the Cold War but could not fathom Kennedy's anti-Katanga policy. There were echoes of Suez in the Congo.

Few colonies came to independence as unprepared as the Congo on June 30, 1960. Belgian colonialism had been harsh and exploitative. Out of a population of fourteen million, there were only seventeen black university graduates, not one a doctor, a lawyer, or an engineer. The hundred thousand Belgian settlers and bureaucrats ran the commerce and administration and expected to keep on doing so for years after independence. Unlike the British or the French, the Belgians provided no period of self-rule to prepare their colony for independence. A week-old National Assembly elected the new leaders—a fiery, irrational prime minister named Patrice Lumumba and a stolid, enigmatic president named Joseph Kasavubu—less than a week before independence. The independence ceremonies did not foster any mood of good feelings. Lumumba invoked "the insults, the blows that we had to submit to . . . because we were Negroes" and warned the Belgians, "Our wounds are too fresh to forget."

The troubles began just five days later in the Léopoldville (now Kinshasa) barracks of the Congolese army known as the Force Publique. This army of 25,000 men did not have a single African commissioned officer; it was commanded by 1,135 Belgians. Angered by the sight of powerful, new black politicians riding around in sleek cars while their own path to prestige was blocked by whites, a group of Congolese soldiers announced they no longer need obey their Belgian officers. Lieutenant General Emile Janssens, the Force Publique commander, tried to quash the mutiny with arrogance. In a blatant and now infamous act of neocolonialism, Janssens assembled the troops and chalked across the blackboard the admonition BEFORE INDEPENDENCE = AFTER INDEPENDENCE. But the soldiers started to sack the canteen, and their mutinous mood soon spread to the Thysville garrison less than a hundred miles away.

As more rioting shook up garrisons throughout the country, the soldiers directed as much of their fury at Lumumba as at their Belgian officers. A frightened Lumumba quickly gave in and dismissed all Belgian officers, appointing his cousin Victor Lundula, a civilian whose only military experience came during a brief stint as medical orderly in the Force Publique, as the new commander with the rank of major general. Joseph Mobutu, a corporal and former journalist, was promoted to chief of staff with the rank of colonel. The instant promotion of hundreds of inexperienced Africans failed to calm the situation, and the undisciplined Force, now known as the Armée Nationale Congolaise (ANC), went on a rampage.

Reports spread of rape and murder of whites throughout the Congo, and thousands of terrified Belgians fled across the borders to

Congo-Brazzaville, Uganda, Angola, and Northern Rhodesia (now Zambia). A Belgian Royal Commission later reported that 291 European women had been raped by marauding Congolese troops. On July 10, Belgium, transporting 5,600 troops to join 3,800 already stationed at its Congolese bases of Kitona and Kamina, intervened to restore order within the former colony.

But the Belgian intervention was unpalatable to many outsiders in the era of emerging Africa. This disdain for Belgium was exacerbated a day later when the Belgians killed more than a dozen Congolese in the town of Matadi and when Moise Tshombe, listening to Belgian advisers from the Union Minière du Haut Katanga, declared the independence of his province of Katanga with its mineral wealth. The Eisenhower administration rejected all suggestions that U.S. troops replace the Belgian troops and encouraged the Congolese government to turn instead to the United Nations. The appeal to the U.N. from both Prime Minister Lumumba and President Kasavubu came two days after Belgium had ordered its troops into the Congo.

☙❧

On July 14, barely two weeks after independence, the U.N. Security Council, called into special session by Hammarskjöld, approved his request to send a U.N. peacekeeping force to the Congo to replace the Belgian troops there and restore order. The vote was eight to zero, with three abstentions—Britain and France, the two main colonial powers in Africa, and Nationalist China. Hammarskjöld pledged that the force would include African troops, fire only in self-defense, and keep out of the internal politics of the Congo.

After the secretary-general rushed phone calls to leaders around the world, troops from Ghana and Tunisia (some Tunisians without ammunition) arrived in the Congo aboard American and British transport planes the next day; troops from Ethiopia and Morocco came the day after. A band and an old black goat, the regimental mascot, led the marching Moroccans out of the airport. Hammarskjöld named Major General Carl Carlsson von Horn of Sweden as commander. Troops from thirty countries continually augmented the U.N. force until it reached peak strength of 19,828 a year later.

From the start, U.N. officials expected maddening difficulties. "This is the craziest operation in history," Hammarskjöld said. "God only knows where it is going to end." He described the U.N. operation as much like giving first aid to a rattlesnake. Politics would circumscribe every military step. "Unfortunately, we were not 'any army';" von Horn wrote later, "we were a United Nations Force in which logic, military principles—even common sense—took second place to political factors." The UN (or ONU, as it was known in the Congo from the initials in French for "United Nations Organization") puzzled the Congolese, who had heard little about it before. "The ONU?" a Congolese official asked Brian Urquhart of the United Nations. "What tribe is that?"

Although Lumumba assumed that the U.N. force would do his bidding, Hammarskjöld soon demonstrated that the Blue Helmets were an international army with its own mandate, taking orders only from him. U.N. troops quickly replaced Belgian troops at airports, radio stations, and highways and fanned out to provincial towns like Stanleyville (now Kisangani), Thysville, Matadi, Luluabourg (now Kananga), and Coquilhatville (now Mbandaka) to impose order. By July 23, a little more than a week after the first contingents arrived, U.N. troops had replaced Belgian troops everywhere except in Katanga and the two Belgian bases.

But the U.N. force was beset with problems. Each country's contingent had different weapons, vehicles, radio systems, and even eating preferences. Confusion could not be avoided. Major General Henry Templar Alexander, the British officer who served as chief of Ghana's defense staff and led the first Ghanaian troops into the Congo, wrote later, "There seemed to be no form of military planning cell in the United Nations Secretariat which could plan and produce the type of military force required to bring peace to a country which had been reduced to chaos overnight. . . . Troops arrived, officers arrived, commanders arrived, and nobody knew quite what they were supposed to do."

Relations with the Armée Nationale Congolaise were nettlesome. With astounding bluffness, General Alexander told Undersecretary-General Ralph Bunche, who served as Hammarskjöld's special representative to the Congo during the first months, "The nigger in the woodpile is the ANC." In his memoirs, Alexander made the same point with more tact. "The United Nations military forces went into the Congo to 'assist' the central government in Léopoldville to maintain law and order," he wrote, "but unfortunately the major law-breakers were the Congolese army."

Rajeshwar Dayal of India, one of Bunche's successors in the Congo, described the ANC as "armed rabble." Anyone who had dealings with the ANC during the 1960s knows what Dayal meant. For many years, Congolese troops wore their feelings of inferiority on their sleeves. An arrested white always knew that survival depended on calming the frantic fears of the handful of soldiers arresting him. When a column of mercenary soldiers approached, some ANC troops would undress, leave their uniforms behind, and flee in underwear. Whenever they felt threatened or defeated, the Congolese soldiers would assuage their humiliation by storming into an undefended village or town, pillaging, raping, and murdering civilians, both white and black. In January 1961, a Stanleyville unit of the ANC murdered twenty-two European missionaries and an unknown number of Africans. The Congolese soldiers would engage an enemy military force only if small enough to overrun.

General Alexander tried to disarm units of the ANC but was prevented by Bunche and other U.N. officials who insisted they had no authority to do so. The fear of disarming, however, may have contributed to later incidents of ANC assaults on small units of U.N. troops. Congolese troops mercilessly clubbed eight Canadian soldiers at the Léopoldville airport and eight U.S. airmen who had ferried U.N. supplies into the Stanleyville airport. More than a year later, Congolese troops murdered forty-four Ghanaian soldiers in Port-Francqui (now Ilebo) and thirteen Italian airmen in Kindu. For a while, Moroccan troops tried to restrain Congolese soldiers, but this stopped after Colonel Mobutu deposed the Lumumba government in a coup on September 14. By then, chaotic events had drawn the U.N. into internal Congolese politics.

In early September 1960, a little more than two months after independence, President Kasavubu and Prime Minister Lumumba attempted to oust each other. Pleading the need for calm and order, Andrew Cordier, the American who succeeded Bunche in the

Congo, sent U.N. troops to occupy the radio station in Léopoldville, shutting off Lumumba's main channel for rousing the capital's Africans to his side. Cordier also closed all major airports in the Congo, preventing a dozen Soviet transport planes from ferrying Congolese troops to Léopoldville to help Lumumba. In the midst of this confusion, Mobutu staged a coup and turned the government over to a committee of young, educated, nonpolitical Congolese.

≫≪

These latest events in the Congo provoked Soviet leader Nikita Khrushchev into a vitriolic attack against Dag Hammarskjöld in the General Assembly in late September 1960. The Soviets had expected the peacekeepers to become a kind of military arm of Lumumba. But they had helped his enemies instead. The Soviet Union blamed the secretary-general for allowing the dismissal of Lumumba and the subsequent expulsion of Soviet bloc diplomats from Léopoldville by the Mobutu government. This was the same session of the General Assembly that would witness Khrushchev a couple of weeks later pounding his shoe upon the table in protest against what he regarded as anti-Soviet attacks by Western delegates. (That incident has become so much part of U.N. lore that the most frequent question thrown at tour guides in U.N. headquarters is still "Where was Khrushchev sitting when he pounded his shoe?")

In the debate on the Congo, Khrushchev insisted that the United States and the colonial powers "have been doing their dirty work in the Congo through the Secretary-General of the United Nations and his staff." "Conditions have clearly matured," he insisted, "to the point where the post of Secretary-General . . . should be abolished." In its place, the Soviet leader proposed a three-part executive unit representing the Western governments, the Soviet Union and its bloc, and the neutralist nations. This proposal, repeated endlessly by the Soviets for almost a decade, became known as the "troika."

At present, Khrushchev said, only one official had the responsibility for carrying out the decisions of the Security Council and the General Assembly—and that was too much to expect of one man. "Let those who believe in saints hold to their opinion," Khrushchev told the General Assembly. "We do not credit such tales." The Soviet leader called on Hammarskjöld to "muster the courage to resign." "There is no room for a man who has violated the elementary principles of justice in such an important post as that of Secretary-General," he said.

Hammarskjöld took the podium to defend himself and, even more important, the institution of the secretary-general. "The man does not count," he said, "the institution does. A weak or nonexistent executive would mean that the United Nations would no longer be able to serve as an effective instrument for active protection of the interests of those many members who need such protection." Since Khrushchev found it impossible to work with him, Hammarskjöld went on, the proper course might be resignation. But, if he did resign, the Soviet Union would insist on replacing him with a troika. "By resigning, I would, therefore, at the present difficult and dangerous juncture throw the organization to the winds," Hammarskjöld said. "I have no right to do so because I have a responsibility to all those states members for which the organization is of decisive importance, a responsibility which overrides all other considerations."

The applause and shouts of approval from the delegates lasted for several minutes. Bunche slipped a note to Hammarskjöld, telling him that it was "the greatest and most spontaneous demonstration in U.N. annals." Hammarskjöld had extended the power of the office of secretary-general well beyond Trygve Lie. The first secretary-general could not survive a Soviet boycott. But, by 1960, Hammarskjöld had demonstrated that, as protector of the principles of the charter and of the rights of the small and vulnerable member states, the institution of the secretary-general—at least as personified in Hammarskjöld— had powers of its own. The secretary-general now had enough prestige to lead the Security Council toward crises and deal with them by carrying out the council's resolutions in his own way. The Security Council could not micromanage him.

※❧

By this time, the United States had decided that the Congo would have no peace unless the erratic, demagogic Lumumba was eliminated. Even though confined to his house and surrounded by a protective cordon of U.N. Moroccan troops, Lumumba, according to the Americans, still had enough charisma to inflame the masses. The CIA dispatched an agent with lethal poison to assassinate him. But before the agent could do his job, the Congolese took care of the matter themselves.

In an attempt to reach his base in Stanleyville, Lumumba slipped past the U.N. guards but was soon captured by Congolese troops. Just a few months later, in January 1961, Mobutu turned Lumumba over to his secessionist enemies in Katanga, where he was severely beaten and shot to death in the presence of two Katangan ministers. U.N. soldiers had watched him arrive in the Katangan capital of Elisabethville (now Lubumbashi) but had done nothing because of their mandate to stay out of Congolese politics. The murder provoked worldwide shock and fury, and the U.N. was castigated for failing to protect Lumumba and prevent his transfer to Katanga. Khrushchev denounced Hammarskjöld as Lumumba's "chief assassin."

More political turmoil followed. Antoine Gizenga set up a Lumumbaist régime in Stanleyville. Khrushchev, still insisting on the replacement of Hammarskjöld by a troika, recognized Gizenga as the legitimate leader of the Congo. Six countries including Morocco and Egypt withdrew their troops from the U.N. force in protest against Hammarskjöld's failure to save Lumumba. Hammarskjöld, who had personally led Swedish U.N. troops into the Katanga in October, called on the Security Council for more authority. Although continually criticized by the Soviet Union, the old European colonial powers, and radical African states, Hammarskjöld had the support of most new African countries and of President Kennedy. The Security Council gave him what he wanted.

☙❧

On February 15, 1961, the council—by a vote of nine to zero, with the Soviet Union and France abstaining—passed a resolution authorizing the United Nations peacekeepers to use force, if necessary, to prevent civil war in the Congo, a little more than seven months after independence. The council had never granted such authority to U.N. peacekeeping troops before and did not do so again until the Somalian and Bosnian missions were authorized in the 1990s. The resolution also authorized the U.N. to bring the various ANC units under discipline and control and to remove all mercenaries and Belgian officers from Katanga.

By then, five armies watched each other in the Congo: the U.N. force of almost twenty thousand posted in small detachments throughout the country; ANC units of seven thousand troops in the Léopoldville area loyal to General Mobutu; ANC units of fifty-five hundred in the Stanleyville area loyal to Gizenga and the memory of Lumumba; ANC units of three thousand troops in South Kasai province loyal to the secessionist movement of Albert Kalonji; and the Katanga Gendarmerie of six thousand troops under Belgian and mercenary officers loyal to Tshombe. The U.N., trying to ease tribal and racial conflicts, set up areas of refuge and neutral zones for civilians and spent a good deal of time rescuing European settlers under siege. While the Blue Helmets were never able to whip the ANC units into order, political maneuvering, especially by American diplomats, managed to fashion a fragile unity of all political factions and regions of the Congo except Katanga by the end of the summer of 1961. It was now time for the U.N. to end the secession of Katanga.

The first assault on Katanga—Operation Morthor—began at 4 A.M. on September 13, 1961, dissipated in recriminations and a humiliating stalemate, and led to the death of Hammarskjöld as he tried to arrange a cease-fire. For several weeks, Conor Cruise O'Brien, the Irish diplomat in charge of U.N. operations in Katanga, had been trying to round up the 208 Belgian officers and 302 mercenaries in the Katangese Gendarmerie and deport them from the Congo. Both Tshombe and the Belgian consul had promised to cooperate, but, by the time of the assault, 104 foreign soldiers were still listed as "missing." O'Brien suspected that they and perhaps many more unknown mercenaries were in hiding, waiting to fight alongside the gendarmerie.

Tshombe, intent on preventing his gendarmerie from turning into a rabble like the ANC, quietly hired mercenaries to replace Belgian soldiers whenever U.N. pressure forced him to let some of them go. "In these matters," he told Major Guy Weber, his Belgian military adviser, "I trust only whites." Tshombe's crew of mercenaries drew on many sources, including French paratroopers fresh from defeat in Algeria, South African and Rhodesian adventurers, Belgian settlers, Italian Fascists, and German veterans of World War II. Most were racists who seemed to enjoy shooting down blacks for pay, but there were also idealists who believed in some kind of multiracial Africa. The mercenaries were often known as *les affreux* (the frightful ones) because of their ferocious attacks in northern Katanga on Baluba tribesmen who opposed Tshombe and his secession.

U.N. officials looked on Tshombe with contempt. He had an infuriating way of acquiescing at attempts to bring Katanga back into the Congo and then reneging, of promising to rid his army of foreigners yet somehow never managing to follow through. "Neither statements of fact nor written engagements could be relied on," O'Brien wrote later. "No contradiction, no detected lie, caused Mr. Tshombe the slightest embarrassment. If caught out in some piece of duplicity—on political prisoners, refugees, mercenaries or anything else—he would show absent-mindedness, tinged, I sometimes imagined, with a paternal compassion for the *naïveté* of anyone who supposed he would tell the truth, if he could derive the slightest advantage from telling anything else." Yet Tshombe also struck many outsiders as a far more able administrator and adroit politician than anyone else in the Congo.

According to O'Brien's version of the events, he and Brigadier K. A. S. Raja, the Indian commander of the military forces in Katanga, received the orders from Mahmoud Khiary of Tunisia, their senior U.N. officer in Léopoldville, only a few hours before the battle. Under Operation Morthor, U.N. officials and their troops (one Swedish battalion, one Irish battalion, and two Indian battalions of Gurkhas and Dogras) would surround the presidential palace of Tshombe, arrest four of his key cabinet members, occupy the key centers of communication (the post office with its telephone and telegraph exchanges and the radio station), raid the files of the offices of Katanga security and the ministry of information, run the Congolese flag up on all public buildings in Elisabethville, and persuade Tshombe, under this pressure, to give up his secession.

As Khiary left the Villa des Roches, the U.N. headquarters in Elisabethville, he told O'Brien, "Above all, no half measures." O'Brien assumed the plan had been approved by Hammarskjöld. But Hammarskjöld, although he had given the plan tentative approval, had expected everyone to wait until he arrived in Léopoldville for final authorization. Operation Morthor was set in motion while the secretary-general was en route to Léopoldville.

As heavy firing broke out in Elisabethville, a panicky Tshombe phoned O'Brien twice. O'Brien recounted his U.N. orders and, while guaranteeing Tshombe's personal safety, asked the Katangese president to make a radio broadcast declaring the secession of Katanga at an end and ordering his soldiers to halt their fire. Tshombe agreed, and an ebullient O'Brien told journalists at 6:30 A.M., "The secession of Katanga has ended. It now is a Congolese province run by the central government." The pronouncement was premature.

No U.N. troops had circled Tshombe's palace. O'Brien attributed this to a breakdown in communication between the Indians and Swedes. English, the lingua franca of the U.N. troops, was a second language to both, and many did not speak it as well as they thought. There were political and military disagreements between the Indians and Swedes as well. "Such are the troubles of an international force," O'Brien said. Instead of making his broadcast ending secession, Tshombe left the palace, hid in the home of the British consul, and then fled to Northern Rhodesia.

Indian soldiers armed with rifles of 1918 vintage tried to take over the post office peacefully by persuading the Katangese gendarmes that they would not be disarmed if they let the U.N. troops in. But a sniper on top of the nearby Belgian consulate building shot and killed an Indian soldier, setting off firing by both sides. "After heavy stiff hand to hand fighting," according to official U.N. dispatches, the Indians overcame the Katangese within an hour, both at the post office and at Radio Katanga. Katanga's new Mercedes armored cars handled "mostly by Belgians in civilian clothes" and cheered by crowds of whites tried to retake the post office and radio station. The Blue Helmets, in their 1940-model Irish armored cars and Swedish armed personnel carriers, repulsed this counterattack, but mortar and automatic-rifle fire by the Katangese demolished the studio beyond repair. Automatic-rifle firing continued in Elisabethville throughout the day. The U.N. troops had managed to arrest only one of the hunted cabinet members, and the Congolese flags did not go up on government buildings.

The Katangese counterattack, bolstered by more white civilians who had taken up arms, intensified the next day. Although they failed to dislodge the U.N. soldiers from downtown Elisabethville, the Katangese heavily damaged the occupied buildings. The Katangese also surrounded 158 Irish troops at their garrison in the nearby mining town of Jadotville (now Likasi) and the 500 Irish and Swedish troops at the old Belgian base of Kamina in northern Katanga. A Katangese Fouga Magister jet fighter piloted by a mercenary bombed and strafed both U.N. headquarters in Elisabethville and the Irish company at Jadotville during the night. The U.N. had no defense against the Fouga. Although the fighting in Elisabethville was stalemated, the U.N. had become the besieged force there, and the Irish troops surrendered at Jadotville five days after the U.N. attack began.

Hammarskjöld arrived in Léopoldville a few hours after the attack began and soon heard the cries of protest from outraged governments. Lord Landsdowne, a special British envoy, warned Hammarskjöld that Prime Minister Harold Macmillan believed only the Communists would benefit from the chaos sure to come out of U.N. attacks on Katanga; Tshombe had to be persuaded peacefully to join the Congo. President Kennedy agreed. Reassuring his critics, Hammarskjöld issued a statement claiming that the U.N. had not tried to attack Katanga but had only defended itself when fired upon by the Katangese. "If this is an accurate account of what took place in Elisabethville on the morning of September 13th," an angry O'Brien wrote in his memoir, "my name is Titus Oates." (Since Titus Oates was the lying, eccentric Anglican priest who caused the deaths of thirty-five innocent people in the seventeenth century by cooking up a phoney tale of a Catholic plot to assassinate the English king, O'Brien was saying, in effect, "If Hammarskjöld is telling the truth, then I'm a crazed liar.")

On September 17, Hammarskjöld decided to fly to Ndola in Northern Rhodesia to meet Tshombe and work out a truce. He also hoped to reconcile Tshombe and Congolese Prime Minister Cyrille Adoula, ending the secession peacefully. To avoid the Fouga, the chartered airplane, a DC-6B, flew at night on a circuitous route without radio contact. After seven hours, the plane reached the Ndola area shortly past midnight, the pilot informing the tower that he could see the airport lights and was descending. The plane then disappeared. A search found the wreckage in a forest a few miles north of Ndola during the day. All thirteen aboard including Hammarskjöld died. Despite widespread suspicions at the time, most analysts now believe the crash was an accident.

🌿🌿

The posthumous publication of *Markings*, however, inspired a school of fanciful, mystic speculation about Hammarskjöld's need for death at that time and premonitions about it. In an article in *Look* Magazine in 1964, John Lindberg, an old professor of Hammarskjöld's in Stockholm, wrote, "In the summer of 1961, he rode, amid the jubilation of the population, to his Congolese Jerusalem. The ninth hour, the hour for death at the cross, was at hand and was now. . . . A week before the end, my wife, with an often proved instinct for the inwardness of events, said to me, 'Now, there is only one way out for Dag—death.' "

This provoked an angry letter from Ralph Bunche to *Look* publisher Gardner Cowles. "Dag Hammarskjöld was introspective and deeply reflective," Bunche wrote, "but he was not a brooder, and he never revealed to those of us who worked closely with him any obsession about power, self-glorification, martyrdom or death. . . . The idea of death as 'the only way out for Dag . . .' when, in fact, he was at the very peak of his career and of his international success, is a sensationally morbid and idiotic fancy of Mr. and Mrs. Lindberg."

Yet a mystical doubt lingered, if not over the cause of the death, at least over the possibility that it was foretold. In an interview three decades later, Per Lind, Hammarskjöld's old friend in the Swedish foreign ministry, said, "What can be discarded are all these fantastic stories that Hammarskjöld himself caused it [his death]." Yet, Lind went on, "about two weeks before the crash, I received a letter here in

Stockholm from him that rather astonished me. It was a brief letter saying that 'in case of need I wish you to take care of my private papers, in my office and my home.' That was the gist of it. Many people have taken this as some kind of proof that he knew that he was going to die, that he was expecting this, that he had a premonition. . . . And some people went further saying that he arranged it. That is ridiculous. But it [the letter] was a remarkable thing anyway."

※ ❦

After the death of Hammarskjöld, Mahmoud Khiary, while insisting that the U.N. still stood by its demands that all mercenaries must leave, then worked out the cease-fire with Tshombe. Both sides exchanged prisoners, and the U.N. troops withdrew from the post office and radio station. The U.N. also agreed to let Katangese gendarmes join U.N. troops at the Elisabethville airport. According to the U.N., eleven U.N. soldiers died in the fighting; the Katangese lost fifty dead. The U.N. had lost Hammarskjöld and achieved nothing with Operation Morthor.

The second battle of Katanga, far more destructive and bloody, provoking far more rage from U.N. critics, erupted less than two months later. Tshombe had proven as stubborn as ever, dismissing mercenaries publicly, then rehiring them surreptitiously. The U N , bolstered by another Security Council resolution authorizing the use of force, reinforced its Katanga units with two Ethiopian battalions (bringing total strength to almost six thousand), new equipment like Ferret armored cars and heavy mortar and 108-millimeter guns, and, most important, an air unit of six Indian Canberra jet bombers, six Swedish Saab jet fighters, and four Ethiopian F-84 jet fighters. American transports ferried most of the new troops and matériel into Katanga. Breaking with the British, the Kennedy administration had finally decided that the forcible suppression of Tshombe was the only hope for averting an instability that could lead to a Communist takeover in the Congo.

There were many sources of tension. In a show of fury at the U.N., Katangese paracommandoes showed up at a party for Tshombe's most prominent American defender, Senator Thomas

Dodd of Connecticut, and seized Brian Urquhart, who had just arrived to take O'Brien's place, and his deputy. The pair were clubbed
mercilessly, the beating breaking Urquhart's nose and cracking some
of his ribs. Threatened with an assault by the U.N. on the presidential
palace, Tshombe interceded with the gendarmes to obtain Urquhart's release. "Better beaten than eaten," Urquhart told reporters.
A Gurkha officer and his driver, however, were killed while searching
for Urquhart. Katangese gendarmes mounted roadblocks throughout
Elisabethville, impeding the free movement of U.N. troops. When
Tshombe defied repeated calls to remove the roadblocks, U Thant,
Hammarskjöld's successor as secretary-general, ordered Brigadier
Raja to clear them by force on December 5. That set off the battle
that lasted two weeks.

The U.N. planes took off from Luluabourg and destroyed all
four Katangese jet planes on the ground at their base in Kolwezi.
With no challenge, the U.N. planes then bombed and strafed targets
in Elisabethville at will. Encircling the city, the U.N. ground forces
attacked the camps of the gendarmerie. Many gendarmes withdrew
into the white residential neighborhoods, and it became difficult to
flush them out without harming civilians and their property. There
were U.N. excesses that made headlines throughout the world. Trying to terrify gendarmes from nearby camps, U.N. troops misfired
many rounds of mortars into the compound of twenty-nine American
Seventh-Day Adventist missionaries and into Prince Leopold Hospital. In another error, the Canberra jets bombed the hospital of a former uranium mine in Shinkolobwe and killed four Africans.
Swooping over Elisabethville, the U.N. jets bombed and strafed the
Roman Catholic cathedral, the museum, and a beauty parlor.

British Prime Minister Macmillan wrote bitterly in his diary,
"Yesterday an Ethiopian soldier shot a Swiss banker in Elisabethville
with a bazooka. No one knows why, and no one cares. But even Swiss
bankers ought to have some rights." Urquhart was troubled as well.
"The moment a peacekeeping force starts killing people it becomes a
part of the conflict it is supposed to be controlling and thus a part of
the problem," he wrote. ". . . I loathed the battle in Elisabethville,
from which no good came for anyone. Many innocent people were
killed or hurt and neither the U.N. nor the mercenaries nor

Tshombe came out of it with any credit." Urquhart described the Indian Canberra bombers as "a menace" and finally, after they had demolished the post office, persuaded Brigadier Raja to call them off.

The U.N. force moved at a snail's pace into Elisabethville. Urquhart attributed the military problems to a lack of discipline and cohesion. He described Brigadier Raja as "a weak Indian commander who was not respected by his subordinates." The Swedes, according to Urquhart, resented the Indians who "being professionals, tended to be patronizing toward the others." He found the Ethiopians "undisciplined, paranoid and dangerous." By December 18, the U.N. controlled much of Elisabethville but had still failed to dislodge the gendarmes from all their strongholds. As they closed in on the heart of the city, the Blue Helmets were hampered by sniper fire from white civilians. The U.N. agreed to a cease-fire when Tshombe cabled President Kennedy a promise to meet with Congolese leaders to discuss a pact unifying the Congo. By then, twenty-one U.N. soldiers, two hundred Katangese, and six white mercenaries had died in the battling. In a few days, Tshombe signed the agreement. But he quickly reneged, and the Katanga secession continued.

The final battle of Katanga came a year later. U Thant kept trying to ease Tshombe back into the Congo through negotiations, but he always seemed to slip out of a compromise at the last moment. The machinations made the secretary-general lose patience with Tshombe and his ministers. Describing the Katangese president as "a very unstable man," U Thant told a news conference, "I don't know what I can do with such a bunch of clowns." With his revenues from Union Minière, Tshombe hired more mercenaries and bought more jet fighters. Firing between the gendarmes and the Blue Helmets broke out again in late December 1962. Once more pleading self-defense, the U.N. launched an offensive designed to rid the Congo of Tshombe and his secession for good. It was called "Operation Grand Slam."

Urquhart had no military complaint this time. "We had, at last, a magnificent military command in Katanga," he wrote. ". . . The commander was Major-General Dewan Prem Chand, a soft-spoken, serious-minded Indian officer. . . . His operational deputy was the commander of the Indian Brigade, Brigadier Reggie Noronha, a cavalry officer, fast, stylish, decisive and with a capacity for the grand gesture. I could have told Tshombe that it was very foolish to mess about with two such formidable professionals. However, mess about he did."

The U.N. troops, supported by aerial strafing and bombing, moved swiftly this time. Brigadier Noronha and his Indian troops, after killing fifty Katangese gendarmes on the outskirts of the city, took control of the gendarmerie headquarters and the downtown area of Elisabethville in a day. Swedish U.N. planes destroyed two British Vampire jets and five converted Harvard trainers on the airfield at Kolwezi, eliminating any threat from the Katanga air force. A day later, Ghanaian and Swedish troops seized the military town of Kamina in the north and Irish troops took over Kipushi, the border town that guarded the flow of traffic from Tshombe's allies in Northern Rhodesia. There was little resistance after then. Within two days, Prem Chand and Noronha led their troops toward the mining towns of Jadotville and Kolwezi across the Lufira River.

The U.N.'s detractors were furious. Senator Dodd called the offensive "a flagrant, inhuman act of aggression." The British and Belgians warned U Thant that if the U.N. crossed the Lufira River, Tshombe's mercenaries would blow up the great Union Minière facilities in Jadotville and Kolwezi. The mercenaries had already destroyed the two bridges on the river. U Thant promised to delay the U.N. troops but later said his message did not reach Prem Chand and Noronha in time. There was no talk of slowing down among U.N. officials in the Congo. "We are not going to make the mistake this time of stopping short," said Ghana's Robert Gardiner, the chief of U.N. operations in the Congo. The two Indian generals forded the river on New Year's night, pushing their vehicles across on makeshift rafts. The surprised Katangese soldiers fled, allowing the Indian troops to enter a practically undefended Jadotville twenty miles north the next day. The mercenaries had run off without destroying the mines. The U.N. now controlled every important town of Katanga except Tshombe's military stronghold of Kolwezi.

Tshombe, escaping to the south on a Rhodesian air force plane and then making his way from Northern Rhodesia back to Kolwezi, broadcast an appeal for a cease-fire and negotiations to end the secession. But U Thant said it was too late for negotiations; he wanted "actions by Mr. Tshombe and not words, written or oral." Tshombe returned to Elisabethville, where he was placed under house arrest by the U.N. and released only after he promised to end the secession. In Kolwezi on January 15, Tshombe sent a message to U Thant, "I am ready to proclaim immediately before the world that Katanga's secession is ended." A formal surrender agreement was signed by Tshombe and General Prem Chand in Elisabethville on January 17. The U.N. had lost only eleven men in the final battle. A few days later, U.N. troops marched into Kolwezi while Tshombe called on his gendarmes to cooperate with the United Nations. Two and a half years after independence and the intervention of the U.N., the Katanga secession was over.

The United Nations peacekeeping force withdrew from the Congo on June 30, 1964, four years after its arrival. The Congo was hardly an ordered society, but there was little left for the U.N. to do. "The United Nations," U Thant said, "cannot permanently protect the Congo, or any other country from the internal tensions and disturbances created by its own organic growth toward unity and nationhood."

☙ ❧

Many ironies trailed the U.N. adventure. A week after the Blue Helmets left, Tshombe, just returned from exile in Europe, was named the new prime minister of the Congo. With avid U.S. support, he hired mercenaries, mainly from South Africa, to lead the Armée Nationale Congolaise against the leftist Lumumbaist rebels in the Eastern Congo. When the Nigerian civil war erupted in 1967, many of the same people who railed against Katanga now supported the secession of Biafra. And, in a final irony, General Mobutu, taking over as president in 1965, eventually succeeded in uniting the Congo and, while doing so, fashioned one of the most tyrannical, corrupt, and avaricious régimes in Africa. But in those confusing times of the early 1960s, Katanga was a blot on the integrity of Africa, and the U.N. succeeded in wiping it out.

The main casualty of the Congo was a grievous loss. Dag Hammarskjöld was awarded the Nobel peace prize for 1961 shortly after his death. For years, diplomats would insist that they were looking for another Dag Hammarskjöld whenever they scoured the lists of candidates for secretary-general. But, despite this insistence, they always seemed to choose someone whom they were sure would give them far less trouble.

Nor did they want to take on another Congo, for, though ending relatively well, the mission had confused and confounded everyone. For almost three decades, U.N. diplomats shied away from military engagements and dispatched peacekeepers to a scene of former conflict only when there was general support for them from all sides. The U.N. would not mount another peace enforcement expedition until the 1990s, when it sent troops to Somalia and assigned some enforcement duties like protecting besieged towns to peacekeepers already in Bosnia. U.N. officials talked about the Somalia and Bosnia operations as if they were unprecedented; everyone had forgotten the bloody Congo by then.

❧ 8 ❧

Adlai Stevenson and the Cuban Missile Crisis: *The U.N. as Theater*

The news that President John F. Kennedy intended to appoint him ambassador to the United Nations was a bitter disappointment to Adlai E. Stevenson. He had expected to be named secretary of state. Although he had twice led his party to defeat in presidential elections, he had done so with honor and distinction and grace and wit, and he was surely the best known and most respected Democratic Party leader in the rest of the world. He probably felt more pain at losing his hopes for secretary of state than he had felt losing two elections to Dwight D. Eisenhower. Stevenson insisted to his friends that he would never accept the job of U.N. ambassador. Exaggerating his own importance in the infant days of the U.N., he said, "I had that job fifteen years ago."

Kennedy intended to dominate international affairs himself, and he did not need or want a second pole of foreign policy-making in his administration. He wanted a quiet technician as secretary of state who would not attract attention away from the White House, and he got just that in Dean Rusk, the president of the Rockefeller Foundation who had served as an assistant secretary of state in the

Truman administration. The Kennedy crowd, in any case, did not believe that the older Stevenson fit in with them. The old joke during the 1952 and 1956 campaigns was that Stevenson would rather make *Bartlett's Familiar Quotations* than be president. Reporters complained often that they could rarely get a copy of his speech in time for the morning newspapers because he spent so many hours rewriting and honing phrases. The Kennedys liked men of action, and Stevenson struck them as an airy-fairy orator and garrulous spinner of philosophy. To make matters worse, Stevenson had failed to climb aboard the Kennedy bandwagon at the Democratic National Convention in Los Angeles but had persisted in holding on to his few delegates in the vain hope that Kennedy could be stopped short of a first ballot victory. Stevenson did campaign for Kennedy later, but, in fact, the new president owed him very little.

Kennedy cajoled Stevenson into accepting the job as U.N. ambassador. The new president described it as one of the three or four most important positions in his administration. He told Stevenson that, as a member of the cabinet, he would be vital in foreign policy-making. After offering the job during a meeting at his home in Georgetown, Kennedy escorted Stevenson to microphones outside and told reporters, "It is my hope, if Governor Stevenson accepts the position, that he will attend cabinet meetings and will serve as a strong voice in foreign policy over its entire range." The president then expected Stevenson to announce his acceptance. Instead Stevenson told reporters that he would mull the offer over and reach a decision "in the very near future." Kennedy was shocked and furious. The incident only confirmed his image of Stevenson indecisiveness. Stevenson did accept the job within a few days, but, by then, the strain of his relationship with the president was irreparable.

The blandishments proved hollow. Stevenson never did become a major force in the making of the Kennedy administration's foreign policy. Secretary Rusk was deferential to Stevenson's feelings. When the president skipped the opening session of the General Assembly, Rusk always stepped aside to let Stevenson deliver the main American speech. But the White House listened to Stevenson infrequently and heeded him even less. He functioned primarily as the stellar mouthpiece for American foreign policy in the world forum.

He performed well, and that was a considerable accomplishment in those days. Newly independent nations from Africa and Asia were doubling the membership of the U.N. (to ninety-nine by 1961), and both the United States and the Soviet Union were trying to line them up. A voice as persuasive and respected as Stevenson's could prove decisive. But all the U.N. talk—and the realization that he had only a minuscule role in policy-making—wore him down. When the State Department instructed him to remain in New York for a debate rather than go home to Illinois one week, he said, "Do I have to stay here for more of that yak-yak? It doesn't mean a thing."

Yet, despite his irritation and frustration, he was one of the greatest boons the U.N. has ever had. When he attended his first session of the Security Council on February 1, 1961, the other ambassadors broke into applause. As John Bartlow Martin put it in his painstaking two-volume biography in 1977, "He gave the U.N. a standing with the American people that it had never enjoyed before (and has not since). . . . It takes nothing away from them to say that not Henry Cabot Lodge or Warren Austin or Arthur Goldberg or any other U.S. representative gave the U.N. the impact on the American people that Stevenson gave it. For none personified so well before the American people the ideal of world order to which the U.N. aspired." For a brief few months, the U.N. had Dag Hammarskjöld at its helm and Adlai Stevenson at his side. They made it easy to believe in the U.N.

꧁꧂

The Security Council did most of its work in public those days, and much of its news was generated when the ambassadors, especially the Soviet and American ambassadors, battled with fiery words and nasty barbs. While diplomats liked to call the Security Council a world forum, it was more like world theater with the most histrionic ambassadors credited with accomplishing the most for their governments. Both the United States and the Soviet Union vied to influence world public opinion, and it was widely assumed that ambassadors who knew how to dominate good drama were powerful assets in the propaganda battles of the Cold War.

In 1960, for example, when the Soviet Union convoked a Security Council meeting to berate the United States for sending U-2 spy planes over Soviet territory, Ambassador Henry Cabot Lodge responded with a surprise stage prop. He had no real defense. The Soviets had shot down U-2 pilot Gary Powers, and even President Eisenhower admitted that Powers was on an espionage mission. So, while television cameras recorded the scene, Ambassador Lodge suddenly pulled a plaque out from beneath the table. The plaque— showing the Great Seal of the United States—had been presented to the U.S. embassy in Moscow by the Soviet-American Friendship Society. Lodge triumphantly showed all the members of the Security Council the exact place in the plaque where a microphone had been hidden by the Soviets. In short, Lodge demonstrated, the Soviet Union was as guilty of espionage as anyone else. It was not much of a revelation or, in fact, of a defense. But it seemed like effective theater at the time.

As ambassador, Stevenson was widely regarded as the champion of the Third World. On most issues, he counseled support of the colonies and the former colonies against the European colonial powers. He also urged Washington to be patient with the so-called neutral nations. He acknowledged that they were apt to blame the United States rather than the Soviet Union on most Cold War issues. But, he said, "I suspect we have no choice but to be patient and philosophical about this astigmatism." In a memorandum to President Kennedy, he explained that, as former colonies, the new neutral nations tended to feel bitter about America's close alliance with the former colonial powers. Though the Kennedy administration was sympathetic to his point of view, he was often overruled on these matters. In the conflict between France and Tunisia over the French naval base at Bizerte in 1961, for example, he proposed that the United States vote for a General Assembly resolution condemning France, but the State Department ordered him to abstain.

Yet principle was more important to him than sympathy for the Third World. When India seized the Portuguese enclave of Goa in 1961, he rose in the Security Council to condemn the self-righteous government of Jawaharlal Nehru. Stevenson went beyond his instructions and heaped scorn on Nehru and his hypocrisy. He sneered at Indian Minister of Defense V. K. Krishna Menon, a familiar figure at the U.N. — "so well known in these halls for his advice on matters of peace and his tireless enjoinders to everyone else to seek the way of compromise." This supposed believer in nonviolence, Stevenson said, "was on the borders of Goa inspecting his troops at the zero hour of invasion." "Let us be perfectly clear what is at stake here, gentlemen," he went on. "It is the question of the use of armed force by one state against another. . . . The Indian tradition of non-violence has inspired the whole world, but this act of force with which we are confronted today mocks the good faith of India's frequent declarations of exalted principle." When the Soviet Union vetoed a resolution condemning India, Stevenson said, "Tonight we are witnessing the first act in a drama which could end with the death of the Organization. The League of Nations died, I remind you, when its members no longer resisted the use of aggressive force."

The speech troubled Clayton Fritchey, Stevenson's press spokesman, who told biographer Martin, "He got carried away. I was shocked. It is one of the few instances where Stevenson was a demagogue. There couldn't be a more smug country than India, but we were worse." Washington, however, was ecstatic over Stevenson's performance. Kennedy, after all, had once described the Indians as "a bunch of sanctimonious bastards," and Stevenson had gone a long way toward tearing them down to size with his words.

The American obsession with Fidel Castro provided the background in 1961 for Stevenson's most humiliating performance at the U.N. and, a year later, for his most memorable performance as well. He had been briefed a week ahead of time but not consulted about the Central Intelligence Agency's invasion of Cuba in April 1961. The plan struck him as wild and cockeyed, but he did not try to prevent it. By the time he was told, it was probably too late to stop it and, in any case, no one in the White House cared whether he liked it or not.

The CIA trained and equipped Cuban exiles at a camp in Guatemala and then led them in an amphibious landing on April

16 at the Bay of Pigs. To mask American involvement, the CIA painted Cuban air force markings on U.S. B-26 bombers flown over Cuba by exile pilots from a field in Nicaragua. These pilots, following a CIA cover story, were officially described as defectors from the Cuban air force turning on Castro. On April 15, when raids on Cuban airfields took place, one plane flew directly from Nicaragua to Florida to provide the cover story; a second, damaged over Cuba, flew to Florida as well because the pilot could not make it all the way back to Nicaragua.

The White House briefers had not informed Stevenson about the cover story, and, accepting it whole, he arose in the Political Committee of the General Assembly and unknowingly lied. He showed delegates a photograph of one of the planes displaying the red star insignia of the Fuerza Aerea Revolucionaria of Cuba. "These pilots and certain other crew members have apparently defected from Castro's tyranny," he said. "No United States personnel participated. No United States government airplanes of any kind participated. These two planes to the best of our knowledge were Castro's own air force planes and, according to the pilots, they took off from Castro's own air force fields." By the time the hapless exile troops clambered ashore at the Bay of Pigs a day later, however, the cover story was exposed as a fraud.

"So the cover blew off," Harlan Cleveland, the assistant secretary of state for international organizations, said years later, "and Adlai was absolutely fit to be tied. He was a rather mild person, really, and tolerant, but he was just furious that his government could have hung him out to dry that way." Stevenson told White House Press Secretary Pierre Salinger later that it was "the most humiliating experience" of his public life. Yet, Stevenson, while defending the Bay of Pigs invasion itself, appeared ready to stretch the truth for the sake of his country. When Cuban Foreign Minister Raul Roa accused the United States of aggression, Stevenson told the Political Committee on April 17, "These charges are totally false, and I deny them categorically. The United States has committed no aggression against Cuba and no offensive has been launched from Florida or from any other part of the United States." That was true, of course, since the CIA invasion had been launched from Guatemala, but it was surely a legalistic subterfuge.

By April 19, three days after the invasion, the exiles had been soundly defeated. The CIA adventure was a debacle. But Stevenson still insisted that it was purely a Cuban affair. "If this was a United States military operation, do you think it would succeed or fail?" he asked rhetorically. "How long do you think that Cuba could resist the military power of the United States? Perhaps the best evidence of the falsity of shrill charges of American aggression in Cuba is the melancholy fact that this blow for freedom has not yet succeeded." Although it was not an American military operation, President Kennedy soon acknowledged that the Bay of Pigs invasion had been American-led. "There is an old saying that victory has a hundred fathers and defeat is an orphan," he told a news conference on April 21, accepting responsibility for the week-old disaster.

Stevenson toyed with the idea of resigning, but he really did not want to leave public life. Kennedy sent emissaries, including National Security Adviser McGeorge Bundy, to New York to calm Stevenson. "Hold his hand," the president told Bundy. Stevenson was probably most calmed by the realization that, despite the lies he had put forth, he still had not lost his credibility at the U.N. "It didn't particularly rub off badly on Stevenson," Cleveland said. "His colleagues at the U.N. sympathized with him and didn't blame him for lying to them." Many had been burned themselves by foreign ministries that changed policies abruptly or set off on mad adventures without informing their ambassadors at the United Nations.

❦

The Cuban missile crisis erupted more than a year and a half later. It is popularly regarded as Adlai Stevenson's finest hour at the United Nations—though the historic record makes it clear that neither he nor the U.N. played major roles. When examined in retrospect, the crisis appears even more frightening than it did then. President Kennedy was prepared to risk nuclear war to eliminate the Russian missiles from Cuba, even though his secretary of defense did not believe they posed any new strategic danger to the United States. The world was saved from horrendous catastrophe because Nikita Khrushchev did not feel that keeping the missiles in Cuba was worth the risk of war. "We're eyeball to eyeball," Secretary of State Rusk said, "and I think the other fellow just blinked." The world never came closer to nuclear disaster than this moment in the Cold War, and, according to all the excited accounts, war was averted only by this blink.

Of course, President Kennedy might have changed course and moderated his determination as zero hour came even closer. The first news stories, inspired by the White House, described an administration of hawks pushing aside a lone dove—Adlai Stevenson—to frighten Khrushchev into accepting their will. But, in fact, the president and his brother, Attorney General Robert F. Kennedy, in the end accepted some of the tenets of the Stevenson arguments that they sneered at in the beginning. They were not as tough as they pretended. But they had set the United States off on a dangerous course. "If indeed war should break out," Khrushchev wrote to Kennedy, "then it would not be in our power to stop it, for such is the logic of war."

But Khrushchev deserves no accolades for wisdom in the crisis, since he started it. The Soviets, before they stopped, were assembling twenty-four launchers for medium-range (630 miles) ballistic missiles and sixteen launchers for intermediate-range (1,100 miles) ballistic missiles in Cuba, with storage spaces nearby for nuclear warheads. "The Americans had surrounded our country with military bases and threatened us with nuclear weapons," Khrushchev said later, "and now they would learn just what it feels like to have enemy missiles pointing at you; we'd be doing nothing more than giving them a little of their own medicine." But he insisted he had no intention of using them offensively: the nuclear missiles were there to protect Cuba. "Only a fool would think we wanted to invade the American continent from Cuba," he said.

American historian Michael R. Beschloss believes Kennedy must share in the blame for the crisis. "Had Kennedy not provoked Khrushchev by repeatedly heralding American nuclear superiority, indulging himself and his officials in talk that caused the Russians to fear a first strike, and suggesting . . . that the United States might invade the island in 1962," Beschloss writes, "it is doubtful that Khrushchev would have felt compelled to take his giant risk on Cuba." It was a foolish risk as well, for the chances of the Soviet

Union assembling all its missile launchers on Cuba before the Americans discovered them at work were slim.

On October 16, Kennedy received photographic proof from the CIA that the Soviets were building the MRBM and IRBM launchers in Cuba and had supplied Castro with IL-28 bombers. The twelve-day crisis began. The president and his brother convened continual meetings of what they called the ExComm—the Executive Committee of the National Security Council—a kind of crisis task force comprising all the key advisers and cabinet members. From the start, President Kennedy was determined to remove the launchers and missiles—even if it took force, even if it risked war. He was not going to be accused by his critics of letting Khrushchev hoodwink him. He accepted the assessment of Secretary of Defense Robert S. McNamara that the missiles would not change the strategic balance at all. If he wanted to, Khrushchev could attempt to wipe out the United States—and, of course, ensure his own country's destruction—by firing intercontinental ballistic missiles from sites in the Soviet Union; he did not need the missiles in Cuba. But Kennedy did not intend to let the Soviet Union push him or the United States around in front of his Republican critics. Kennedy had to show he was a strong leader willing to shoulder risks. His brother told him, "I just don't think there was any choice. If you hadn't acted, you would have been impeached." The president agreed.

Although a majority of the members of the ExComm at first advised an air strike wiping out the missile sites in Cuba, a consensus later formed in favor of a blockade preventing Soviet ships from bringing any more weapons into the island. A sneak air attack troubled sensibilities. "I now know how Tojo felt when he was planning Pearl Harbor," said Robert Kennedy. The ExComm decided that if the blockade, accompanied by secret and public admonitions, did not persuade Khrushchev to backtrack, the United States could then launch air strikes. All the people around Kennedy realized that war could come from an American-Soviet skirmish at sea or from the launching of a Soviet missile that escaped destruction in an air strike. The United States had so many more nuclear warheads than the Soviets that it surely would have won the war. But victory would have been Pyrrhic amid the devastation of both sides.

Stevenson shuttled down to Washington for some though not all of the ExComm meetings, but his counsel received little open support; some of his views, because of their logic, prevailed in the end, however. "Let's not go into an air strike until we have explored the possibilities of a peaceful solution," Stevenson said. In a note, he told Kennedy, "I feel you should have made it clear that the existence of nuclear missile bases anywhere is negotiable before we start anything." The president read the note and remarked sarcastically to his special counsel, Theodore C. Sorensen, "Tell me which side he is on." In the discussions, Stevenson proposed that Kennedy offer something to Khrushchev. Perhaps the United States could abandon the U.S. naval base in Guantánamo Bay, Cuba, if the Soviets dismantled their missile sites. The U.N. ambassador also suggested that Kennedy might announce that the United States was ready to negotiate the elimination of NATO missile bases in Italy and Turkey in any general disarmament agreement with the Soviet Union.

Stevenson said afterward that "most of those fellows will probably consider me a coward for the rest of my life for what I said today, but perhaps we need a coward in the room when we are talking about a nuclear war." Although Kennedy told Sorensen, "You have to admire Adlai — he sticks to his position even when everyone is jumping on him," the president rejected the proposals and sometimes belittled Stevenson behind his back. He had no intention of announcing possible concessions before Khrushchev gave in. Robert Kennedy told his brother that Stevenson was "not strong enough or tough enough to be representing us at the U.N. at a time like this." The president thought his brother was exaggerating Stevenson's supposed weakness but agreed to send John J. McCloy to New York to steel Stevenson's position. McCloy, the Republican chairman of the Chase Manhattan Bank and the former U.S. high commissioner in Berlin, had the reputation of a tough Cold Warrior, and Stevenson resented his presence.

On October 22, President Kennedy dispatched a harsh letter to Khrushchev via Soviet Ambassador Anatoli Dobrynin. The president reminded the Soviet leader that he had been warned by Kennedy at their summit at Vienna that "the United States could not tolerate any action on your part which in a major way disturbed the existing overall balance of power in the world." As for the Cuban missiles, Kennedy said sternly, "I must tell you that the United States is determined that this threat to the security of this hemisphere be removed."

An hour later, the president informed the nation on television that "unmistakable evidence has established the fact that a series of offensive missile sites is now in preparation in that imprisoned island" of Cuba. He said the missiles could hit any city between Peru and the Hudson Bay. He called the buildup "a deliberately provocative and unjustified change in the status quo which cannot be accepted by this country, if our courage and our commitments are ever to be trusted again by either friend or foe." He announced three steps: a "quarantine"—a euphemism he used because a naval blockade was regarded as an act of war—on shipments of military equipment into Cuba; a warning that "further action will be justified" if the quarantine fails to end the threat; and a pledge that any attack on any country in the Western Hemisphere by a missile from Cuba would require "a full retaliatory strike upon the Soviet Union." He demanded that Khrushchev "abandon this course of world domination" and announced that the United States would ask for an emergency meeting of the U.N. Security Council. "The greatest danger of all," he said, "would be to do nothing."

The president ordered fifty-six American warships to encircle Cuba, a dozen Polaris submarines with nuclear missiles to rush toward the coast of the Soviet Union, the Strategic Air Command's bomber fleet to go on alert, and military personnel to prepare more than two hundred intercontinental ballistic missiles in the United States for firing.

Kennedy's speech stunned the world. "In my memory," Secretary-General U Thant wrote in his memoirs, "it was the grimmest and gravest speech ever made by a head of state. . . . The President's militant thrust at the Soviet Union as the party responsible for the crisis, and his unconcealed commitment to act alone against the missile threat to his country, came as a thunderbolt." The secretary-general was filled with doubts and foreboding. "Even if the President's revelations were correct," he said, "would it not be wiser, I thought, to ask Chairman Khrushchev privately to do what he was publicly asked to do? . . . And was the United States, the most powerful country in the world, prepared to plunge the world into a nuclear holocaust? . . . I was more deeply troubled than I had ever been in my life. . . . I wondered whether the President's vigor and vitality—and the vehemence of his reaction—were reassuring or frightening."

The emergency meeting of the Security Council began the day after the speech with Stevenson and Soviet Ambassador Valerian Zorin exchanging insults and accusations. While Stevenson condemned the Soviet Union for carting missiles into Cuba, Zorin condemned the United States for its blockade of the island. Each introduced resolutions condemning the other. On the third day, while television cameras recorded it all, Stevenson rose in rebuttal.

"I want to say to you, Mr. Zorin, that I do not have your talent for obfuscation, for distortion, for confusing language and for double talk," Stevenson began. "And I must confess to you that I am glad I do not. . . . The other day, Mr. Zorin, I remind you that you did not deny the existence of these weapons. Indeed, we heard that they had suddenly become defensive weapons. But today, again if I heard you correctly, you now say they do not exist, or that we haven't proved they exist, with another fine flood of rhetorical scorn. All right, sir, let me ask you one simple question: Do you, Ambassador Zorin, deny that the U.S.S.R. has placed and is placing medium and intermediate range missiles and sites in Cuba? Yes or no—don't wait for the translation—yes or no."

Despite the solemnity of the mood, many ambassadors could not stifle their laughter at the sudden demand by Stevenson for a reply without waiting for the interpretation. "I am not in an American court of law," Zorin replied, "and therefore do not wish to answer a question put to me in the manner of a prosecuting counsel. You will receive the answer in due course in my capacity as representative of the Soviet Union."

"You are in the courtroom of world opinion right now," Stevenson said, "and you can answer 'Yes' or 'No.' You have denied that they exist—and I want to know whether I have understood you correctly."

"Please continue your statement, Mr. Stevenson. You will receive the answer in due course."

"I am prepared to wait for my answer until hell freezes over, if that's your decision," Stevenson said. "And I am also prepared to present the evidence in this room."

It was time to show the world the U-2 photographs of the Soviet missile sites in Cuba. The Americans, Harlan Cleveland recalled, had made "a very good tactical decision not to use them in the opening speech, to wait until we were challenged, and then roll them out as rebuttal. Zorin absolutely fell like a ripe apple into our hands because he said, in effect, 'Who says there are missiles in Cuba?' . . . And then at a signal—I mean we had this all worked out ahead of time—doors flew open, easels were rolled in and so forth—it was a media event of the first water. And I think that the drama of that . . . worked, as far as anything can work in politics, perfectly, and was very persuasive to everybody, including U Thant." "I never knew Adlai had it in him," said President Kennedy. "Too bad he didn't show a little more of this steam in the 1956 campaign."

Nothing else in Stevenson's long career as U.N. ambassador would attract as much notice as his "until hell freezes over" speech and his dramatic show of U-2 photographs, which, unlike those of the Bay of Pigs, were deadly accurate this time. As numerous analysts have pointed out since, Stevenson's words lacked logic. President Kennedy was not prepared to wait until hell froze over. The crisis was moving swiftly to its climax. But, as John Bartlow Martin said, "though faulty in logic, [the speech's] political effect was enormous. The net impression was that at last somebody had told the Communists to go to hell."

※※

In the meantime, U Thant intervened in the crisis, addressing an identical appeal to Khrushchev and Kennedy for suspension of the arms shipments and the quarantine for two to three weeks "to give time to the parties concerned to meet and discuss with a view to finding a peaceful solution of the problem." This elicited some byzantine responses. Ambassador Zorin swiftly dismissed the appeal and castigated U Thant for failing to put all the blame on the United States. But an embarrassed Zorin discovered a few hours later that

Khrushchev had accepted the appeal. Kennedy, on the other hand, rejected it but decided to use U Thant to ward Khrushchev off confrontation. Stevenson persuaded U Thant to ask Khrushchev in a second letter to instruct his ships to stay away from the American interception area "for a limited time only." The wording, in fact, was drafted at the State Department, Assistant Secretary Cleveland revealed years later. Khrushchev accepted U Thant's proposal, the first indication to the White House that he was seeking a way out of the crisis. Kennedy, answering a second appeal from U Thant, grudgingly agreed not to bother the Soviet ships if they stayed back.

But the real negotiations were going on in reams of pages transmitted between Kennedy and Khrushchev. The tone was belligerent, nasty, sometimes full of invective. Khrushchev accused the United States of "outright banditry . . . the folly of degenerate imperialism . . . an act of aggression pushing mankind toward the abyss of a missile nuclear war." On October 27, however, a rambling, obviously rushed letter arrived from Khrushchev. "If the President and Government of the United States were to give assurances that the U.S.A. itself would not participate in an attack on Cuba and would restrain others from this kind of action, if you would recall your fleet, this would immediately change everything," Khrushchev wrote. "The questions of armaments would disappear, since, if there is no threat, then armaments are a burden for every people. . . . Let us therefore show statesmanlike wisdom. I propose: we, for our part, will declare that our ships bound for Cuba will not carry any kind of armaments. You would declare that the United States will not invade Cuba with its forces and will not support any kind of forces that might intend to carry out an invasion of Cuba." Feelers for a deal of this kind were reaching the White House from other sources, including U Thant.

But, before Kennedy could reply to this letter, another letter from Khrushchev, broadcast over Radio Moscow, reached the White House. Khrushchev now demanded that the United States remove its missiles from Turkey. President Kennedy chose to reply to the earlier letter and, at least publicly, ignore the latest one. If Khrushchev would dismantle and remove all his missiles from Cuba, Kennedy wrote, the United States would end the quarantine and pledge not to invade Cuba. The White House called this "the Trollope ploy" after the tendency of the Victorian heroines of Anthony Trollope to hear only what they wanted to hear and accept proposals of marriage from men who did not realize they were proposing.

At the same time, Robert Kennedy, meeting secretly with Ambassador Dobrynin, assured the Soviets that the missiles would be removed from Turkey. But he added that the United States would never acknowledge that this was part of the deal and, in fact, would cancel the withdrawal of these missiles if the Soviet Union boasted that it was part of the deal. (President Kennedy, however, had decided to accept a Turkey-Cuba missile swap in public if his brother's private assurances proved inadequate.) On October 28, the reply came from Khrushchev: He trusted President Kennedy's pledge of no invasion and had issued an order to dismantle, crate, and return the missiles to the Soviet Union. The crisis was over.

&

Stevenson, with McCloy at his side, now had the job of working out the details of dismantling the missiles and a system of verification. Stevenson suggested that he expand the talks and take up broad disarmament issues with the Soviet negotiator, Deputy Foreign Minister V. V. Kuznetsov, but the suggestion only angered Kennedy. The president sent Stevenson severe instructions to stick to the issue of the Soviet missiles and bombers in Cuba and nothing else. Secretary-General U Thant flew to Havana to try to persuade Fidel Castro to accept either U.N. or International Red Cross inspections of the missile sites. But a weary, almost distraught Castro refused, calling inspections an infringement of Cuban sovereignty. The Kennedy administration finally decided to rely on inspections by American reconnaissance planes. Castro, despite his anger over losing his missile defense, did not try to shoot down these planes. Khrushchev also agreed to let the Americans observe and count the IL-28 bombers as the ships carrying them left Cuba. The Americans and Soviets soon informed U Thant that the Cuban crisis should be removed from the Security Council's agenda.

Stevenson received a depressing blow a few weeks after the crisis when the *Saturday Evening Post* published an article by Washington journalists Stewart Alsop and Charles Bartlett that painted him as the odd and wimpish man out on the Kennedy team that managed the crisis. Alsop and Bartlett said that only Stevenson dissented from the ExComm's decision to blockade Cuba. "There is disagreement in retrospect about what Stevenson really wanted," the writers said, before quoting "a nonadmiring official" who told them, "Adlai wanted a Munich. He wanted to trade the Turkish, Italian and British missile bases for the Cuban bases." The magazine ran a full-page photograph of Stevenson with the caption, "Stevenson was strong during the U.N. debate, but inside the White House the hard-liners thought he was soft." The writers ignored the fact that, in the end, ExComm had accepted Stevenson's plea to give up the surprise air attack and look for a peaceful solution first. Bartlett was a long-time intimate friend of President Kennedy, and it was widely assumed that the article represented the thinking of the White House. The writers, of course, were not told that President Kennedy had secretly assured Khrushchev that he would remove the missiles from Turkey.

There is little doubt that the president had talked with Bartlett and did feel that Stevenson had seemed like a querulous dissenter at the ExComm meetings. The president grew irritated at the controversy over the article, especially when Stevenson appeared on the *Today* television show to defend himself. But Kennedy did not want to lose Stevenson as U.N. ambassador and, after a good deal of rewriting, sent Stevenson a public letter, addressed to "Dear Adlai." "This is just a note to tell you again how deeply I regret the unfortunate stir which has arisen over the statements contained in the Saturday Evening Post article," Kennedy said. "I think you know how greatly we have all admired your performance at the United Nations in general and during the Security Council discussions and private negotiations connected with the Cuban crisis in particular. . . . It goes without saying that you have my fullest confidence and best wishes."

In later assessments, both Stevenson and U Thant insisted that the United Nations had made a vital contribution to ending the crisis. Speaking on his own ABC-TV show, *Adlai Stevenson Reports*, the ambassador said that the U.N. "performed in the classic manner in which it was intended to perform." "It provided a forum for the parties to expose their grievances," he said. "It afforded a means of marshalling world opinion. And it provided an opportunity to the United

Nations, to the Secretary-General to offer mediation and concilia-
tion." In his memoirs, the secretary-general elaborated on the same
themes. "All three parties directly involved knew from the beginning
they could not ignore the World Organization . . . ," he wrote. "As
subsequent developments show, the debates in the Security Council
had tremendous impact in turning the general opinion of a large
number of member governments in favor of finding an alternative to
war; the acceptance by the Soviet Union and the United States of my
suggestion helped avert an armed clash at sea, and the fact that both
the Soviet Union and the United States agreed to the inspection role
of the United Nations is evidence of a potential of considerable importance for the Organization in the future."

The achievements enumerated by Stevenson and U Thant cannot be denied, but, when examined in the enormity of the crisis, they
are relatively minor. The most terrifying confrontation of the Cold
War was settled by the two main protagonists themselves. President
Kennedy chose to deal with the crisis by threatening Khrushchev directly and threatening him with a nuclear war that the U.N. would
have been powerless to prevent. Kennedy did not go to the U.N. until
he had made up his mind on the course to follow, and nothing that
happened at the U.N. changed that course. The theater of the Security Council—especially when played by Adlai Stevenson with all his
reputation, influence, and rhetorical skill—surely did sway public
opinion in much of the world to the side of the United States, but it is
not clear that public opinion mattered in persuading Khrushchev to
back down and dismantle the missile sites. U Thant served less as a
mediator than as a conduit for proposals that the United States felt it
could not make in public. In fact, if President Kennedy had been
forced to make the withdrawal of the American missiles from Turkey
public, he planned to do so by persuading U Thant to suggest it first.
The United States still looked on the U.N. as a useful tool in American foreign policy—not as an independent force of its own.

☙❧

Stevenson never again won the praise and attention that were
his during the Cuban missile crisis debates at the Security Council.
Undersecretary of State George Ball, an old friend of Stevenson, told

John Bartlow Martin, "After the Cuban missile crisis Adlai was only going through the motions. His role had become ritualistic. From then on he knew that he was not going to have an impact on foreign policy—which was what was most important to him. . . . It was an unhappy life, certainly not his finest hour. I loved Adlai but by the time he died I felt he was almost a caricature of himself—a hollow man. . . . History had passed him by. His life had passed him by. He had no place to go. He talked about leaving the U.N. but he had no place to go."

After Kennedy's assassination, President Lyndon B. Johnson kept Stevenson on as U.N. ambassador, but he had no influence on Vietnam policy, no influence on Johnson's decision to intervene in the Dominican Republic. He had high hopes at first since he and Johnson were of the same generation and had known each other for years. But, by 1965, he complained that he had been reduced to a "defense counsel" at the U.N., fending off attacks, while taking almost no part in policy-making in Washington.

❧ 9 ❧

U Thant and the Quest for Peace in Vietnam

The Soviet Union did not want U Thant or anyone else to succeed Dag Hammarskjöld in 1961; as mentioned in chapter 7, they wanted a troika—three secretaries-general representing the Capitalist World, the Communist World, and the Third World. Premier Nikita Khrushchev felt that the Soviet Union had been tricked by Dag Hammarskjöld, a bureaucrat from a neutral country who ended up, in the Soviet view, hand in glove with Washington. "While there are neutral countries," Khrushchev said, "there are no neutral men." But the Americans felt that a troika would only paralyze the Secretariat and probably destroy the U.N. The idea did not even appeal to the Third World. The new countries of Asia and Africa did not want a junior place alongside two superpowers in a triumvirate. They felt it was time for one of their own to take on the whole job alone. They therefore lobbied for a single secretary-general—so long as he came from the Third World.

Adlai Stevenson persuaded the Security Council and the Soviet Union to shelve the troika proposal, but the Soviets then tried to salvage a shadow of the original with another idea: The secretary-general would have to surround himself with a coterie of advisers representing the three blocs. This plan was acceptable to the United States, but there were weeks of wrangling about the number and nationality of these advisers. One ambassador even suggested fifteen— to accommodate a host of regions and ideologies—but the Security Council could not settle on a formula.

The field of candidates for the job of secretary-general narrowed to two: Ambassador Mongi Slim of Tunisia and Ambassador U Thant of Burma (now Myanma). According to Brian Urquhart, they were the only two people that Hammarskjöld had looked on as possible successors. Slim had problems: The Soviets thought he was too Western, the Israelis regarded him as allied to their enemies, and the French still wanted to punish Tunisia over the Bizerte base. U Thant was less controversial, although there were French objections because he had been chairman of the Afro-Asian committee on Algerian independence and Arab objections because of the close relations between Burma and Israel. A French diplomat even derided U Thant as too short and as an ignoramus in the French language. When the calumny reached the ears of the five-foot-seven U Thant, he retorted, according to his memoirs, that "I was taller than Napoleon, and . . . he did not even speak English."

The Security Council finally selected U Thant on November 3, 1961, to complete the term of Hammarskjöld. The General Assembly confirmed him on the same day. The impasse had been broken by a Stevenson compromise: U Thant would be named acting secretary-general rather than secretary-general and would promise to consider geography in naming undersecretaries-general who would offer him advice that he was not bound to heed. He later named eight undersecretaries-general, including Ralph Bunche and a Soviet bureaucrat. In 1962, the Security Council and General Assembly removed "acting" from his title and elected him to a five-year term (including the thirteen months already served). He won reelection for five years in 1966 and retired in 1971.

U Thant is probably the least remembered or recognized secretary-general in U.N. history. The Johnson administration treated him with contempt for his search for peace in Vietnam and with ridicule for his failure to prevent the Six-Day War. Urquhart, who wrote many of his speeches and reports, has remained one of his few staunch defenders. U Thant, Urquhart wrote, was "a decent, brave and responsible man" who was "virtually written out of history" in the West after serving as a useful scapegoat. A quiet man who believed in living simply and attracting little attention, he probably suffered in reputation most when compared to the image of his dynamic predecessor.

U (the letter simply means "Mister" in the Burmese language) Thant, fifty-two when he succeeded Hammarskjöld, liked to wear well-tailored suits and smoke Burmese cheroot cigars. "As a Buddhist," he wrote in his memoirs, "I was trained to be tolerant of everything except intolerance." He practiced *bhavana*, a form of meditation, every day and tried to achieve *metta* (goodwill), *karuna* (compassion), *mudita* (sympathetic joy), and *upekka* (equilibrium). "I believe that I have attained a greater degree of emotional equilibrium than most people," he wrote. "This explains why I received the tragic news of the sudden death (in a traffic accident) of my only son, Tin Maung Thant, on May 21, 1962, with minimal emotional reaction. For are not birth and death the two phases of the same life process?" He also believed in astrology and told a skeptical Ralph Bunche once that the stars, especially the movements of Saturn, had foretold Lyndon Johnson's decision in 1968 to halt the bombing of North Vietnam. Despite U Thant's passive demeanor, Bunche found that he was as thin-skinned as Hammarskjöld and took criticism just as hard. But Hammarskjöld, Bunche noted, "was more of a fighter—he got angry and belligerent as well as hurt." U Thant, according to Urquhart, "never lost his temper."

U Thant was not a well-known statesman when he took over as secretary-general. He began his career as a teacher of history and English at Pantanaw High School in the Irrawaddy delta region of Burma in the late 1920s. U Nu, later a leader in the successful campaign for Burmese independence from Britain, was the school's headmaster. U Thant, allying himself with U Nu's movement, left the school and became a prolific writer of anticolonial articles for newspapers and magazines. When Burma was granted independence in 1948, his friend and colleague U Nu became its first premier. U Thant held several posts in the government, mainly as a counselor to the premier. In 1957, Premier U Nu appointed U Thant as Burma's ambassador to the United Nations.

U Thant was not fearful of involving himself in difficult and volatile problems like Vietnam and the Cuban missile crisis. Despite right-wing and European outcries, he finished the job that Dag Hammarskjöld had begun of forcibly putting down the secession of Katanga. He believed that "the Secretary-General must always be prepared to take an initiative, no matter what the consequences to his office or to him personally may be, if he sincerely believes that it might mean the difference between peace and war." He had long identified "with the cause of small nations, poor nations, newly independent nations, and nations struggling for independence," and he believed that he and they shared the same philosophy: The U.N. was the defender of the rights and liberties of the small, poor, and weak. But he also had a restrictive, almost legalistic concept of his role, and he sometimes disappointed others by his lack of action. Despite the mounting deaths, he refused to intervene in the Nigerian civil war because it was an internal matter. And some analysts believe that the Six-Day War could have been averted if he had managed to hold the U.N. soldiers in place in the Sinai in the face of Nasser's demand that they go.

U Thant was the secretary-general who sent the first Blue Helmets to the Mediterranean island of Cyprus, now the classic example of U.N. peacekeeping in action. This hapless island, just forty miles from the Turkish mainland, had a population of seven hundred thousand, 80 percent of Greek descent, 20 percent Turkish descent. Since the late nineteenth century, the Greek Cypriots had agitated for enosis—union with Greece—while the Turkish Cypriots, backed by the Turkish government, resisted a union that would render them even more vulnerable in a larger country. Cyprus was granted independence from Britain in 1960 with a constitution that guaranteed political rights to the Turkish Cypriot minority. The vice presidency and 30 percent of the cabinet and parliamentary seats were allotted to the Turkish Cypriots. In 1963, Archbishop Makarios III, the president, tried to eliminate these guarantees, arguing that they made the divisions of the island worse. His attempt set off bloody communal fighting.

The British, as guarantors of the constitution, put together a peacekeeping force, but it failed to calm the agitation. In March 1964, the Security Council asked U Thant to set up a replacement peacekeeping force and appoint a mediator. "This essentially dumped the problem in my lap," the secretary-general said. U Thant then essentially dumped the problem in Ralph Bunche's lap, and Bunche proceeded to set up the peacekeeping force in Cyprus with troops from Canada, Finland, Ireland, and Sweden. "If you get in there, you'll never get out," Bunche told the Canadian ambassador, a joke that proved prescient. Bunche avoided the mistakes of the Congo operation: There was no hint that the peacekeepers were there to help the Cyprus government, and the troops received strict orders to avoid use of firearms if possible. Bunche also chose the unwieldy acronym UNFICYP (United Nations Force in Cyprus).

U Thant surely did not realize how long the classic peacekeeping operation initiated in his régime would last. UNFICYP was still in operation as the U.N. approached its fiftieth anniversary. For more than thirty years, the peacekeepers patrolled cease-fire lines between the belligerents while repeated attempts at mediation failed. The cease-fire lines became more dramatic and definite in 1974 when a coup led by Greek officers seeking union with Greece overthrew Makarios for a while, prompting an invasion by the Turkish army. The Turks swiftly occupied 40 percent of the island, and the peacekeepers, who never numbered more than 6,400 and dwindled to a thousand or so in 1995, patrolled the new lines after then. Although there were 165 Blue Helmet deaths in thirty years, Cyprus was considered the kind of operation of limited danger that the U.N. did best. So long as the U.N. stood between them, the two sides usually held back their fire. Many U.N. officials lost patience, however, fearing that so long as the U.N. was there to avert bloodshed, the belligerents would always balk at reaching a settlement. The Security Council, however, was still unwilling in 1995 to test the theory and risk another bloodbath in Cyprus.

U Thant believed in aggressively pushing "the good offices" of the secretary-general into crises so that the antagonists could have a neutral force for mediation or a neutral conduit for negotiation. His "good offices" proved a useful though minor element in the Cuban missile crisis; the Kennedy administration was prepared to use him even more if Khrushchev had not backed down. But, all in all, his record from personal interventions in crises was spotty. He failed in his attempt to encourage a peaceful settlement in Vietnam and, in the end, became an annoying irritant to the Johnson administration. But his Vietnam venture was a noble failure, though still clouded in angry invective and controversy.

The Vietnam War had its roots in French colonialism and the French failure, despite American military assistance, to defeat the Communist-led independence forces in Vietnam. After the French garrison at Dien Bien Phu surrendered to Ho Chi Minh's forces in 1954, French Premier Pierre Mendès-France negotiated a settlement in Geneva. The Geneva Accord provided that Ho would control North Vietnam pending elections throughout the country supervised by an International Control Commission made up of representatives from India, Poland, and Canada.

There is no doubt that Ho, the most popular nationalist throughout Vietnam, would have won the elections, but they were never held. The South Vietnam government of Ngo Dinh Diem, imposed and supported by the Eisenhower administration, refused to take part in any elections. The Communist Vietcong, encouraged by North Vietnam, rebelled against Diem, and Vietnam was soon at war again. For almost twenty years, American governments preached that this was another Korea; if South Vietnam fell, the rest of Southeast Asia would fall to Communism like collapsing dominoes. While President Kennedy committed almost 20,000 advisers and troops to the battle, President Johnson escalated the number of troops until more than 550,000 Americans battled the Vietcong. By the time the war ended in 1975 with the defeat of the Americans and then the South Vietnamese, almost 60,000 Americans had died in Vietnam. Vietnamese casualties, of course, were far greater.

U Thant felt a duty to try to end the war even though the Geneva Accord had been negotiated outside the United Nations. His views on American participation in the war were clear from the beginning. "I had held all along that the real issue of the war was not whether the political aims of U.S. policy were right or wrong; the issue was the American *conduct* of the war," he wrote in his memoirs. "Even if the United States were right politically, it was, in my view, immoral to wage a war of this kind." He told a news conference in Paris in April 1964, "Military methods have failed to solve the problem. They did not solve it in 1954 [when the French army tried and failed to squelch the Vietnam independence movement], and I do not see any reason why they would succeed ten years later. As I see the problem in Southeast Asia, it is not essentially military, it is political; and therefore, political and diplomatic means alone, in my view, can solve it." He brought the issue up whenever he met world leaders like President Charles de Gaulle of France, Premier Khrushchev of the Soviet Union, and President Lyndon B. Johnson of the United States.

The secretary-general believed that his relations with Johnson were close. On visits to New York, Johnson would call suddenly and announce without any warning that he was on his way over to the U.N. for a chat. "I do not remember having met any head of state or head of government so informal and so warm toward me, and at the same time so juvenile in his concept of international developments," U Thant said. "He once told me that if South Vietnam were to fall to the communists, then the next target would be Hawaii!"

U Thant's relations with Khrushchev were also warm and close. When they first met near Yalta in 1962, the Soviet premier loaned the slim secretary-general a pair of his own bathing suits and invited him to swim in the Black Sea. "What trunks!" U Thant said. "The ones he gave me would fit a Japanese Sumo wrestler with a fifty-inch waist. . . . I somehow managed to tuck the trunks around my waist as I would a Burmese *longyi*." The men were so different in size that the picture is hard to imagine: a whale frolicking in the water with a seal. Since he spoke no Russian and Khrushchev no English, U Thant described his thirty minutes in the Black Sea as "the most memorable, and at the same time the most boring, I had ever spent with a head of state." But he left the Soviet Union with the feeling that he had met a man "with genuine emotional, temperamental, and verbal links with working class people." In later meetings, Khrushchev encouraged U Thant to intervene in the Vietnam War.

On August 6, 1964, President Johnson invited U Thant to Washington for an official visit. At a State Department luncheon that day, hosted by Secretary of State Dean Rusk and attended by Undersecretary of State Averell Harriman, Assistant Secretary of State William Bundy, U.N. Ambassador Adlai Stevenson, and others, U Thant brought up Vietnam. "Although Vietnam was not officially on the agenda of either the Security Council or the General Assembly," wrote Stevenson's biographer, John Bartlow Martin, "it overshadowed everything the U.N. did as it overshadowed everything the Administration and the Congress did." According to U Thant's account, he told the Americans that he believed it would be useful if emissaries of the United States and North Vietnam could meet for private conversations without a third party present. He said he knew Ho Chi Minh, the leader of North Vietnam. This seemed to be a hint that U Thant might be able to arrange a meeting, but he "did not make any specific proposals." U Thant left the luncheon, however, persuaded that "Mr. Rusk and his colleagues were receptive to the idea."

President Johnson laid the hospitality on thick. U Thant called the White House experience that day "the most unforgettable in my ten-year experience as Secretary-General." Accompanied by Stevenson and Bunche, U Thant arrived by helicopter as a U.S. Marine Corps band played on the South Lawn. President Johnson and Lady Bird Johnson welcomed him in the Rose Garden, and then U Thant met with Johnson and some aides in the Oval Office. The secretary-general told the president that Ho Chi Minh was more deeply influenced by French culture than Communism and that it might be worthwhile to attempt private contact with him. Ho was probably more pro-Moscow now than pro-Beijing, U Thant said. This discourse evidently struck Johnson and the others as naïve. Johnson told him, "We are ready to get out tomorrow if they [the Communists] will behave." More than two hundred guests—cabinet members, senators, congressmen, ambassadors, actors, journalists, businessmen, ministers, and labor leaders—attended the formal dinner in U Thant's honor that evening.

U Thant returned to New York convinced that he had the authority to approach Ho Chi Minh. He instructed his Soviet under-secretary, Vladimir Suslov, to ask his government to pass an oral mes-sage to Ho that U Thant believed "it would be in the interest of peace if an emissary of Hanoi would have face-to-face talks with one from Washington, without any publicity and without the participation of any third party." Three weeks later, Suslov told him that Hanoi had agreed. U Thant immediately informed Adlai Stevenson who, ac-cording to U Thant, welcomed the news and promised to relay it to Washington.

Stevenson, however, informed U Thant in mid-October that new turns in foreign policy would be impossible during Johnson's presidential election campaign against Barry Goldwater; it would be best to shelve the plan for a secret meeting until the election ended. After Johnson's landslide victory, Stevenson told U Thant that Wash-ington, checking another source, did not believe Hanoi was serious about a meeting. The other source turned out to be the Canadian member of the International Control Commission for Vietnam who, according to U Thant, had no links to Ho Chi Minh. After a hospital stay and a vacation forced on him by stomach ulcers, U Thant ap-proached Stevenson's deputy, Charles W. Yost, early in 1965 only to discover that Yost knew nothing about the matter. Stevenson was re-porting to Washington on this issue by phone and had left no record of it with members of his mission.

There appeared to be a change of mood in mid-January. Steven-son asked U Thant where a meeting might be held. U Thant, after contacting the Burmese government, proposed Rangoon and sug-gested that the American ambassador there meet with an emissary from North Vietnam. But the change of mood did not last long. Ste-venson informed U Thant on January 30 that Washington had de-cided not to take part in such a meeting. The Americans feared that it could not be kept secret and, once publicized, would demoralize the South Vietnamese government and trigger its downfall. U Thant said that Stevenson was clearly disappointed. It has never been clear, however, how hard Stevenson pushed the U Thant plan in a Wash-ington suspicious of the secretary-general, and it is doubtful that he personally informed Johnson. Washington obviously never took the proposal seriously. On February 7, American planes began bombing

North Vietnam, and Hanoi announced it would not take part in any talks with the United States so long as the bombing continued.

A frustrated U Thant was sure that Washington had toyed with him. Alluding to his private talks on Vietnam, he told a February 24 news conference that vital information about the war was being withheld from the American people. "I have been conducting private discussions on this question of Vietnam for a long time," he said. ". . . Of course, it will not be very helpful at this stage to reveal even some parts or some features of the negotiations I have conducted. . . . I am sure that the great American people, if only they knew the true facts and the background to the developments in South Vietnam, will agree with me that further bloodshed is unnecessary. And also that the political and diplomatic method of discussions and negotiations alone can create conditions which will enable the United States to withdraw gracefully from that part of the world. As you know, in times of war and of hostilities, the first casualty is truth." In the eyes of Washington, these words would destroy whatever usefulness he had as a mediator or go-between in Vietnam. U Thant understood this but felt he had to speak out. Rusk got so angry that he phoned him and said, "Who do you think you are, a country?"

On instructions from the State Department, Stevenson met U Thant and Bunche and criticized the secretary-general harshly. He accused U Thant of a breach of trust, for their talks had been confidential and should not have been revealed. He added that President Johnson was very upset by U Thant's remark about the lack of truth. He said that the U.N.'s prestige had fallen to an all-time low in Washington and that it would now be difficult for American officials to talk frankly with U Thant in the future. U Thant replied that he was sorry he had caused Stevenson and Washington embarrassment. But he warned Stevenson that most Asian leaders were convinced that the Communist chances for victory would only improve as the war worsened. This meeting took place on the eve of some of the great American escalations. During 1965, the numbers of American troops would increase eightfold from 23,000 to 185,000.

U Thant encountered President Johnson again in the San Francisco Opera House at ceremonies commemorating the twentieth anniversary of the United Nations on June 25, 1965. Johnson decided to confer with U Thant alone in a small room adjoining the opera hall and asked Stevenson to leave. Bunche encountered a red-faced Stevenson storming out of the room. "He does not want me present," Stevenson told Bunche. Johnson and U Thant met for more than an hour, and the president, according to U Thant's account, was in "a serious, even sour, mood." Johnson said that, because of his esteem for U Thant and the United Nations, he had hosted the biggest dinner ever held in the White House the previous August. He had wanted to tell the whole world that he looked on U Thant as a man of peace and the U.N. as the only hope for peace. And now he was distressed that his honored guest was criticizing his Vietnam policy.

The secretary-general recounted the whole story of his peace initiative and his contact with Hanoi. Johnson gave U Thant the impression that he had found out about the initiative only recently and had known nothing while it was going on. He repeated the hoary rationale that the Saigon government would have collapsed if the United States had proceeded. The president then told U Thant that Adlai Stevenson "was just an idealist with his head in the clouds." He had lost two presidential elections and didn't understand public opinion. "His evaluation of events, both domestic and foreign," the president said, "usually turned out to be incorrect." Averell Harriman, the president said, was ready to go anywhere in the world on behalf of the U.S. government to talk with emissaries of North Vietnam. Johnson also said that he had set aside one billion dollars to rehabilitate both North and South Vietnam when the war ended. Public opinion was very important, he stressed, and American public opinion favored the bombing of North Vietnam. He also said that he had planned to boycott the twentieth anniversary celebration because the U.N. was so critical of his Vietnam policies. Many congressmen had urged him to stay away, but Secretary of State Dean Rusk and Ambassador Stevenson had urged him to go, and he had yielded to their insistence.

It was obvious why the president did not want Adlai Stevenson in the same room. By then, however, Stevenson probably knew that Johnson — just like the Kennedys — regarded him as an idealist with his head in the clouds. A little more than two weeks later, on July 14, 1965, while walking in London with his long-time friend and associate, Marietta Tree, discussing with her what he might do if he left the U.N., Stevenson complained of feeling faint and then reeled over backward, striking his head on the pavement. He had died of a massive heart attack at the age of sixty-five. Both the United Nations and the U.S. Congress devoted a full day to eulogies. The U.N., at least in its first fifty years, would never again have an American ambassador of such worldwide renown.

❧

Dean Rusk had only contempt for U Thant and his story of a peace initiative. In 1967, addressing a group of American educators, Rusk said, "You have heard about the end-of-'64 beginning-of-'65 business when peace was about to break out in Rangoon. . . . Really, what happens on these matters is basically this: there are an awful lot of candidates for the Nobel Peace Prize running around the world these days. . . . They don't understand what they hear." His analysis evoked a good deal of laughter.

Rusk was even harsher in his memoirs published in 1990, twenty-five years after the initiative failed. His denunciation had the air of a rather overblown postmortem—since he obviously never thought the initiative was worth much of his time in the first place. Rusk said there was never any proof of any initiative. The Soviet undersecretary who had been U Thant's channel for messages, Rusk said, was a KGB spy who might have been conducting some kind of "clandestine operation for propaganda purposes." U Thant never gave Washington a copy of any message he had sent or received. "All we had were U Thant's guarded hints that if we could go to Rangoon, Hanoi would join us there," Rusk said. In his infamous news conference of February 24, 1965, according to the former secretary of state, U Thant had misrepresented the situation.

"Possibly U Thant himself was the victim of misinformation or simply wishful thinking," Rusk wrote, "but frankly, I thought he had lied like a sailor. I never had much respect for U Thant's integrity. He probably knew that he never had a message from Hanoi that pointed toward peace. Sometimes intermediaries will say things to each side that go beyond the facts, hoping that somehow this will get the two sides together."

Not only had U Thant damaged American prestige and increased the American credibility gap, Rusk said, but he also had hurt relations between Stevenson and Rusk. "Desperate to find a way toward peace," Rusk said, "Adlai was impatient with me and didn't think we were being responsive. Our conflict was rather sharp. Stevenson publicly took a position fostered by U Thant which, as far as I was concerned, was just a cock-and-bull story." Rusk also denounced a contention by U Thant in his memoirs that President Johnson had confirmed to the secretary-general at a meeting in 1966 that he had not been informed of the initiative while it was pursued. "If that is U Thant's story," Rusk said, "either U Thant or Lyndon Johnson did not tell the truth. I prefer to think it was U Thant because Johnson was kept up-to-date on these developments. I briefed him specifically on this so-called Rangoon Initiative."

⁂

Contempt from Washington did not stop U Thant from continually trying to use his "good offices" to help end the Vietnam War. He kept offering proposals for peace and making pleas for the United States to end the bombing. In 1967, he met North Vietnamese emissaries in Rangoon but came out with nothing that might appeal to the Johnson administration. U Thant called the war "more violent, more cruel, more damaging to human life and property, more harmful to relations among the great powers, and more perilous to the whole world" than any other war that had taken place since the end of World War II. Yet neither he nor the United Nations could do anything about it. The U.N., in fact, would remain marginalized throughout the peace negotiations that produced the withdrawal of the American forces and the debacle that followed with the fall of Saigon in April 1975.

The U.N., moreover, was often afflicted with impotence even when it faced lesser trials. The war that erupted between India and Pakistan over the disputed province of Kashmir in August 1965 seemed like the kind of conflagration the U.N. was ideally equipped to put out. The U.N. had posted observers along cease-fire lines in Kashmir since the two countries first battled there in 1948. Diplomats looked on both India and Pakistan as ideal member states always striving to strengthen the U.N. U Thant set off to both countries in September 1965 with some hope that he could mediate a settlement.

The trip was considered so important that President Johnson offered to loan U Thant one of his presidential Boeing 707 planes. But U Thant was too embarrassed to accept. He told Ralph Bunche it "would be far too luxurious for me." With his staff of only four, including Brian Urquhart, the secretary-general said, the large jet plane "would be almost empty." So U Thant and his group went by commercial plane until they reached Teheran and found that airlines were not flying into Pakistan. He then accepted use of the propeller-driven Convair of the American military attaché in Teheran.

A good deal of warmth infused the conversations of U Thant with his interlocutors. The secretary-general seemed to wander over many extraneous matters like the art and literature of Buddhism, but he continually prodded his hosts as well to agree to a cease-fire. Pakistan President Ayub Khan, with his clipped British accent, no-nonsense air, brush mustache, and six-foot-three frame, impressed U Thant as "the DeGaulle of Asia." Urquhart described Ayub Khan as "the quintessential field marshal" who wore "the best and most expensive-looking shoes I have ever seen." Foreign Minister Zulfikar Ali Bhutto arranged for the secretary-general to take time out to visit Taxila, seat of the oldest Buddhist university in the world. That fulfilled "one of my life's ambitions," U Thant said. He described himself as "speechless with awe and veneration at the spectacle" of the ruin of Taxila with rows of sandstone statues of Buddha. Bhutto later presented U Thant with "an exquisite standing statue of the Buddha" from his personal collection.

In India, U Thant called on President Sarvepalli Radhakrishnan. "Meeting him meant more than meeting the president of the most populous democracy in the world, for before me was a great philosopher and a teacher," U Thant said. "It was a spiritual experience." They discussed the *Dhammapada*, perhaps the most influential of all books in Buddhist literature, which Radhakrishnan had translated from Sanskrit into English. U Thant then called on Prime Minister Lal Bahadur Shastri "at his modest home." Shastri, U Thant said, was "the direct antithesis of President Ayub Khan . . . quite unlike a formidable field marshal." The prime minister was "a short man with a simple demeanor." Despite this demeanor, he was as forceful as Ayub Khan in discussing Kashmir.

When U Thant returned to New York more than a week later, Arthur J. Goldberg, who had left his place on the U.S. Supreme Court to succeed Stevenson as U.N. ambassador, led the Security Council to John F. Kennedy International Airport to welcome the secretary-general back, an unprecedented tribute. But U Thant returned empty-handed. Both sides had refused U Thant's first call for an unconditional cease-fire. His second appeal had been accepted by Indian Prime Minister Shastri but not by Pakistani President Ayub Khan. He had issued a third call, and the replies, which came in after his return to New York, showed no change in the Pakistani position. "I had now played all my cards," U Thant said. "There was nothing more I could do than to report to the Council that the situation was deadlocked." The deadlock was finally broken by Soviet Premier Alexey Kosygin, who brought both Shastri and Khan to Tashkent in January 1966 and persuaded them to sign a peace agreement.

The frustration over the marginalization of the U.N. from the Vietnam War and the failures of the U.N. in a number of political conflicts led many U.N. diplomats and officials in these days to look for other responsibilities for the U.N. The preamble of the Charter of the United Nations, largely written by American poet Archibald MacLeish, begins, "We the peoples of the United Nations determined to save succeeding generations from the scourge of war. . . ." It was assumed at the beginning that this was the main role of the U.N. But the preamble also states that the peoples of the United Nations are determined "to promote social progress and better standards of life in larger freedom" and "to employ international machinery for the promotion of the economic and social advancement of all peoples." These secondary goals began to assume primary importance, especially as the poor nations of Asia and Africa swelled the ranks of the U.N.

"I felt very strongly when I assumed the duties of Secretary-General," U Thant wrote in his memoirs, "that it is no longer morally acceptable or politically expedient for the more advanced nations to ignore the backwardness and poverty of the others." When President Kennedy proposed that the 1960s be designated the Decade of Development, U Thant and the General Assembly endorsed the idea enthusiastically. Noting that the charter had created the Economic and Social Council within the U.N. and that the U.N. had started creating specialized agencies like the U.N. Development Program (UNDP), the U.N. Children's Fund (UNICEF), and the U.N. Educational, Scientific, and Cultural Organization (UNESCO), U Thant said that the U.N., "for the first time in history, provided mankind with mechanisms that would seek to improve the life of every man, woman and child on earth. This was a goal perhaps more revolutionary than any political revolution in history." With the membership going well over one hundred, Brian Urquhart said, "the agenda of the U.N. shifted and widened to include subjects scarcely dreamed of at its inception—development, population, food, environment, water, and other global problems."

After he retired, Ambassador Goldberg warned the U.N. not to stray from its original purpose. "The staff of the U.N.," he said, "because they despair of political solutions to world problems, emphasize economic programs instead. These programs are all to the good. But these programs should go on independently at the U.N. . . . The real test of the U.N. is political—what it can do in political terms to assure peace and security. Its accomplishments in these areas is a mixed bag. However, if the U.N. were junked, we'd have to recreate it tomorrow." There was a good deal of wise counsel in the assessment of Goldberg. Humanitarian relief and economic development were prideful duties of the U.N., but its most vital work still lay in trying to keep the peace, even if it failed far more often than it succeeded.

❧ 10 ❧

The Six-Day War

At 10 P.M. on the night of Tuesday, May 16, 1967, General Indar Jit Rikhye of India, commander of the United Nations Emergency Force (UNEF) on the Egyptian side of the border with Israel, received an obscure, cryptic message from General Mahmoud Fawzi, chief of staff of the armed forces of the United Arab Republic (as Egypt called itself in those days). The fateful message, its English awry, demanded that the U.N. pull its troops out of the observation posts (OPs) in the Sinai so that Egyptian troops could take their place. The U.N. Blue Helmets had taken positions along the border after the Suez Crisis in 1956 to keep the peace between Egypt and Israel.

"To your information," wrote General Fawzi, "I gave my instructions to all UAR armed forces to be ready for action against Israel the moment it might carry out any aggressive action against any Arab country. Due to these instructions our troops are already concentrated in Sinai on our eastern borders. For the sake of complete secure [security] of all U.N. troops which install OPs along our borders, I request that you issue your orders to withdraw all these troops immediately. . . . Inform back the fulfillment of this request. Yours . . ."

The real reason for this demand was never clear. Egyptian President Gamal Abdel Nasser insisted throughout the crisis that he had to move his troops to the Israeli border because Israel had amassed a dozen or so brigades on the Syrian border. This was based on false intelligence supplied by Soviet Ambassador Dmitri Pojidaev in Cairo. The U.N. informed Nasser several times that their observers had found no mass of Israeli troops, but Nasser spurned these assurances. With popular grumbling about the poor state of the economy and with other Arabs taunting him about his weakness, Nasser may have felt the time had come to sound bellicose. Or, newly armed by the Soviet Union, with an armada of planes and tanks greater than that of Israel, Nasser may have felt that the time had truly come to wage war on Israel again.

Within two days of the Fawzi demand, Secretary-General U Thant shocked many world leaders by announcing the complete withdrawal of the emergency force (the first U.N. peacekeeping troops ever deployed). The decision was widely condemned at the time. With their buffer gone, nerves exacerbated and rhetoric ever more fiery, the Israelis and the Arabs marched inexorably into another conflagration. Within three weeks, the Six-Day War erupted, ending in an astoundingly swift and overwhelming Israeli triumph—a victory, however, that turned bitter and onerous in the next quarter of a century and compounded the instability of the Mideast.

Politicians and journalists excoriated U Thant. President Johnson described himself as dismayed over the "hurried withdrawal." Secretary of State Dean Rusk called U Thant's actions "disastrous." British Prime Minister Harold Wilson deplored the force's "disappearance . . . almost overnight." His predecessor, Alec Douglas-Home, said it was "a dreadful mistake." *New York Times* foreign affairs columnist C. L. Sulzberger concluded that U Thant "had used his international prestige with the objectivity of a spurned lover and the dynamism of a noodle." Syndicated columnist Joseph Alsop derided the act as "poltroonery." Israeli Foreign Minister Abba Eban was contemptuous. "What is the use of the fire brigade which vanishes from the scene as soon as the first smoke and flames appear?" he told the U.N. General Assembly. When war broke out, the *Spectator* of London headlined its editorial U THANT'S WAR.

U Thant had his defenders, most notably Brian Urquhart, his thoughtful and dynamic associate. He ridiculed the attacks on U Thant as "humbug" and "hypocritical and escapist nonsense." Urquhart made the case in his memoirs that U Thant had no legal grounds for acting differently and, even more important, that the Egyptian army of President Nasser would have easily pushed aside the thirty-four hundred lightly armed U.N. troops if they had tried to resist. Urquhart's argument assumed, of course, that Nasser intended to head into battle whether the U.N. liked it or not. Although U Thant detractors doubt it, there is much evidence that this was true. Yet, even if it were, U Thant still must be faulted for handling the crisis with too much pedantry and too little imagination. His performance was far from agile, far from astute, and it contributed to a darkening of the image of the U.N. and the office of secretary-general.

Since he took orders solely from the U.N., General Rikhye rightly refused to submit to the withdrawal demand of General Fawzi and instead relayed the letter to New York. U Thant immediately called in Egyptian Ambassador Mohammed Awad El Kony, dressed in a dinner jacket for a formal dinner at the Asia Society, and warned him that the demand could lead to war. El Kony, however, said he knew nothing about Fawzi's letter. During the next day, U Thant handed Ambassador El Kony an aide-mémoire that summarized the secretary-general's views on the Egyptian demand. In retrospect, the document seems out of step with the enormity of the crisis, for it offered to give everything away with hardly a murmur of protest.

❧

The aide-mémoire acknowledged that the U.N. had no authority to keep troops on Egyptian soil without the consent of the Egyptian government. Under a cardinal rule of peacekeeping (though bent in the Congo and ignored later in Somalia), the U.N. did not send troops anywhere without the consent of the antagonists. "If that consent should be withdrawn or so qualified as to make it impossible for the force to function effectively, the force, of course, will be withdrawn," U Thant said. The aide-mémoire then threatened Egypt: The U.N. would accept no partial or temporary withdrawal. If the

Egyptians wanted some but not all U.N. troops to move so that Egyptian troops could be redeployed, the U.N. would reject that demand and withdraw all its forces permanently. On top of this, U Thant chided the Egyptians for sending their first request to the U.N. commander on the field. The proper procedure, U Thant said, was a direct request to the secretary-general from the government of Egypt.

Critics found grievous faults in U Thant's aide-mémoire. The assertion that Egypt had full authority to expel the U.N. troops was debatable. Dag Hammarskjöld had managed to limit that authority in 1956. In negotiating the agreement to allow the entry of the U.N. peacekeepers after the Suez crisis, Hammarskjöld persuaded Nasser to accept what became known as the "good faith" clause. It stated that the Egyptian government, while exercising its sovereign rights on any matter concerning the presence of the U.N. troops, "will be guided, in good faith, by its acceptance of General Assembly resolution 1000" — the resolution setting up the U.N. force.

In a private memorandum circulated later to a few associates and diplomats, Hammarskjöld interpreted the "good faith" clause to mean that the Egyptians could not ask the U.N. troops "to withdraw before the completion of the tasks" set down by the resolution. But what were these "tasks"? The resolution was vague — "to secure and supervise the cessation of hostilities." If this phrase signified some kind of negotiated settlement or permanent stability between Egypt and Israel, the tasks obviously had not been completed by 1967. The Hammarskjöld-Nasser "good faith" agreement thus appeared to limit Egypt's authority to force the withdrawal of the Blue Helmets.

More than a week after the Six-Day War ended, U Thant was embarrassed when Ernest A. Gross, a former deputy American ambassador to the U.N., released his copy of Hammarskjöld's private memorandum. In a public reply, overly defensive in tone, U Thant said that Gross's release of a document "of a purely private character and . . . supposedly secret in nature" raised "some question of ethics and good faith." He said that the document had never been shown to Nasser and that the Egyptian government "knew nothing about it and was in no way bound by it." Moreover, the secretary-general said, it was out of date. The tasks that Hammarskjöld and Nasser had in mind in 1956 involved the replacement of British, French, and Israeli troops by the peacekeepers—tasks completed a decade ago. While this contention cast some doubt on the validity of the logic in the Hammarskjöld memorandum, the memorandum was still persuasive evidence that at the least U Thant should have hesitated before embracing Egyptian authority whole.

The U Thant aide-mémoire probably erred as well by threatening to withdraw all the troops permanently even if Nasser demanded only a partial redeployment. This sounded almost like a dare. At best, it was a bluff that failed, a flawed attempt to shock Nasser into status quo.

❧❦

Much depends on what Nasser really intended. If he was all out for war from the start, nothing would have stopped him. But Nasser afterward insisted that he had not been. He told Dean Rusk that he had wanted a partial withdrawal, not a complete one. When all the U.N. troops left, he was forced to move his own soldiers into the vacuum. Once in Sharm al-Sheikh, which controlled the Strait of Tiran, he had to blockade Israeli shipping. "What could I do?" he told Rusk. "These were Israeli ships. I couldn't let them pass. I had to close the Strait of Tiran." Rusk called this "a feeble excuse." Repeating this story to Eric Rouleau of the French newspaper *Le Monde* in 1970, Nasser said that U Thant, under the influence of Ralph Bunche, had withdrawn all the forces in order to entice the Egyptians into Sharm al-Sheikh. "We fell into the trap that was set for us," Nasser said. According to another account, Nasser wanted the original message from General Fawzi to demand that General Rikhye redeploy his troops, not withdraw them, but the courier had left with the original message before Nasser could change it.

All this, of course, has the ring of convenient revisionism by Nasser in the wake of a disaster brought on only by himself. Despite these postwar excuses, Nasser never turned off his fiery, bellicose, incessant oratory during the crisis. He could have stepped backward if he really wanted to. Yet there also is no doubt that Thant's aide-mémoire made it dangerously easy for him to demand U.N. withdrawal.

⁓

For four weeks, U Thant and the U.N. failed to prevent the war or stop it from running its course. Events moved swiftly. During the forty-eight hours after the Fawzi letter, the secretary-general asked Israeli Ambassador Gideon Rafael to allow the peacekeepers to move to his side of the border, but the diplomat refused, repeating the long-standing Israeli insistence that this would affront sovereignty. Rafael told the secretary-general dismissively that Israel did not intend to accept U.N. discards from Egypt. "Israel is not the Salvation Army," he said. U Thant wrote later that war might have been averted if Israel had agreed to the deployment, even for a short while. In Cairo, Egyptian Foreign Minister Mahmoud Riad called in the ambassadors from those countries supplying troops to the U.N. force and told them their soldiers had to leave. India and Yugoslavia, whose troops made up almost half the force, announced their withdrawal without waiting for orders from New York. Egyptian soldiers entered several U.N. camps in the Sinai and forced peacekeepers out.

At noon on May 18, U Thant received the official Egyptian reply to his aide-mémoire of the day before. The note from Foreign Minister Riad followed the procedure set down by U Thant. It said that "the government of the United Arab Republic has the honor to inform Your Excellency that it has decided to terminate the presence of the United Nations Emergency Force from the territory of the United Arab Republic and Gaza Strip." Urquhart had written an appeal from U Thant to Nasser for reconsideration of the decision, but Ambassador El Kony warned the secretary-general that such an appeal would only infuriate Nasser and strike him as hostile and unacceptable. U Thant decided not to send it.

The secretary-general met with ten ambassadors who either belonged to a special UNEF advisory committee or provided troops to the force. The Canadian ambassador, backed by two others, argued that it was up to the U.N. alone to decide the fate of its peacekeepers. But U Thant was adamant that he had no choice but to comply with the Egyptian demand for withdrawal. Neither U Thant nor the others exercised their right to call an emergency meeting of the Security

Council or the General Assembly to consider the issue. A few hours later, U Thant wrote Riad that the U.N. would comply with the Egyptian demand but added, "In all frankness, may I advise you that I have serious misgivings about it."

U Thant decided to fly to Cairo to discuss the crisis with Nasser. He had met Nasser several times before and regarded him as simple, charming, polite, and somewhat shy. The secretary-general wanted to take Ralph Bunche along, but the Egyptians vetoed him because he was American. While U Thant was still en route, Nasser announced that he had closed the Strait of Tiran to Israeli ships and other ships carrying goods to Israel. By replacing the peacekeepers with his own troops in Sharm al-Sheikh, Nasser now controlled the Strait of Tiran that led to the Gulf of Aqaba and the Israeli port of Eilat. Eilat had become Israel's second port (Tel Aviv on the Mediterranean was the first) and the entry for oil from the Middle East, especially Iran. A blockade was regarded as an act of war under international law, and everyone assumed that Israel would not accept this without a battle.

In a speech to the Egyptian armed forces announcing the blockade, Nasser repeated his accusation that Israel had amassed eleven to thirteen brigades on the Syrian border. "We are now face to face with Israel," he said. Nasser also said that if the U.N. force had refused to withdraw, "we would have regarded it as a hostile force and forcibly disarmed it." "We are definitely capable of doing such a job," he added. Bristling with Soviet arms, Nasser obviously felt confident about his new military prowess. "The Jews threatened war," he said. "We tell them: You are welcome, we are ready for war."

U Thant arrived in Cairo with a proposal similar to his Cuban missile crisis proposal. If Egypt would lift its blockade for two weeks, he would ask Israel to halt its use of the Gulf of Aqaba for two weeks as well. That would allow time for negotiation. Nasser agreed, but there was never any chance that the Israelis would agree, for they believed there was nothing to gain from delay. U Thant told Nasser that he was surprised at the imposition of the blockade for it made war inevitable. He also chided Nasser for making the announcement while the secretary-general was en route to Cairo. Nasser repeated that Egypt had no choice but to impose the blockade because of Israeli threats of aggression. As for the timing, Nasser implored, it would have looked like the Egyptians were snubbing U Thant if they had delayed the announcement until after he left. They would not have wanted to do that. U Thant left Cairo with very little.

※꽃

Both sides mobilized for war and talked of little else. Posters appeared in Cairo showing an Egyptian strangling a Jew cowering behind an evil American. A headline in the *Al Ahram* newspaper, edited by Nasser's old friend Mohammed Hassanein Heikal, cried out WAR IS INEVITABLE. King Hussein of Jordan, derided by Nasser only a few weeks earlier as a traitor to the Arab cause, signed a defense pact with Nasser. Nasser promised the destruction of Israel but added he would be patient. "I can wait a year or ten years," he said. But he warned Israelis by radio: "We face you in battle and are burning with desire to start in order to obtain revenge. This will make the world realize what the Arabs are and what the Jews are." He told the Egyptian National Assembly, "We are now ready to confront Israel. . . . We are not afraid of the United States and its threats, of Britain and her threats, or of the entire Western world and its partiality to Israel."

Israel was menaced by rearmed Arab forces with more planes and tanks and far more troops than the Jewish state could muster. A small land of 2.5 million surrounded by hostile Arab countries with a population of 110 million, Israel had a citizen army, and its economy could not afford prolonged mobilization. As adult males left their jobs to take up arms and prepare for war, high school pupils delivered the mail and collected the garbage. Lost production in factories and farms drained fifteen million to twenty million dollars from the economy every day. Israel waited while American Ambassador Arthur Goldberg tried to put together a United Nations majority that would guarantee the right of Israeli shipping to bypass Nasser's blockade. But it could not wait very long.

In New York, Ambassador Goldberg struggled in the Security Council to win approval of a resolution that would declare the Gulf of Aqaba an international waterway that Nasser had no right to blockade. Britain supported it, but France and Canada insisted that Nasser had the legal right to close the gulf. Nasser condemned the resolution before it was ever put to a vote. He said he would regard any resolution that interfered with his blockade as "a preliminary to an act of war." In the words of Israeli Foreign Minister Eban, "There was peril for Israel wherever it looked. Its manpower had been hastily mobilized. Its economy and commerce were beating with feeble pulses. Its streets were dark and empty. There was an apocalyptic air of approaching peril. And Israel faced this danger alone."

≈≈

At 8 A.M., Israeli time, Monday, June 5, Major General Mordechai Hod, the commander of the Israeli air force, issued his battle order. "Soldiers of the Air Force," it began, "the swashbuckling Egyptian Army is moving against us to annihilate our people. . . . Fly on, attack the enemy, pursue him to ruination, draw his fangs, scatter him in the wilderness, so that the people of Israel may live in peace in our land, and the future generations be secured." In their preemptive attack, the Israeli jets—French Mirage and Mystère fighter-bombers—flew west over the Mediterranean well beyond Egypt and then banked south, turning back toward Egypt from the west. Flying low to avoid radar, the Israeli jets caught most of the planes of the Egyptian air force parked neatly at their airfields and destroyed them. The planes of Egypt's allies—Jordan, Iraq, and Syria—were blasted as well in similar surprise attacks. Within four hours of the first day, Israel had destroyed more than four hundred planes, the bulk of Arab airpower.

An hour after the first attack, a call from Ralph Bunche woke the secretary-general. "U Thant, war has broken out," Bunche said. It was 3 A.M., New York time. U Thant, who lived in the elegant Riverdale section of the Bronx, left his home at 3:45 A.M. and headed for U.N. headquarters. For the first time in his memory, he had left home without his morning *bhavana*. In Washington, the Johnson administration was surprised by the breakout of the war. "We were shocked as well, and angry as hell, when the Israelis launched their surprise offensive," Secretary of State Dean Rusk wrote in his memoirs. The Americans thought they could have persuaded Nasser to lift the blockade if the Israelis had waited. U Thant summarized what was known and issued a report to an emergency meeting of the Security Council at 9:30 A.M. It was the first of 1,099 reports that he would issue about the war and its aftermath during his last four years as secretary-general. U Thant also told the council that Israeli artillery and planes had attacked two U.N. camps and a U.N. convoy in Egypt during the first day and that Jordanian soldiers had taken over U.N. headquarters at Government House in the Arab area of Jerusalem. A total of fifteen peacekeepers, all preparing for evacuation, would die during the Israeli attacks that week.

By Tuesday, the second day of the war, Cairo Radio broadcast its excuse for Egyptian setbacks: American and British warplanes were protecting Israel with "an air umbrella" and joining the Israeli air force in its attacks on Arab cities and airfields. The American ambassador reported to Washington that Foreign Minister Riad seemed to believe this wild accusation. Egypt broke off diplomatic relations with the United States. Accepting the Egyptian charges of American participation in the war, Algeria, Sudan, Syria, Iraq, Yemen, and Mauritania broke off relations as well. The Security Council unanimously passed a resolution calling for a cease-fire, but it would prove to be only the first of several unheeded resolutions to come out of the council during the brief war. Passage of the resolution came only after the Soviet Union, evidently troubled by the false Arab charges of U.S. and British involvement in the war, decided to abandon a pro-Arab resolution in favor of one that favored neither side. Jordan accepted the cease-fire, but the Israelis, who had warned King Hussein to stay out of the war, did not intend to stop.

By Wednesday, the third day of the war, Israeli troops defeated Jordan's Arab Legion, occupied the West Bank, and seized the Arab section of Jerusalem. Israeli soldiers caressed and kissed the stones of the Wailing Wall in Jerusalem, the only remnant left of the ancient temple of Solomon, the holiest relic of Judaism. "We have taken the city of God," said General Shlomo Goren, the chief rabbi of the armed forces. "We are entering the messianic era for Jewish people." Moshe Dayan, the minister of defense, stood in front of the Wailing Wall, which Jordan had barred to Israelis, and promised, "We have

British Prime Minister Winston Churchill, U.S. President Franklin D. Roosevelt, and Roosevelt's son Elliot aboard the H.M.S. *Prince of Wales*, August 14, 1941, for the meeting that produced the Atlantic Charter.

All photographs are printed courtesy of the United Nations.

Soviet Foreign Minister V. M. Molotov, U.S. Secretary of State Edward Stettinius, and British Foreign Secretary Anthony Eden confer at the San Francisco conference, May 1, 1945. *(Rosenberg)*

Delegates of the Big Five — the United States, the Soviet Union, Britain, France, and China — confer in San Francisco, May 29, 1945.

Ralph Bunche of the United States, acting U.N. mediator for Palestine, confers with the chief of the U.N. observer team, Major General Aage Lundström of Sweden, in Haifa, 1948.

United Nations headquarters. *(A. Birizzi)*

Yugoslav troops, part of the U.N. peacekeeping force, on patrol in the Sinai, El 'Arish, Egypt, January 1957.

Secretary-General Hammarskjöld inspects the Brazilian battalion of the U.N. peacekeeping force in the Sinai, Rafa, Egypt, December 1958.

Soviet Premier Nikita Khrushchev in animated discussion at a General Assembly meeting, September 26, 1960. Marshal Tito of Yugoslavia, in the light-colored jacket, is among those listening. *(Y. Nagata)*

Secretary-General Hammarskjöld in Katanga in the Congo, August 14, 1960.

Secretary-General Kurt Waldheim visits U.N. peacekeepers assigned to southern Lebanon, April 18, 1978. *(J. Isaac)*

Secretary-General Javier Pérez de Cuéllar visits Namibia in advance of
U.N.-assisted elections, Windhoek, Namibia, April 1989. *(M. Grant)*

A Canadian medic with the U.N. peacekeepers in Cambodia examines an elderly man, March 2, 1993. *(J. Isaac)*

Secretary-General Boutros-Ghali and a French officer at the Baidoa Orphanage in Somalia, October 1993. The orphanage is run by the private Irish organization GOAL with the support of the U.N. *(F. Ribere)*

Eritrean women dance in celebration of the U.N.-supervised referendum in which Eritrea votes to separate from Ethiopia; Adi Segdo, Eritrea, April 1993. *(M. Grant)*

Secretary-General Boutros-Ghali and North Korean Deputy Foreign Minister Choe U Jin in the demilitarized zone between North and South Korea, Panmunjom, December 24, 1993. *(J. Bu)*

Nelson Mandela, who was elected president of South Africa in U.N.-monitored elections, speaks at a rally in Cape Town on the day before his inauguration, May 10, 1994. *(C. Sattleburger)*

returned to the holiest of our holy places, never to depart from it again." Jordanian casualties came to three thousand dead, wounded, and missing. The Security Council adopted a Soviet resolution demanding an end to the fighting by 8 P.M., Greenwich mean time, that day.

By Thursday, the fourth day of the war, Israel stormed all the way across the Sinai to the Suez Canal and trapped the Egyptian army in the desert. Egyptian casualties came to more than twelve thousand dead, wounded, and missing. The Egyptians had lost seven hundred tanks and almost four hundred planes. Egypt accepted the U.N. cease-fire, tantamount to a surrender. The Security Council meetings were growing more vituperative with Soviet Ambassador Nikolai T. Fedorenko heaping insults upon the Israelis and the Americans.

By Friday, the fifth day of the war, Nasser announced his resignation, a clever ruse to rekindle popularity. "We cannot hide from ourselves the fact that we have met with a grave setback in the last few days," Nasser said in a radio broadcast to the nation. ". . . I tell you truthfully that I am ready to assume the entire responsibility. . . . I have decided to give up completely and finally every official post and every political role and to return to the ranks of the public to do my duty with them like every other citizen." Almost on signal, tens of thousands of Egyptians streamed into the streets of Cairo chanting "Nasser! Nasser! Nasser!" Women threw dirt on their heads to signify their mourning. The vice president refused to accept Nasser's resignation. The National Assembly voted 360 to nothing to refuse it as well. Faced with these shows of support, Nasser relented. "I feel that the people's will cannot be refused," he told the National Assembly. "Therefore I have decided to stay where people want me to stay until all traces of aggression are erased." The Security Council passed a third resolution calling for a cease-fire. Syria accepted it, but Israeli troops continued to advance.

By Saturday, the sixth and final day of the war, Israel defeated Syria, chasing its troops from the Golan Heights, a mountainous site from which the Syrians had rained shells down on Israeli farmlands below for years. The Security Council met in an emergency session at 4 A.M., New York time, amid reports that Israel was bombing and advancing on Damascus. Soviet Ambassador Fedorenko announced that his government had broken off relations with Israel. Moshe Dayan asked General Odd Bull of Norway, chief of staff of the U.N. observers in the Mideast, to make arrangements for a cease-fire. General Bull proposed a cease-fire at 4:30 P.M., GMT. Both Syria and Israel accepted. Israel now occupied the Golan Heights, the Sinai, East Jerusalem, Gaza, and the West Bank. "The war is over," said Moshe Dayan. "Now the trouble begins."

※ ※

The Security Council labored during the next few weeks to put together a resolution that might set down a formula for permanent peace. It would obviously be futile for the council to demand only that the Israelis give up the land seized in battle. Israel had abandoned its conquests under international pressure in 1956 only to face increasing Arab hostility and a second war a little more than a decade later. Much of the credit for the 1967 resolution belonged to American Ambassador Arthur J. Goldberg, who had spent many years as a labor lawyer before serving on the Supreme Court. "Goldberg was certainly the best negotiator I have ever seen, at the U.N. or anywhere else," wrote Seymour Maxwell Finger, one of his associates at the American mission to the U.N. "He was always thoroughly prepared; knowledgeable on all aspects of the issue; aware of what arguments the other side was likely to make; judicious in weighing the strengths and weaknesses of the respective positions; clear in exposition; and calm, patient, and scrupulously honest." Lord Caradon, the British ambassador, introduced Resolution 242—adopted unanimously by the Security Council on November 22, 1967—but Goldberg wrote most of it and negotiated many of the details with Soviet Deputy Foreign Minister Vasily Kuznetzov. Though known as a Zionist sympathizer, Goldberg managed to persuade Egyptian Ambassador El Kony and other Arab diplomats of his fairness in drafting the resolution.

Resolution 242—perhaps the best-known Security Council resolution in the first fifty years of the U.N.—stated that "a just and lasting peace in the Middle East" should include the application of two principles: (1) "withdrawal of Israeli armed forces from territories occupied in the recent conflict," and (2) "acknowledgment of the sovereignty, territorial integrity and political independence of every state in the area and their right to live in peace within secure and recognized boundaries free from threats or acts of force." In short, the resolution called for withdrawal of Israeli troops in exchange for recognition of Israel and the renunciation of all threats to destroy it. "The aims of the two sides do not conflict," Lord Caradon told the Security Council. "They converge. They supplement and support each other. To imagine that one can be secured without the other is a delusion. They are of equal validity and equal necessity."

There were a couple of ambiguities. Although Arab politicians often insisted that the resolution provided for withdrawal from all the occupied territories, it actually called for withdrawal "from territories occupied" without specifying how many. The resolution also did not state which came first—withdrawal or recognition. Arab politicians would insist later that recognition of Israel could come only after it withdrew from the territories. The resolution, however, implied that the two acts would take place simultaneously. The resolution left a good deal of room for negotiation, and it became the basis for the Camp David talks that produced the Israeli-Egyptian peace treaty in 1979 and the secret talks that ended with the peace agreement between Israel and the Palestine Liberation Organization in 1993. In both cases, however, negotiations took place outside the U.N.

For Israelis, the resounding triumph of the Six-Day War engendered a euphoria about the strength and mystique of their nation. They had stood alone and smote the menace around them. They now had slabs of territory to absorb attacks should the enemy be foolish enough to persist. But victory also instilled a dangerous contempt within them for the vanquished. Every household could show snapshots of tanks abandoned in the desert by frightened Egyptians. Nor were the slabs of territory a complete blessing. More than a million Palestinian Arabs lived there, and the Israelis had now become occupiers of hostile land.

The victory against a larger and heavily armed foe was so swift and sure that it aroused enthusiastic admiration worldwide. There was no doubt about the cheering in the United States and much of

Europe. The Associated Press, the most evenhanded of all American news organizations, could not suppress its excitement in a specially produced book on the war, *Lightning Out of Israel*. "Now, suddenly," related the AP writers as they described the second day of the war, "it seemed that tiny, outnumbered Israel was bigger than life-size; overnight David had outgrown Goliath. With breathless precision, with grim thoroughness, the Israeli war machine ground on through Tuesday." Even elsewhere, where governments bristled over the Israeli triumph, peoples could not hide their glee. Africans listening to shortwave broadcasts cheered the Israelis onward from afar even while authoritarian African governments, oblivious to public opinion, contemplated support for their Arab brothers. Sudan joined Egypt in breaking relations with the United States, but some Sudanese intellectuals acknowledged that deep down they had felt a pang of joy when they heard that the Israelis had wiped out the air force of the overbearing Egyptians.

But unabashed admiration did not last very long. As the years wore on, Palestinian and Arab persistence succeeded in swaying sentiment against Israel in the Third World and in pockets of supposedly progressive thinking elsewhere. Israel took on the guise of a colonial power suppressing the Palestine people. Israel found itself lumped with South Africa in condemnations. Even the repulsion at Arab terror did not always squelch this mood. Israeli settlements in the occupied territory and the open Israeli contempt for Palestine aspirations did not help. As the Third World took a commanding majority in U.N. membership and thus the General Assembly (there were 127 members by the end of 1967), the organization lined up against the little land it had once created out of sympathy and justice. The American veto in the Security Council served as Israel's only shield at the U.N.

The Six-Day War intensified the Israeli disdain for the United Nations. Israeli leaders had long ago decided that they could not trust the security of their country to the U.N. Even during the country's birth year of 1948, when the U.N. was known by the acronym UNO (for "United Nations Organization") in Israel, Premier David Ben-Gurion had set the tone with his dismissive appraisal of its significance. "UNO, schmuno," he said. The Six-Day War only proved how ineffectual the U.N. could be. In the Israeli view of things, a wimpish U Thant, with barely a protest, had removed his barrier of peacekeepers and allowed Nasser to march toward the Gulf of Aqaba and choke an Israeli lifeline. U.N. resolutions always seemed to take something from Israel and offer nothing in exchange. Unlike the dénouement of the Suez crisis in 1956, the Israelis did not intend to give up their conquered territory in 1967. The Israelis also felt that the U.N. provided the Arabs with a convenient escape from dealing directly with Israel. So long as U.N. resolutions ended wars and U.N. peacekeepers patrolled cease-fire lines, the Arabs did not have to negotiate directly with Israel for an armistice and peace. With the image of U Thant's cowardice implanted in their minds, the Israelis intended to have as little as possible to do with the U.N. from now on. The anti-Israeli bias in the General Assembly only strengthened Israel's anti-U.N. attitude.

For the United Nations, the Six-Day War was a devastating blow. The first U.N. peacekeeping force had stood on guard for a decade and then failed its terrible time of testing. "We all labored under a crushing sense of failure," Brian Urquhart wrote. "I believe that both U Thant and Bunche suffered irreparable psychological damage from this episode, and the physical health of both steadily declined after it." Ralph Bunche had created the United Nations Emergency Force, and, as Urquhart put it, he saw much of his life's work destroyed within a few days. Bunche retired in June 1971 and died six months later at the age of sixty-eight. In his eulogy, U Thant told the General Assembly that Bunche was "an international institution in his own right, transcending both nationality and race in a way that is achieved by very few."

The Arab-Israeli conflict would no longer occupy the U.N. as obsessively as it once did. The U.N. played a role during the 1973 Yom Kippur War when Egypt and Syria almost defeated Israel in a surprise attack. But, quickly rearmed by the Americans, a bloodied Israel counterattacked and drove across the Suez Canal to the west and almost to Damascus in the north. This war came near to triggering a terrifying clash of superpowers as the Soviet Union threatened to send troops and the United States put its military forces on alert. In the end, Secretary of State Henry Kissinger brokered a deal in Moscow that allowed the Security Council to declare a cease-fire that was accepted by the Arabs and Israelis. To patrol cease-fire lines after the war, the U.N. created a second U.N. Emergency Force in the western Sinai and a new force of peacekeepers on the Golan Heights. Syria allowed the Golan Heights force only after Kissinger flew to Damascus to pressure and persuade President Hafez al-Assad. Secretary-General Kurt Waldheim, who had succeeded U Thant, was hardly a major player. The 1973 war made it clear that the Arab-Israeli conflict had now become an issue for great powers who did not need the U.N. very much in their wheeling and dealing.

Shut out of most Cold War conflicts and now bereft of much of the Israeli problem—the kind of problem that Harry Truman once said we had the U.N. for—the United Nations entered an era that was surely the nadir of its first fifty years. Paralysis, Third World cant, the hypocritical anti-American ranting of ambassadors from little tyrannies, corruption and waste—all these somehow became the hallmark of the U.N. during the 1970s and early 1980s. Some Americans wondered whether there ought to be a United Nations after all.

❧ 11 ❧

Kurt Waldheim:
The Big Lie

In December 1971, when Kurt Waldheim of Austria was elected as the fourth secretary-general of the United Nations, his main rival was Max Jakobson of Finland, the first choice of the United States. But the Soviet Union had vetoed Jakobson, spreading the word they had done so because he was Jewish and thus unacceptable to the Arab world. In those days, it was known that Waldheim, like many other Austrians, had served as an officer in the German army during World War II. Daniel Patrick Moynihan, a member of the American delegation to the General Assembly, noted sardonically that, "faced with a choice between anti-Semitism and anti-fascism, the Russians came down on the side of enduring values"—age-old Russian anti-Semitism. Moynihan remarked to American Ambassador George Bush, "Our candidate had been a Jewish socialist, but we settled for a German infantry officer."

Moynihan's wit would have metamorphosed into fury if he had known the full story. Waldheim had hidden most of it. He had joined two Nazi organizations during his youth. As a second lieutenant in World War II, he had been assigned to a German army unit in the

Balkans that had rounded up thousands of Jews in Greece for deportation to Auschwitz and had killed thousands of innocent villagers in Greece and Yugoslavia as reprisals for attacks by the "Partisans," as Resistance fighters were known during the occupation. The commander, General Alexander Löhr, also an Austrian, had been executed as a war criminal after the war. The Yugoslav government had accused Waldheim as well of war crimes. The official document of the United Nations War Crimes Commission, charging Waldheim with "murder" and "putting hostages to death," was still in the rarely consulted archives of the U.N.

There is no doubt that Waldheim would never have been elected secretary-general if this information had been public at the time. But the former Austrian foreign minister, who campaigned long and hard for the job, lied about his past in memoirs, interviews, articles, and official biographies. While acknowledging that he had served with the German army, Waldheim insisted that he had gone back to the university to study law in 1942 after he was wounded on the Russian front. He never mentioned his later reassignment to the Balkans.

In retrospect, it seems like a fortuitous metaphor for the United Nations to be led during the 1970s by a Nazi and a liar. The fortunes and esteem of the U.N. never sank lower. Many Americans and Europeans developed contempt for the world organization. The sales of UNICEF Christmas cards started to dwindle. Newspapers berated UNESCO so often during the 1970s for trying to hamper the Western press that President Reagan could pull out in 1984 with hardly a protest from anyone. New Yorkers grumbled about having a cauldron of anti-Semitism within their midst. Gallup poll approval ratings for the U.N. plummeted. The disdain for the U.N. culminated with the sarcasm of Deputy Ambassador Charles Lichenstein, who exploded at delegates in 1983 for complaining about the treatment of diplomats in the United States. Lichenstein lectured the complainers that if they did not like their treatment they should "seriously consider removing themselves and this organization from the soil of the United States." "We will put no impediment in your way," he went on, "and we will be at dockside bidding you a fond farewell as you set off into the sunset." Lichenstein, of course, confused his geography—as they set sail in the East River they would reach no sunset—but there was no confusion about his distaste.

In her book *Countenance of Truth*, Shirley Hazzard, the short-story writer and former U.N. employee who has dissected the organization in both fact and fiction, tried to make the case that Waldheim's past was far more than a metaphor. She implied (without using the word *blackmail*) that those who knew the truth—evidently, the Soviets above all—may have blackmailed Waldheim into avoiding human rights and other issues that might have proven embarrassing to the blackmailers. The blackmail did not have to be overt; the mere fear that he could be exposed by the Soviets might have been enough to rein him in. She cited Waldheim's failure to cry out against North Vietnamese treatment of refugees after the Vietnam War, his condemnation of the dramatic Israeli raid on Entebbe that freed Israeli hostages in 1976, his hesitancy about protesting the Polish government's jailing of a young Polish U.N. staff member while she was visiting friends in Warsaw, and his refusal to say anything about the vast imprisonment of political dissidents in the Soviet Union. Hazzard acknowledged that other secretaries-general have been as fretful as Waldheim about offending governments. But she wrote "there were indications that his extreme receptivity to national pressures possibly originated . . . in compulsions beyond the acknowledged sphere of U.N. weakness." His timid responses to abuses of rights and censorship, she said, "invite the suspicion that he acted out of fear."

The most thorough amassing of documentary evidence about Waldheim in World War II was made by Robert Edwin Herzstein, a professor of history at the University of South Carolina. His early research was financed by the World Jewish Congress, the *New York Times*, and ABC News. These findings fed the sensational accusations made by the World Jewish Congress against Waldheim in 1986 as he campaigned for the presidency of Austria. Herzstein's careful sifting of the documentation made it clear that Waldheim was probably not a war criminal but an ambitious young intelligence officer who prepared situation reports that were used by war criminals as they planned their brutal reprisals against Greek and Yugoslav resisters. By sweeping this out of his biography, Waldheim lived a lie for more than forty years. He compounded the deplorable falseness by refusing to acknowledge any wrong when finally exposed and by throwing up a succession of phoney denials until forced each time by the weight of evidence to peel away a little more of his lie.

The lie and the guilt probably influenced his work as secretary-general and ensured, as Hazzard concluded, that he would be a cautious administrator unwilling to provoke controversy. Yet there is no hard evidence to prove this. We cannot be certain that those who knew his past blackmailed him into mediocrity and insensitivity. Though cautious, he was an adequate and active secretary-general who filled the office while the U.N. limped along during its most impotent and hypocritical moments. Perhaps a smarter secretary-general with less baggage from World War II and more imagination could have talked the General Assembly out of passing its infamous and harmful "Zionism Is Racism" resolution, but we will never know for sure. At a time when the rest of the U.N. behaved badly, Waldheim never made up for it by trying like Dag Hammarskjöld to assume the role of a moral force. Of course, if Waldheim had posed as a great moral force, he would have proven even more of a fraud than he turned out to be.

❧❦

Kurt Waldheim, blond and a lanky six foot four, was nineteen years old when Adolf Hitler's troops overran Austria in March 1938 on the eve of World War II. The German-speaking Austria was immediately annexed to Nazi Germany in what was known as *Anschluss*. Many outsiders looked on Austria as the first victim of Hitler. But Hitler was Austrian himself, and his first conquest was not a totally unwilling victim. Union with Germany had long been advocated by some Austrian politicians. A half-million Austrians lined the Ringstrasse to cheer Hitler's triumphal entry into Vienna, and a quarter of a million crowded alongside the New Hofburg palace to hear his balcony speech.

The Gestapo swiftly arrested Kurt Waldheim's father, Walter Waldheim, as an anti-Nazi. He had been a prominent supporter of the conservative Christian Social Party that opposed *Anschluss*. He was released after a day or two but dismissed from his job as superintendent of schools in Tulln. Kurt Waldheim's scholarship to the Consular Academy in Vienna was canceled as well. But relatives put together enough money so that the future foreign minister and U.N. secretary-general could continue studies at the academy, a training school for diplomats.

German army records discovered by Herzstein revealed that Kurt Waldheim joined the National Socialist (Nazi) German Students League on April 1, 1938, two weeks after Hitler entered Vienna. Despite the records, Waldheim later denied that he was a member of the league. Waldheim had spent a year of military service in the Austrian army in 1937 before enrolling in the Consular Academy and was still obligated for more training after the annexation by Germany. The Austrian army by then had become the German army. He took several more months of training during 1938, spending some time in the cavalry and some time with German forces occupying the German-speaking Sudetenland of what was then Czechoslovakia.

In November 1938, shortly after Kristallnacht in Germany, the time of wholesale Nazi smashing of Jewish shops, homes, and synagogues, Waldheim, according to German army records, joined a cavalry unit of the Sturmabteilung (the S.A.). Literally the Storm Troopers, the S.A. were better known as the Brownshirts, the young Nazi thugs who violently enforced the party's edicts and whims. The Brownshirts were among those who forced Jews to clean the gutters and public latrines in Vienna after the Anschluss. Waldheim, however, contended later that his unit was merely a riding club made up of Consular Academy students. This prompted Austrian Chancellor Fred Sinowatz to joke to reporters, "I accept what Herr Waldheim says: that he was not himself a member of the S.A., only his horse was." Membership in the S.A. was not counted as a criminal act by the United Nations War Crimes Commission. It concluded that many Austrians felt compelled to join to safeguard their positions and advance their careers.

When World War II broke out, Waldheim, commissioned a lieutenant, saw action on both the French and Russian fronts. In December 1941, a week before his twenty-third birthday, he was wounded in Russia, his right thigh torn by shrapnel from a grenade.

After treatment at field hospitals in Minsk and Vienna, he returned home to recuperate. For years, Waldheim maintained that this ended his military career. Unfit for military service, he said, he then studied law at the University of Vienna. The German army did allow Waldheim to begin his studies at the university and gave him school leave from time to time afterward so that he could earn a doctorate in law in 1944. But, according to the records found by Herzstein, Waldheim, declared fit for service after his recuperation, reported back to the German army for duty in March 1942.

Waldheim found himself assigned to the troubled Balkans as part of the quartermaster department of General Friedrich Stahl's Battle Group West Bosnia. The Partisans of Tito had routed the fascist Croatian army on the Kozara plateau, and Stahl had taken over from the Croatians. The German commander decided to denude the plateau of its civilian population and thus prevent them from harboring the Partisans. While killing thirty-four hundred Partisans, the Germans rounded up tens of thousands of civilians, mostly Serbs, shooting, according to German army orders, all those "caught with weapons or who have fought against German or Croatian troops . . . as well as those proven to have taken active part in the revolt." Those who were not shot were either deported to labor camps in Germany and Norway if they were strong enough or, if they were not, turned over to Croatian authorities for possible execution. Herzstein estimated that more than sixty-five thousand people were killed in action, executed afterward, or shipped off to labor camp. The German suppression of Kozara is regarded as one of the worst massacres of the Yugoslav occupation.

Waldheim's role in this is not clear. After denying any knowledge of the massacre at first, he later acknowledged that he was with Stahl's group but only as a clerical supply officer for the army. But Herzstein said that Waldheim's quartermaster unit, during the Kozara massacre, "collated statistics regarding the number of prisoners, then surveyed the number of trucks and railway cars available to deport them." Croatian leader Ante Pavelić awarded Waldheim the Silver Medal of the Crown of King Zvonimir with Oak Leaves "for courage in the battle against rebels in West Bosnia in the spring and summer of 1942." The Croatians, according to Herzstein, "only gave the medal to people who actively helped them. Waldheim could not have received the medal for routine bookkeeping tasks carried out for the German forces alone." By the end of the year, Waldheim was commissioned a first lieutenant.

After working as an interpreter to ease communication between German and Italian officers, Waldheim was posted to Athens as a deputy operations officer in a German team helping the Italian army deal with Greek Partisans. This duty provided Herzstein with the only evidence—very slim and rather indirect evidence—that linked Waldheim to the Holocaust, Hitler's attempt to exterminate the Jews. A document signed by Waldheim showed that he had routinely passed on intelligence about the Jews of the Greek island of Ionnina to the German unit that eventually rounded up and deported two thousand Jews from the island to the death camps. Waldheim told reporters in 1986, "I swear to you that I did not have the slightest thing to do with the deportation of the Jews. I just learned about these things from recent newspaper reports. . . . I know it sounds improbable, but I did not know about it." Herzstein found this ignorance implausible and concluded harshly that "in properly transmitting information about the disposition of Jews in occupied territories . . . the deputy operations officer . . . played a small but necessary role in the smooth execution of Hitler's Final Solution."

During the last year and a half of war, Waldheim served as an intelligence officer in Army Group E, commanded by General Alexander Löhr, a fellow Austrian. Based first at Arsakli outside Salonika in Greece and then in Sarajevo in Yugoslavia, Waldheim's task was to prepare papers describing the situation in the field for study by the command. He had to evaluate the reports pouring into headquarters and analyze them. Sometimes he even briefed General Löhr in person. Assigned to keep the Partisans of Greece and Yugoslavia in check, Löhr settled on brutal reprisals as his main tactic. German soldiers killed 720 men and destroyed the monastery in the village of Kalavryta. After Partisans fired on a German truck convoy, a regiment of the S.S. (Schutzstaffel), the Blackshirt Nazi security police, murdered 215 civilians, including 9 infants, in the village of Clissura. By January 1944, the Germans had destroyed 485 villages in Greece. There were 762,000 homeless Greeks as a result.

Waldheim, in an act of courage, protested the reprisals, though not on moral grounds. At the end of one of his reports, he wrote, "The reprisal measures imposed in response to acts of sabotage and ambush have, despite their severity, failed to achieve any noteworthy success. . . . On the contrary, exaggerated reprisal measures undertaken without a more precise examination of the objective situation have only caused embitterment and have been useful to the [Partisan] bands." He sent this report to the chief of the general staff of Army Group E with copies to the S.S. Although his thorough and careful reporting and analyses may have provided some of the information that provoked reprisals, he evidently would not have ordered them himself.

After the war ended in May 1945, the Americans kept Waldheim in a prisoner-of-war camp for almost a month because he had been an intelligence officer under General Löhr's command. But, finding no evidence of war crimes, the Americans released him. After working for a few months as an assistant judge in Baden, Waldheim started anew as a diplomat, finding a post as personal diplomatic secretary to Karl Gruber, the acting foreign minister. Austria remained under Allied occupation until 1955, and the Allies supervised an Austrian "denazification" program designed to eliminate Austrian Nazis from public life. Waldheim prepared affidavits stating that he would not have been allowed to complete his studies or begin his legal career without membership in the Nazi Students League and the Brownshirt Cavalry Corps. Overloaded with cases, the denazification commissions cleared Waldheim without any hearing or any requests for details of his military career.

In 1947, the Yugoslav government of Tito intensified its investigation of the brutality of Army Group E during the war and executed its commander, General Löhr, for war crimes. In December of that year, the Yugoslav State Commission for the Determination of Crimes Committed by the Occupying Forces and Their Collaborators sent an *odluka*, or indictment, against Waldheim to the United Nations War Crimes Commission in London. The *odluka* charged that Lieutenant Waldheim was "responsible for the preparation and issuing of . . . criminal orders while his group operated in Yugoslavia." These orders, the indictment went on, caused "murders and massacres, execution of hostages, deliberate destruction of property, burning of settlements." Waldheim, the Yugoslav commission said, "is a war criminal. Arrest and imprisonment of this defendant is mandatory under Article 4, Paragraph V of the Yugoslav Code on criminal activities against the people and the state, and his extradition to the Yugoslav authorities is obligatory." Yugoslavia later added evidence from a German prisoner of war still in its hands. The POW, who had served as a clerk in Löhr's army, was quoted as saying, "I remember certain persons have been murdered at Sarajevo in November 1944. They were executed according to the order given by Waldheim in retaliation for desertion from the German Army of some other persons."

In February 1948, the War Crimes Commission, just before disbanding itself, approved the placing of Waldheim's name on its list of war criminals. He was charged with "murder" and with "putting hostages to death" from April 1944 to May 1945 in "all parts of Yugoslavia." The document described Waldheim and the intelligence staff as "the means for the massacre of numerous sections of the Serb population." Waldheim's name was placed automatically on the Central Registry of War Criminals and Security Suspects. His file— along with all the others of the War Crimes Commission—ended up in the storage bins of the U.N.

The War Crimes Commission document dealing with Waldheim—Case # R/N/684—is the most damaging evidence against him and the U.N. Not only did the U.N. elect an accused war criminal as secretary-general in 1971, but it did so with the ruinous document lying somewhere in its stores. Herzstein concluded, however, that the Yugoslav indictment was a politically motivated concoction based on flimsy evidence. In his book *Waldheim: The Missing Years*, Herzstein said that the Yugoslavs, angry about a border dispute with Austria, planned to use the indictment to embarrass Gruber, Waldheim's boss, at one of a series of international conferences deciding the future of Austria. The plan, according to Herzstein, was to attack Gruber by accusing him of keeping a Nazi war criminal at his side. But Waldheim had been transferred to the Austrian legation in Paris before the conference that the Yugoslavs planned to disrupt with their finger-pointing. With Waldheim gone, they failed to raise the issue and, in fact, never bothered to press Austria later for his extradition. They did not do so, according to Herzstein, because they knew the evidence against Waldheim was weak and largely manufactured.

ꙮꙮ

In any event, none of this derogatory detail surfaced as Waldheim rose steadily in the ranks of the foreign ministry and of the conservative People's Party. In a little more than two decades, he served in a variety of important diplomatic and political posts including ambassador to Canada, director general of the foreign ministry for political affairs, ambassador to the United Nations, and foreign minister. In 1970, he ran as the People's Party candidate for president of Austria but lost. In a break with U.N. tradition, he and Jakobson openly lobbied to succeed U Thant as secretary-general in 1971.

The Soviets wanted Gunnar Jarring, the former Mideast mediator and the Swedish ambassador to Moscow, but withdrew his nomination in the face of a threatened veto by the Chinese Communists (who had entered the U.N. only a few weeks earlier). The Nixon administration supported Jakobson, without pushing too hard, but both he and Argentine Ambassador Carlos Ortíz de Rozas were vetoed by the Russians. The Chinese, calling for a secretary-general from the Third World, vetoed Waldheim at first but relented on a second ballot, ensuring his election. Jakobson was upset, for he believed that Washington had promised the Finns that Ambassador George Bush would veto all other candidates "till the cows come home," hoping that the Soviets would change their minds about Jakobson under the pressure. Assistant Secretary of State Joseph J. Sisco said the United States did not defend Jakobson by vetoing everyone else because the tactic would only have stiffened Russian opposition. Although the Russians hinted that they had vetoed the Finnish ambassador because their Arab allies would not work with a Jew, Jakobson said years later that he believed the real reason was that "Moscow thought I would be too strong a Secretary-General in the tradition of Dag Hammarskjöld and . . . was worried that the prestige of the office would strengthen Finland's concept of neutrality."

It is difficult to assess Kurt Waldheim as secretary-general in the light of all that manifested itself later about his past. Not too much was expected of him when elected in any case, though most diplomats assumed he would prove more active and agile than U Thant. Syndicated columnist Joseph Kraft denounced the choice at the time, describing Waldheim as "a man almost certain to bring the office of Secretary-General down to the low estate already reached by the Security Council and the General Assembly." "He is superficial and without strong moral force," Kraft wrote. ". . . He has done nothing of note except be pliant with all comers, beginning with the Nazis whom he served in World War II."

Pliancy was surely his hallmark. "The press used to call him 'The Headwaiter,'" recalled Don Shannon, who covered the U.N. for the *Los Angeles Times* during the entire Waldheim reign. "He always stood there as if he were wringing his hands on a towel, asking what he could do for the powerful countries." Assistant Secretary Sisco described him as a man who gave in to pressures from the Soviet Union and counterpressures from the United States. "He did not have a strong independent commitment to the institution *per se* as a Dag Hammarskjöld—a sharp contrast," said Sisco. A measured yet damning assessment came from Brian Urquhart, who served as one of his undersecretaries-general. "Waldheim was an energetic, ambitious mediocrity," he wrote in his memoirs. "In fact he did rather better as Secretary-General than I had anticipated and demonstrated determination and even, on occasion, courage, but he lacked the qualities of vision, integrity, inspiration, and leadership that the United Nations so desperately needs."

Waldheim faced two enormous difficulties as secretary-general: The Third World had taken over the U.N., and Henry Kissinger had bypassed it. With new African and Asian states swelling the membership to almost three times the original number, the United States and the West could no longer make the General Assembly do their bidding. The watershed was reached just a few weeks before Waldheim's election when the United States failed to keep Communist China out of the U.N. For twenty-one years, the United States had choked

every attempt to take China's seat from Chiang Kai-shek and give it
to Mao Tse-tung. There was an absurdity in this stance: It meant that
the Nationalists who administered no more than the island of Taiwan had the power of veto in the Security Council, while the Communists who controlled all of mainland China did not even have a
seat in the U.N. Many governments chafed under the pressure from
Washington to maintain the absurdity. But they usually gave in. The
Americans employed a parliamentary maneuver to make it somewhat palatable for others to support them. The Americans would insist that the seating of the Chinese Communists was an "important
question" requiring a two-thirds majority. A majority of the General
Assembly would usually vote with the United States on this procedural issue. The Chinese Communists would then win a majority of
votes but fall short of the required two-thirds.

Ambassador George Bush was instructed to pursue the same
strategy in 1971. The absurdity was heightened that year because Kissinger, President Nixon's national security adviser, was in Beijing preparing the way for a presidential visit even while Bush was cajoling
ambassadors to support Washington's anti-Beijing stance. Bush
failed. On the key vote on October 25, 1971, the General Assembly
defeated the American resolution declaring the issue an "important
question" by a vote of fifty-nine to fifty-five, with fifteen abstentions.
The assembly then voted by a margin of seventy-six to thirty-five, with
seventeen abstentions, to approve an Albanian resolution seating the
Chinese Communists in place of the Chinese Nationalists and thus
oust Taiwan from the U.N. The Chinese Communists had fallen
short of the two-thirds, but that no longer mattered. American domination of the General Assembly had come to its end.

Third World ambassadors rose and jumped with joy; a few even
danced in the aisles. Diplomats cheered, embraced each other, and
clapped their hands in an ecstatic rhythmic beat. The outburst had
less to do with admiration for the Chinese Communists than the
need to show Washington who was running the show now—a kind of
self-indulgent, childish symbolism. With a touch of hyperbole, Ambassador Bush denounced the vote as "a moment of infamy." Nixon
was furious. White House Press Secretary Ron Ziegler told reporters
that the spectacle of "cheering, handclapping and dancing" and the

shocking demonstration of "undisguised glee" and "personal animosity" had outraged the president. Ziegler warned that such behavior "could very seriously impair support for the United Nations in the country and in the Congress." Ambassador Salim Ahmed Salim of Tanzania, who had led some of the frolicking diplomats in a victory dance, would pay for his exuberance when the time came to elect a successor to Waldheim.

As national security adviser and later secretary of state, Kissinger was the architect of President Nixon's policy of détente with the Soviet Union. The time had come for the United States to treat the Soviet Union not as an implacable foe but as an enemy with whom cooperation could be negotiated on some issues. Kissinger believed that links to China gave the United States an opening to persuade the Soviet Union to ease tensions in certain areas. The Russians looked on China as almost as great an enemy as the United States and did not want both allied against them. Kissinger hoped that the cooperation on manageable issues could be used "as leverage to modify Soviet behavior in areas in which the two countries were at loggerheads." The tenets of détente would be worked out in bilateral negotiations in Moscow and Washington, not at the U.N.

Détente allowed Kissinger to maneuver in the Middle East, weakening Soviet influence by making the United States the prime mover in the peace process. This also diminished the United Nations, for the Mideast had once been its main province. Kissinger simply did not need the U.N., except perhaps to rubber-stamp agreements that he had worked out or to implement them in the way he set down. The passive role of the U.N. continued even after Kissinger left the scene. During the Carter administration, peace between Egypt and Israel was negotiated at Camp David in Maryland, not alongside the East River in New York. Kissinger did not have a high opinion of the U.N. in any case. He told Samuel De Palma, the assistant secretary of state for international organizations, "Don't bother me with that U.N. crap." At most, Kissinger praised it faintly as "a convenient meeting place for diplomats and a useful forum for the exchange of ideas." While he credited the U.N. with performing "important technical functions," he concluded that "it failed to fulfill the underlying premise of collective security—the prevention of war and collective resistance to aggression." He would not even credit the U.N. with any achievement in the Suez Canal crisis, for he disagreed with Eisenhower and Dulles for "manhandling our closest allies." He thought it was deplorable that the United States had failed to reduce the scope of Soviet adventurism then. "I was convinced that we would pay heavily in the years ahead for our shortsighted playing to the gallery," he wrote in his memoirs.

❧

During all the Waldheim years, the U.N. mounted only three new peacekeeping missions, all in the Mideast. Two came out of the 1973 Yom Kippur War and were largely Kissinger creations. Kissinger flew to Moscow to negotiate a cease-fire resolution that would stop the fighting on the Egyptian front. He then went on to Israel to warn Prime Minister Golda Meir that further arms shipments from the U.S. to replenish the matériel lost in the war depended on her acceptance of the cease-fire resolution; this was a bitter blow, for the Israelis were about to destroy the Egyptian Third Army in the Sinai, but she gave in. The Soviet-American resolution was presented to the Security Council and, of course, accepted. This produced the second United Nations Emergency Force in the Sinai. The Blue Helmets returned to the area they had abandoned under U Thant's orders on the eve of the Six-Day War.

Months of shuttle diplomacy by Kissinger between Damascus and Jerusalem produced the U.N. Disengagement Observer Force on the Golan Heights that Israel had seized from Syria. Under Kissinger's prodding, the two sides signed an agreement in Geneva in May 1974 that asked Waldheim to set up the force that would occupy most of the area and attempt to prevent a resumption of fighting. The agreement was then forwarded to the Security Council in New York, which, of course, approved it. The lack of U.N. input in both these cases was understandable. As Mona Ghali, an analyst for the Henry L. Stimson Center, put it in a study of U.N. peacekeeping, "Given the bipolarity of the international system at the time, plus the American view that the U.N. had transformed itself into the Third World's

soap box, and Israel's open contempt for the Organization, it is difficult to see how the U.N. could have operated any differently."

The third peacekeeping force—the U.N. Interim Force in Lebanon—also came out of American diplomacy. President Jimmy
Carter was upset when Israel invaded southern Lebanon in March
1978 intent on breaking the power of the Palestine Liberation Organization (PLO) there. Carter feared that the invasion would embarrass Egyptian President Anwar Sadat and thus upset the peace talks
between Egypt and Israel. So American Ambassador Andrew Young
introduced a resolution calling for a cease-fire, withdrawal of the Israeli troops, and a U.N. force to supervise the withdrawal. The Security Council passed the resolution twelve to nothing, with the Soviet
Union and Czechoslovakia abstaining and China not voting. (The
size of the council had expanded from eleven to fifteen in the mid-
1960s to reflect some of the increased membership in the U.N.) Israel
never accepted this mission, which proved ineffectual. The Israeli
Defense Force simply shoved the Blue Helmets aside in their next
invasion of Lebanon in 1982.

Despite the U.N.'s impotence, Waldheim was an active secretary-general; he worked hard, traveled a good deal, communicated
with leaders, strove for attention, and blathered to reporters even
when he had nothing to say. As a former German army officer, he
had little chance of ingratiating himself with the Israelis, but he
squandered even that little chance on a visit to Israel in 1973 when
he refused to wear a hat or a yarmulke inside Yad Vashem, the hallowed
Israeli monument to the Holocaust. The *Jerusalem Post* headlined an
editorial about the trip to Israel A VISIT WITH NO PURPOSE.

Cyprus erupted again in 1974, the conflagration drawing in the
Turkish army, which occupied the northern part of the island. The
fighting caught twenty-three hundred peacekeepers spread throughout the country. The peacekeepers arranged local cease-fires in various villages, provided relief to fleeing civilians, evacuated foreign
diplomats and their families, and occupied the Nicosia airport. A
Greek Cypriot mob, sure that the United States sided with Turkey,

sacked the U.S. embassy in Nicosia and murdered the ambassador. Waldheim kept the Blue Helmets on the island and then redeployed them to patrol the new cease-fire lines.

Waldheim tried to work out a settlement that would lead to independence for South-West Africa (or, as it would be known in a few years, Namibia), but he failed to convince outsiders that the time was ripe. He was always conscious of the limitations of his office. "All I have is moral power," he said in 1977. "I have nothing behind me. . . . I have not got the power to force anyone to do anything." Upon hearing that, the *Times* of London described Waldheim as "the spokesman for the largest body in the world equipped with the least number of teeth."

William E. Schaufele Jr., an American diplomat who had served as ambassador to Upper Volta before joining the U.S. mission at the U.N., noted that Waldheim was so intent on pleasing African countries that he rarely brought their problems to the U.N. "You know that in all the time I was there, only one African issue, outside of southern Africa, was brought to the U.N.," Schaufele said. ". . . I often used to wonder why Waldheim didn't get involved in more African issues on his own initiative, but he was sensitive to the Africans not wanting to bring their issues to the U.N." African diplomats might be incensed at the killings in Burundi and Uganda, but they feared that raising them at the U.N. would embarrass Africa as a whole.

In Teheran in 1978, Waldheim complained to the shah of Iran that he had not been permitted to speak with dissidents. "I will not have any guest of mine waste a single minute on these ridiculous people," the shah replied. A couple of years later, after the shah had lost the throne, Waldheim was back trying to persuade the most radical of these dissidents to release the American hostages held in the U.S. embassy. The Iranians posted insulting photos throughout the city of Waldheim kissing the hand of the shah's twin sister. The Iranians forced him to spend much of his time talking with victims of the shah's secret police and witnessing relics of the oppression. Obliged to visit a cemetery to lay wreaths on the graves of "revolutionary martyrs," he found an angry mob swarming around his car. They jumped and pounded on the roof, he recalled in his memoirs, "their faces twisted in a frenzy of hatred." His U.N. security guard swerved the car and headed through the graves to the helicopter that had brought them to the cemetery. The frustrated mob, Waldheim said, was "in hot pursuit" and "we got away by the skin of our teeth." Led to a hectic meeting of the revolutionary council in a darkened room, his entreaties to release the hostages got nowhere. The Iranians did not even let him see them.

Waldheim campaigned vigorously and unashamedly in 1981 to become the first secretary-general elected to a third term. "During the General Assembly session," Urquhart wrote, "Waldheim's performance became a general joke, as he buttonholed and cajoled and wheedled everyone in sight. Ministers and diplomats scurried nervously along the corridors, dreading the familiar grasp of the Secretary-General's hand on their elbow." His Nazi associations were still hidden. The United States supported him, but the Chinese wanted a candidate from the Third World and vetoed Waldheim. Ambassador Salim Salim of Tanzania, however, the leading Third World candidate, had a formidable opponent. George Bush, now vice president, remembered Salim's victory dance ten years earlier when the General Assembly defied the United States and voted to admit the Chinese Communists. Ambassador Jeane Kirkpatrick was prepared to veto Salim if he could garner the needed nine votes. Both he and Waldheim had to withdraw. In the end, the Security Council settled on a compromise, Javier Pérez de Cuéllar of Peru, a retired undersecretary-general. Unlike Waldheim, Pérez de Cuéllar had not campaigned at all; in fact, he sat out the voting back home in Peru.

꿪꿲

The Waldheim scandal broke five years later while he was running for the presidency of Austria. Even the little that was then known about his past was enough to trouble the World Jewish Congress and its secretary-general, Israel Singer, an American born in Austria, about the idea of Waldheim reigning over Austria. Professor Herzstein was commissioned to sift through various archives and uncover the truth. There had been rumors that linked Waldheim to the deportation of forty thousand Jews from Salonika. Herzstein found no evidence of this, but he did document the hidden, missing years that Waldheim had spent in the Balkans attached to the German army units suppressing the Partisans. The news was released by the World Jewish Congress in New York on March 3, 1986, in the midst of the Austrian presidential campaign.

Waldheim offered lame excuses. He had done nothing wrong. He had a clear conscience. He had nothing to do with deportations. He had held a minor bureaucratic job. He had never mentioned his duty in the Balkans because it was so unimportant. "I did my duty in a German uniform," he said. "So did most everyone else of my generation. In any case, no one can prove that I ever personally committed anything that could be called a crime." The accusations probably helped his campaign. Austrians closed ranks to defend him. Austrian Jews felt the wrath of his defenders. In Vienna, Nazi hunter Simon Wiesenthal, who defended Waldheim as innocent of war crimes, said that Austria had experienced its "biggest wave of anti-Semitism in 40 years." Waldheim led all candidates with 49.6 percent of the vote in the first round on May 4 and then swept to victory with 53.9 percent in the second round on June 8. When Waldheim was inaugurated in July, the United States embassy showed its displeasure by sending the deputy chief of mission rather than the ambassador or some high official from Washington like Vice President Bush to the ceremonies. Ironically, the representative was Felix S. Bloch, the diplomat later hounded out of the State Department on suspicion of passing documents to Soviet agents.

Almost a year after the inauguration, U.S. Attorney General Edwin Meese III placed the name of Waldheim on the U.S. "Watch List." That meant that the president of Austria would be prohibited from entering the United States—unless he received an exemption from the president or secretary of state. Terry Eastland, Meese's chief spokesman, said, "The evidence collected . . . establishes a prima facie case that Kurt Waldheim assisted or otherwise participated in the persecution of persons because of race, religion, national origin or political opinion." Most of the evidence uncovered by Herzstein was cited. But a Justice Department official added that Waldheim was responsible "for approving and disseminating propaganda, including the most vicious anti-Semitic tirades you could imagine." In response, President Waldheim told the Austrian people on television, "Let me say in all simplicity but also with clarity that cannot be misunderstood: I have a clear conscience."

In hopes of clearing Waldheim's name, Austrian Foreign Minister Alois Mock asked a Commission of Historians led by Swiss military historian Hans-Rudolf Kurz to investigate the case. After meeting for twenty-seven days, the commission concluded in 1988 that Waldheim had voluntarily joined two Nazi organizations, filled an important leadership role as an intelligence officer with the German army, prepared guidelines for the interrogation of captured Allied commandoes, and probably contributed to the deportation of prisoners and refugees in the Kozara campaign. The commission said that Waldheim bore no direct responsibility for war crimes, but he knew about the crimes, did nothing to prevent them, and failed to distance himself from them. The commission's report elicited a defense that admitted more than ever before. "Practically every soldier in the Balkans knew that reprisal actions were carried out," Waldheim said. "The fact that, as a staff officer, I was, here and there, better informed could be true, but I did not volunteer for the job. I pay the deepest respect to all those who offered resistance. But I ask for understanding for the hundreds of thousands who did not but were still not personally guilty. We certainly didn't do any more than try to survive the war. Yes, I admit I wanted to survive."

※ ❦

During the General Assembly meetings in the fall of 1994, Austrian Foreign Minister Mock handed a letter to Secretary-General Boutros Boutros-Ghali asking that the U.N. invite former Secretary-General Waldheim to attend the fiftieth anniversary celebrations in New York in October 1995. That raised the specter of the U.S. Immigration and Naturalization Service refusing entry to a guest of the U.N. for the celebrations. After several months of deliberations, Boutros-Ghali announced, without explanation, that Waldheim would not be invited for the fiftieth anniversary. To ease the embarrassment, however, Boutros-Ghali decided to cross Pérez de Cuéllar, the only other former secretary-general alive, off the list as well. Pérez de Cuéllar said he understood.

❧ 12 ❧

Zionism Is Racism

Bella Abzug, the irrepressible, tough-talking, stocky congresswoman from New York City, wearing a wide-brimmed, flowery hat as usual, rushed menacingly toward an Arab delegate at the First United Nations Conference on Women in the Tlateloco conference center of Mexico City in June of 1975. On behalf of the Arabs, Third World delegates had just proposed adding a clause to the U.N.'s first declaration of rights for women. That clause—its relevance to women rather remote—would call for the elimination of Zionism. Abzug, furious, muttering aloud that Zionism had nothing to do with women's issues, accosted the Arab delegate, who, like most Arab delegates at this conference, was a male.

Abzug thundered at him, "Why do you mix all these political issues into the conference?"

Raising his eyebrows slightly to show his disdain, the Arab replied with a question of his own. "What kind of conference do you think this is?"

"A conference on the equal rights of women," she shouted.

He laughed at her. "You can look for equal rights somewhere else," he said.

The amendment condemning Zionism filled many delegates from the industrialized countries with shivers of despair. They knew that a political battle over Israel would spoil all the good that might come out of the conference. At the least, it would hog most of the publicity. Feminists had worked hard to persuade the U.N. to convene a women's conference and felt frustrated and angry over the prospect of it shriveling beneath a furious conflict that had nothing to do with women's issues. Françoise Giroud, the French minister of women's affairs and a former newsmagazine editor, pleaded with the Third World delegates not to embroil themselves in Arab-Israeli issues. "Throughout history women have fought for men in their revolutions," she said, "and, when the revolutions were over, women have ended up cooking and making coffee again."

But the amendment, supported by the Third World and by the Soviet Union and its satellites, passed easily. The conference approved it by a vote of sixty-one to twenty-three, with twenty-five countries abstaining. "If Zionism is to be included in the final declaration," T. W. M. Tirikatene-Sullivan of New Zealand protested, "we cannot understand why sexism was not included." In the end, only the United States and Israel voted against the declaration as a whole, which, in its more relevant clauses, called for the elimination of "all obstacles that stand in the way of enjoyment by women of equal status with men." The conference, with American support, also passed a ten-year "world plan of action" — devoid of foolish political slogans — that simply proposed steps to improve the economic lot of women.

As the conference closed, some American delegates and U.N. officials begged reporters to emphasize all the good that had come out of the conference rather than the rancor over Zionism. Helvi Sipila of Finland, the highest-ranking woman official of the U.N. and the secretary-general of the conference, even tried to paint the Zionism amendment as a healthy sign for women. She argued lamely that the controversy showed governments now trusted their female diplomats to take up the same issues as male diplomats. Most news stories, however, stressed that the conference had foundered on an issue that had nothing to do with the rights of women.

Barbara M. White, a diplomat of ambassador rank assigned to the U.S. Mission to the United Nations and a delegate in Mexico City, shared the enthusiasm of those diplomats who felt that the women's conference had been an overall success despite the unpleasantness over Zionism. In a State Department cable summing up the conference, she wrote, "The U.S. achieved its principal objective: passage of a world plan of action. . . . As was inevitable, the conference was politicized to a degree . . . but not to such a degree that it failed to take action on the women's issues. . . . Our 'no' vote was based on unacceptable references to Zionism. . . . While regrettable that the 'no' vote was necessary, and particularly unfortunate that we were isolated in company only with Israel, I do not consider it of great importance to the outcome of the conference."

ᪿᪿ

Daniel Patrick Moynihan, the new American ambassador to the U.N., read the cable while in Geneva, allowed his anger to brim beyond control, and fired a sarcastic response to his staff in New York. A politician and professor of literary flourish, a thinker and writer of great insight, though afflicted with occasional flashes of obscurity, Ambassador Moynihan cabled that he could not understand how the United States had voted against the conference's declaration of human rights if it was so inspiring and, at the same time, how the declaration could be so inspiring if the United States had voted against it. He closed the cable with an aphorism from Benjamin Disraeli, the nineteenth-century British prime minister: "Few ideas are correct ones, and which they are none can tell, but with words we govern men."

"My cable was received with puzzlement at the U.S. mission in New York," Moynihan wrote later. "No one could understand what I had in mind. What I had in mind was that the Declaration of Mexico . . . was a totalitarian tract. . . . It was the language of a wholly politicized world, of a permanently mobilized society in which all interests were subservient to and ultimately placed in the service of the political objectives of the state. . . . But there was no one at the U.S. mission who seemed to have the vaguest perception of any of this. To the contrary, they had persuaded themselves that their job as diplomats was to get along with other diplomats. And so, like Ambassador White, they made their way from one conference to the next, painfully anxious to please, willingly associating themselves with the most outrageous assaults on principles they should have been defending." For Moynihan, the Zionism condemnation was not a small blot on the successful record of the conference but devastating proof of the conference's failure. If he had been at Mexico City, he would have shouted his contempt with such venom that no one would have been deluded into calling the conference a success.

The stage would thus soon be set for one of the great battle royals of the United Nations—Ambassador Moynihan versus the Third World. Moynihan, the future Democratic senator from New York, then forty-eight, had worked for both Democratic and Republican administrations in Washington and had developed a penchant in both for stirring up trouble with his words and ideas. As an assistant secretary of labor for policy planning and research in the Johnson administration in 1965, he published a prescient report, *The Negro Family: A Case for National Action,* which concluded that the instability of black family life was a root cause of many of the black social problems in the United States. He called for unemotional study of such problems as black illegitimacy and poor performance on intelligence tests. The Moynihan report was denounced roundly by many civil rights leaders, including the Reverend Martin Luther King Jr., and it took another twenty years before scholars would finally dust off the report and begin to heed Moynihan's admonition to examine these problems without cant. In 1970, while an assistant to the president for urban affairs, he sent a memo to President Nixon suggesting that the time had come to treat the issue of race with "benign neglect." The brouhaha over his report on the Negro family may have prompted his mood and the unfortunate phrase. Whatever the motivation, this remark, leaked to the press, proved hard to live down.

After serving as Nixon's ambassador to India, he attracted the attention of President Ford and Secretary of State Henry A. Kissinger in 1975 with a long magazine article, "The United States in Opposition." Moynihan argued that the Third World, stuffed with British Fabian Socialist ideas, had mounted an anti-American campaign to take wealth from the industrialized states and distribute it to the developing nations. It was time for the United States to go into opposition and stand up for itself and democracy against "a world order dominated arithmetically by the countries of the Third World." "It is time," he went on, ". . . that the American spokesman came to be feared in international forums for the truths he might tell." Above all, these truths would lay bare the crimes and injustices of the governments that dared to come to the U.N. and criticize the United States. Although Kissinger was lukewarm about the idea of a human rights zealot in the job, Ford offered Moynihan the post of ambassador to the U.N.

Moynihan resisted the appointment at first. Reeling off a catalogue of renowned ambassadors to the U.N., he said he had seen Adlai E. Stevenson humiliated, Arthur J. Goldberg betrayed, George W. Ball diminished, Charles Yost ignored, George Bush traduced, and John Scali savaged. He told Helmut Sonnenfeldt, the State Department counselor, that he would not tolerate being lied to by Secretary of State Kissinger. "You do not understand," Sonnenfeldt admonished Moynihan. "Henry does not lie because it is in his interest. He lies because it is in his nature." Moynihan accepted the appointment and was sworn in on June 30, 1975.

❧❧

As the Third World increased its numbers in the U.N., several leaders realized that if they and their colleagues held ranks, they could control debate and resolutions in the General Assembly. Of course, the General Assembly could inflict wounds only with words. But words, as Moynihan tried to explain in his cable to his staff, have a power of their own. The Third World still had no real authority within the Security Council. But the Security Council accomplished little these days, for it was paralyzed by the Cold War: the United States and the Soviet Union had the power to veto each other within the council or settle matters between themselves outside the council. The General Assembly had become the U.N.'s main field of battle.

The developing countries organized themselves in 1968 into a bloc called the Group of 77, but the bloc did not coalesce until the 1970s when its numbers climbed to well over a hundred, an overwhelming majority of the total membership of 142 in 1975. (U.N.

membership had grown from 51 in 1945 to 82 in 1958 to 115 in 1964 and would increase further to 158 in 1984 and 185 in 1995.) Despite the bloated size, the members still persisted in calling themselves the Group of 77. The hardening of their views came in the fourth non-aligned summit conference in Algiers in September 1973.

A Third World ideology formed in Algiers. The leaders adopted Mexican President Luis Echeverría Alvarez's call for a New International Economic Order that would break the monopolies of the transnational companies of the neo-imperialist powers. The Third World had justifiable economic grievances. The prices of manufactured imports kept rising while the prices of their exports of raw materials and farm produce for the most part fell. Industrialized markets kept Third World products out with high tariffs. But the Third World accepted all kinds of radical, unreasonable tenets in the new ideology: The Third World must look on the United States and the old imperial powers as its real enemies; the former colonies must struggle against the menace of cultural imperialism as hard as they once struggled against old-style imperialism; the poor countries must support the cartel of OPEC (the Organization of Petroleum Exporting Countries) as a demonstration of Third World power, no matter how much its price increases hurt poor countries; the Third World must rail against injustice in two pariahs—South Africa and Israel—and accept injustice everywhere else.

Perhaps most important, Third World countries agreed that they could not afford to split ranks on any of these issues, for fear of diluting their power. Rosemary Righter, who became an exacting critic of the U.N. as diplomatic correspondent for the *Sunday Times* of London in the late 1970s and 1980s, wrote in the 1990s that the Algiers summit "established Third World solidarity as a galvanizing political principle and provided it with its sacred texts." "Derogation from the scriptures in the pursuit of national self-interest became unthinkable," she went on. "Heresy might be entertained in private, but public departures from the faith were inconceivable." Algerian Foreign Minister Abdelaziz Bouteflika and other Algerian diplomats kept the Group of 77 united at sessions of the General Assembly. "They ran it with a whip hand," said W. Tapley Bennett Jr., Moynihan's deputy ambassador. "They'd have these meetings, and if they had trouble, they'd just stay until after midnight, after some of the more comfortable non-aligned had gone home. Then the Algerians would ram their measures through; they would tyrannize some of the milder Africans. I would say there was one year—and I don't think this is too much of an exaggeration—when in many ways the single most influential country at the U.N. was Algeria: more than ourselves, more than the Russians, more than the British, just because they had this vehicle at their beck and call, and used it."

In 1974, American Ambassador John Scali, the former Associated Press and ABC-TV News diplomatic correspondent, warned the Third World that their "tyranny of the majority" would work against them. Instead of browbeating countries like the United States into accepting its bidding, the Third World would drive the United States and others into negotiating their international problems outside the U.N. But the warning was not heeded.

Hypocrisy governed the tyranny of the majority. In 1972, for example, the government of Burundi, controlled by the minority Tutsi tribe, tried to eliminate the entire modern class of the majority Hutu people. All those with some education, government jobs, or money were to be killed. The government prepared lists of intended victims. A large number simply received a summons in an orderly way to report to the police at a certain time. The Tutsis then took them away for execution. The Hutus made up 85 percent of the population in this central African country, but they offered little resistance. The government probably killed somewhere between one hundred thousand and two hundred thousand Hutus that year. If the white tribe of South Africa had ever tried to eliminate the entire modern class of Zulus and Xhosas, the outcry at the U.N. would have been terrifying and heart-rending. Nothing, in fact, ever perpetrated by the oppressive white South African government compared with the genocide of Burundi. Yet the Burundi killings were never discussed at the General Assembly. The Burundi ambassador, in fact, had the effrontery to list himself as one of the sponsors of the annual resolutions condemning South Africa.

The hypocrisy was underscored for Moynihan in 1975 by the appearance of Field Marshal Idi Amin Dada, the president of Uganda, during the weeks of speechifying that open the annual session of the General Assembly. President of the Organization of African Unity that year, Amin was one of the great shames of Africa. He had much blood on his hands, imprisoning and executing his enemies with unabashed glee. He had deported every man, woman, and child of Asian descent in his country—almost two hundred thousand—in an act of cruelty not seen since Ferdinand and Isabella expelled the Jews from Spain in 1492.

His news conferences were jousts of bizarre hilarity. In a typical session with foreign correspondents in Entebbe in February 1973, for example, he began with words of admiration for Prime Minister Edward Heath of Britain. "Mr. Heath is my best friend," said Amin. "Great Britain has one of the best prime ministers. He is like Hitler. I like him very much. He is very strong." A German correspondent then asked him to talk a bit more about his admiration for Adolf Hitler. Amin, after all, had once sent a cable to Secretary General Kurt Waldheim praising Hitler for trying to exterminate the Jews. "Oh, no," Amin replied, "not Hitler. I meant Winston Churchill. Mr. Heath is like Winston Churchill. Please make that Churchill. I don't want to quarrel with my friends. I don't want to open a second-line front against me." Then he laughed heartily. An enormous man, six foot three and weighing more than 250 pounds, he always seemed like a country bumpkin out of place. If reporters did not know about the blood on his ham hands, they might have mistaken him for a peasant philosopher with a flair for comic, self-deprecating absurdity. Anyone who believed in Africa would wring his or her hands in shame at the despicable antics of Amin. Yet Africa refused to do anything about him until 1979 when President Julius Nyerere of neighboring Tanzania, one of Africa's f w leaders of conscience, sent troops into Uganda and drove the menace off his throne.

Amin's speech to the General Assembly, obviously written for him by an aide, was devoid of Amin's quaint bumpkinlike English. But the ideas were clearly his own. "The United States' persistent support for Israel stems from the sad history of colonization," he said. "The United States of America has been colonized by the Zionists who hold all the tools of development and power. They own virtually all the banking institutions, the major manufacturing and processing industries and the major means of communication, and have so much infiltrated the CIA that they are posing a great threat to nations and peoples which may be opposed to the atrocious Zionist movement. They have turned the CIA into a murder squad to eliminate any form of just resistance anywhere in the world. . . . How can we expect freedom, peace and justice in the world when such a powerful nation as the United States of America is in the hands of the Zionists? . . . I call for the expulsion of Israel from the United Nations and the extinction of Israel as a state." Ambassadors applauded Amin throughout the speech and stood up for a final ovation at the end. Since newspapers had grown tired of U.N. rhetoric, the speech was not widely reported.

Moynihan was not in the hall of the General Assembly but heard the speech by radio hookup in the U.S. mission across the street. No word of condemnation of the speech came from Washington, and Moynihan decided to tell the world himself what it ought to think about Marshal Amin and his strictures. In a couple of days, Moynihan addressed the AFL-CIO convention in San Francisco with scathing words, all written on the flight that morning from New York. "Every day, on every side, we are assailed [at the U.N.]," Moynihan said. "There are those in this country whose pleasure, or profit, it is to believe that our assailants are motivated by what is wrong about us. They are wrong. We are assailed because of what is right about us. We are assailed because we are a democracy. . . . It is no accident that on Wednesday His Excellency Field Marshal Al Hadji Amin Dada . . . called for 'the extinction of Israel as a state.' And it is no accident, I fear, that this 'racist murderer'—as one of our leading newspapers called him this morning—is head of the Organization of African Unity. For Israel is a democracy and it is simply the fact that despotisms will seek whatever opportunities come to hand to destroy that which threatens them most, which is democracy." The speech had not been cleared by the State Department.

A headline on the front page of the *New York Times* the next morning summarized the speech succinctly: "Moynihan Assails Uganda President—Delegate to U.N. Endorses Description of Amin as 'Racist Murderer.' " Third World delegates were furious at Moynihan. Ambassador Tiamiou Adjibade of Dahomey arose in the General Assembly to denounce Moynihan's speech as "verging on irresponsibility" and indicative of "a grave unawareness which is liable to vitiate dangerously relations between the United States and members of the O.A.U." To smooth relations, the staff of the U.N. mission prepared a press release for Moynihan stating that he had no quarrel with those words of Amin that "earned wide approval" but that he dissented from those that were "morally offensive." Moynihan refused to issue the release because "not one goddamn thing Amin had said had won my wide approval."

☙❧

The battle over Zionism then erupted in what is known as the Third Committee of the General Assembly. The Assembly divides its work among six committees, the Third dealing with "social, humanitarian and cultural issues." The Soviet Union, twenty-one Muslim countries, Cuba, Guinea, Mali, and Dahomey suddenly introduced a resolution in the Third Committee declaring that "Zionism is a form of racism and racial discrimination." Since racism was anathema to the United Nations and since Zionism was the name of the movement that established a homeland for the Jews in their biblical lands, Moynihan interpreted the resolution as denying the right of Israel to exist. He also looked on the resolution as part of a Soviet conspiracy to disrupt any moves toward peace in the Middle East. The sponsors, however, sold the resolution as a symbol of Third World solidarity, not as a step toward exterminating Israel or enhancing Soviet influence.

Despite the vote on Zionism at the women's conference in Mexico City and similar votes at other conferences, neither Washington nor Israel had expected the issue to come up in the U.N. General Assembly. But Moynihan quickly teamed with Israeli Ambassador Chaim Herzog to battle against the resolution. Herzog, the son of the chief rabbi of Ireland, had fought with the British army during World War II. After emigrating to Israel, he served as director of military intelligence and as military governor of the West Bank before his appointment as U.N. ambassador. Moynihan and Herzog successfully persuaded European ambassadors to back them and tried to peel African and Latin American ambassadors off the Third World majority. But they failed to get even enough support to postpone a vote. Moynihan believed that Arab "blandishments"—bribes in one way or another—kept many Third World countries in line, and he miscalculated by assuming that Latin American countries would feel obliged to join him because of their Jewish minorities.

In the Third Committee debate on October 17, Leonard Garment, one of Moynihan's deputies, warned the Third World, "I choose my words carefully when I say that this is an obscene act. . . . In fairness to ourselves we must also issue a warning. This resolution places the work of the United Nations in jeopardy." Sure of defeat, Herzog arose. "This . . . is a sad day for the United Nations," the Israeli ambassador said. "The Jewish people will not forget this scene nor this vote. We are a small people with a long and proud history. . . . We shall survive this shameless exhibition. But we, the Jewish people, will not forget . . . those who voted to attack our religion and our faith. We shall never forget." It is doubtful that many ambassadors listened closely to these speeches. The Third Committee passed the resolution by a vote of seventy to twenty-nine, with twenty-seven abstentions. Moynihan stepped over to the seat of Herzog and embraced him. "Fuck 'em!" Moynihan said. The delegates left to change for the annual ball of the United Nations Association at the Waldorf-Astoria. Secretary-General Waldheim, according to Moynihan, "waltzed with imperial *éclat.*"

Third Committee action is only a stage in the U.N. process. But, since every member of the General Assembly has the right to take part in a committee vote, the Third Committee seemed to presage final approval by the General Assembly, barring some sort of last-minute parliamentary maneuver. The General Assembly met a few weeks later, on November 10, 1975, to consider final passage of the resolution. Belgium, attempting a last-ditch parliamentary maneuver, tried to shelve the vote for the year but lost sixty-seven to fifty-five, with fifteen abstentions. Herzog made another impassioned speech that few of the majority bothered to hear. "It is symbolic that this debate, which may well prove to be a turning point in the fortunes of the United Nations and a decisive factor as to the possible continued existence of this Organization," he began, "should take place on November 10th. Tonight, 37 years ago, has gone down in history as *Kris-*

tallnacht or The Night of the Crystals. This was the night on the 10th of November 1938 when Hitler's Nazi storm troopers launched a coordinated attack on the Jewish community in Germany, burnt the synagogues in all its cities and made bonfires in the street of the Holy Books and Scrolls of the Holy Law and Bible." When he finished speaking, Herzog took a copy of the resolution in his hands and tore it in half.

The State Department let Moynihan make his speech without any clearance from Washington. Moynihan wrote it with the help of Norman Podhoretz, the editor of *Commentary* magazine, which had published Moynihan's article on the United States in opposition. After a few preliminary remarks, he issued a cry of defiance: "The United States rises to declare before the General Assembly of the United Nations, and before the world, that it does not acknowledge, it will not abide by, it will never acquiesce in this infamous act." "As this day will live in infamy," Moynihan went on, "it behooves those who sought to avert it to declare their thoughts so that historians will know that we fought here . . . and that while we lost, we fought with full knowledge of what indeed would be lost. . . . The terrible lie that has been told here today will have terrible consequences. Not only will people begin to say, indeed they have already begun to say, that the United Nations is a place where lies are told. Far more serious, grave and perhaps irreparable harm will be done to the cause of human rights." Moynihan closed by repeating his defiant beginning: The United States would never acknowledge, abide by, or acquiesce in this infamous act. The final vote followed the Third Committee vote closely. The U.N. General Assembly passed the resolution by a vote of seventy-two to thirty-five, with thirty-two abstentions.

Final passage of the resolution by the General Assembly was a disaster for the United Nations. Secretary-General Waldheim knew this but refused to condemn the resolution. "As the General Assembly, composed of representatives of sovereign states, is one of the main organs of the United Nations, it is not for the Secretary General publicly to criticize its decisions, even if he personally believes they are wrong," he explained years later. In their frustration, many critics began to wonder whether the confrontational tactics of Moynihan had contributed to the disaster. Some believed that a more soothing

American ambassador might have talked the Third World out of its foolishness.

The most damning analysis came from British Ambassador Ivor Richard, whom Moynihan described as "a hugely fat, thoroughly likeable, rather cynical politician." In a speech to the United Nations Association, Richard said that Europeans had not experienced the same furor over the Zionism vote as Americans. "This is not due to any lesser feeling on our part about the issue of anti-Semitism," he said. "It is more due to the fact that we have managed to avoid reacting to the vote in purely ideological and emotional terms." Looked at coldly, he said, the vote showed that the Third World was not a monolith. "The cracks are deepening," he said, "and the divisions becoming more apparent." He said that, despite the General Assembly vote, the notion that "Zionism is racism is an absurd proposition, rejected by most of the world." The vote should be seen in that context. In short, foolish acts by foolish bodies should not be taken seriously.

❧ ❧

Richard moved on to more personal grounds in his analysis. In an obvious allusion to Moynihan tactics, Ambassador Richard said, "I do not see it [the U.N.] as a confrontational arena in which to 'take on' those countries whose political systems and ideology are different from mine. I spend a lot of time preventing rows at the U.N. — not looking for them. Whatever else the place is, it is not the OK Corral, and I am hardly Wyatt Earp." The ambassador mentioned no names, but his audience knew who did act as if he were Wyatt Earp in the OK Corral.

Several other critics accepted the thesis that Moynihan's antics had lost the day. Seymour Maxwell Finger, a professor and a retired American diplomat who had worked for the U.S. Mission to the U.N. for fifteen years, suggested that Moynihan's "flamboyant, demagogic style" may have helped pass the resolution. "Several African representatives tried to get the Zionism issue sidetracked," Finger wrote, "but they told me that Moynihan's flamboyant statements handicapped their efforts. An African ambassador who had been Moynihan's classmate at the London School of Economics said privately that he and many of his colleagues resented the way the U.S. representative talked down to them. The Libyan ambassador, who led the drive to define Zionism as racism, told Ambassador Piero Vinci of Italy that he could never have succeeded if Moynihan had not provoked so much resentment among the African delegates." Rita A. Hauser, a Republican lawyer who had served as an American delegate to the U.N. Human Rights Commission, insisted that the resolution "could easily have been buried in the Third Committee." "Moynihan, instead, seized on it as a direct confrontational 'obscenity' . . . ," she went on. "By doing that he compelled the issue to the table, which to me is a folly when you don't have the votes."

Moynihan had staunch defenders as well. An avalanche of letters from the public endorsed his battle against the resolution. *Time* magazine wrote that "as a sort of ambassadorial fighting Irishman, Pat Moynihan has become an American pop hero." "He was controversial, you know, and he meant to be," said Deputy Ambassador Bennett. "He said things that needed to be said. We were being pushed around, and I think what he did was good. . . . I don't see myself obligated to help everybody in the world if they're busy kicking us in the teeth all the time." His defenders probably made more sense than his detractors. Anyone who watched the machinations of the U.N. Conference on Women, where American delegates did try in vain to soothe Third World delegates into reason, would have doubted Moynihan's chances of burying the Zionism resolution even if he had assumed the gentle guise of Florence Nightingale instead of Wyatt Earp.

Moynihan suspected at first that Secretary Kissinger was behind the British ambassador's speech and the campaign against his tactics. He felt less sure about this later and finally accepted Kissinger's assurances that he had not inspired the speech. But Moynihan still resented the secretary of state's failure to come to his defense. Feeling a growing lack of support from both Kissinger and President Ford, Moynihan resigned the following February and soon announced his candidacy for the U.S. Senate. His defender, Ambassador Bennett, said, "I think toward the end probably he realized that he was carrying it too far, and so I've often said, if people ask me, I think Pat Moynihan came at the right time and went at the right time."

❦

For the Third World, passage of the resolution amounted to a self-indulgent, adolescent act of folly. It accomplished nothing practical for the cause of the Palestinians, and it hurt the United Nations, the Third World's main vehicle for attention. The U.N. was now an object of ridicule in its host country, the one that paid 25 percent of its regular budget and more than 30 percent of its peacekeeping budget. Nothing in U.N. history so diminished the organization in the eyes of Americans as the vote for the Zionist resolution. The U.N. looked like a warren of Third World crazies, and some Americans wondered why their government spent any money on it at all.

Many governments voted for the resolution without thinking about the consequences and were shocked by the intense reaction. Mexico, for example, had voted for the resolution to help President Echeverría position himself as a champion of the Third World. He had embarked some months earlier on a campaign to succeed Kurt Waldheim as secretary-general. It was not a well-planned campaign; some of his aides were surprised to learn that the Security Council with its Big Power vetoes, not the Third World-controlled General Assembly, actually selected the secretary-general. Mexico had clearly voted for the resolution as a symbol of its solidarity with the Third World and as a sign of its independence from the United States.

Of the seventy-two countries that voted for the resolution, none was in a more vulnerable position than Mexico. Tourism was a major industry, accounting for 14 percent of Mexico's foreign exchange earnings, and most of the tourists came from the United States. As soon as the General Assembly passed the resolution, American Jewish groups announced a boycott of Mexico. American organizations canceled plans to hold conventions in Mexico out of deference to their Jewish members. There were thirty thousand hotel cancelations in a single week. President Echeverría suddenly put down his Third World shield and dispatched his Secretary of Foreign Relations,

Emilio O. Rabasa, to Israel to lay a wreath at the grave of Theodor Herzl, the founder of Zionism. At a three-hour meeting with American and Canadian Jewish leaders in Mexico City a month after the vote, Echeverría promised that Mexico would never vote that way again. But the pledge came too late. It would take years for Mexico to regain its tourist losses.

※ ❦

The low esteem for the U.N. in the 1970s would encourage some American interest groups to propose pulling out of it altogether. In the early 1980s, the conservative Heritage Foundation, the most influential think tank advising the Reagan administration, published a study concluding that "a world without the U.N. would be a better world." "What the United Nations has come to resemble most," wrote Burton Yale Pines, vice president of the foundation, "is a House of Mirrors at an amusement park. Like a House of Mirrors, the U.N. distorts reality — exaggerating some things, diminishing others and obscuring most." Pines wrote that "the United Nations is an organization out of control." He said it had become "exceedingly anti-U.S., anti-West and anti-free enterprise" and had betrayed "the spirit and substance of its own Charter." He accused it of failing "as a peacekeeper and protector of human rights" and said that "inefficiency, cronyism, high pay, lavish expense accounts and even corruption and illiteracy have become the all too common characteristics of the Secretariat and other U.N. bureaucracies."

This was an extreme view. Neither President Reagan nor the Congress ever seriously considered withdrawal. Yet, helped by the posturing of the Third World, the critics succeeded in fixing an image in the American mind of a blathering, incompetent, corrupt United Nations. This made it easy for the United States to punish the U.N. with delays and reductions in payment of annual assessments during the 1980s and to pull out of the U.N. Educational, Scientific, and Cultural Organization (UNESCO) with barely a whimper of protest. Even in the 1990s, when the U.N. won renewed support in the United States, that old image of blather, incompetence, and corruption still rushed to the fore whenever anything went wrong.

After Moynihan, both Presidents Ford and Carter tried a new approach to the U.N., an attempt at accommodation of the Third World. Ford appointed William W. Scranton, a soft-spoken former governor of Pennsylvania, and Carter appointed Andrew Young, the former congressman and former aide to the Reverend Martin Luther King Jr. Young was the first black to serve as American ambassador to the U.N., and he wooed the Third World assiduously, especially the Africans. Young, in fact, sometimes went overboard in identifying himself with the Third World—accusing his own country of detaining thousands of political prisoners, castigating Russia, Britain, and Sweden as racist, and meeting secretly with a representative of the Palestine Liberation Organization (PLO) at the U.N. The mood upset Republican civil rights lawyer Rita Hauser. "I went over to the mission once for a meeting during his time, and I was really shocked," she said. "There were Black Power posters on the walls, and there were Third World, PLO posters and all that stuff."

The good feelings generated by Young did not power any basic change in the attitude of the Third World. "In retrospect, I feel that we didn't get from the nonaligned generally in the General Assembly . . . the kind of reciprocity that we should have," said Young's deputy ambassador, James F. Leonard. "Most of them were genuinely grateful for the important things we did, but they tended to be prisoners of positions that were taken, in some cases, under direct Cuban and hostile non-aligned influence. . . . Very early in the Carter Administration, the nonaligned showed a weakness and a willingness to be led by their worst elements. I've held this against them ever since." In any case, the era of accommodation did not last very long. In 1981, President Reagan appointed Jeane J. Kirkpatrick, a neoconservative professor, as U.N. ambassador, and she felt it was time to return to the days of Pat Moynihan confrontation in the OK Corral.

❧❧

It took sixteen years before the General Assembly would revoke the resolution branding Zionism a form of racism and racial discrimination. The vote came less than a year after the victory over Iraq in the Persian Gulf War. It was a heady, exciting time when the U.N.

felt more powerful and focused than ever before, when the United States and Russia learned to act as one, when the nonaligned countries groped for a new purpose and even a new name. Intense pressure from President Bush and American Ambassador Thomas R. Pickering prepared the way for the vote. The General Assembly revoked the old, contentious resolution on December 16, 1991, by a vote of 111 to 25, with 13 countries abstaining. "It is more than time to consign one of the last relics of the Cold War to the dustbin of history," said Deputy Secretary of State Lawrence S. Eagleburger. After the vote, Senator Pat Moynihan of New York rushed onto the floor of the General Assembly, happily shaking hands with many delegates.

❧ 13 ❧

UNESCO:
Defenses of Peace
in the Minds of Men

When the United States lashed out
at UNESCO (the United Nations Educational, Scientific, and Cultural Organization) during the 1980s, it lashed out at a favorite son
turned prodigal. The Truman administration had demonstrated its
enthusiasm for the idea of UNESCO by sending prestigious American poet and playwright Archibald MacLeish to London in November 1945 to lead the American delegation to its organizing
conference. MacLeish, a former assistant secretary of state who had
crafted the wonderful preamble to the U.N. Charter in San Francisco a few months earlier, wrote the opening lines of the UNESCO
constitution as well: "Since wars begin in the minds of men, it is in
the minds of men that the defenses of peace must be constructed."

MacLeish looked on UNESCO as the intellectual steel for the
U.N. itself. In the preamble to the charter, his opening lines etched
the true purpose of the United Nations. The preamble began by declaiming that "we the peoples of the United Nations" are "determined to save succeeding generations from the scourge of war,
which twice in our lifetime has brought untold sorrow to mankind."

MacLeish believed that UNESCO—by educating the peoples of the world about each other—would help "root out the prejudice and ignorance which have separated them in the past." Alongside the U.N. Charter itself, UNESCO would serve as a second key for unlocking "the great dream of peace through understanding." Playwright and novelist J. B. Priestly, a member of the British delegation, called the London meeting "the most underrated conference in all history."

UNESCO opened for business at the Sorbonne in Paris a year later with delegates ironing out the final details. Former French Prime Minister Léon Blum presided at the session, proclaiming, "I have faith in UNESCO because I have faith in peace." Blum proposed MacLeish as the first director-general. But MacLeish begged off, for, he said, he "had run out of oxygen" and needed to return to academic life and his writing. British biologist Julian Huxley, the brother of novelist Aldous Huxley, was elected instead. MacLeish agreed to serve on the executive council, but resigned four months later, fearful, according to his biographer Scott Donaldson, that UNESCO might turn into "a bureaucratic educational operation."

UNESCO was not the only U.N. special agency in those early days. The U.N. revived the International Labor Organization (ILO), founded in 1919, and created the World Health Organization (WHO) and the Food and Agriculture Organization (FAO). Several international technical agencies dating from the nineteenth century—dealing with telecommunications, meteorology, and postal matters—were revived as well. And, most important, politicians and economists, meeting in Bretton Woods, New Hampshire, in 1944, a month before the Dumbarton Oaks conference, signed the treaties that set up the World Bank and International Monetary Fund (IMF), laying down a new financial system for the postwar world.

These agencies fulfilled some of the auxiliary goals of the U.N. Charter. Although the founders assumed that eliminating "the scourge of war" was the primary work of the U.N., they also set down several vague and less heroic goals like "promoting social progress and better standards of life in larger freedom." According to the charter, the U.N. would work toward economic and social development, health improvement, cultural and educational cooperation, and universal respect for human rights and fundamental freedoms. There was a theory behind all this, reflected in MacLeish's belief that UNESCO could help root out the underlying causes of war. The organizers hoped that the lessons learned in cooperating about matters like health, food, refugees, and telecommunications would make it easier for governments to cooperate on more complex and abrasive political issues like the prevention of war.

※彣

The mission and rationale of the agencies changed after the decolonization of the European empires during the 1960s. Third World governments demanded technical assistance from the U.N. as they struggled to escape their poverty. The specialized agencies proved an important source of experts. With their new influence and, in fact, new majority in the General Assembly, the new governments persuaded the industrialized nations to join them in creating the U.N. Development Program (UNDP), which used funds donated by the rich nations to fund technical assistance programs of the agencies. The Third World also created the U.N. Conference on Trade and Development (UNCTAD) to articulate theories of economic development.

With the Security Council moribund as a result of the Cold War and the incompetence that allowed the Arab-Israeli issue to slip into the hands of other peacemakers, the United Nations took on the guise in the 1970s and 1980s of an organization more concerned with economic and social issues than peace and war. U.N. boosters would defend the organization from criticism by pointing to its accomplishments in health, refugee care, literacy, child labor standards, and the like. "The United Nations has had some success," Rosemary Righter, chief editorialist of the *Times* of London, wrote dismissively in her 1994 book, *Utopia Lost*, "in persuading the broader public that it had another face—the UNICEF Christmas card face—to compensate for paralysis in the Security Council and the acrimony of General Assembly debates." By citing UNICEF (the U.N. Children's Fund) as her image, Righter mocked the best known of all U.N. programs because of its seeming success in healing and feeding children and its appeals for contributions through the worldwide sale of Christmas cards. In any case, no matter what the founders intended, the U.N., through its agencies and special programs, spent many times more money on social and economic issues than on peacekeeping and the prevention of war.

Egged on by increasing frustration over their failures in economic development, Third World governments began to look on the U.N. system of agencies and special programs in the 1970s not just as a resource for technical assistance but as a vehicle to change and radicalize the debate over economic development. Expanding on the ideas of Argentine economist Raúl Prebisch, the first secretary-general of the U.N. Conference on Trade and Development, Third World governments, joined by the Soviet Union and its satellites, stridently advocated a New International Economic Order.

Prebisch insisted that the free-market system doomed the Third World to the sale of commodities at decreasing prices while the cost of manufactured imports from the industrialized world increased in price. To break this cycle, the New International Economic Order— extolled by Mexican President Luis Echeverría during his failed campaign to succeed Kurt Waldheim as secretary-general—called for a transfer of resources from the industrialized to the developing worlds by smashing the hold of the transnational corporations, elevating the price of commodities through Third World cartels, protecting neophyte industry in the Third World, and opening Europe and North America to Third World products. These demands, requiring strong government interference in the market, rushed headlong into the barrier of free-world ideology—a barrier reinforced when conservative ideologues British Prime Minister Margaret Thatcher and American President Ronald Reagan assumed office in 1979 and 1981.

❧

The strident demands accomplished little beyond irritating the governments of the industrialized countries. Governments that together paid 75 percent of a budget chafed whenever they were outvoted on Third World economic issues by a two-thirds majority that together paid less than 1 percent of that budget. Nor did it seem to make sense when countries with a total population of only ninety million could outvote countries with a total population of almost five billion. The irritation was exacerbated when the Third World countries began to inject political vendettas into U.N. conferences on social and economic issues—like the foolish condemnation of Zionism at the First U.N. Conference on Women in 1975. The United States withdrew from the International Labor Organization (ILO) in 1977 because of its obsession with "political issues which are quite beyond the competence and mandate of the organization." The Americans returned in 1980, however, when the ILO promised to abstain from political adventurism.

The irritation led Americans and Europeans to look more closely and coldly at the proliferation of U.N. agencies and programs. The original charter, bolstered by Third World pressures, spawned an enormous number of agencies, programs, and special bodies with a dizzying array of acronyms that made up what bureaucrats called "the U.N. family." By the 1990s, the U.N. family had nineteen specialized agencies (counting the World Bank and IMF), fifteen programs, and seven smaller "special bodies." The patriarch—the traditional New York–headquartered U.N. comprising the Security Council, the General Assembly, the Economic and Social Council, and the secretary-general and his staff—was dwarfed in size and spending by all the other U.N. family operations. At the end of 1991, for example, almost three times as many bureaucrats worked in the various agencies and programs (thirty-nine thousand) as in the U.N. Secretariat (fourteen thousand). These statistics, moreover, did not include the staffs of the World Bank and the International Monetary Fund (IMF), for these two agencies had become so independent of the U.N. over the years that they were usually excluded from the official charts listing "the U.N. family" (see Appendix III).

Righter, echoing many critics, wrote that the U.N. system defied logical analysis. Much of the U.N. family was out of control, with the agencies acting like separate fiefdoms often led by arrogant barons. The U.N. Economic and Social Council, under the charter, had the responsibility of bringing all the specialized agencies and programs "into relationship with the United Nations"—supervising and presumably controlling them in some way. But this proved impossible. Although they filed reports with the Economic and Social

Council, the agencies were autonomous bodies governing their own memberships and budgets. The U.N. secretary-general could neither appoint nor fire their directors-general.

In theory, the secretary-general and U.N. headquarters had more control over a group of other programs like the U.N. Development Program (UNDP), the U.N. Children's Fund (UNICEF), and the Office of the U.N. High Commissioner for Refugees (UNHCR). They were subsidiary bodies of the U.N. with budgets provided by the General Assembly or by voluntary contributions from governments and the public. Unlike what happened in the specialized agencies, the secretary-general appointed the directors of these subsidiary bodies, and the General Assembly had the power to alter their work or even abolish them. In practice, however, these programs usually operated much like the specialized agencies—without interference from the General Assembly or the secretary-general.

The system lent itself to waste, corruption, and bureaucratic tyrannies. Europeans and Americans, annoyed by the Third World's manipulation of the U.N., started to take notice of its institutional faults. Journalists snooped around and came up with numerous articles about mismanagement and worse at the United Nations. These were bolstered by U.S. government and congressional reports demanding reform. Most anecdotes about flagrant abuses came out of the agencies, not out of the Secretariat in New York, but the public did not make any distinction between the U.N. and its "family." Such articles still appeared in the 1990s in newspapers as important as the *Washington Post* and the *Sunday Times* of London.

No one could doubt the tales of bloated bureaucracies, graft, and waste. Yet it sometimes seemed that the journalists, forgetting the multinational and multiethnic character of the U.N., wrote as if nothing would satisfy them except a bureaucracy staffed by the kind of efficient and Calvinist civil servants that only a country like Switzerland could produce. Moreover, ethnocentrism ruled the journalistic definition of waste; official U.N. publications with ludicrous titles were often derided by contemptuous American journalists who forgot that a subject of no importance to them might prove of vital importance to someone elsewhere in the world.

Nevertheless, there is no doubt that many grievous and uncontrollable faults besmirched the agencies, and UNESCO was a prime offender. A cold and tough American attitude—shorn of patience or tolerance—was renewed in the early 1980s when Jeane Kirkpatrick, President Reagan's ambassador to the U.N., decided to emulate Daniel Patrick Moynihan as a scold of the Third World. Although the Heritage Foundation—the think tank with the most influence on the Reagan administration—declared it time to get out of the U.N. altogether, Ambassador Kirkpatrick never advocated so foolish or controversial a step. But the Reagan administration, spoiling for a fight with the irascible, unreasonable, smug Third World, decided to take on UNESCO and make of it a pitiful example. The battle was as effortless for the Reagan administration as the invasion of Grenada.

🌿🌿

Two issues made UNESCO an easy target for the Reagan administration: the New World Information and Communication Order and the stewardship of Amadou-Mahtar M'Bow of Senegal, the stubborn, egotistical director-general of UNESCO. The cries for a new information order came out of an obvious imbalance. Information and communication were monopolized by the industrialized West. The United States and Europe, for example, controlled the worldwide wire services: the Associated Press (American), United Press International (American), Reuter (British), and Agence France Presse (French). Almost every newspaper—except those of the Soviet bloc—took one of these services. The rest of the world saw the problems and accomplishments and failures of the Third World through the eyes of Americans and Europeans. Third Worlders, in fact, saw other Third Worlders through these same eyes. Advocates of the new information order insisted that the monopoly of news agencies often ignored or distorted news from Africa, Asia, and Latin America. The critics also complained that the West had similar monopolies on television, movies, records, book publishing, and other forms of communication.

The New World Information and Communication Order fit neatly into the New International Economic Order advocated by the Third World. Communications was an industrialized product like any other controlled by the transnational corporations, and Third World countries needed to defend themselves against it. Moreover, Third World leaders believed they were handicapped in trying to persuade others of the justice of their views when information about these views were funneled through channels controlled by the industrialized countries. If the poor countries broke this monopoly, they might be able to win more converts to their cause.

These information and communications problems outlined by the Third World were difficult to deny. When the Third World proposed a few ameliorative measures—like American and European funding of a new wire service to report Third World news—the industrialized governments agreed to help. But the proponents of the new information order had a panoply of more radical solutions, and these infuriated the major newspapers and wire services of the democratic countries of Europe and North America.

The main trouble was context. The proposals were put forward mainly by autocratic Third World governments joined by the Soviet Union and its Eastern European satellites. These countries kept their own newspapers under their thumbs and routinely harassed and expelled foreign correspondents trying to report the news. It was hard to credit their sincerity. For this reason, Moynihan believed that the issue should have been squashed immediately. "If we had any sense in these matters," he said, "the minute the subject arose in UNESCO, we would have said there is nothing to discuss because there are only about 35 countries which have freedom of the press, and the rest don't."

The examples of Third World and Soviet contempt for the foreign press were innumerable. Ugandan soldiers murdered Nicholas Stroh of the *Washington Star* in 1971, probably under the direct orders of Idi Amin. In 1975, Peru expelled AP Lima correspondent Edith Lederer, giving her a week's notice. In 1976, the Philippines refused to allow Arnold Zeitlin, an AP correspondent based in Manila, to return to his office from a trip abroad because his reporting had been "endangering the security and prestige" of the country. In 1977, Pakistani police detained Lewis Simons of the *Washington Post* at Lahore airport for 32 hours after he tried to enter the country and then expelled him as "a banned person." The Soviet Union arrested

Los Angeles Times Moscow correspondent Robert Toth in 1977, accused him of collecting political and military secrets, interrogated him for several days, and threatened to bar him from leaving the country as scheduled before bowing to pressure from Washington and relenting. These examples are culled from scores of similar Third World and Soviet bloc incidents in the 1970s. No matter what they said in the councils of UNESCO, countries like Nigeria and Ethiopia, which cleared their capitals of all foreign correspondents in 1977, did not want better reporting of their activities; they wanted no reporting.

In this context, it was difficult for American and European editors to accept any proposal put forth by these enemies of a free press, no matter how high-minded or innocuous the rhetoric sounded. Proposals to license journalists, ostensibly for their own protection, were viewed as heavy-handed attempts to control reporting by refusing licenses to those journalists deemed undesirable by a government. Editors suspected the motives of politicians who insisted that newspapers and magazines should be obligated to print the replies of all those who felt that news articles "had seriously prejudiced their effort to strengthen peace . . . , to promote human rights, or to counter racialism, apartheid and incitement to war." Calls for the media to "contribute to promoting the just cause of peoples struggling for freedom and independence" sounded like dictums from on high about what and what not to print.

Director-General M'Bow allowed UNESCO to serve as the proving ground and battleground for the New World Information and Communication Order. The phrase was coined at a UNESCO meeting of mass communications experts in Montréal in 1969. The strongest statement on the issue, however, came not from UNESCO but from a symposium on information convened by the Non-Aligned Movement in Tunis in 1976. The conference's final report said that the monopolized media "tend to distort news from the non-aligned countries, either by falsifying it or by remaining totally silent in the many cases of success achieved in the different fields by peoples of the non-aligned countries." As a result, the report went on, "it is the duty of the non-aligned countries and other developing countries to change the situation and obtain the decolonization of information and initiate a new international order of information." These words brimmed with the notion that sovereign governments have the right to control the flow of information in and out of their countries.

None of the official UNESCO pronouncements—those approved by its entire membership—ever had the same stridency as those coming out of the Tunis symposium. UNESCO, for example, never officially supported the licensing of journalists. In 1978, the General Conference of UNESCO issued a declaration stating that "the mass media have an important contribution to make to the strengthening of peace and international understanding and in countering racialism, apartheid and incitement to war." The declaration was so watered down that in the end even the United States gave it reluctant support, hoping that this would end the matter. But M'Bow and the UNESCO Secretariat kept the issue alive in the late 1970s and early 1980s through a series of symposiums, committees, and reports on the new information order.

The debate often limped in confusion. "I was asked this morning if I could define the NWICO [New World Information and Communication Order] in fifty words or less," Professor George Reedy of Marquette University, the former White House press secretary for President Lyndon B. Johnson, told a symposium in 1984, "and I had to answer that I could not define it in fifty thousand words or less. . . . We have had so many years of discussion in which everybody has turned their backs to each other and talked to the walls."

American and European journalists finally lost patience with the jabbering and interference. The debate itself was harmful, journalists believed, for it encouraged Third World governments to justify and intensify their harassment of foreign correspondents. A warning came from the *New York Times* in 1980. "American journalism values its freedom from official scrutiny and control more than it values UNESCO, or even the United Nations," the *Times* said in an editorial. In 1981, a conference of Western journalists organized at Talloires, France, by the World Press Freedom Committee and Tufts University declared that the "time has come within UNESCO and other intergovernmental bodies to abandon attempts at regulating news content and formulating rules for the press."

Americans like to personalize and demonize their enemy in
war, and the autocratic Amadou-Mahtar M'Bow made that easy to
do in the war against UNESCO. His career before coming to
UNESCO, however, had hardly seemed demonic. M'Bow, fifty-nine
years old when elected to his second six-year term as UNESCO
director-general in 1980, spoke only the Wolof language when he entered the French primary school in Louga in the arid peanut-growing
area of eastern Senegal in 1929. His early school days in one of the
poorest areas of Africa came during the worldwide Depression, and
he once told an interviewer, "For me hunger is no rhetorical expression. One must have lived through it to understand its horror." Joining first the French army and then the Free French forces of Charles
de Gaulle during World War II, he ended the war as the first African
technical sergeant in the French air force. He remained in Paris after
the war, earning a degree in tropical geography from the University
of Paris and winning election as president of the Association of African Students in Paris and as secretary-general of the Federation of
Black African Students in France.

Returning to Senegal in the 1950s, he was soon selected by the
French colonial government to direct the UNESCO-sponsored Department of Fundamental Education, a program for rural schooling.
Active in the political party led by Leopold Senghor, M'Bow was
named minister of education and culture in the pre-independence,
self-government cabinet of 1957. He resigned a year later, however,
because he regarded Senghor as too moderate in his dealings with
the French. Senghor had decided to campaign in a referendum for
approval of President de Gaulle's 1958 constitution that would keep
self-governing colonies like Senegal in some kind of association with
France. M'Bow agitated for Senghor to follow the radical Sekou
Toure of Guinea and campaign against the constitution and for independence. Senghor proved wiser than both M'Bow and Toure.
When Guinea rejected the constitution in the referendum, a furious
de Gaulle thrust Guinea into immediate independence and crippled
it by withdrawing all French equipment, administrators, specialists,
and financial aid at once. The French even ripped out the telephone
lines and destroyed the prison records. De Gaulle, meanwhile, lavished aid on Senghor's Senegal, which voted for association with

France, and then rewarded him with a smooth transition to independence two years later.

Politically weak, the once radical M'Bow taught history and education at Dakar and Saint Louis in Senegal for a few years and then, back in favor with the immensely popular President Senghor, returned to the cabinet as minister of education in 1966. Forced to tighten the budget in a recession brought on by plummeting peanut prices, M'Bow slashed subsidies for lycée and university students. Rampaging students mobbed the streets of Dakar in protest, and the violence prompted Senghor to move M'Bow to another cabinet post. M'Bow, sure his political career was now over, accepted an offer from Director-General Rene Maheu in 1970 to join UNESCO as assistant director-general for education. In 1974, M'Bow succeeded Maheu, a Frenchman, and assumed the honor of serving as the first black African chief of a major U.N. agency.

Once in power, M'Bow caught the imperious disease afflicting many of the all-powerful U.N. agency directors. He ordered the construction of a lavish penthouse for himself on top of U.N. headquarters on the left bank of Paris. "Am I supposed to live in a hut in the middle of Paris just because I am an African?" he said when questioned about the penthouse. He courted the loyalty of Third World members of the UNESCO executive board by plying them with fellowships and cultural trips. He dealt harshly with dissent. When a representative from the U.N. Development Program criticized UNESCO for failing to finish some technical assistance projects on time, M'Bow cut him off at a meeting of the UNESCO executive board. "I'm not going to allow everybody to criticize everything," he said. He banished from his way those bureaucrats who differed with him. When he could not fire them because of their protection as international civil servants, he kept them on the payroll but gave them absolutely nothing to do.

M'Bow identified himself and UNESCO with the New World Information and Communication Order at a time when the Third World was luxuriating in its power at the U.N. He was not prescient enough to see how this could hurt UNESCO. Nor was he wise enough to sense something terribly discordant in an information program that alienated all the major editors in Europe and the United

States. He began to describe attacks on the information order and UNESCO as personal attacks upon himself. In 1983, when Gregory J. Newell, the young and inexperienced assistant secretary of state for international organizations, and Jean Gerard, the American ambassador to UNESCO, informed him that the United States would not accept an increase in spending in the latest budget, M'Bow angrily warned the Americans to stop treating him "like an American black who has no rights." Newell and Gerard stormed out of the meeting, the incident solidifying Newell's attitude as the leading advocate within the State Department for withdrawal.

Critics accused M'Bow of mismanagement. The *Economist*, the British newsmagazine, described the UNESCO staff in 1983 as "trampled by a mixture of nepotism, maladministration, reverse racism, and an apparently incorrigible tilt toward the hardliners of the Third World." Rodolfo Stavenhagen told the *Economist* that he had just quit his job as head of the UNESCO social science division because of "the atmosphere of distrust, denunciation, and a sort of bureaucratic terrorism which has led to total intellectual suffocation."

In December of 1983, Secretary of State George P. Shultz announced that the United States would withdraw from UNESCO at the end of the next year unless the agency reformed itself. A State Department memorandum cited as grievances UNESCO's anti-Western tone, its advocacy for a new information order that threatened "a free press and a free market," its receptivity to "statist, collectivist solutions," and its rejection of sound management procedures.

Assistant Secretary Newell and Ambassador Gerard insisted that their grievances were not personal—M'Bow himself was not the problem. "Neither his resignation nor his staying is the issue," said Gerard. There was a good deal of truth in this position. The Reagan administration wanted to punish the Third World and the United Nations far more than it wanted to punish some African bureaucratic tyrant. Washington believed that previous administrations had allowed the anti-Americanism of the Third World to go too far. As American Ambassador Kirkpatrick told a congressional committee, "The United States sunk slowly to a position so impotent and isolated

. . . that we could not even protect ourselves against the attacks of arrogant dictators who are dependent on us for help." As part of its belittling of the U.N., the Reagan administration wielded the power of its purse. Washington withheld a percentage of its annual assessment of dues for the regular U.N. budget to pressure the organization into making administrative reforms. The administration also stopped contributing money to the U.N. Population Fund as punishment for funding projects in a country like China that had an active abortion program. The Reagan administration believed that its policies had reduced the level of anti-American noise in the General Assembly and that its withdrawal from UNESCO wold prove the most potent sign of its tough campaign against the U.N.

But a resignation by M'Bow—the ultimate reform, after all— might have made it difficult for Washington to implement its threat. That, in fact, was probably the only chance for UNESCO to prevent the loss of its most important member state, the loss of 25 percent of UNESCO's budget. But M'Bow, while willing to order a few lukewarm reforms, had no intention of resigning. He looked on himself as the champion of the Third World, taking on its most powerful adversary. In a sense, he was waging the battle that he had once tried to persuade Leopold Senghor to wage against Charles de Gaulle.

But 1984 proved a public relations disaster for M'Bow. He hired an American firm to lobby in Washington for UNESCO at a cost of fifteen thousand dollars a month plus expenses. The funds came out of a special account filled by the agency's share of proceeds from a UNESCO record album marketed every year in France for the benefit of cancer research. While 90 percent did reach the French Cancer Research Society, 10 percent ended up in UNESCO's special fund. The French public was furious when news accounts revealed that M'Bow used 10 percent of the profits on cancer benefit sales to lobby the U.S. government. The U.S. General Accounting Office issued its assessment of UNESCO during the year, finding lax supervision, inadequate control of the payroll, and overconcentration of power in the hands of M'Bow. When two UNESCO internal task forces completed their reports on the problems of UNESCO, M'Bow released the report on management reform but not the one on program reform. Critics suspected that the suppressed report proposed dropping the new information order. M'Bow refused to talk to the press at all during 1984.

The director-general, however, did write a strange yet revealing letter to *Le Monde* in which he likened himself to the Jews who were hounded and finally murdered by the Nazis and their allies in the 1930s and 1940s. "Yesterday the anti-Semites belittled the Jews for their supposed greed, their traditions, their clannishness and even their caftan coat," M'Bow wrote. "Today the journalist of *Le Monde* attributes to me . . . an eagerness for gain, a guilty penchant for my roots, a spirit of favoritism towards friends and politicians of my continent." A *Le Monde* article had described his wearing of a traditional Senegalese robe—the grand boubou—on ceremonial occasions. M'Bow said that *Le Monde* had brought up the robe "just the way people before World War II would bring up the side curls of Orthodox Jews."

As threatened, the Reagan administration withdrew from UNESCO at the end of 1984. It did so to the general approval of American editorial writers, still smarting under the attacks by the New World Information and Communication Order. Britain and Singapore followed the Americans out of UNESCO a year later. "It is sad," said Timothy Raison, the British minister of state for overseas development, "that an organization which began with such high hopes . . . should have gone so wrong." George Foulkes, a member of the Labour Party opposition, lamented that the move by Prime Minister Thatcher's government was "a kick in the teeth for the Third World."

After the American withdrawal, many European diplomats and UNESCO officials believed that the resignation or dismissal of M'Bow was the only hope for an eventual return of the United States and a future for the agency. In October 1986, M'Bow appeared to give in to the pressure when he announced, "I am not going to ask for a third term." That sounded like he planned to retire at the end of his second term in November 1987, but some skeptics insisted that the phrasing left him enough room to make the race if others asked him. In a rare reception for reporters at UNESCO, he said his candidacy did not matter anyway. "There will be a North-South crisis inside UNESCO," he said, using the jargon for a conflict between the industrialized and developing nations, "no matter who is director general." In the end, the skeptics proved right, and M'Bow, pleading the entreaties from various governments, announced that he would seek a third term after all.

On the eve of the election meetings of the fifty-member executive board in October 1987, West Germany and Switzerland said they would quit if M'Bow won a third term. Japan, the Netherlands, and Canada indicated they would follow. M'Bow, nevertheless, expected to put together enough Third World and Communist bloc votes to win. In fact, M'Bow led all candidates on the first three ballots, coming within three votes of the required twenty-six-vote majority. He failed only because the Communist votes, in a crushing surprise, were not cast in his favor. This was the fruit of the "new thinking" that Soviet leader Mikhail S. Gorbachev promised in his foreign policy. His aides explained to American reporters that the United States and the Soviet Union really had more in common with each other than either had with the Third World. Abandoned by the Communists, M'Bow withdrew, accusing the Western countries of returning "to the methods of blackmail, disinformation and also pressure of all sorts." The executive board selected Federico Mayor, a biochemist and former Spanish minister of education, as M'Bow's successor.

※ ※

UNESCO had become so marginal an agency for Americans that the significance of M'Bow's defeat and Mayor's election was little noted at the time. It was the strongest sign that the Cold War was coming to an end at the United Nations and that the Security Council could now start acting in a way that the founders of the U.N. somewhat intended. The United States had laid low one of the major agencies of the U.N. in the mid-1980s, but this paled next to the news that the Soviet Union was now ready to join the United States in trying to order the world. Although the Reagan administration intended to deliver a body blow to the U.N. with the withdrawal, the UNESCO episode actually ended with a good deal of hope for a revitalized United Nations.

Mayor took over UNESCO and tried hard to entice the United

States back. He dropped the New World Information and Communication Order, reduced staff, reformed management, and turned the agency's attention to matters that would attract an American audience, like the history of the Nazi Holocaust against the Jews. By 1993, a Clinton administration task force, made up of representatives of the major departments of the U.S. government dealing with foreign affairs, recommended that the United States return to UNESCO. But President Bill Clinton, evidently concerned about pockets of opposition in Congress, hesitated, unwilling to risk a political battle over an issue as insignificant as rejoining UNESCO. These pockets became far more powerful in 1995 when the Republicans took over both the Senate and the House of Representatives. As the fiftieth anniversary celebrations approached, Clinton had still not taken the United States back into UNESCO.

❧ 14 ❧

Javier Pérez de Cuéllar and the End of the Cold War

In the fall of 1982, after a few months on the job, sixty-two-year-old Javier Pérez de Cuéllar, assisted by a long-time associate, Undersecretary-General Brian Urquhart, issued his first report as secretary-general on the work of the United Nations. No international civil servant could rival this pair in their clearheaded understanding of the organization. They never let their fierce attachment to the U.N. and its history get in the way of their cold eye. Hardly anyone outside the U.N. read the reports of secretaries-general in those days. The U.N. with all its cant and posturing had become too boring. But, if they had read Pérez de Cuéllar's first report, they would have been astounded at its frankness.

Pérez de Cuéllar described the Security Council as "unable to take decisive action to resolve international conflicts." He said that its resolutions, even when passed unanimously, "are increasingly defied or ignored by those that feel themselves strong enough to do so." The founders intended the council to employ stern measures to ensure world peace but, the new secretary-general lamented, alluding to the Cold War, "the prospect of realizing such measures is now deemed

almost impossible in our divided international community." He concluded, "We are perilously near to a new international anarchy."

The secretary-general said that his most urgent goal was to render the United Nations capable of carrying out its primary function—"collective action for peace and security." "Without such a
system," he said, "the world community will remain powerless to
deal with military adventures which threaten the very fabric of international peace." Yet the Security Council was so impotent that most
countries in conflict no longer bothered to take their troubles there.
"The Council too often finds itself on the sidelines at a time when
. . . its possibilities should be used to the maximum," he said.

Pérez de Cuéllar pleaded with the United States and the Soviet
Union to make the Security Council work. "Whatever their relations
may be outside the United Nations," he said, "the permanent members . . . share a sacred trust that should not go by default owing to
their bilateral differences." Without much evident conviction, he
called on all countries to strengthen the United Nations in practical
ways so that it could be used "as an essential institution in a stormy
and uncertain world."

In the fall of 1991, a few months before his retirement, the seventy-one-year-old Pérez de Cuéllar issued his final report as secretary-
general on the work of the United Nations. He did so this time
without the help of Urquhart, who had retired a few years earlier.
The mood of Pérez de Cuéllar was so optimistic now that the contrast with his first report seemed almost histrionic. Instead of invoking
international anarchy, he now hailed the "renaissance" of the U.N.,
"the end of the long season of stagnation." The world was transforming itself day by day, and "at no point in this time of tumult has the
United Nations failed to keep pace with historic change." He cata-
logued a series of success stories—and of significant innovations in
peacekeeping. While "some discordant notes . . . are still audible,"
he said, "the effectiveness of the United Nations can no longer be in
doubt."

The outgoing secretary-general felt the need to deflate some of
his own euphoria. "A Panglossian frame of mind is hardly appropriate for the United Nations," he said. While it was true that the Security Council was cured of paralysis, he went on, "the United Nations

is now entering uncharted territories and undertaking tasks of a kind unforseen in its original design." But he could not suppress his mood completely. "None of these difficulties," he concluded, ". . . diminishes the metamorphosis of the United Nations." Its newfound potency, he believed, "testifies to the resilience of the human spirit."

❧

Pérez de Cuéllar was not alone, of course, in dramatic metamorphosis of rhetoric during the 1980s. President Ronald Reagan had assumed office in 1981 with a dark and forbidding image of his enemy. Describing the goal of the Soviet Union as a one-world Communist state, Reagan told his first news conference, "The only morality they recognize is what will further their cause, meaning they reserve to themselves the right to commit any crime, to lie, to cheat, in order to attain that." In a speech to the National Association of Evangelicals in Orlando, Florida, in 1983, he delivered his famous characterization of the Soviet Union as "the evil empire." Declaiming that the Communists since Lenin had preached "everything is moral that is necessary for the annihilation of the old exploiting social order," Reagan said it was wrong to blame both sides equally for the arms race during the Cold War. To do so, he said, was "to ignore the facts of history and the aggressive impulses of an evil empire." Those who "simply call the arms race a giant misunderstanding," Reagan insisted, remove themselves "from the struggle between right and wrong, good and evil."

If there ever was an "evil empire," the walled fortress of the Kremlin lay at the heart of it, shadowed with brutal history from dark medieval princes and Ivan the Terrible to Joseph Stalin. Ronald Reagan entered that fortress for the first time on a dazzling, sunlit Moscow afternoon in May of 1988. But Reagan stepped into the heart of the evil empire without any tremulous foreboding. Beaming with his patented smile of good feelings, he eagerly grasped the hand of Soviet leader Mikhail S. Gorbachev within the ornate splendor of the Hall of Saint George in the Great Palace of the Kremlin. It was the fourth summit meeting of the two powerful statesmen.

A couple of days later, Gorbachev guided Reagan on a walking

tour of Red Square and the Kremlin grounds. The president put his
arm around Gorbachev in Red Square and mused, "I'm glad we are
standing here together like this." A few minutes later, Gorbachev led
Reagan to a thirty-nine-ton cannon dating from 1586 that stands in a
plaza on the Kremlin grounds. A handful of reporters and a Soviet
television crew clustered around the cannon when the two leaders
approached. "Do you still believe you are in the evil empire?" a British journalist called out. "No," Reagan replied, surely and quickly.
"Why not?" several reporters asked. Reagan hesitated, leaned his
head to one side, and thought a bit. Gorbachev tried to prompt him.
"Are you happy with that concept?" he asked in Russian. Reagan
then said to the reporters, "You are talking about another time, another era." Only five years had passed since his Orlando speech.

A little more than a year later, on the night of November 9,
1989, the Berlin Wall, that most solid and disheartening of all sym-
bols of the Cold War, would fall, as East Germany opened the gates
and tens of thousands of joyous Berliners hacked away at the brick
and its graffiti. The twentieth century, a century of extraordinary moments, some of them so terrible and cruel as to defy imagination,
hurtled to its close with yet another breathtaking moment—this one
so joyous and blessed as to defy imagination. The Cold War died in
the late 1980s without bloodshed and without rancor. Soviet Communism released its hold on Eastern Europe and its internal empire
and then collapsed like a balloon chasing the swift escape of its own
air. Both the heady optimism of Pérez de Cuéllar and the Reagan
shedding of dark shibboleths about the Soviet Union reflected the
same phenomenon—the end of the Cold War.

≈≈≈

The turn in the fortunes of the United Nations did not come
automatically. Yet Pérez de Cuéllar was so self-effacing as secretary-
general that it has been hard to credit him with guiding the turn.
Don Shannon of the *Los Angeles Times*, who covered the two terms
of Pérez de Cuéllar, found him a well-meaning but ineffectual diplomat, a leader who so "lacked any kind of forceful personality" that he
could never generate excitement for an issue. When he left the Sec-

retariat Building every day, he would politely and patiently reply in any of three languages (he had learned French as a child from his governess) to the questions posed by reporters but in tones so soft that it became a strenuous task to pry his words out of the tape. Rosemary Righter, the British editorial writer, caught his public image when she revived an old description of him as a man "who wouldn't make waves if he fell out of a boat." She ridiculed the public praise for him by some American diplomats in his last few years in office. Until that flurry of praise, she wrote with scorn, his "grey manner, low profile and evident inaptitude for administrative reform had singularly failed to inspire enthusiasm."

His self-effacing manner, however, may have left a false impression. Some analysts like Cameron R. Hume, an American diplomat who wrote a remarkable study of Security Council diplomacy during the Pérez de Cuéllar decade, believed that he served the United Nations well with a skillful, accomplished though muted performance behind the scenes. A tenacious and patient diplomat, he cajoled the great powers into molding their use of U.N. institutions to fit changing times. He did so, of course, without fanfare, without attention to himself. "He was a quiet, serious person," Brian Urquhart wrote, "who knew who he was, had no pretensions or election debts, and wanted to get on with the job, which he already knew a great deal about. He liked short and decisive conversations, and was uninterested (perhaps too much so) in his public 'image,' which saved a great deal of time. With him I never felt the embarrassment or apprehension I had sometimes experienced when listening to Waldheim talking to visitors." In his quiet, laborious way, Pérez de Cuéllar set in motion some of the most significant peacekeeping operations of the post–Cold War era like those in Namibia, El Salvador, and Cambodia.

Javier Pérez de Cuéllar of Peru came to office with long experience in the U.N. In fact, he was a member of the Peruvian delegation to the first session of the General Assembly in London in 1946. After a quarter of a century of diplomatic service, including two years as ambassador to the Soviet Union, he returned to the U.N., this time in New York, as the Peruvian ambassador in 1971. In 1975, Secretary-General Kurt Waldheim appointed him as special representative to Cyprus. While he failed to work out a permanent settlement between the Greek and Turkish Cypriots, Pérez de Cuéllar was credited with defusing the tension enough to allow the two sides to withdraw their weaponry behind U.N.-patrolled cease-fire lines. After a little more than a year back in the Peruvian diplomatic service, he was named an undersecretary-general by Waldheim in 1979. In 1981, he retired as undersecretary-general and as a Peruvian diplomat as well. He was resting on a beach in Peru near the end of the year while the Security Council struggled for six weeks to pick a secretary-general. He did not campaign at all.

After rounds of veto by China eliminated Waldheim's bid for a third term and rounds of veto by the United States stopped Tanzanian Foreign Minister Salim Ahmed Salim, the Security Council considered nine other candidates—including Jorge Illueca of Panama, Radha Krishna Ramphul of Mauritius, Prince Sadruddin Aga Khan, and Pérez de Cuéllar. An African diplomat described Pérez de Cuéllar as "everyone's last choice." But he proved the only nominee who could avoid a veto by one of the Big Five. He was, as Bernard D. Nossiter of the *New York Times* put it, "the candidate with the fewest strikes against him." The Soviet Union, always fearful that Latin Americans were lackeys of the United States, knew Pérez de Cuéllar as an ambassador to Moscow and decided to abstain rather than veto him. The new U.N. chief was probably the most cultured secretary-general since Hammarskjöld. Pérez de Cuéllar wrote poetry and prided himself on rereading the works of such Spanish and Latin American others as Miguel de Cervantes, Miguel de Unamuno y Jugo, José Ortega y Gasset, Jorge Luis Borges, and Gabriel García Márquez.

The Falklands War quickly pulled the first Latin American secretary-general into troubled seas. On April 3, 1982, an Argentine force of five thousand troops invaded the British Falkland Islands—or, as the Argentines called them, the Malvinas—an archipelago of two hundred islands 250 miles off the Atlantic coast of Argentina. Ownership had been disputed since the British seized the islands in

1833. The Falklands—with a total area about the size of Jamaica in the Caribbean—were widely recognized as Argentine territory then. But Great Britain, the world's strongest naval power, occupied the islands to prevent rival American whalers and seal hunters from using them. The British expelled the few hundred Argentine settlers and replaced them with British. At the time of the 1982 invasion, there were perhaps two thousand people on the Falklands, mostly sheep farmers. These British settlers did not want to become Argentine.

British Ambassador Anthony Parsons quickly asked for a meeting of the Security Council and won approval of a resolution calling on the Argentines to withdraw immediately and begin negotiations on the future of the Falklands. This early support for the British, however, lessened with time as Prime Minister Margaret Thatcher dispatched a seaborne force to drive the Argentines out of the Falklands. There was no doubt that the Argentines had embarked on a foolish aggression—even if their claims to the islands were probably valid, though a century and a half out of date. But the idea of the British mounting an armada to defeat the heirs of Spain rankled many Latins with the historical memory of British triumphs over Spain on the seas in earlier centuries. Moreover, they argued that various Western Hemisphere defense pacts guaranteed that all, including the United States, would unite to drive off any attack by an outside power. This mood was tempered somewhat by a widespread enmity for Argentine arrogance throughout Latin America; Brazilian officials, for example, while they would not say so publicly, were overjoyed at the prospect of the British humiliating the overbearing Argentines.

The issue confused American officialdom. While Secretary of State Alexander Haig felt that the United States would have no choice in the end but to support its NATO ally, U.N. Ambassador Jeane Kirkpatrick, who had written articles and monographs about Argentina, was sympathetic to the Argentine position. Kirkpatrick, in fact, had tried to talk British Ambassador Parsons out of taking the matter to the Security Council, for she believed that the Argentines would be more susceptible to quiet persuasion if not attacked in public. Haig decided to anoint himself chief mediator and began an enervating series of flights, shuttling from Buenos Aires to London four times, in hopes of preventing bloodshed. By the end of April, however, Haig withdrew, announcing that Argentina had rejected his proposal for a settlement and that the United States would now publicly support the British position. Pérez de Cuéllar, who had been pushed to the sidelines by the Haig shuttle, took over as chief mediator.

The secretary-general met separately every day in his thirty-eighth-floor offices with Argentine Deputy Foreign Minister Enrique Ros and British Ambassador Parsons and put together proposals of his own in mid-May to break the impasse. These proposals called for an interim solution: withdrawal of the Argentine troops, redeployment of the British fleet, and the start of negotiations. The secretary-general presented this package to Argentine Foreign Minister Nicanor Costa Ménendez and British Foreign Secretary Francis Pym and received what he thought was agreement from both sides. But snags developed quickly. "I received texts which did not reflect this agreement," Pérez de Cuéllar reported to the Security Council. "I immediately telephoned President [Leopoldo] Galtieri in Buenos Aires and Prime Minister Thatcher in London and asked them to overcome their differences." But he got nowhere.

The problem was mostly Argentine reluctance. Ambassador Kirkpatrick met with Costa Ménendez and Ros several times, trying to persuade them to accept the secretary-general's proposals without condition. At one stage, there was a suggestion that three flags could fly over the Falklands: those of the United Nations, Britain, and Argentina. Kirkpatrick pleaded with the Argentines to accept, for the arrangement at least moved Argentina a step closer toward sovereignty over the islands. But the Argentines would accept only if their flag flew higher than the others.

Her meetings with the Argentines angered Haig, for he did not want the United States, a backer of Britain, seen in the Argentine camp. He derided Kirkpatrick as "mentally and emotionally incapable of thinking clearly on this issue." She retorted that he was insensitive to the feelings of Latin Americans. In the end, she failed to break down the Argentine stubbornness, and the secretary-general announced the ignominious end of his mediation attempt on May 20. The British troops landed in the Falklands the next day and subdued and expelled the Argentines in a few weeks. The humiliation forced the military junta to resign, a withdrawal that allowed the return of democratic civilian rule to Argentina. A thousand lives—a little more than seven hundred of them Argentine—were lost during the war.

※ ❧

This was not an auspicious beginning for the first secretary-general from Latin America. He had failed to avert war on a vital Latin issue that was not even encumbered by the Cold War. It was hardly an advertisement for his vaunted diplomatic skills. Pérez de Cuéllar later turned his attention to the Iran-Iraq war, which began in Waldheim's administration, not his own, but still persisted, killing and maiming tens of thousands. On the surface, Pérez de Cuéllar was no more successful at stopping the bloodshed in Iran and Iraq than he had been in the Falklands. But he encouraged a change in procedures that proved vital for the work of the Security Council.

The war erupted in September 1980 when Saddam Hussein sent Iraqi troops to occupy disputed territory within Iran. At issue was the nub of land on the Shatt al Arab waterway formed by the confluence of the Tigris and Euphrates Rivers near Basra. This land juts between Iran and Kuwait and gives Iraq its only outlet on the Persian Gulf. Without it, Iraq would be landlocked. Although the waterway was recognized internationally as the boundary between the two countries, Iraq had long claimed both sides of the waterway. Saddam, much as he seized Kuwait ten years later, decided to take the ninety square miles of disputed territory by force. Relations had been embittered for some time. The Iraqi president, at the request of the shah of Iran, had expelled the Ayatollah Khomeini from his exile base in southern Iraq in 1978. Since then, the ayatollah spewed forth only contempt for Saddam, disdaining him as a "deviated person . . . completely uninformed about Islam." Iraq, after all, had a secular government, anathema to the ayatollah who had created an Islamic state in Iran. Saddam Hussein suspected that the Iranians were the perpetrators of a series of terrorist bomb attacks within Iraq, and he deported tens of thousands of Iranians back to Iran in 1980.

At the time of the invasion, Iran, still holding fifty-two American diplomats as hostages, was probably the world's most isolated society, a pariah with few friends. While U.N. officials and diplomats would not stand up and cheer Iraqi aggression, many surely hoped in private that the Iraqis would bloody Iran swiftly and teach the ayatollah that his kind of evil engendered its own retribution. American Secretary of State Edmund S. Muskie met with Soviet Foreign Minister Andrey Gromyko and announced that both the United States (the enemy of Iran) and the Soviet Union (the supplier of Iraq) would remain neutral in the war. The Security Council did little more than plead lamely for a cease-fire and welcome Secretary-General Kurt Waldheim's decision to send former Swedish Prime Minister Olof Palme to the area on a fruitless quest for a cease-fire and a settlement. The Iranians refused to believe that the detention of the American hostages weakened their case. Iranian Prime Minister Mohammed Ali Rajai, according to Kurt Waldheim, "could not understand why the Iranians, so evidently the victims of aggression, did not get a more sympathetic reception."

But Iraq did not teach Iran any punitive lesson. The more populous Iran counterattacked and drove inside Iraq with a force of one hundred thousand—half regular army, half revolutionary guard and youth brigades. Many units attacked without protective armor. Iraq retaliated with artillery, air raids, and poison gas. Pérez de Cuéllar traveled to both Teheran and Baghdad in 1985 in a futile attempt to mediate a settlement. Having driven the Iraqis out of their country, the Iranians did not intend to settle easily. They now demanded $150 billion in reparations, the condemnation of Iraq as an aggressor, the ouster of Saddam Hussein, and Iraqi recognition of Iran's right to the disputed territory. "Peace with the criminal is a crime against Islam," said the ayatollah.

Despite quadruple bypass heart surgery at the Mount Sinai Medical Center in New York in 1986, Pérez de Cuéllar was elected for a second term that year. The war still raged with massive losses of life and became even more complex as the United States, which shared intelligence with Iraq as part of a "tilt" toward Saddam Hussein, also sold more than two thousand missiles to Iran as part of the infamous Iran-contra scandal. The United States also put the American flag on Kuwaiti tankers and sent warships to the Persian Gulf to protect these tankers against an attack by either side.

In his first news conference after the start of his second term in January 1987, Pérez de Cuéllar told skeptical reporters that the United States and the Soviet Union must work together to put an end to the war. "They are the two most powerful countries," he said. "They have to show that they can deal with problems where the Security Council has a role to play. If I assume that they are not going to agree on something, what is the use of having a Security Council?" These words signaled that the secretary-general intended to take advantage of the new rhetoric coming from Gorbachev and his diplomats.

Pérez de Cuéllar brought the ambassadors of the Big Five into his office and encouraged them to meet periodically behind closed doors to see if they could come up with some proposals to end the war. The ambassadors accepted the idea and began to meet secretly and leisurely every few weeks at British Ambassador John Thompson's residence on Beekman Place near the U.N. The mood of the sessions was probably leavened by the presence of amiable, polyglot General Vernon A. Walters, the American ambassador known for his affinity for easing conversation with a good anecdote.

It is hard now to sense the enormity of the innovation then. Perez de Cuéllar had done no more than propose that these diplomats behave as most diplomats usually behave—by conducting their business quietly behind closed doors. But that was not the way the Security Council normally did its business then. Ambassador Kirkpatrick described the Security Council as "a body before which certain melodramas are played out." "It's not paralysis," she went on. "There is a lot of activity. It's a sound and light show in which a country is identified as villain and victim." Some of the most exciting events of the Security Council in the past—Henry Cabot Lodge's brandishing of the bugged embassy plaque, Adlai Stevenson's "until hell freezes over" speech—were all played out in public as theater. Except when it met privately to mull over candidates for secretary-general, the Security Council almost always met in public and, of course, accomplished little in the 1970s and 1980s.

Pérez de Cuéllar's proposal also encouraged the Big Five to value their own strength. If they could agree on a course of action, there was almost no way to stop it. The other ten members of the

Security Council—the rotating members who had no veto—might grumble, but the Big Five had enough influence to sway at least four votes to their side and obtain the required nine votes for passage of a resolution. Power at the U.N. could pass from the Third World and the General Assembly to the Big Five and the Security Council. The ten nonpermanent members of the council, in fact, did protest when they found out about the secret meetings of the Big Five on the Iran-Iraq war. The Big Five, after working out their position, then met privately with the others and accepted some of the useful amendments.

In a couple of years, the method of operation spawned by Pérez de Cuéllar to deal with the Iran-Iraq war would become the habit of the Security Council. In the 1990s, the Security Council ambassadors would find themselves meeting almost every day behind closed doors—sometimes all together, sometimes in caucuses of the Big Five or of the nonaligned or even of what became known as the non-nonaligned—to set a course of U.N. action on the mounting number of problems that reached them. The secrecy was conducive to action. These meetings, however, whether secret or not, would have accomplished little in Cold War days. Pérez de Cuéllar sensed in 1987 that the time had come when the United States and the Soviet Union could engage in real diplomacy.

It took almost six months for the Security Council, after numerous private consultations, to emerge in public and pass a strong resolution on the war. The resolution, approved unanimously in July 1987, demanded an immediate cease-fire, ordered Iran and Iraq to withdraw to prewar boundaries, asked the secretary-general to dispatch a force of observers to supervise the cease-fire, urged an immediate exchange of prisoners, and called on Iran and Iraq to cooperate with Pérez de Cuéllar in mediation "to achieve a comprehensive, just and honorable settlement." The Security Council passed the resolution under authority of Chapter 7 of the U.N. Charter. This would allow the council to authorize force later if Iran and Iraq ignored the demands. Secretary of State George P. Shultz, who represented the United States at the session, hailed Pérez de Cuéllar for his "crucial role in catalyzing the unprecedented process that led to the adoption of this resolution." Heeding the call of the secretary-general, Shultz said, the Security Council "as a whole has functioned in the collegial spirit envisioned by the founders of the United Nations at its creation."

Pérez de Cuéllar flew to Baghdad and Teheran but again failed to fashion a cease-fire. Since withdrawal would pull the Iranians out of Iraq, Saddam Hussein accepted it, but Iran did not. The United States wanted the Security Council to follow through with sanctions against Iran, especially an arms embargo. But the Soviet Union and China would not agree. While the Big Five continued to meet in private, they were now divided and thus incapable of action. This impasse remained until the spring of 1988, when an arms embargo against Iran became a lost cause. Iraq launched a new offensive that drove the Iranians out of Iraq and back into Iran. With Iraq bombing cities and using poison gas, Security Council ambassadors did not feel like punishing Iran anymore. The Iranians won even more sympathy in July 1988 when the American cruiser *Vincennes* accidentally shot down a commercial Iranian flight, Iran Air 655, killing the 290 persons abroad.

The battling would soon end. Iraq said it did not intend to hold on to any Iranian territory beyond the disputed boundary. "We will not give the Iranians this card to play with in mobilizing their population," said Iraqi Deputy Foreign Minster Nizar Hamdoon. "If they want to continue the war, they will have to explain to their people why they are attacking us because we are stopping at the international border." Iran gave in and accepted a cease-fire, blaming the United States for its plight. The Iranians cited the American destruction of the Iran Air flight as proof that the aggression against Iran had "now gained unprecedented dimensions." The United States, according to President Ali Khamenei, would wreak more terror upon Iran if it did not give in. Khamenei wrote Pérez de Cuéllar that his country now accepted the cease-fire resolution. Pérez de Cuéllar organized a U.N. force of observers to supervise the cease-fire that commenced on August 20, 1988—eight years after the war started and a full year after the Security Council resolution demanding the cease-fire.

✿❧

The war ended not because of Pérez de Cuéllar's diplomatic artistry or the Security Council's newfound delight in hush-hush palaver but only because the two sides had finally had enough of the awful battles. Yet this did not diminish what the Security Council had accomplished. American diplomat Cameron R. Hume, who took part in many of the negotiations, wrote, "The most important accomplishment of the process that led to the adoption of 598 [the cease-fire resolution] was that the permanent members kept talking." ". . . The Soviet Union and the United States showed that they placed a higher value than previously on their bilateral relationship," he went on. ". . . To the extent that the Security Council became a place for the major powers to find a meeting of the minds on issues of collective security, it could function as the United Nations' founders had intended." Excitement over the U.N. acting as the founders envisioned would be expressed again and again by many analysts and ambassadors in the next few years.

The outside world would gain its first real image of the U.N.'s transformation during the Persian Gulf War of 1990–91. Although U.N. diplomacy during the war fulfilled all that Pérez de Cuéllar had hoped and preached to the Security Council in the mid-1980s, the secretary-general was not a key actor in this monumental event. A case can be made, in fact, that U.N. participation was somewhat less than it seemed. (All this will be explored in the next chapter.)

✿❧

Pérez de Cuéllar made a second contribution to the future of the U.N.—a new kind of peacekeeping. This, too, reflected the collapse of the Cold War. With the United States and the Soviet Union cooperating rather than plotting against each other through proxy governments and rebellions, some regional wars diminished and became ripe for negotiation. The troubles of Namibia, Angola, Mozambique, Cambodia, Nicaragua, and even El Salvador suddenly seemed amenable to solution. In the past, U.N. peacekeepers—with the glaring exception of those in the old Congo—spent most of their time manning cease-fire lines while belligerents negotiated endlessly for a peace settlement beyond reach. Under Pérez de Cuéllar, the U.N. started deploying peacekeepers to countries after the signing of a peace agreement. Aside from supervising cease-fire lines, the U.N. now found itself overseeing elections, monitoring human rights violations, disarming military units, and shoring up institutions. Only a few like the Namibia and Nicaragua missions were completed during Pérez de Cuéllar's administration, but almost all were conceived then.

The mission to Namibia was a startling success, brimming with symbolism. For decades, South Africa had defied the U.N., refusing to allow independence for its trusteeship of South-West Africa. The South Africans had taken over the German colony during World War I and administered it afterward as a League of Nations mandate. After World War II, however, South Africa refused to acknowledge the transfer of South-West Africa from the League of Nations to the U.N. South Africa insisted that South West Africa was a territory of South Africa, not a trusteeship administered by South Africa on behalf of the U.N. This legal conflict solidified the anti–South Africa atmosphere within a United Nations already offended by the racist apartheid policies of the country. A series of U.N. condemnations and sanctions made South Africa a pariah among nations.

With the Cold War winding down, however, U.S. Assistant Secretary of State Chester A. Crocker managed in 1988 to broker an independence deal for South-West Africa (soon to be renamed Namibia) in which Cuba agreed to withdraw its troops from neighboring Angola and South Africa agreed to withdraw its troops from South-West Africa. The South African whites accepted the deal because guerrilla warfare had made the territory too costly in casualties to administer, the withdrawal of Cubans promised stability in the region, and a ferment in white Afrikaner thinking had started to question the sense of apartheid.

Although South Africa was suspicious of the U.N. because of its incessant antiapartheid rhetoric over the years, it agreed to a mission of forty-five hundred U.N. peacekeepers to oversee the transfer of power to an independent Namibia in March 1990. The peacekeepers

supervised the ceasefire, the withdrawal of outside troops, and national elections. The smoothness of the operation contributed, at
least in a small way, to the mood in Pretoria that would lead to the
abandonment of apartheid and make the U.N. an acceptable source
of election monitors when South Africa held its democratic multiracial elections in 1994.

☙❧

But the most remarkable U.N. achievement during these years
was probably the mission to El Salvador. A civil war had raged in El
Salvador for more than a decade with the United States bolstering
the government at a cost of a million dollars a day and the Soviet
Union arming the rebel FMLN *(Frente Faribundo Marti para la Lib-
eracion Nacional)* guerrillas through Nicaragua and Cuba. It was a
tenet of Reagan administration policy that it would never let El Salvador go Communist the way the Carter administration, in the Reagan administration view, let Nicaragua go Communist. But the
United States had a flawed ally in El Salvador, and American diplomats had to help the Salvadoreans cover up some notorious military
atrocities. In November 1989, the guerrillas struck the capital of San
Salvador in their largest offensive of the war. While bringing the war
to the heartland of the Salvadorean Establishment, the rebels failed
to set off the popular uprising that they had expected. But the military, while fending off the offensive, alienated many Americans by
bombing poor neighborhoods suspected of hiding the guerrillas and
by murdering six Spanish Jesuit priests accused of sympathizing with
the FMLN. Salvadorean President Alfredo Cristiani and the rebel
comandantes realized that the time had come to talk about peace. By
then, perhaps seventy-five thousand people had lost their lives in the
tiny country with a population of five million.

Since 1984, sometimes over Washington's objections, the leaders of Central America and its neighbors had been meeting periodically in hopes of negotiating peace settlements that would end the
civil wars in Nicaragua, El Salvador, and Guatemala. A 1987 peace
plan put forth by President Oscar Arias of Costa Rica (who won the
Nobel peace prize for his efforts) eventually led to U.N. supervision

of elections in Nicaragua that ousted the Sandinistas from power in 1989 and to U.N. demobilization of the United States–backed contra rebels. The peace process in both Nicaragua and El Salvador would have foundered if both the Soviet Union and the United States had not decided it was time to withhold support from their rebellious clients in Central America.

The Salvadorean government and the FMLN met for almost two years under U.N. mediation. Pérez de Cuéllar's personal representative for Central America, the urbane Alvaro de Soto of Peru, did most of the work of shuttling between delegations and bringing the two sides together for negotiations in various sites like Geneva, Caracas, Mexico City, New York, and San Jose, Costa Rica. President Cristiani, ignoring denunciations from extreme elements in his own political party, took part in some of the negotiations himself. So did Pérez de Cuéllar. Later, Cristiani said that the participation of the U.N. was crucial. "The U.N. made it very difficult for either side to get up from the table and leave," he said. With so many Salvadoreans hoping for peace, the side that quit the talks and defied the U.N. would be hurt politically.

Over the months, the two warring sides agreed on what amounted to a revolution in El Salvador: reduced armed forces including the dismissal of those guilty of human rights violations, creation of a new civil police force to replace the paramilitary police force responsible for many of the worst human rights offenses, disarming of the FMLN, observation by outsiders of the next election, monitoring of human rights, an outside Commission of Truth to delve into some of the terrible atrocities of the war, and land distribution to FMLN guerrillas—all of this overseen by a U.N. peacekeeping force. By the last day of 1991, however, full agreement had not been reached.

That day was the last day for Pérez de Cuéllar as secretary-general. He had plans to leave that evening for a vacation in the Bahamas. Aides had gathered in his office to wish him farewell. But the secretary-general said he was not leaving yet. "I think it is my duty to stay as long as I see my presence is of some use," he told the staff. "I cannot leave right now." He told reporters, "It is a race against time." He evidently was prepared to stop the clock, if necessary—a legal fiction that would make believe that the year and his term had not expired at midnight. But that did not prove necessary. The two sides reached agreement just before midnight that New Year's Eve. There is little doubt that both wanted agreement to come while a fellow Latin American headed the U.N. The first word to the press came not from the U.N. but the United States. Assistant Secretary of State Bernard Aronson, monitoring the talks, came out and told reporters that agreement had been reached. "To the Salvadorean people," Aronson said, "it's the best New Year's present they could have. . . . Both sides know that the war is over." "I feel very proud," said Pérez de Cuéllar, "not just of myself but also of my colleagues and friends who participated in the Salvadorean negotiating effort."

The U.N. mission would last until mid-1995. Implementation of the agreement was not always smooth. The Salvadorean government, pleading a lack of funds, had still failed to provide land to more than a small percentage of FMLN fighters by 1995. Political violence had not been eliminated. Yet the achievements were remarkable. One could sense that immediately at the new U.S. embassy compound in San Salvador, a complex of ugly, brutish buildings surrounded by concrete walls like a prison. The enormous compound, opened in 1992, was designed during the war to intimidate the FMLN by driving home the American might that stood behind the Salvadorean government. Yet, only a few months after the embassy opened, the American chargé d'affaires included former FMLN *comandantes* on the guest lists of his cocktail parties for prominent Salvadorean politicians. Clean-shaven, neatly combed, sipping drinks, the former *comandantes* did not look out of place on the grounds of the once-despised Americans. Peace had come to El Salvador, a prideful U.N. success in the wake of the Cold War.

❧ 15 ❧

The Persian Gulf War

Canadian Ambassador Yves Fortier, a member of the Security Council on that hectic night when Iraq invaded Kuwait, described the Persian Gulf War later as "a classic case" in the way the United Nations was supposed to react to naked aggression. "It was Political Science 101," said Fortier. Sitting in his Ford Foundation office around the corner from the U.N., Brian Urquhart, the former undersecretary-general, called the war "the first exercise in the unanimous collective security that we've been talking about since the days of Woodrow Wilson." Secretary-General Javier Pérez de Cuéllar tempered some of this euphoric excitement. "It was not a United Nations war," he told the European Parliament in Strasbourg. "General Schwarzkopf was not wearing a blue helmet." But it was hard to temper the euphoria too much. The United Nations, belittled for much of two decades, had suddenly proven itself and won new respect and admiration. Not since those days at Hunter College did the American public feel so much that the United Nations really counted.

In a few years, there would be disappointments, reassessments, even renewed disdain. Some analysts began to accept former Secretary of State Henry A. Kissinger's postwar assessment that "historians will in all likelihood treat the Gulf crisis as a special case rather than as a watershed." Yet the two concepts did not exclude each other. Whether special case or not, the Gulf War could still be a watershed. By changing the way the U.N. operated, the war was surely a crucial event. But the diplomacy about the war needs to be examined in some detail to make clear what it achieved for the United Nations, at least in the 1990s, and where, in fact, it sowed seeds for a nettlesome future.

☙ ❧

In the early hours before dawn of August 2, 1990, Saddam Hussein dispatched the first of one hundred thousand troops across the southern border of Iraq to seize the tiny but oil wealthy emirate of Kuwait. Most troops belonged to his well-trained and tested Republican Guard. Iraq had long claimed Kuwait as "an integral part of the Iraqi Republic," even though it had been ruled separately by Britain as a protectorate from 1899 until its independence in 1961. In less than four hours, the troops, rushing down a superhighway and bolstered by other troops ferried into the seaport by helicopter, entered the capital of Kuwait City. In a day, they controlled half the emirate; in two days, all of it.

The occupation shocked President George W. Bush and his advisers in the White House. Although there had been alerts from U.S. intelligence, the president did not believe that Iraq, enervated from a decade of war with Iran, would stir up so much trouble on another border. At the most, there was a suspicion that Saddam Hussein might seize some bits of disputed territory on the border. Even on that score, Egypt and Saudi Arabia had assured Washington that they were mediating the border dispute. Ambassador April Glaspie had confronted Saddam Hussein in Baghdad but, acting under instructions from Washington, sounded somewhat Milquetoast in her warning against provoking trouble. The shock was heightened for Bush because he had been trying to woo Iraq back into respectability for more than a year. The Bush administration had even cut red tape and pressured agencies to approve questionable exports to Iraq that eventually made their way into Saddam Hussein's enormous program for producing weapons of mass destruction. It is not surprising that news of the Iraqi aggression struck at Bush like a sting.

U.N. Ambassador Thomas R. Pickering and his wife were guests at a small dinner hosted by retired American diplomat Thomas Enders, now an investment banker, in honor of departing British Ambassador Crispin Tickell at the Carlyle Hotel in New York during the evening of August 1. At 10 P.M., the dinner was interrupted by an urgent phone call from Undersecretary of State Robert M. Kimmitt to Pickering. Since it was summer and daylight saving time, there were nine hours' time difference between Kuwait and New York. By the time Kimmitt phoned Pickering, the invasion was six hours old, and the Iraqi troops had overrun much of Kuwait and entered Kuwait City. Kimmitt told Pickering that President Bush wanted a resolution as soon as possible from the Security Council condemning the aggression.

Pickering, then fifty-eight, was one of the most experienced and admired ambassadors in the American foreign service. He had served tours as ambassador to Jordan, Nigeria, El Salvador, and Israel before President Bush named him U.N. ambassador in 1989, only the second career diplomat to fill that post. Bush, a former U.N. ambassador himself, broke with tradition and did not grant Pickering cabinet status. That probably reflected Bush's own experience. As the U.N. ambassador, Bush had worked hard at cultivating friendships with the other ambassadors, even those from the smallest and least significant countries. That demanded a good deal of his time. Most U.N. ambassadors, unlike Bush, had not devoted that kind of time to New York, preferring to shuttle to Washington for more glamorous cabinet meetings and strategy conferences with key policy-makers. Bush, evidently persuaded that Pickering should concentrate on the ins and outs of politicking within the U.N., decided not to distract him with a seat in the cabinet. Pickering, a tall, balding, affable man with an inquisitive and incisive mind, yet wise and confident enough to listen to the views of others, set a standard of performance that later U.N. ambassadors would have difficulty matching.

Pickering, en route to the U.S. mission, used the car phone to

start a flurry of urgent calls that would last far into the night. He
alerted Romanian Ambassador Aurel-Dragos Munteanu, who had
begun his turn as the month-long president of the Security Council
just that day, and told him that the United States would probably ask
for an emergency meeting of the council that night. For a while, he
could not locate a key player, Mohammad Abulhasan, the ambassador from Kuwait. Pickering finally tracked him down at a dinner in
honor of the Bahrain ambassador at the Russian Tea Room alongside
Carnegie Hall. Abulhasan, who had not yet heard of the invasion,
quickly agreed to join the United States in demanding an emergency
meeting and hurried toward U.N. headquarters. Pickering then
called Kimmitt back, and the two discussed what a resolution should
say. The State Department faxed a draft to Pickering, and the ambassador set out to corral the votes.

The ambassadors sat down at 1:30 A.M. to begin their consultations behind closed doors. The Iraqi aggression was so blatant that it
was not difficult to persuade many ambassadors to condemn it. But
Pickering wanted as close to unanimous approval of the American
resolution as possible. Ethiopian Ambassador Tesfaye Tadesse tried
for several hours in vain to reach the foreign ministry in Addis Ababa
for instructions. He finally gave up and, recalling those days in 1936
when Emperor Haile Selassie pleaded with an unheeding League of
Nations to stop the Italian invasion of Ethiopia, decided to cosponsor
the resolution on his own initiative. Ambassador Abdalla Al-Ashtal of
Yemen also failed to obtain instructions from home. Unlike Tadesse,
Al-Ashtal decided not to take part in the vote at all, not even to
abstain.

At 5 A.M., Ambassador Munteanu called a formal meeting of the
Security Council to order. "The world is watching what we do here
and will not be satisfied with vacillation or procrastination," said
Pickering. The American resolution, cosponsored by eight others,
was short and direct. It condemned the Iraqi invasion of Kuwait, demanded the immediate and unconditional withdrawal of all Iraqi
troops, and called on the two countries to begin immediate negotiations over their differences. The Security Council, according to the
resolution, acted under the authority of Chapter 7 of the U.N. Charter. That meant that the council had the right to impose economic

sanctions later and even to remove the troops by force if Iraq defied the U.N. The resolution was approved by a vote of fourteen to nothing, with Yemen not taking part. Even Cuba voted in favor of the American resolution. The emergency meeting ended shortly after 6 A.M., barely twelve hours into the war. Never in the history of the U.N. had aggression been condemned more swiftly.

From the beginning, President Bush wanted to dislodge the Iraqi troops. His resolve was strengthened by a meeting with British Prime Minister Margaret Thatcher in Aspen, Colorado, and by the pleadings of some members of his team. Thatcher likened Saddam Hussein's aggression to Hitler's ravenous greed for European territory during the 1930s. Deputy Secretary of State Lawrence Eagleburger warned that American acquiescence to Iraqi aggression would embolden tyrants like Mu'ammar al-Gadhafi of Libya and Kim Il Sung of North Korea. "It is absolutely essential," Eagleburger said, "that the U.S.—collectively if possible, but individually if necessary—not only put a stop to this aggression but roll it back." But General Colin Powell, the chairman of the Joint Chiefs of Staff, did not believe that saving Kuwait was worth the risk; he counseled that America's first priority was defense of Saudi Arabia.

Bush agreed that defending Saudi Arabia and the rest of Persian Gulf oil from Iraqi aggression had first priority. A week after the invasion, Bush announced the launch of Operation Desert Shield, the eventual dispatch of 230,000 American troops to Saudi Arabia to discourage any new adventures by Saddam Hussein. "I took this action," he said, "to assist the Saudi Arabian government in the defense of its homeland. . . . The mission of our troops is wholly defensive." He said he was counting on U.N. economic sanctions to drive the Iraqis back from Kuwait. Ambassador Pickering informed the U.N. that the troops were being deployed in aid of American allies under the right of self-defense guaranteed by the U.N. Charter.

But Bush also instructed the Pentagon to prepare for a war as well. Despite the cautions from General Powell, the president was determined to beat back and humiliate Saddam Hussein. "This touches some deep inner core," a White House aide told New Yorker writer Elizabeth Drew. "He was deeply offended by the aggression against Kuwait." Critics of the president, however, winced when he announced to the world that Saddam Hussein was "going to get his ass kicked." It sounded like an adolescent trying to prove his ascent from wimpery. Yet, whatever the motivation, Bush never wavered from his determination to right an injustice. The only question was how. The president gave sanctions a chance to work first but not much of a chance, for he did not have faith in them.

By chance, Secretary of State James A. Baker III was in Russia on official business when the Iraqis invaded. The issue was a delicate one, for Iraq had been one of Russia's links to the Mideast, its main client there for military sales. Some Russian diplomats did not want to lose this friendship. But Foreign Minister Eduard Shevardnadze insisted that Russia must stand beside the United States in its denunciation of aggression. In a joint statement, issued just two days after the invasion, Baker and Shevardnadze said that "governments that engage in blatant aggression must know that the international community cannot and will not acquiesce in or facilitate aggression." This cooperation was cemented at the U.N. by the representation there. Yuli Vorontsov, the Russian ambassador, was as experienced, nuanced, and outgoing as Pickering. He had served as a junior diplomat with the Soviet mission to the U.N. when the Security Council was a den of recriminations in the 1960s, and he did not intend to repeat any of those unpleasant encounters.

※※

From August 2 until November 29, the Security Council passed twelve tough resolutions dealing with Iraqi aggression, a crescendo that should have made Saddam Hussein realize that he faced disaster if he did not yield. A key resolution, passed only five days after the invasion, slapped a total embargo on all trade (except for basic food and medicine) with Iraq, including a ban on the purchase of Iraqi oil and on the sale of arms to Saddam Hussein. Iraqi Ambassador Abdul Amir Al-Anbari cried out that the embargo was illegal because it had been forced through the Security Council by the United States. "Anything imposed by force and threat is not legitimate under the principles of the Charter," he said. But Pickering told the Security Council, "Iraq must learn that its disregard for international law will have crippling political and economic costs." Russia voted for the sanctions even though, as a Russian diplomat told the other ambassadors, it "affects a whole set of relationships between us and Iraq that have been developing for many years now." The Security Council imposed the trade embargo by a vote of thirteen to nothing, with Cuba and Yemen abstaining.

The resolutions were mainly written in Washington, faxed to New York and then distributed by Pickering to the other ambassadors. But Pickering proved a master at guiding the resolutions through the council and shading each nuance when necessary to pull along any reluctant ambassador. Reminiscing about him later, ambassadors remembered Pickering as a diplomat in perpetual motion, an amiable magician, wheeling and dealing. His right hand seemed to dip constantly into his pocket to pull out one substitute resolution after another. Every few minutes, he would snap open a cellular phone to whisper at Washington. He dominated the Security Council in a way that no American ambassador, not even Adlai Stevenson, had ever done before. Despite the bitter clamor from Iraqi Ambassador Al-Anbari, Pickering never seemed to ram a resolution through the council. "He knew how to negotiate with the members so they would feel part of the process," said a French diplomat. "He might change a word here, a word there, nothing substantive, but it would enable a delegate to save face." He phoned Washington often to persuade the State Department to accept the word changes as a price for support. Five of the twelve resolutions were passed by the unanimous vote of the fifteen ambassadors. Cuba voted against three of the resolutions, and Yemen against two. There were no other negative votes.

Pickering took a backseat, however, on the most important resolution of all—the one that authorized the Persian Gulf War. That was handled by Secretary Baker. Although he reportedly had doubts about the impending war and shared many of General Powell's worries and hesitations, Baker was, above all, a Bush loyalist. The Bush administration had upset U.N. diplomats and officials in mid-August by announcing it intended to stop ships by force if they attempted to circumvent sanctions. Secretary-General Pérez de Cuéllar objected. "Only the United Nations, through its Security Council resolutions, can really decide about a blockade," he said. President Bush finally relented, and the Security Council, in a late August session that ended just before dawn, passed an American-sponsored resolution authorizing the use of force to stop sanctions-busters at sea. In view of that precedent, the U.S. could hardly go to war against Iraq without obtaining U.N. approval first. Once President Bush decided he had no alternative but to use force to dislodge the Iraqi troops, he instructed Pickering to seek U.N. authorization and dispatched Baker to cement the votes.

In early November, Baker set off for several capitals of governments on the Security Council to shore up support. He also met Chinese Foreign Minister Qian Qichen in the Chinese town of Urumqi near the Russian border, and the foreign ministers of Ethiopia, Ivory Coast, and Zaire in Geneva. He consulted with everyone, in fact, except the Cubans. In San'a, the capital of Yemen, President Ali Abdallah Salih, turned him down. "We do not support the presence of foreign forces in the region," he said. But Baker did not meet rejection anywhere else. A bellicose pronouncement came from British Prime Minister Thatcher during the trip. She told the House of Commons, "Either he [Saddam Hussein] gets out of Kuwait soon or we and our allies will remove him by force, and he will go down to defeat with all its consequences. He has been warned."

President Bush cast some doubt about whether he really needed a U.N. resolution—even while he sought one. He told a news conference that the United States already had the right to remove the Iraqis by force. "But we've been great believers in going to the United Nations," he said. "And I think one of the major successes has been the ability to have world opinion totally on our side because of U.N. action."

Secretary Baker presided over the Security Council on November 29, 1990. Foreign ministers represented thirteen of the governments on the council. It was the second council meeting at the level of foreign ministers that year; in the previous forty-five years of the U.N., there had only been two other meetings where a majority of the council were represented by their foreign ministers: ceremonial sessions on the twenty-fifth anniversary of the U.N. in 1970 and on the fortieth anniversary in 1985. "With the Cold War behind us,"

Baker said, "we now have a chance to build the world which was envisioned . . . by the founders of the United Nations. We have the chance to make the Security Council and this United Nations true instruments for peace and for justice across the globe." The American-sponsored resolution authorized "member states cooperating with the government of Kuwait . . . to use all necessary means to uphold and implement" the August 2 resolution that demanded the immediate and unconditional withdrawal of the Iraqi troops from Kuwait. The new resolution allowed Saddam Hussein until January 15—almost seven weeks from then—to comply. This grace period was inserted at the request of Soviet President Mikhail Gorbachev to allow a final surge of diplomatic pressure to make the Iraqi president see the light.

Iraqi Ambassador Al-Anbari mocked President Bush's oft-stated contention that the removal of Iraqi troops from Kuwait would represent a victory for the "new world order." "Where is that new international order?" he said. "Is it the massing of American forces and their deployment in the Gulf region? Is it the threats of the invasion and destruction of Iraq." Cuban Foreign Minister Isidóro Malmierca said he opposed giving "the United States and its allies *carte blanche*." But Shevardnadze said that "the universal value of freedom and democracy for man, for society and for international relations . . . must be protected and upheld." The Security Council passed the resolution by a vote of twelve to two. Cuba and Yemen cast the negative votes while China abstained. Baker proclaimed that this resolution and the eleven preceding resolutions had created "a new fact: a newly effective United Nations Security Council, free of the constraints of the Cold War."

❧❧

Bush worked assiduously to put together a coalition of military force to help oust Iraq from Kuwait. Saudi Arabia, Britain, and, after a change of defense ministers, France agreed to furnish key air combat and ground forces. Smaller units came from two dozen other countries like Egypt and Spain. American military strength would, of course, power the coalition. The Pentagon churned out plans for a military offensive even while President Bush talked about economic sanctions in public. As early as October 11, in fact, Bush and his advisers had concluded at a White House meeting that they would have to use military force to drive out the Iraqis. Bush's wrath and rhetoric intensified against Saddam Hussein. On November 1, he called Iraq's alleged atrocities against Kuwait "outrageous acts of barbarism." "I don't think Hitler ever participated in anything of that nature," he said.

At a news conference on November 8—three weeks before the Security Council resolution authorizing the use of "all necessary means" to push out Iraq—the president announced the dispatch of more American troops to Saudi Arabia. "I have today directed the Secretary of Defense to increase the size of U.S. forces committed to Desert Shield to insure that the coalition has an adequate offensive military option should that be necessary to achieve our common goals," he said. ". . . Iraq's brutality, aggression and violations of international law cannot be allowed to succeed." The numbers of American soldiers would almost double to four hundred thousand. American intelligence believed that Saddam had an army of a million with more than four hundred thousand in and around Kuwait. Bush told reporters the next day that he still hoped sanctions would work but "I have not ruled out the use of force at all."

Although the last Security Council resolution left room for diplomacy to head off war, it did not leave room for compromise. Bush insisted that Saddam Hussein had no choice but to surrender to the Security Council resolutions and get out of Kuwait. The American president was in no mood for any face-saving compromises—like the convening of a Mideast conference on the Palestinians or continued Iraqi occupation of a few tidbits of disputed territory—that would give Saddam Hussein a veneer of phoney victory as he withdrew. It is not clear that the Iraqi president would have withdrawn even if granted some face-saving compromises, but they were never among Bush's cards. The Russians and French did suggest tentative compromises but aroused only disapproving grunts from both the White House and Baghdad.

❧

At the end of November, to demonstrate that he was ready "to go the extra mile for peace," President Bush announced that he was prepared to send Secretary of State Baker to Baghdad to look Saddam Hussein in the eye and explain that the Americans and their allies were dead serious about the U.N.'s January 15 deadline. The Iraqi president countered that Secretary Baker could come to Baghdad on January 12 but not before. This date was too close to the deadline to be taken seriously; the White House derided it as a delaying tactic. In the end, Bush agreed to arrangements for Baker to meet in Geneva on January 12 with Iraqi Foreign Minister Tariq Aziz, the urbane Christian who served as Saddam Hussein's chief spokesman to the West. This raised some hopes, but only among the gullible.

Accompanied by a few aides, Baker and Aziz met on January 12 in a conference room in Geneva's Hotel Intercontinental near the Palais des Nations, the headquarters of the old League of Nations and now the main headquarters for U.N. operations in Europe. "Would you mind if I smoked?" Aziz asked. "No," Baker replied, "as long as it's not a Cuban cigar." Aziz took out his cigarettes. Baker then handed Aziz a letter from President Bush and asked him to deliver it to Saddam Hussein. Aziz said he would have to read it first. In the letter, Bush said to Saddam Hussein, "Unless you withdraw from Kuwait completely and without condition, you will lose more than Kuwait. What is at issue here is not the future of Kuwait . . . but rather the future of Iraq. This choice is yours to make." After reading it, Aziz told Baker, "I regret that I cannot accept this letter. The tone is not appropriate for a head of state."

The two officials then sparred for more than six hours in a futile debate that repeated old positions and offered nothing new. After the meeting, President Bush told a news conference in Washington, "I sent Secretary Jim Baker to Geneva, not to negotiate, but to communicate, and I wanted Iraqi leaders to know just how determined we are that the Iraqi forces leave Kuwait without condition or further delay." Bush described the Iraqi response to Baker as "a total stiff-arm . . . a total rebuff."

On that same day, Bush won authorization from a troubled and divided Congress for military action. Daniel Patrick Moynihan, the former U.N. ambassador, now a senator from New York, told the Senate that the crisis did not "necessitate the confrontation of the largest set of armed forces since World War II." "Nothing large happened," he said. "A nasty little country invaded a little but just as nasty country. . . . Suddenly our institutions are acting as if to say, 'Oh, my God, we missed World War III. Maybe we can have it now here.' " But the Senate approved the resolution by a vote of 52 to 47, the House by a vote of 250 to 183. The resolution authorized the president to use American armed forces to push Iraq out of Kuwait provided he determined that all peaceful means had failed.

In fact, there was only one real peaceful step left, and it was not much of one. Secretary-General Pérez de Cuéllar arrived in Baghdad on the night of January 12. Aziz, just back from Geneva, greeted the secretary-general at Saddam International Airport. "I am bringing the will of the international community for a peaceful solution," Pérez de Cuéllar said. But the secretary-general, bound by the U.N. resolutions, felt he could not propose anything but an unconditional Iraqi withdrawal. After meeting with Saddam Hussein the next day, he left Baghdad, telling reporters at the airport, "I don't see any reason for hope." His talks with Saddam Hussein, he said, were "polite but, unfortunately, unsuccessful." A few hours before the deadline, on the night of January 15, the secretary-general issued a last-minute public appeal for Iraqi troops to leave Kuwait. It was, of course, ignored. There was nothing left but war. The White House wanted the anti-Iraq coalition's forces to fly the U.N. flag, but Pérez de Cuéllar refused. He reportedly did not want a repeat of the Korean War model where the American-led troops invoked the name of the U.N. but tolerated no interference from the U.N.

❧❧

At 3 A.M., Iraq time, on January 17, 1991 (7 P.M. the night before, in Washington), an American F-117A Stealth fighter hurled a two-thousand-pound, laser-guided bomb at the antenna-topped roof of the International Telephone and Telegraph Building in downtown Baghdad. Within seconds, another Stealth fighter sent a similar bomb at the Tower for Wire and Wireless Communications in Baghdad. The world's war against Saddam Hussein—officially named Desert Storm—was under way. The old warhorses of the U.S. Strategic Air Command, the eight-engine B-52 bombers, flying from Barksdale Air Force Base, Louisiana, almost eighteen hours away, unleashed their cruise missiles at strategic targets. Tomahawk cruise missiles, launched from U.S. Navy ships in the Persian Gulf and the Red Sea, descended on Baghdad. F-15 and F-16 fighters, F-4G Wild Weasels, British Tornadoes, and Apache Attack helicopters joined the aerial pounding.

Within the first three hours, more than 400 combat aircraft, supported by 160 tankers and command planes, attacked Iraq. Their targets were command centers, communications buildings, government ministries, early warning radar posts, air defense equipment, Scud missile launchers, oil refineries, and air bases throughout the country, as well as the presidential palace and other strategic sites in Baghdad. "The great showdown has begun," Saddam Hussein told Iraqis that morning. "The mother of all battles is under way."

The incessant bombing continued for five weeks, crippling the infrastructure of Iraq and wearing away the inner will of the Iraqi soldier. After the first week, General Powell made it clear what was in store for the Iraqi army. "Our strategy to go after this army is very, very simple," he told a televised news conference at the Pentagon. "First we are going to cut it off. And then we are going to kill it." The American-led high-tech air war went so well that Secretary of Defense Dick Cheney called it the most successful air campaign in the history of the world.

Saddam Hussein could mark only a few slight turns in his favor. While his defenses failed to stop the American-led coalition's bombing, he managed to fire Scud missiles of his own at cities in Israel. He obviously hoped to break up the coalition by changing the nature of the war into a struggle between the Arab world and Israel. Although the indiscriminate Scud attacks terrified and infuriated the Israelis, Prime Minister Yitzhak Shamir heeded American pleas to stay out of the war. In another burst of effrontery, the Iraqi president sent a battalion of seven hundred troops and forty-five tanks into Saudi Arabia to take over the border town of Khafji. The Iraqis held the town for thirty-six hours before they were routed out by Saudi and Qatari troops and U.S. Marine helicopters.

The United Nations had no role in the war, but some U.N. officials and ambassadors hoped for a brief moment that they might bring it to a close in February and avert the carnage of an American-led ground offensive. Soviet special envoy Yevgeny Primakov, a Middle East specialist and former *Pravda* correspondent, returned to Moscow from a diplomatic mission to Baghdad with a plan for Iraq to start withdrawal one day after a cease-fire was declared. Under the plan, officially approved by Aziz on a quick trip to Moscow but still awaiting ratification from Saddam Hussein, the Iraqis promised to complete their withdrawal from Kuwait City within four days and the rest of the country within twenty-one days. According to Primakov, Iraq was sick of the bombing and ready to surrender. Gorbachev informed Bush of the prospects on the night of February 21, and the Security Council decided to meet in closed session the next morning to discuss the Soviet-brokered plan. Pérez de Cuéllar felt so upbeat that he ordered Marrack Goulding, the undersecretary for political affairs and the chief of peacekeeping, to ask several governments if they could provide troops to monitor any withdrawal.

President Bush did not like the Primakov plan. It bristled with too many Saddam Hussein conditions for what sounded like a slow and triumphant withdrawal. Bush preempted any U.N. consideration of the plan by proclaiming an ultimatum to Saddam Hussein to start leaving Kuwait City within twenty-four hours or face annihilation. White House Press Secretary Marlin Fitzwater explained that the Iraqis had two days to complete their withdrawal from the capital and seven days to get out of Kuwait altogether. There would be no cease-fire, but the United States promised to refrain from attacks on retreating troops. Security Council ambassadors received news of the ultimatum as they headed toward their consultation room. Cigar-wielding Cuban Ambassador Ricardo Alarcón protested to reporters, "It's humiliating to the Security Council. We haven't even met, and we have been told by the United States that we have a deadline by noon tomorrow. The big sheriff is deciding what we do." Others shared Alarcón's feeling but did not say so publicly. They knew that their meeting was pointless, and they knew as well that Saddam Hussein would not be stampeded out of Kuwait by Bush's ultimatum. The Iraqi units would soon shatter under the fury of the ground offensive.

≈≈

The ground war began before dawn on February 24, Iraqi time, a few hours after the ultimatum expired. The offensive succeeded beyond the most optimistic hopes of the American generals. The marines, augmented by Arab troops, struck northward and raced toward Kuwait City. U.S. Army divisions with their British and French allies, all having moved secretly westward in the last ten days, struck across the Iraqi border in a flanking movement designed to shut off an Iraqi retreat. Iraqi troops reeled under the double assault and fled from Kuwait in tanks, military vehicles, and stolen trucks and cars, heading toward the southern Iraqi city of Basra for refuge. Allied planes bombarded the retreating Iraqis. The bombing left one long Iraqi column of more than a thousand burned-out cars, trucks, tanks, and other vehicles with the bodies of two hundred to three hundred Iraqis lying nearby. American television and newspapers ran fearful images of the devastation and dubbed the scene "the highway of death." Sights like these troubled the conscience of Americans. For months, American officialdom had described the enemy as the fourth largest army in the world. But the Iraqis were no match for the Americans and fell to pieces under the onslaught.

On the afternoon of February 27, President Bush, General Powell, Secretary of State Baker, Secretary of Defense Cheney, British Foreign Secretary Douglas Hurd, and others assembled in the Oval Office of the White House to decide the fate of the war. According to the account of Michael Gordon and General Bernard E. Trainor in their history of the war, the president wanted to know when Powell and his field commander, General H. Norman Schwarzkopf, felt they could end the war. General Powell, whose military ideology embraced attack with overwhelming force followed by quick withdrawal without any nettlesome occupation, told Bush, "We are in the home stretch. . . . Norm and I would like to finish tomorrow, a five-day war." The president agreed. "We do not want to lose anything now with charges of brutalization," he said. "We do not want to screw this up with a sloppy, muddied ending." Addressing the nation on television, Bush said that the war would end the next day, February 27, 1991, one hundred hours after the start of the ground offensive.

Most analysts concluded later that Bush had ended the war too soon. The U.S. had chased Saddam Hussein out of Kuwait. But the military trap was opened before it could shut off the escape of tens of thousands of Republican Guard troops. Saddam Hussein, though he reigned over a crippled country, had enough military force to put down rebellions by the Kurds in the north and the Shiites in the south and keep himself in power.

But Americans felt euphoric about their massive victory. The mood was enhanced by the astonishingly low number of American casualties: 119 killed, 10 missing, and 330 wounded in action, with 72 dead from accidents and other causes outside the battling. The total of Iraqi military dead was estimated by the U.S. Defense Intelligence Agency at between 50,000 and 150,000. Despite the extent of the victory, the mood at the U.N. was troubled, especially among Third World countries who suddenly felt impotent in a world organization largely controlled by the United States with the support of its new ally, the Soviet Union (soon to break up into Russia and a varied cluster of independent republics). "It is not necessarily my view," said Chinmaya R. Gharekhan, the cautious Indian ambassador, a member of the Security Council, "but there is a perception in the United Nations, widespread throughout, that the United States used the Security Council."

Bush strengthened that perception when he told four Arab journalists in a postwar interview that he might have pursued the war against Iraq even if he had failed to win U.N. blessing. Bush was obviously in an expansive mood. "I might have said to hell with them [the Iraqis]," he said. "It's right and wrong. It's good and evil. He's evil. Our cause is right. And without the United Nations, [I might have] sent a considerable force to help." In fact, Bush, unsure he had enough votes, soon ignored the Security Council and on his own ordered U.S. troops into northern Iraq to help provide relief for the Kurds. The U.S., Britain, and France also decided they needed no U.N. approval when they imposed a no-fly zone in northern Iraq to prevent Saddam Hussein from airlifting troops to suppress the Kurds and a similar zone in the south later to protect the Shiite Muslims.

※ ఙ

Led by Ambassador Pickering, the Security Council imposed a peace on Iraq that was as harsh as that imposed on defeated Germany by the Treaty of Versailles after World War I. The key resolution, approved on March 3, was so long that ambassadors, borrowing an image from Saddam Hussein's rhetoric, called it "the mother of all resolutions." The resolution was approved by a majority of twelve, with Cuba opposed and Ecuador and Yemen abstaining. Although Iraq had fled from Kuwait, it had done so only reluctantly and under the power of a thunderous onslaught, and all sanctions were therefore kept in place by the resolution.

To lift the sanctions, Iraq had to comply with a series of tough-minded conditions. The most significant was the obliteration of all its programs for the development and production of nuclear, chemical, biological, and other weapons of mass destruction. In what Iraqi officialdom regarded as a humiliating affront to sovereignty, Iraq also had to allow a system of U.N. monitoring that would ensure it never produced these weapons again. Only after the weapons programs were permanently stifled, according to the resolution, could Iraq sell its oil. For months, the stubborn Iraqis struggled to delay and outwit the U.N. Special Commission charged with eliminating Saddam Hussein's programs for these terrible weapons. But the Iraqis, under the threat of renewed coalition air attacks, reluctantly gave in to the blandishments of Rolf Ekeus, the Swedish diplomat who headed the Special Commission. By mid-1995, Iraq appeared close to full compliance with the demands of the resolution on weapons of mass destruction.

The postwar attitude of the Bush administration left U.N. diplomats puzzled about its commitment to the United Nations. In a speech to the American Newspaper Publishers Association in May, two months after the war's end, Deputy National Security Adviser Robert M. Gates pronounced the administration's attitude about lifting sanctions. "Saddam is discredited and cannot be redeemed," Gates said. "His leadership will never be accepted by the world community and, therefore, Iraqis will pay the price while he remains in power. All possible sanctions will be maintained until he is gone. Any easing of sanctions will be considered only when there is a new government." This attitude was somewhat understandable. Many critics decried the American failure to oust Saddam Hussein from power during the war. Bush had glibly compared the Iraqi dictator to Hitler; at times, Bush called him worse than Hitler. No one had ever contemplated a defeated Germany after World War II with Hitler still at the helm. Yet, if Bush's comparison was apt, he had allowed the modern-day Hitler to remain in power in Iraq. The Gates threat, cleared by the White House, amounted to a promise that the United States now hoped to oust Saddam Hussein through sanctions.

The Gates speech upset the Pickering mission at the U.N. The war-ending resolution contained no demand that Iraq somehow rid itself of Saddam Hussein. The White House proclamation of such a demand seemed to hold the resolution in contempt. "The United States has been punctilious about staying within the resolutions up to now," said an aide to Pickering. "In general, it [the Gates threat] goes beyond the resolution." Pickering, forced to defend the new White House doctrine publicly, insisted that Gates had allowed some flexibility by stating that "all possible sanctions" would be kept in place. But the Bush administration clearly did not want to look flexible, and its attitude left the later Clinton administration little room to maneuver.

U.N. officials and diplomats were shocked to learn a few weeks later that the Bush administration had decided to remove Pickering from the U.N. and transfer him to India. Unlike Adlai Stevenson, Pickering was not encumbered by a paralyzed Security Council good for nothing but theatrics, and the difference probably made Pickering the most effective American ambassador ever to serve at the U.N. His removal struck the U.N. like a crude slap. Secretary of State Baker, however, told the Senate the change was simply part of a policy to rotate ambassadors every three years. But no one at the U.N. believed that. "It's pretty thin, isn't it?" said a French diplomat.

In a sense, Pickering had done his work too well. He accomplished all that Washington wanted but did so rather independently. Baker and his aides did not look kindly on initiative; they felt the need to control events and underlings. John R. Bolton, the assistant secretary of state for international organizations and Pickering's superior on the department's organizational charts, reportedly complained that Pickering, when carrying out orders from Washington, would move from A to C as instructed but would usually do so without following the department's order to go through B. Even more important, Pickering irritated Margaret Tutwiler, the department spokeswoman and a long-time confidante of Baker. "Pickering would say things at the United Nations," said an aide to one of the State Department's key policy-makers, "that were not contrary to State Department policy and might even have logically followed State Department policy but had not been specifically approved by the top people. . . . As a result, Tutwiler got upset when she was asked questions about something that Pickering said and [she] did not know what to reply. These people do not like someone who is out of their control." This attitude was so obvious that Henry Kissinger introduced the departing Pickering at a luncheon for businessmen as "our distinguished ambassador—too distinguished for some people."

A few days before his inauguration as president, Bill Clinton broke with the inflexible policy of the Bush administration and held out hope to Saddam Hussein that the United States might look on him differently if he mended his ways. "I always tell everybody," Clinton said in an interview with the *New York Times*, " 'I'm a Baptist. I believe in deathbed conversions.' If he wants a different relationship with the United States and with the United Nations, all he has to do is change his behavior." But this note was roundly condemned by his critics, and President Clinton soon discovered that there were no political dividends in smoothing relations with Saddam Hussein and a good many dividends in standing up to him. The American public was obviously pleased when Clinton bombed a Baghdad intelligence center in June 1993 in retaliation for an alleged Iraqi assassination attempt against former President Bush while visiting Kuwait.

As for sanctions, the Clinton administration did move away from the simplistic policy of keeping them in place so long as Saddam Hussein ruled Iraq. But the legalistic policy set down by American Ambassador Madeleine K. Albright was clearly honed for the same result. Under the American plan, Saddam Hussein would not be allowed to sell oil even if he did comply with all the conditions in the war-ending resolution. Instead, these sanctions would be lifted only when Saddam Hussein complied with all the conditions set down by all the resolutions—such conditions as recognizing the boundary worked out by a demarcation commission, accounting for missing Kuwaitis, paying compensation to all those hurt financially by the war, and so on. Otherwise, the Americans argued, there would be no way of knowing if the Iraqis were sincere about accepting perpetual U.N. inspection. The American stubbornness upset other members of the Security Council, especially France and Russia. They wanted to start buying oil from Iraq soon; they also insisted that the sanctions were hurting the Iraqi people without weakening Saddam Hussein's hold on the country. The Security Council appeared headed for a showdown on this issue, perhaps in late 1995.

꧁꧂

It became fashionable a few years after the Persian Gulf War to downgrade its importance. That was inevitable, since George Bush had oversold it with all his talk about a new international order. Victory in the Persian Gulf did not create such an order. There was little doubt that the special circumstances of the war—a blatant act of aggression, a despotic leader easy to demonize, an American president prepared to commit enormous resources for a distant war, a Russia so disoriented by sudden weakness that it acquiesced in all the United States did—would be difficult to duplicate. An American-led coalition of nations might not find it so easy to squelch a tyrant in the future.

Yet the Persian Gulf War made the Security Council feel the glory of its own strength. Even without the Persian Gulf War, of course, the Security Council would have evolved into a far stronger body than it had been during the Cold War. But the dramatic ejection of the Iraqis from Kuwait gave the Security Council an exciting confidence. Provided the Big Five agreed or at least withheld their veto, provided five or six or seven others joined the Big Five, the Security Council felt it could literally attempt to do anything. The Persian Gulf expanded the horizon of the Security Council and, in fact, made election to it one of the grand prizes of U.N. membership. The newly found power probably led the Security Council to attempt far more than it could manage. But, even when some failures tempered a good deal of optimism, there was little doubt that the Security Council had become what Roosevelt wanted—the heart of the U.N.

The Gulf War, however, also had a troublesome side for the U.N. The Security Council realized its potential and achieved the most when the United States decided to lead it. As a result, the war solidified the American notion that the U.N. worked best when it did what the United States wanted. This encouraged American critics to harp on any later attempt by the White House to lead the U.N. in new directions if these directions smacked more of multilateralism than of American national interest. Americans acted as if the U.N. were their U.N. At the slightest hint that it might not be theirs alone, Americans tended to turn their backs on the United Nations and shun it.

❧ 16 ❧

Boutros Boutros-Ghali

Boutros Boutros-Ghali startled a rare news conference in May 1994 by declaring that he might seek a second five-year term as secretary-general of the United Nations. "The question will be raised in 1996," said the seventy-one-year-old former Egyptian diplomat and law professor, "and it will depend on my physical capacities. If I am feeling in shape, quite honestly, I will say yes. On the other hand . . . if I don't feel well enough, then I won't request a second term." Until then, he had insisted that he did not intend to stand for a second term, a stance that allowed him to wield his independence like a shield of honor. Why had he changed his mind? "I believe that only stupid people don't change their mind," he replied.

The announcement infuriated Clinton administration officials, provoking mutterings in private about the fortunes of a snowball in hell. Boutros-Ghali's relations with American diplomats and officials had been tense for some time, and many were so exasperated with him that they intended to recommend a veto if he submitted to a vote in 1996.

There was a good deal of irony in this. The United States did not favor Boutros-Ghali the first time around but for far different reasons. In 1991, he simply did not measure up to the standards that Bush administration officials had set for the new secretary-general after the Persian Gulf War. He struck them as too elderly, too frail, too passive, too laconic, and too old-fashioned for the dynamic image on their minds. It was time for the U.N. to be led by someone with both weight and pizzazz.

President Bush's own personal choice was Canadian Prime Minister Brian Mulroney, the garrulous and congenial Irish-Quebecker whose popularity was plummeting at home. But a furious protest from Third World ambassadors undercut Mulroney so badly that the embarrassed Canadians soon withdrew his candidacy. The Third Worlders insisted it was Africa's turn to fill the job. While the White House began a lackadaisical search for another suitable candidate, the State Department, wary of offending Egypt, voted perfunctorily for Boutros-Ghali on a succession of ballots, sure that he would never get the required nine votes to win. This proved a miscalculation. On November 21, 1991, while the Americans still searched, the Security Council elected Boutros-Ghali as the sixth secretary-general.

As secretary-general, Boutros-Ghali certainly did not exhibit any of the flair or dynamism that American officials once sought. But, inward and moody and sometimes disdainful, Boutros-Ghali became the most stubbornly independent secretary-general in the half-century history of the United Nations. He made the secretary-general an international player in a way that had not been seen since the days of Dag Hammarskjöld and the crisis in the Congo. While he did not have the same reverence and affection, Boutros-Ghali proved at least as active as Hammarskjöld in crises and just as effective at expanding the role of the office. He was not the passive bureaucrat that fretful American officials once expected. The Clinton administration, in fact, soon wished that he were.

Boutros-Ghali's activism alarmed critics and prompted many to exaggerate his role. Former Assistant Secretary of State Richard L. Armitage and former U.N. Ambassador Jeane Kirkpatrick accused him of trying to become "chief executive officer of the world" and "the world's commander-in-chief." This widespread perception made it easy to turn him into a scapegoat. The Clinton administration succeeded in deluding the American public into believing it was Boutros-Ghali alone who led American soldiers to disaster in Somalia. Bosnians blamed Boutros-Ghali and the U.N. for the international paralysis that permitted Serbian aggression and ethnic cleansing to go on so long. His disdain for such emotion and lapses of logic only infuriated his critics and sharpened their barbs.

Boutros-Ghali was no smooth-talking diplomat. He ran the U.N. with the instincts of a suspicious politician and the brilliance of a former professor whose mind could absorb data and order it into policy alternatives with breathtaking ease. Once his logic pointed the way, he usually followed it consistently, even to a fault. He was so jealous of his independence that he did not even reward the early supporters like France and the African governments that ensured his election. A Christian Copt whose rise to the top was always blocked in Muslim Egypt, he did not expect more than meager rewards for his services. He knew how to shrug off insults. Nothing at the U.N. compared with the vitriol heaped upon him by the Arab world for negotiating the Israeli-Egyptian peace treaty. He knew that his power was limited. As secretary-general, he depended on governments to supply him with troops for battle. He had no constituencies of voters to rally when powers like the United States slapped him down. Yet he refused to shrink within these limitations.

❦❦

Boutros Boutros-Ghali was born in Cairo on November 14, 1922, an heir of a land-rich, influential Coptic Christian family, the grandson of a prime minister assassinated a dozen years before. He grew up in the enormous mansion that had been the home of his grandfather, a house of a hundred rooms in a once-elegant neighborhood of Cairo that had started to decay.

His odd double-drum name, which critics sometimes mocked and comics like David Letterman repeated for laughs, reflected a twin tribute to his grandfather. Boutros Pasha Ghali was gunned down in 1910 by Ibrahim Nasif Wardani, a European-educated pharmacist and radical Muslim nationalist protesting the prime minister's supposed closeness to the British colonial power. It was a time of tension between Muslims and Copts, and Cairo crowds hailed the killing with a chant, "May God bless Wardani who killed Ghali the Nazarene." In memory of the martyr, the Ghali family adopted his first name, Boutros ("Peter" in the Coptic language), as part of the family name. In further honor of the assassinated prime minister more than a decade later, the parents of a new grandson decided to name him Boutros as well.

Everyone assumed that the young Boutros Boutros-Ghali would follow the family tradition of public service. "When I was a young boy," he recalled, "our family built a church in Cairo in honor of my grandfather. It was called Boutrosia. His tomb was inside. There was written on the tomb, 'God is witness that I served my country to my best ability.' There was even a painting of my grandmother offering the Church to the Virgin Mary. For a small boy to see such things creates an impact. I felt that I must have a political career, that I would betray the tradition of our family if I didn't play a political role." Although he preferred literature as a subject, he studied law at the University of Cairo, a must for an Egyptian entering politics in those days.

As a student he took part in the successful parliamentary electoral campaigns of a pair of cousins, the sons of his uncle Nagib, then minister of agriculture. Using the family mansion as headquarters, he walked the streets of the neighborhood, knocking on doors, whipping up rallies, handing out money. So certain did a political career seem that a girlfriend once showed him a picture of a young man who resembled him somewhat. It was a photo of Jawaharlal Nehru taken in the early years of the century. "You have the same birthday, the 14th of November," she said, "and you will have the same destiny."

His family was proud of its European sophistication. Some fanciful gossipers, in fact, tried later to portray Boutros-Ghali as the model for the wealthy Copt Nessim in Lawrence Durrell's *The Alexandria Quartet*. Although Boutros-Ghali like Nessim was married to a woman from a Jewish family in Alexandria, he would have been far too young to serve as any kind of a model for Durrell. Yet an outsider could probably understand Boutros-Ghali better by trying to transplant the French-speaking, elite, ecumenical atmosphere of the Dur-

rell novels into the high society of Cairo in the 1940s. It was natural in
this milieu for a wealthy scholar like Boutros-Ghali to study for his
Ph.D. in international relations at the Sorbonne in Paris.

When he returned to Cairo in 1949, he quickly joined the political science faculty of the University of Cairo, a possible springboard
for national politics. But a coup led by Colonel Gamal Abdel Nasser
overthrew the monarchy three years later. By 1954, Nasser assumed
full power and ushered in an era of fervent Arab nationalism that
seemed to exclude Copts from government, especially those closely
identified with the old régime. Land reform decrees confiscated the
family's vast holdings throughout Egypt, leaving the Boutros-Ghalis
landless though still wealthy. Teaching quickly became an end in
itself for the young professor. He remained at the university for
twenty-eight years, heading its political science department, editing a
foreign affairs journal, frequently lecturing abroad in such universi-
ties as Columbia, Princeton, the Sorbonne, and Uppsala (in Sweden), and establishing a worldwide reputation as a specialist in
international law.

In 1977, President Anwar Sadat, Nasser's successor, decided to
open channels to the Coptic community by appointing prominent
Copts to his cabinet. Professor Boutros-Ghali was named a minister
of state for foreign affairs. Within a month, Sadat surprised the world
by announcing he would fly to Jerusalem. The foreign minister and
deputy foreign minister resigned in protest. Sadat swiftly promoted
Boutros-Ghali to acting foreign minister and took him along instead.

Rumors spread that the idea for the trip had come from the
Coptic professor in the first place. "I would be proud to have been
the one," he said later, "but it is not true. What happened? I had
written an article that sooner or later we would have to coexist with
Israel and I had organized a round table on the subject. When Sadat
asked me to come to Jerusalem, the Israelis opened their files and
read that I had written the article and decided that I was the brain
behind the visit of Sadat. But it was not true."

Boutros-Ghali was a key negotiator at the Camp David talks that
produced the 1979 Israeli-Egyptian peace treaty. For this, he was vilified in the Arab world for more than a decade as "the academic engineer of Arab surrender." Enemies invoked the memory of his

grandfather, railing at the assassinated prime minister for supposedly selling out the Sudan to the British at the turn of the century. Extremists denounced the "family of traitors" and demanded the death as well of the grandson, Boutros Boutros-Ghali. Palestine Liberation Organization (PLO) Chairman Yasser Arafat stood up at the summit conference of nonaligned nations in Havana in 1979 and shouted, "Sadat had no courage to come here and has sent his puppet instead, the traitor Boutros-Ghali."

Despite the significance of his duties, Boutros-Ghali remained minister of state for foreign affairs for fourteen years, never rising to foreign minister. In May 1991, President Hosni Mubarak named him deputy prime minister for foreign affairs, a largely honorific post designed to enhance his image during the quiet but effective campaign that led to his election as U.N. secretary-general a half-year later.

᠁

Boutros-Ghali insisted in interviews that he had never felt the humiliation of discrimination against Copts. "I have never felt any kind of feeling of being a minority, like Jews feel and Negroes feel," he said. "I'm not saying there is no discrimination. I am saying that because of the wealth of my family, I have never felt any. But I have Coptic students who say there is discrimination. I have Coptic friends who say there is discrimination." Yet there was little doubt that successive governments refused to anoint him as foreign minister only because he was Copt.

His years of political maneuvering while a minority in an Islamic government—albeit a privileged minority—held a key to understanding the mood of his administration at the U.N. A veteran American diplomat described Boutros-Ghali as "the perpetual outsider, the Court Jew" who has accumulated power by trusting no one. "There is a joke," said an ambassador on the Security Council, "that whenever the Secretary-General wants to look for someone he can trust, he stands up on his two feet, walks across the room to the wall, and looks into the mirror." Brian Urquhart, the former undersecretary-general, once proposed that the secretary-general appoint four deputy secretaries-general to lighten the workload. Boutros-

Ghali did not appoint any, for fear of diminishing the authority of his office. Some glib critics insisted that Boutros-Ghali tried to do everything himself. The U.N.'s responsibilities had become too vast and onerous for that, of course, but it was true that he did not delegate authority easily, dismissed aides who displeased him swiftly, and, unlike Hammarskjöld, kept no one of the stature of Ralph Bunche by his side.

He was ever the professor, teaching others a lesson. He continually scolded African ambassadors, for example, for failing to keep informed on issues that matter to Africa or for failing to acknowledge the reality of their continent's woeful state. In one well-publicized incident, he chided the Security Council for blindly accepting a European Community proposal on Bosnia without consulting him or studying it carefully. Most of the fifteen ambassadors on the Security Council felt slighted by him, persuaded that he regarded them as minor bureaucrats. His predecessor, Javier Pérez de Cuéllar, attended most of the private consultations of the Security Council. Boutros-Ghali rarely showed up, looking on the sessions as wasteful for a secretary-general forced to plan and administer the feverish post–Cold War expansion of U.N. missions worldwide.

The secretary-general was a poor public communicator. He was stiff and awkward at formal news conferences. He preferred occasional private sessions with journalists who asked him thoughtful questions that demanded professorial answers. Most reporters who covered the U.N. were out of this loop and resented it. He performed well on French television, where the format lent itself to lengthy conversation. But he performed poorly on American television: his command of English was inferior to his flawless French, and interviewers confused him when they kept interrupting in their breathless hunt for sound bites.

Although he sometimes lost his temper with associates and diplomats who crossed him, Boutros-Ghali could be charming and witty in private. He socialized rarely, watched little if any television, and burrowed at his work at home until midnight every day. After more than three years in New York, he once complained, he had yet to catch a play or a movie or a concert. "I am a monk," he joked. He was oblivious to the momentary celebrities and sensational gossip that caught the fancy of everyone around him. He told several ambassadors that he consulted a doctor about a painful knee during the 1994 Winter Olympics. The genial doctor offered three possible diagnoses: the pain could have come from arthritis, gout, or "a blow from Tonya." "Tonya?" the secretary-general asked in puzzlement. "What's that?" His top aides complained that he wanted them as workaholic as himself, sometimes ordering a report at nine-thirty at night and complaining when it was not on his desk at nine-thirty the next morning. Many aides looked on him as an unreasonable taskmaster.

Even his most contemptuous critics did not deny Boutros-Ghali's brilliance as an analyst of international crises. He dissected a problem from many angles before coming to a conclusion. But, once he made up his mind, he acted decisively and held his point of view. His consistency was astounding in an era when politicians veered from side to side week by week to complement public opinion charts. He was not, however, so quixotic as to refuse adjusting to reality. He continually modified his missions and sometimes stepped into forbidding territory to satisfy the demands of powerful members of the Security Council like the United States. But he did so while sticking to his broad philosophical understanding of an issue. His conclusions about the nature of problems in Somalia, Bosnia, and South Africa did not change from the first months of his administration. This consistency came from both stubbornness and intellectual arrogance. Though he may not have had the political means to impose his point of view, he was convinced that his analysis, at least in theory, was usually right.

Boutros-Ghali was often criticized for failing to whip the Secretariat into shape. Foundations and newspapers continually denounced the U.N. Secretariat as overladen, overpaid, and underworked. Reports and newspaper editors always demanded reform. Some of this was overblown. There were bound to be inefficiencies and confusions in a polyglot bureaucracy culled from 185 countries. Some of the civil servants were as astute, efficient, and resourceful as any in Washington and European capitals. But it is also true that an overhaul would surely have gotten rid of deadwood and revitalized the bureaucracy.

Boutros-Ghali cut down the ludicrous number of undersecretaries-general and reduced the rest of the staff when he took office but seemed to lose interest in the problem afterward. "I don't think managerial issues are his favorite issues," American Ambassador Madeleine K. Albright told Julia Preston of the *Washington Post.* "He had some very good ideas at the beginning but got bogged down." He also found that he had to spend an enormous amount of his time on peacekeeping and peace enforcement—matters far more vital for the future of the U.N.

※※

The United Nations has no more important work than peacekeeping. In its first forty years, the Security Council authorized only thirteen peacekeeping operations. In the fifth decade, another twenty were launched, half of them under Boutros-Ghali. As of December 1994, the U.N. operated seventeen peacekeeping missions with seventy-three thousand troops and police at an annual cost of $3.6 billion—more than three times the cost of the regular $1 billion U.N. budget covering all other activities. Boutros-Ghali's term as secretary-general would surely be defined by his use of peacekeeping.

A close examination of his role in peacekeeping revealed a surprising quality: his caution. In June 1992, after six months on the job, Boutros-Ghali presented his "Agenda for Peace," fulfilling a request from a summit meeting of the Security Council that he set down his proposals to improve "the capacity of the United Nations for preventive diplomacy, for peacemaking and for peacekeeping." The secretary-general spent a total of forty hours poring over and revising the drafts prepared by aides, and the final fifty-two-page manuscript was widely regarded as his personal testament and blueprint.

While his "Agenda for Peace" was an innovative statement, it mainly proposed that U.N. peacekeepers go on with what they had been doing—the traditional monitoring of cease-fire lines like those on Cyprus and the Golan Heights and the more recent and complex work in missions like Cambodia and El Salvador that involved the supervision of elections and shoring up of institutions.

The agenda broke ground at the U.N. with only three proposals:

(1) "preventive deployment" of troops to an area of potential crisis when a worried government asks for them to discourage an outbreak of hostilities, (2) agreements with governments to set aside special troops for possible rapid deployment by the U.N. in peacekeeping and other military missions, and (3) use of peace-enforcement troops, more heavily armed than peacemakers, for dangerous military missions like the forcible maintenance of a cease-fire. None of these ideas was very radical; they were in harmony with the proposals that issued from a host of think tanks in the 1990s.

Three of the post–Cold War peacekeeping missions—Cambodia, Somalia, and Bosnia—each deployed more than twenty thousand troops in the field, U.N. operations on a scale not seen since the years of the Congo crisis. The Cambodia operation, initiated by Pérez de Cuéllar but presided over mainly by Boutros-Ghali, was regarded as a relative success, although the U.N., while organizing meaningful elections, failed to reduce the armies of the contending factions. This left the Khmer Rouge with enough arms to keep its territory in virtual insurrection against the government

※ ※

The Somalia experience underscored Boutros-Ghali's tenacity, even in the face of badgering by so powerful a country as the United States. It also showed him realistically aware of the U.N.'s limitations. When President Bush offered to send more than twenty thousand marines to Somalia at the end of 1992, the secretary-general set down clearly what he saw as the only way to rip out the roots of the catastrophe. To ensure a permanent end to the crippling violence, he told the Security Council in a letter, "it would be necessary for at least the heavy weapons of the organized factions to be neutralized and brought under international control and for the irregular forces and gangs to be disarmed."

Boutros-Ghali clearly wanted the U.S. to complete the job without him. He finally agreed, under American pressure, to take over the operation in May 1993 but, as he wrote Ambassador Madeleine Albright in a confidential letter that month, he was "uneasy" over the gap between the strength of the departing U.S.-led task force and his own weak peacekeepers (even though they would be bolstered by some American forces).

The Somalia mission took a disastrous turn with the futile manhunt for General Mohamed Farah Aideed and the raid on October 3 that left eighteen U.S. Rangers dead. The secretary-general was probably shortsighted in allowing his special representative, retired American Admiral Jonathan Howe, to bog the mission down in the manhunt for Aideed after his minions ambushed and killed twenty-five Pakistani peacekeepers. But the United States and the rest of the Security Council supported the manhunt as well—at least until it began to sour.

With Congress and the public upset by the U.N. misadventure, Clinton announced that he would withdraw all Americans by March 31. A frustrated and betrayed Boutros-Ghali began berating the United States in a series of speeches for failing to stay the course. But there was nothing he could do about it.

彩彩

The Bosnia mission illustrated two somewhat contradictory qualities of Boutros-Ghali—an acceptance of the hypocritical manipulation of the U.N. by the United States and Europe to hide their lack of conviction and a stubborn insistence that he is an independent player on the world stage.

From the start, Boutros-Ghali was reluctant to involve the U.N. in Bosnia, knowing that it was hopeless to ask peacekeepers to act as impartial observers and enemies of Serbian aggression at the same time. But he could not resist the need of the United States and Europe to use the U.N. to show that they were doing something about the horror.

At the end of 1992, the secretary-general acknowledged that the U.N. was being manipulated by the United States and Europe to quiet domestic public opinion, but he was philosophical about this situation. "This is diplomacy," he said. "The U.N. has been created to help the member states solve their problems. If you will solve problems by adopting certain resolutions that are more spectacular than practical, if this can help diffuse tension, why not?" But he also acknowledged the danger. "I don't say that it doesn't hurt the U.N.," he went on. "I am saying that the U.N. has been created to do this. It can hurt the U.N., certainly. If you adopt a very practical resolution and the U.N., for different reasons, is not able to implement it, this will hurt the U.N.."

As the terrible crisis persisted, he became more troubled by the danger to U.N. credibility. But this did not stop him from assuming—with all its risks—a central role in the use of air power authorized by the Security Council. This troubled many diplomats, officials, and analysts. Some worried that Boutros-Ghali had involved himself too much in military issues that were outside the competence of a secretary-general. Others feared that Boutros-Ghali, with his preference for negotiations over military action, would stand in the way of bombing even if all governments clamored for it. In the end, he tried to make it clear that he was no more reluctant than NATO to use airpower. Yet his representative on the scene, Yasushi Akashi of Japan, delayed and even vetoed air attacks enough times to make the U.N. look more cowardly than any of the other actors in the face of Serbian aggression.

The months of paralysis over Bosnia damaged the U.N. markedly. During the Gorazde siege, for example, conservative columnist George Will derided the U.N. as "a moral cipher" with a "pretense that it can play a role for which it is incurably unsuited, that of peacemaker." In the long run, both Bosnia and Somalia will surely be regarded as flawed or even failed U.N. missions. If so, they were dragged down by the lack of resolve in the United States and Europe, not by the failings of the secretary-general. But the reputation of Boutros-Ghali suffered nevertheless.

≈

The frustrations of Somalia and Bosnia led Boutros-Ghali to issue a reassessment of his "Agenda for Peace" in January 1995. He did not alter his original assumptions about the need for peace enforcement, but he faced the political reality of dwindling support. "Enforcement action at present is beyond the capacity of the United Nations except on a very limited scale," he wrote. "It would be folly to attempt to alter this reality at the present time." As he told a news conference, "If the peace enforcement operation is limited to 2,000—4,000 soldiers, we have the capacity to carry it out." Otherwise, he said, the U.N. had to authorize others to do the job in its name, the way the United States organized the coalition that chased Saddam Hussein out of Kuwait. Boutros-Ghali made it clear that the problem of peace enforcement was not in its conception but in the lack of support. He berated U.N. members for failing to provide troops when needed, and he castigated the Security Council for trying to "micro-manage" peacekeeping and peace enforcement operations. To help meet the demand for emergency help, he also proposed the establishment of a U.N. rapid reaction force available for instant call-up.

The reassessment did not please Washington. Ambassador Albright accused Boutros-Ghali of trying to "arrogate more power" to himself with the proposed rapid reaction force, and she took exception to the report's penchant for blaming U.N. failures on Security Council micro-management and lack of support from others. "I think we have to guard against saying that every time there is a success it is due to the United Nations, and every time there is a failure it is due to the member states," she told reporters. Albright belittled the report even before Boutros-Ghali had a chance to explain it at his news conference, and this American breach of protocol appeared to anger him.

In a speech a few weeks after President Clinton decided to pull the American troops out of Somalia, Boutros-Ghali said, "I need the United States. The United Nations needs the United States. Finding the right relationship between the U.N. and the U.S. may be one of the most important tasks of our time." That relationship deteriorated during the Boutros-Ghali era.

There were raised voices and barbed words in meetings of the secretary-general and Ambassador Albright, bristling correspondence between him and Secretary of State Warren Christopher, and public rebukes by both sides. When Boutros-Ghali sent a letter to Israeli Prime Minister Yitzhak Rabin after the Hebron massacre suggesting "*some* kind of United Nations presence" in the occupied territories, Albright's press attaché, James P. Rubin, took the unusual step of issuing a pronouncement that "we do not think the Secretary-General's suggestion is particularly helpful or useful."

The horrors of Rwanda provoked a new conflict between Boutros-Ghali and the Clinton administration in May 1994. While the secretary-general demanded immediate action by the Security Council, Ambassador Albright made Rwanda the first test of Clinton's Presidential Policy Directive 25, the administration's new strict guidelines curtailing American participation in—and even support of—U.N. peacekeeping. Albright pressured the Security Council into delaying the dispatch of a full contingent of five thousand peace-keepers to Rwanda until the secretary-general could satisfy the ambassadors that the new Clinton conditions had been met. "Sending a U.N. force into the maelstrom of Rwanda without a sound plan of operations would be folly," she told the House Foreign Affairs Committee the next day.

※ ⚘

Clinton administration officials insisted that the work of a secretary-general should be purely administrative; he should not be initiating diplomatic moves, setting policy, or implementing Security Council resolutions like a prime minister. "The Secretary-General often oversteps his role," said a U.S. official, "and some of the things he does are counterproductive." Not only did this complicate delicate international problems like the Mideast peace process, the official went on, but "it gives critics like Senator [Robert] Dole an opportunity to lambast the United Nations and hurt the constituency for the U.N. in the United States."

Boutros-Ghali sometimes sounded as if he agreed that his role should be limited. He liked to describe himself as the servant of the Security Council and often proclaimed his political weakness. Asked about his course of action after the Americans withdrew from Somalia, the secretary-general replied, "I can do nothing. I have no army. I have no money. I have no experts. I am borrowing everything. If the member states don't want [to do something], what can I do?"

Yet Boutros-Ghali knew that the American concept of a secretary-general who administrated and took orders was untenable in an era racked by dangerous ethnic conflicts that no government, certainly not the Clinton administration, wanted to handle on its own. The Security Council constantly dealt with these problems by dumping them in the lap of the secretary-general, asking him to report back with an analysis and recommendations. The Security Council had no staff and rarely contradicted Boutros-Ghali's findings and proposals about Cyprus, Angola, Mozambique, Western Sahara, Georgia, and other areas of past and present conflict.

When Boutros-Ghali described himself as a servant of the Security Council, he meant that only in the sense that John Major is a servant of Parliament. Boutros-Ghali understood, of course, that the Security Council was the most powerful body of the U.N., the ultimate source of policy. Yet he saw himself as the independent prod, the catalyst, the guide of policy, and the executor of decisions. "You must be an activist," he told David Frost in an interview, "because we are living in acceleration of history, and there is a daily revolution. And if you will be able to cope with this daily revolution, we must, we must be an activist. You cannot be neutral. You cannot be passive, waiting what will be the direction of the member states. You have to push everybody."

The U.N. Charter set down the secretary-general's powers in sketchy and vague language. It did call him "the chief administrative officer of the organization" but did not—as the Americans might like—limit him to that. His independence derived mainly from Article 99, which stated, in its entirety, "The Secretary-General may bring to the attention of the Security Council any matter which in his opinion may threaten the maintenance of international peace and security." In the early days of the U.N. almost a half-century ago, that did not seem like much. In fact, three months after the first meeting of the Security Council, Secretary-General Trygve Lie angered many of its members by daring to submit a memorandum on his own initiative.

The authority of the office evolved enormously since that precedent, but its reach never extended as far as it did during the 1990s. Boutros-Ghali was quick to establish the secretary-general as an independent power within the U.N. system. His predecessor, Javier Pérez de Cuéllar, would circulate drafts of his reports to the Big Five to make sure they had no objections before he submitted the final report to the Security Council as a whole. Boutros-Ghali ended that practice immediately. His refusal to attend the closed-door consultations of the Security Council—a refusal that annoyed the ambassadors—was another way of establishing independence. "Of course he finds it boring and has other things to do," said a U.N. official. "But, if he were really a servant of the Security Council, he would go even though it was boring." Another practice that irritated the ambassadors—his penchant for phoning their foreign ministers rather than consulting them—drove home that he regarded his own status as greater than theirs. His assertion of the independence of his office will surely count as Boutros-Ghali's most important legacy.

But his skills as a communicator and diplomat were so tentative that he aroused a good deal of ill will and resentment and misunderstanding. These were substantial faults. Boutros-Ghali wanted to transform the United Nations on many fronts, making it a major factor in development, social justice, and environment just the way it was now a major actor in trying to order the chaos spawned by dozens of nasty, ethnic wars. Yet he was never able to articulate for the public, whether within the United States or out, what changes he wanted to see and how he intended to make them. Perhaps even more important, he failed to make outsiders understand the limits imposed upon the U.N. in crisis-torn countries like Bosnia, Somalia, and Rwanda. The Bosnia mission became an object of worldwide ridicule, but the secretary-general was never able to make an impact with the U.N.'s side of the story.

❧ 17 ❧

The Somalia Debacle

On January 5, 1993, Secretary-General Boutros Boutros-Ghali lectured the Somalia warlords gathered for a peace conference in the Ethiopian capital of Addis Ababa. It had been a trying week for Boutros-Ghali. The minions of Somalia chieftain Mohamed Farah Aideed had surrounded the U.N. compound in the Somali capital of Mogadishu a couple of days earlier, pelting it with garbage and rocks and crying out curses and forcing the visiting secretary-general to abandon plans to stop at the compound for a meeting with the U.N. staff there. The crowd of several hundred shouted that the secretary-general favored Aideed's enemies. They intoned "Boutros-Ghali—Down!" and handed out leaflets to visiting journalists that proclaimed in English that they did not want "the Egyptian farmer" in their country. The peace conference opened the next day in discord and recrimination, and Boutros-Ghali, about to depart from Addis Ababa for Egypt, used a final news conference to admonish the Somalis.

The secretary-general tried to make the warlords understand that the outsiders now in Somalia—the U.S. Marines, the U.N., the humanitarian relief organizations—offered Somalia a last chance for peace. The outsiders did not want anything from their country. They would not back one side or the other for gain. If the Somalis failed to reconcile and fashion a workable, peaceful government, the outsiders would surely pack up and go. "The Cold War is finished," he said. "Nobody wants control over Somalia. . . . Some Somalis believe Somalia has strategic importance. That's not true. . . . No one is interested in Somalia, not for strategic reasons, not for oil, not for gold. . . . There can be a real *drame* [using the French word for tragedy] some day: The world could forget Somalia in a few minutes."

But there was no logic to Somalia then. Old Africa hands used to believe that Somalia was blessed because it had escaped the curse of tribalism. Unlike most countries in Africa, Somalia had one tribe, one religion, and one language. Yet now clans and subclans were warring, and even that did not explain the inane horror. "Not only are they from the same tribe," said a U.N. official who knew Somalia well. "Not only do they speak the same language and have the same ethnicity. There is not one single shred of difference between them ideologically. They are only interested in power, and it cannot be shared."

The roots of the Somalia crisis lay in the repressive twenty-one-year rule of General Mohamed Siad Barre. A heavily nomadic, near desert land of seven million, Somalia had been known since independence in 1960 as an impoverished but noisy neighbor in the horn of Africa. Made up of the old British Somaliland and Italian Somaliland, Somalia continually boasted of its intent to swallow up Djibouti (the old French Somaliland), the Northern Frontier District of Kenya, and the Ogaden province of Ethiopia because mostly Somalis lived or trekked there. A bloody war with Ethiopia was fought intermittently over decades. At first the United States backed Ethiopia, while the Soviet Union backed Somalia. When the Ethiopians overthrew Emperor Haile Selassie and rejected his ties with the United States, the Soviets switched their support to Ethiopia. The United States felt it had no choice then but to switch as well and line up with the Somalis, supplying extensive military and economic aid. Somalia was awash with weaponry when civil war erupted in the late 1980s.

Barre, who seized power in a coup in 1969, was a southerner

who favored his own clan; the northerners in the old British Somaliland chafed under his rule. When a rebellion broke out in the north,
Barre tried to suppress it with a terrible bombardment of cities and
civilians. The main city of Hargeisa lay in rubble after the onslaught,
thousands of civilians died, and three hundred thousand refugees
fled to Ethiopia. Barre's fearful fury led him to depend even more on
his own clan, alienating the other clans and subclans in the south
until they, too, took up arms against him. On January 27, 1991, Siad
Barre fled Mogadishu and headed south toward Bardera with his
army. The news was not much noticed outside for it came during the
height of the Persian Gulf War.

Siad Barre tried to regroup and retake Mogadishu but was
driven back by General Aideed. When Barre was finally routed, seeking refuge in Nigeria, the warlords who ousted him then fell upon
each other. Aideed probably led the strongest of the factions, but it
was not strong enough to control the country. Aideed, however,
looked upon himself as the savior of Somalia and therefore entitled
to rule. A former general in the Somali army, Aideed had long been
mistrusted by Siad Barre. The dictator, in fact, had imprisoned him
for seven years and then exiled him to India as ambassador. Aideed
returned in time to lead a rebel militia against Siad Barre in the civil
war.

Aideed's main rival in Mogadishu was Ali Mahdi Mohamed, a
Mogadishu businessman and hotel owner whose forces controlled
northern Mogadishu while Aideed's forces controlled the more strategic southern quarters of the capital. Aideed's fiefdom included the
docks on the sea and the airport. Aideed and Ali Mahdi were both
members of the United Somali Congress and of the Hawiye clan that
prevailed in Mogadishu, but Aideed belonged to the Habar-Gedir
subclan and Ali Mahdi to the Abgal subclan. The governments of
Djibouti, Egypt, and Italy brokered a conference in May 1991 in
Djibouti, at which Ali Mahdi declared himself president of Somalia
and appointed a cabinet. But Aideed, who had been elected party
chairman at a conference of the United Somali Congress, boycotted
the Djibouti meeting as rigged against him.

The civil war ravaged the crops and cattle and terrorized relief workers and merchants trying to distribute food to the starving. By early 1992, Médecins Sans Frontières, the French humanitarian group, one of the few organizations functioning there, described Mogadishu as "a ravaged city . . . forgotten by the international community." A U.N. report called Somalia "a human disaster of appalling magnitude" and "a nightmare of bloodshed and brutality." But the rest of the world took little notice, for there were no foreign journalists in the capital and few diplomats. The United States had evacuated its embassy just before Siad Barre fled. Boutros-Ghali, who tried to follow the situation in Somalia closely, chided the ambassadors of the Security Council for ignoring Somalia while fretting for hours about Bosnia. He accused them of caring more about white Muslims than black Muslims. According to some sources, he even accused them of dealing with "a rich man's war in Yugoslavia while not lifting a finger to save Somalia from disintegration."

Under this pressure, the Security Council voted in late April to authorize a U.N. peacekeeping mission to Somalia, but its implementation depended on the approval of the warlords, and a contingent of five hundred lightly armed Pakistani soldiers did not arrive until September. By then, James Kunder of the U.S. Agency for International Development, the first American official to reach Somalia in eighteen months, had described the situation as "the world's worst humanitarian disaster." He warned that three out of every four children under the age of five might die within six months if the food and medicine did not reach the starving and sick.

At the end of August, President George Bush authorized an American airlift of food into Mombasa. For six months, the American planes flew tens of thousands of metric tons of food from Mombasa on the coast of Kenya to Somalia, sometimes reaching thin airstrips alongside minuscule towns in the most famine-stricken areas of Somalia. The American airlift galvanized a new international effort to rush food into the country for distribution by private humanitarian groups. But looting and hijacking were rampant. Gunmen extorted landing fees from the planes. Relief workers had to hire "technicals"—jeeps and Land Rovers mounted with heavy weapons and guarded by Somali gunmen, all listed on expense accounts as "technical assistance" to mask the embarrassing fact that charitable organizations were hiring gunmen. These gunmen demanded exorbitant fees to protect the supplies from other armed Somalis who looked just like the guards on the "technicals" and carried the same kind of weapons. It had all the markings of a Mafia protection racket. Much of the food and other supplies—perhaps 15 percent to 40 percent—never reached the people who needed it.

The secretary-general had sent Mohamed Sahnoun, an experienced and astute Algerian diplomat, to Somalia as his special representative in March. Sahnoun worked assiduously in the enervating atmosphere to persuade Aideed and the other warlords to accept the presence of the peacekeepers. But the Algerian became more and more incensed at the lumbering pace of inept U.N. bureaucrats who shipped out an inadequate amount of supplies to the ravaged country. Moreover, the Pakistanis did not have the numbers, the weapons, and the mandate to impose peace on Mogadishu and the rest of the country. They proved an ineffectual force. Sahnoun assuaged his frustration on American television, berating the bureaucracy that employed him. This angered Boutros-Ghali, who fired off a reprimand in October that provoked Sahnoun into firing back a letter of resignation. Diplomats tried to persuade Sahnoun to rescind the resignation and Boutros-Ghali to refuse it, but the two stubborn men, friends for years, would not budge, and Sahnoun left Somalia. The U.N. operation, meager as it was, only deteriorated after then.

As U.N., American, and private relief officials sent out calls of distress, American and European television began to take notice. Camera crews flew in with relief workers to hunt for the most distressing scenes. Images of potbellied, stick-limbed, wide-eyed, skull-faced children crammed television screens. Reporters did not have to hunt for sensationalism; it engulfed them and made them numb with anger and hopelessness. There is probably no more horrific sight for even the most hardened journalist than a malnourished, listless wisp of a child, so frail and destined for death that its tiny body will keel over without a whimper at the flick of someone's finger.

In late November 1992, after his defeat for reelection and two months before the inauguration of Bill Clinton, President Bush

bowed to mounting pressure from the press, Congress, and relief organizations to somehow save Somalia. In a kind of last hurrah as
commander in chief, Bush informed Boutros-Ghali that the United
States was ready to dispatch up to thirty thousand troops to Somalia.
Although there were U.N. officials who believed the Somalia disaster
was the kind of job the U.N. could do on its own, the secretary-
general did not agree. In his view, nothing short of an American intervention would work. But he did not want another arrangement
like that of the Persian Gulf crisis in which the Americans obtained
carte blanche from the U.N. to fight a war and then turned their back
on the world organization while doing so. The secretary-general proposed an elaborate set of restrictions, strategic goals, and reporting
requirements for the American-led mission. This was accepted in
principle by both the Security Council and the U.S. government.

By a unanimous vote, the Security Council passed a resolution
on December 3 authorizing the dispatch of the American-led force.
It was an exciting moment for Americans as they envisioned their
troops marching to the rescue of those woeful children on television.
But the resolution harbored a festering controversy over disarmament. In a letter to the Security Council before the vote, Boutros-
Ghali had insisted that military force was required "to ensure, on a
lasting basis, that the current violence against the international relief
effort was brought to an end." "To achieve this," he went on, "it
would be necessary for at least the heavy weapons of the organized
factions to be neutralized and brought under international control
and for the irregular forces and gangs to be disarmed." But the resolution passed by the Security Council was far less explicit about disarmament. It did say, however, that the Security Council endorsed the
recommendation in the secretary-general's letter "to establish a secure environment for humanitarian relief operations in Somalia as
soon as possible." When asked why the resolution did not instruct the
troops to disarm the warlords, French Ambassador Jean-Bernard Mérimée told reporters that the phrase "to establish a secure environment" meant exactly that. Boutros-Ghali agreed. But George Bush
did not.

Boutros-Ghali quickly wrote President Bush that the U.N.
could not take over from the American-led forces until they had created the "inescapable condition" of "a secure environment." The

secretary-general accepted that it was the U.N.'s role to try to mediate a political settlement among the warring factions. But he expected the Americans to encourage this process by disarming the factions. It was not enough for the Americans to provide security only for the delivery of food. The letter infuriated the Bush administration. Assistant Secretary of State John Bolton told a *New York Times* reporter that the secretary-general was trying to change the goalposts in the middle of a game. The United States did not intend a general disarmament in Somalia. The American troops would make sure that food and medicine were distributed without interference. If the Somalis kept their weapons out of the sight of the American troops, no one would take them away. The interpretation of Boutros-Ghali was probably closer to the intent of the resolution than the narrow American view. As a practical matter, however, there was no way for the U.N. to force the United States to do what it did not want to do.

President Bush appointed Robert B. Oakley, a former ambassador to Somalia, as his special envoy. Oakley, a gangling, active man of strong opinions and quotable quips, rushed immediately to Mogadishu to persuade Aideed and Ali Mahdi to withhold their fire while the American troops and their allies came ashore in Somalia. The two warlords were easily persuaded, for neither wanted to tangle then with the Americans. When the first marines of Operation Restore Hope—as the Bush administration called the intervention—rushed onto the beaches of Mogadishu, they were met only by the blinding floodlights of American television crews recording the historic moment. The ludicrous scenes of heavily armed, puzzled American marines blinking at television lights and cameras provoked some public rage at the networks. But they had filmed the scenes only because the Pentagon had advised their correspondents of the exact moment of the invasion.

By January, the intervention force numbered more than 38,000: 25,400 American soldiers and marines and 12,900 troops from France, Canada, Belgium, Italy, Morocco, and other countries. Arriving at the airport, a visitor would behold an astounding sea of tanks, armored personnel carriers, trucks, and jeeps reaching to the horizon. In retrospect, there is no doubt that this enormous, American-led military force could have disarmed the factions with relative ease. But the opportunity was passed over. President Bush did not want to risk even minimal casualties that might drum up public and congressional opposition to a mission that enjoyed enthusiastic approval. The Americans did seize heavy weapons that were either visible or causing trouble. Oakley tried to persuade the warlords to give up their "technicals." Ali Mahdi turned over his to the intervention force for storage, but Aideed claimed that his "technicals" had disappeared. They had actually left Mogadishu to hide while preparing for future battles. Since the Americans did not regard disarmament as one of their duties, Oakley did not argue with Aideed about this obvious subterfuge. Weapons squirreled away for another day were nobody's business.

In a few months, the foreign forces had transformed the atmosphere of Somalia. Violence vanished wherever the soldiers patrolled. The military unclogged the port and managed the airlift. Relief workers now had adequate stocks of grain and other foods and managed to get them swiftly to the needy. The end of famine was in sight, and the International Committee of the Red Cross prepared to close down its feeding stations. There were dangerous clouds. The marines and soldiers had frightened many armed Somalis out of the towns, and they soon terrorized the countryside as marauding bandits. Yet, all in all, the Americans congratulated themselves on a job well done, and Washington called for the U.N. to take over the operation.

As the Clinton administration replaced the Bush administration, the Pentagon prepared plans for what it called a "seamless" takeover by the U.N. in Somalia. The Pentagon planners envisioned a large and tough U.N. force heavily influenced by American ideas and more or less run by Americans. U.S. diplomats and military officers leaned heavily on U.N. officials to make sure that they accepted the American plan. Marrack Goulding, the British diplomat in charge of peacekeeping, did not like the aggressive role mapped out by the Americans for the peacekeepers. The Americans managed to persuade Boutros-Ghali to replace him with Kofi Annan of Ghana as chief peacekeeper; Goulding did not suffer but moved up into the crucial post of undersecretary-general for political affairs. The Americans described the soft-spoken, thoughtful Annan as "more flexible" than Goulding, for Annan accepted the American view that the new U.N. operation should have authority under Chapter 7 of the charter to enforce the peace.

The Americans also handpicked the chief personnel. An American, Rear Admiral Jonathan T. Howe, who had served on the National Security Council in the Bush White House, would be the secretary-general's special representative, the official in overall charge of the operation. Lieutenant General Cevik Bir of Turkey, well known to Americans within NATO, would serve as military commander, with Major General Thomas M. Montgomery of the U.S. Army as his deputy commander. The American troops within the U.N. operation—three thousand in logistics plus a Quick Reaction Force of thirteen hundred—would report directly to General Montgomery rather than General Bir. Boutros-Ghali gave in to these American demands. The new U.N. operation would be tailormade for the United States.

Yet Boutros-Ghali hesitated to take over. Ambassador Oakley publicly berated him for moving too slowly. When General Bir, the U.N. military commander, arrived in Mogadishu in late February, Oakley told reporters that he could not understand why it had taken so long for Bir to get there. But Boutros-Ghali complained in a report to the Security Council a few weeks later that the American-led force had failed to establish a secure environment in Somalia. The presence of the troops did improve security and allow unimpeded distribution of food and medicine, the secretary-general said. But, he went on, "this improvement can not yet be regarded as irreversible and conditions are still volatile. . . . Disarmament is far from complete."

Nevertheless, the Security Council in late March authorized a U.N. takeover in May with a force of twenty-eight thousand plus the American Quick Reaction Force equipped with helicopters, tanks, Bradley assault vehicles, and trucks. Tired of what they regarded as U.N. foot-dragging, the Americans started to withdraw even before the U.N. took over. In a letter to American Ambassador Madeleine K. Albright, Boutros-Ghali accused the United States of pulling its troops out so quickly that the U.N. could not fill the gap in time to prevent further deterioration in security. "I have no alternative but to accept the transfer of command," he wrote. But, he went on in a remonstrating tone, ". . . you would agree with me that the transfer is taking place in less than ideal circumstances. The bulk of the United States contingents and their equipment have been withdrawn before they could be replaced by contingents of other countries."

⁂

The U.N. took over officially on May 4, 1993. It was in some ways an unprecedented moment. For the first time since the days of the Congo crisis and the Katanga secession, U.N. peacekeepers had Security Council authority to invade a sovereign country and impose peace and stability there by force. In the Congo days, however, the authority for the peacekeepers to war on Katanga had been vague and confused. U.N. commanders insisted continually that they were acting in self-defense. The Security Council wanted no such confusion now. The Security Council clearly intended the new peacekeepers to march on the warlords if that were needed to end chaos in Somalia. Yet, despite a drumbeat of U.N. rhetoric about this new power, the American public and Congress did not understand that the new peacekeepers were actually peace enforcers. When American peacekeepers died in the turmoil, America felt shocked and betrayed.

Admiral Howe was viewed with suspicion at first by the secretary-general's aides. He was, after all, deeply involved in official U.S. political-military policy for many years, and these policies had bruised Boutros-Ghali for several months. Holding a Ph.D. from the Fletcher School of Law and Diplomacy and author of a book, *Multicrises: Seapower and Global Politics in the Missile Age*, Howe had served as director of politico-military affairs in the State Department for two years and as a member of the National Security Council in the White House in the administrations of both Presidents Richard Nixon and George Bush. As a deputy to Brent Scowcroft, Bush's national security adviser, Howe had worked closely with Anthony Lake, President Clinton's national security adviser, during the transition from one administration to the other, and Lake had recommended him for the top U.N. position in Somalia. Despite this extensive political background, Howe's detractors would later belittle him as politically naïve and puritanical in Somalia. But Howe adapted himself to U.N. policy with a zest that surprised and pleased Boutros-Ghali. "He is more like one of us than an American," confided an aide to the secretary-general.

Admiral Howe's most significant antagonist would prove to be General Aideed. The two military officers were both fifty-seven years old when the crisis pitted them against each other. Although a warlord, Aideed derived his strength not from weaponry alone but from his support within the Habar-Gedir subclan. In fact, the subclan leaders had called him back from India to lead their forces in the struggle against Siad Barre. Aideed struck many outsiders as too erratic to trust. But U.N. Special Representative Sahnoun and U.S. Ambassador Oakley had both managed to develop a rapport by alternately cajoling and accommodating him. In his book-length account of the American and U.N. Somalia interventions, Oakley treated Howe with some disdain for failing to woo Aideed. It is not clear, however, that this would have worked for Howe. Unlike Sahnoun and Oakley, Howe had orders to disarm the warlords and their gangs, and it would have been difficult if not impossible to cajole Aideed into doing this voluntarily. Aideed, moreover, may simply have concluded by then that the time was ripe to take on the U.N. and show who was the real boss in Somalia.

Aideed evidently concluded soon enough that the U.N.'s policies and its disarmament campaign would weaken him and marginalize him from Somali politics. A rift developed when the U.N. dropped support for a peace conference that Aideed convened for central Somalia. He had been negotiating logistics, agenda, and participants with April Glaspie, the former American ambassador to Iraq who was now Howe's political adviser. Tom Farer, an American University law professor who served as a consultant to the U.N. mission, said that "Glaspie . . . openly manifested sympathy for one of Aideed's most important political opponents . . . and was less than discreet about her hostility to Aideed." Once accused of being too gentle with Saddam Hussein, Glaspie was now accused of being too tough with Aideed. Admiral Howe, however, insisted that the U.N. withdrew support because Aideed kept reneging on his promises during the negotiations. "Aideed was playing all kinds of little games within games," Howe went on. He denied that the U.N. had played favorites. "It was Aideed who changed sides against us," he said.

Radio Mogadishu, controlled by Aideed, began a hate campaign, lambasting the U.N. and the United States as aggressors intent on colonizing Somalia and turning it back into a trusteeship. The radio exhorted Somalis to recall a glorious past when they resisted foreign domination. An angry U.N. staff drew up plans to shut down the radio if it kept up such attacks. On June 5, Pakistani peacekeepers made what they called a routine inspection of five sites where Aideed's militia had agreed to store weapons. One site was within the same building as Radio Mogadishu. A U.S. special forces team accompanied the Pakistanis on that inspection, presumably to figure out the best way to knock out the radio facilities in the future. Rumors spread throughout Aideed's zone that the U.N. was about to seize Radio Mogadishu.

Hostile crowds formed throughout southern Mogadishu, setting up roadblocks to prevent the Pakistanis from returning to their barracks after the inspections. Aideed's militiamen mingled in the crowds, kept behind women and children, and then fired at the U.N. peacekeepers. Pakistani units were ambushed in other areas of the city. The fury of the Aideed weaponry surprised the U N. At the end of the day, twenty-four Pakistanis were dead and fifty-seven injured. Another six were captured, one of them dying in detention. The U.N. hunt for Aideed would now begin.

On the very next day, June 6, an angry and unanimous Security Council passed an unprecedented resolution authorizing the secretary-general "to take all necessary measures against all those responsible for the armed attacks . . . including those responsible for publicly inciting such attacks." Howe could now arrest and detain Aideed if, of course, he could catch him. Justifying the manhunt, Howe told the people of Somalia that the "gallant soldiers of the Pakistan brigade . . . were murdered as they sought to serve the neediest people in the city." He said that "twelve of the soldiers were helping unload food at a feeding station when they were foully attacked by cowards who placed women and children in front of armed men." The Security Council resolution, he went on, reflected "the world's outrage at these unprovoked attacks."

For four months, the U.N. fought a war with the elusive Aideed and his militia. At Howe's request, the United States sent four hundred Rangers and Delta Force antiterrorist commandoes and equipped them with powerful Cobra helicopter gunships. The Rangers and commandoes were under the direct command and control of the U.S. Central Command in Tampa, Florida, and thus not officially part of the U.N. mission at all. Howe announced a twenty-five-thousand-dollar bounty for the capture of Aideed. In a raid on what the U.N. called Aideed's "command and control facilities" on July 12, a half-dozen U.S. Cobra gunships fired sixteen antitank missiles into the house of Abdi Qeybdiid, the Aideed minister of defense. The aim was to kill everyone inside. Somalia sources claimed that more than seventy people died, mostly politicians and clan elders. When four journalists arrived to cover the raid, a crowd turned on them and killed them. As the street war intensified, there were hundreds of Somali casualties. U.N. casualties rose as well with Americans, Nigerians, more Pakistanis, and others among the dead.

The bloodshed began to trouble some members of Congress who could not fathom so much killing in a U.N. peacekeeping mission. But Ambassador Albright defended Howe's war on Aideed in an August Op-Ed piece in the *New York Times*. "The decision we must make is whether to pull up stakes and allow Somalia to fall back into the abyss or to stay the course and help lift the country and its people from the category of a failed state into that of an emerging democracy," she wrote. "For Somalia's sake, and ours, we must persevere."

By mid-September the Clinton administration had second thoughts about the killing and the futile manhunt. In New York for the opening session of the 1993 General Assembly, Secretary of State Warren Christopher handed Boutros-Ghali a secret document outlining American proposals for a new U.N. approach in Somalia. Christopher called for the U.N. to declare a cease-fire in the Mogadishu street war and open talks with Aideed's faction for a political settlement. But the secretary of state did not propose any pardon for Aideed. Instead, he laid down a scheme—evidently already in motion—in which the leaders of Ethiopia and Eritrea would arrange for Aideed's voluntary departure and exile. He assured the secretary-general that the Rangers would remain in Somalia until "those

wanted by the U.N. for murdering peacekeepers" were either captured or exiled.

In a lengthy written reply a few days later, Boutros-Ghali
doubted whether Ethiopia and Eritrea would succeed in persuading
Aideed to depart. Although he ignored the call for a cease-fire, the
secretary-general told Christopher that he had asked Admiral Howe
to put together an interim government that would include representatives from Aideed's subclan. But he repeated his long-standing position that "our efforts to restore peace and prosperity in Somalia will
not succeed unless we can disarm the clans and factions." Boutros-
Ghali recognized that public opinion might persuade governments
to lose enthusiasm for the Somalia mission and force the Security
Council to withdraw entirely or at least abandon south Mogadishu to
Aideed. But, he went on, "let us have no illusions about what the
consequences would be." "Not only would that condemn the people
of Somalia to a resumption of civil war and all the horrors that would
result," he said. "It would also represent a humbling of the United
Nations . . ." He said this would have "a devastating effect" on the
capacity of the U.N. to contribute to a better world.

The United States could have called off the hunt for Aideed and
his lieutenants anytime it wanted. The Delta commandoes and
Rangers, who carried out the hunt, were under the command of
Major General William F. Garrison, who reported directly to the
Central Command. But no one in Washington ordered General
Garrison to rein in his mission. On Sunday afternoon, October 3, a
fleet of helicopters swooped down on a building on Hiwadag Street
in south Mogadishu, unloading Delta commandoes and Rangers
who rushed inside and swiftly arrested twenty-four associates of Aideed. Two were so high ranking that the Americans looked on the
raid at first as a mission accomplished. General Garrison had hoped
that the capture of top lieutenants would smoke Aideed out of his
hiding places.

But heavily armed Aideed militia men rushed to the scene and
shot down one helicopter with a rocket-propelled grenade. About 90
Rangers and commandoes moved to the fallen helicopter a couple of
blocks away in hopes of saving the crew. They formed a perimeter
around the area to protect the crew while waiting for help. General

Garrison ordered a convoy of trucks, which had just picked up the Somali prisoners, to head back toward the downed helicopter, but the trucks were halted by Somali gunfire. Soon a second helicopter crashed a half-mile away. Soldiers trying to reach the wreckage were killed by snipers. The Quick Reaction Force—made up of soldiers from the U.S. Army's Tenth Mountain Division—tried but failed at first to get past Somali ambushes and rescue the Rangers and commandoes. Later in the night, they regrouped and tried again, this time with tanks borrowed from Malaysian peacekeepers and armored personnel carriers from the Pakistanis. By 7 A.M., fifteen hours after the raid began, the survivors were rescued. There were 18 Americans and 1 Malaysian dead, and 84 Americans and seven Malaysians wounded. The Somalis counted 312 dead and 814 wounded. The humiliation of the Americans was driven home on American television by scenes of Somalis dragging a dead American body through the streets and by images of a terrified captured American pilot.

The shock of the American losses, etched on television, galvanized President Clinton into a decision to withdraw all American troops from Somalia. Clinton administration aides whispered that the White House had known practically nothing about what was going on in Somalia and publicly blamed Boutros-Ghali and the U.N. for leading American soldiers into a debacle. Newspaper editorialists picked up this note of outrage. President Clinton did not blame Boutros-Ghali. But, in a televised speech to the nation two days after the star-crossed raid, the president announced that new American forces en route to Somalia "will be under American command." This, of course, left the false impression that the troops already there were not under American command.

The deployment of new troops to Somalia was a prelude to withdrawal. The president shocked Boutros-Ghali by announcing that all Americans troops would leave Somalia by March 31, 1994. The American intervention would come to an end then. The president said the extra troops heading toward Somalia would stay long enough to protect the other American troops as they prepared to withdraw. He underscored his rejection of Boutros-Ghali by asking Ambassador Oakley to return to Somalia and try to work out a political settlement with all the clans and factions. Oakley had infuriated

Boutros-Ghali in the early days of 1993 with his drumbeat insistence that the secretary-general was dragging his feet on taking over the operation in Somalia. Clinton told Congress that the hunt for Aideed would be called off while Oakley tried to broker a settlement.

The American decision to withdraw crippled the Somalia operation and made all U.N. peacekeeping suspect in the eyes of Americans. The name Somalia became a buzzword for failure. Whenever the Security Council discussed a new peacekeeping venture, critics raised the specter of another Somali debacle. The Clinton administration issued stringent new guidelines for American participation or even support of U.N. peacekeeping. If these guidelines were followed strictly, the United States would never support another peacekeeping operation again. The Americans, in fact, had to close their eyes to their own guidelines in 1994 when they persuaded the Security Council to vote for a new peacekeeping venture in Haiti.

Boutros-Ghali had scant success trying to persuade other countries to take the place of the Americans in Somalia. As Kofi Annan, the chief of peacekeeping, put it, "Other presidents and prime ministers are going to have difficulty explaining to their people that the American president is removing his troops because it is too dangerous but is encouraging them to send their own troops." In the end, Boutros-Ghali cobbled together a Third World force, largely from Pakistan and his own native Egypt.

The United Nations entered a long and tortuous retreat; each step backward became a new humiliation. In late November, the Security Council suspended all charges against Aideed and his lieutenants and appointed a commission headed by Chief Justice Matthew S. W. Ngulube of Zambia to determine who was responsible for the murderous ambush of the Pakistanis, the incident that had triggered the manhunt. The commission reached the conclusion months later that Aideed and his faction were indeed, as everyone suspected, the culprits, although it also accused Howe and his advisers of naïveté in dealing with Aideed. By then, Howe had left Somalia, and Aideed had long since returned to public life, holding news conferences, issuing threats, still plotting an ascent to power. Despite the findings of the commission, the Security Council made no attempt this time to punish Aideed.

In February 1994, shortly before the Americans withdrew, the Security Council changed the mandate of the peacekeepers. No longer were they in Somalia with the lofty aim of disarming the warlords and enforcing peace. They now would protect roads, ports, and airstrips, guard relief workers, and fire their weapons only in self-defense. Without the use of any force, the peacekeepers would encourage disarmament, relying "on the cooperation of the Somali parties." If interclan fighting broke out, the peacekeepers would not interfere. They would only retain the right to defend themselves from harm. Ambassador Albright told the other ambassadors that the resolution "states clearly what many of us have been saying for months: the people of Somalia must bear the responsibility for national reconciliation and the reconstruction of their own country." But she, of course, had seemed to say just the opposite in her Op-Ed piece in the *New York Times* six months earlier.

As the months went by, the U.N. seemed to accomplish little but feed wages and looted goods into the economy. Aideed and Ali Mahdi moved no closer to reconciliation. The United States, which paid 30 percent of the cost, decried the waste of money. In September 1994, when the Security Council voted to extend the mission for another month, Ambassador Albright abstained. "In the face of Somali intransigence and unwillingness to reach political agreement," she said, "[the U.N.] cannot continue to maintain 15,000 troops in Somalia and spend over $2.5 million a day." By November, the rest of the council agreed. Preparing an ignominious end to a grand adventure, the Security Council voted unanimously to pull out of Somalia by March 31, 1995. Ambassador Albright insisted that the intervention had not been a failure. The U.N., she said, had saved "hundreds of thousands of lives . . . from starvation" and had "offered a helping hand and, in the face of often violent opposition, firmly held that hand open for over two years, ready and willing to help." Another Security Council ambassador, however, confided, "We are doing exactly what the Americans did in Viet Nam—declaring victory and getting out."

Calling it Operation United Shield, the United States sent Lieutenant General Anthony C. Zinni and eighteen hundred marines to protect the U.N. peacekeepers as they withdrew from Mogadishu. At 1 A.M., Mogadishu time, Friday, March 3, 1995, General Zinni and his marines and the last peacekeepers, all Pakistanis, left their redoubt on a Mogadishu beach in amphibious assault craft for four U.S. Navy ships waiting four miles offshore. The marines had spent seventy-three hours onshore and had suffered no casualties. The end came almost twenty-six months after the first marines had come ashore at Mogadishu in President George Bush's Operation Restore Hope. The U.N. compound in Mogadishu, modernized over the months with one hundred million dollars' worth of streetlights, sewage systems, and other equipment, was now so looted that it lay in ruins. The rest of Somalia was in far better shape than it had been when the first marines landed. "Harvests have been plentiful," wrote William Finnegan of the New Yorker, "hunger has been banished, and trade is brisk in the towns and cities." But the warlords were still not reconciled to each other, and many Somalis feared that the famine and its horror would return if the warlords took each other on again. The secretary-general's warning had become prophetic. The world seemed ready to forget Somalia in a few minutes. But the failure of the intervention—a failure of both the U.N. and the United States—would not be forgotten.

❦ 18 ❦

Alibi: *The U.N. in Bosnia*

Replying to questions after a speech to a banquet in mid-1992, Thomas R. Pickering, the departing American ambassador to the U.N., described the U.S. government's policy on Bosnia. "If Europe leads, we will follow," he said. "If Europe does not lead, we will also follow." His cutting wit reflected the confusion and paralysis of the United States and Western Europe in dealing with the most brutal conflagration in Europe since the end of World War II. The United States had left it up to Europe to deal with the catastrophe. When Europe failed, the United States had little useful to suggest. No European or American government wanted to risk losing hundreds of lives to save Bosnia.

By the end of 1994, the Security Council had issued well over a hundred resolutions and official statements on the crisis in the former Yugoslavia. Most focused on Bosnia, and few changed the course of the war. Governments often whipped the Security Council into a resolution, in fact, mainly to assuage public opinion at home. Europeans and Americans were outraged by the aggression and brutality in Bosnia, but they did not want their sons to die in a long and dangerous intervention there. So governments made their publics feel better by encouraging a show of action in the U.N. In August 1992, for example, the Security Council called upon all member states to take "all measures necessary" to facilitate the delivery of humanitarian aid to Sarajevo and the rest of Bosnia. This was the kind of wording that allowed President Bush to pursue the Persian Gulf War. When the Security Council passed a similar resolution for Bosnia, it was front-page news throughout the United States. But no American president or any other leader ever pursued a war against the Serb aggressors in Bosnia. The resolution was never implemented.

The U.N. could point to credible achievements in Bosnia, Croatia, and Macedonia—the three countries that it dealt with in the former Yugoslavia. Protected by the peacekeepers, the Office of the U.N. High Commissioner for Refugees (UNHCR) had organized a relief operation that managed winter after winter to prevent starvation in Sarajevo and the government-held enclaves of Bosnia. By talking and threatening its way through an endless succession of cease-fires and broken cease-fires, the U.N. had somehow managed to tone down the intensity of the Serb shelling and sniping of Sarajevo and other besieged towns. The U.N. also had managed to prevent the war from spreading. The work of the peacekeepers was arduous and fraught with danger. By the end of March 1995, 149 peacekeepers had been killed and 1,366 wounded in the former Yugoslavia. But the U.N. had failed to do what many Americans and Europeans would have liked to see. The U.N. had failed to turn back aggression, recover conquered territory, and end the war. The U.N., of course, had neither the power nor the authority to do so. It could do no more than the United States and Europe wished.

At a dispirited symposium of scholars and U.N. officials at Princeton University in October 1993, José-Maria Mendiluce of Spain, the former UNHCR chief in Bosnia, revealed that relief workers sometimes felt that their mission had amounted to little more than "an alibi" for the Western world. Whenever anyone demanded to know what they had done to stop the war, European and American politicians, hiding their guilt, could point to the presence of the U.N. and insist they had done all they could.

The war was fanned by demagogues. Tito and his Communist Party had held together a Yugoslavia that was driven by ethnic differences that politicians found easy to exploit after he died in 1980. The main conflict had long been between the Eastern Orthodox Serbs and the Roman Catholic Croats, an enmity exacerbated by World War II when the Nazi Germans set up the fascist Croat *Ustasha* state that slaughtered tens of thousands of Serbs; estimates of the death toll run from 350,000 to 750,000. The Serbs, the most populous people in Yugoslavia, did not intend to forget this or any other injustice. "Their tragic defect," wrote Warren Zimmermann, the American ambassador to Yugoslavia from 1989 to 1992, "is an obsession with their own history." He said the Serbs had "a lugubrious, paranoid and Serbo-centric view of the past."

The crisis was rooted in the emergence of Slobodan Milošević, an authoritarian banker who came to power in 1987 as leader of the Serbian League of Communists and was later elected president of Serbia. Milošević's demagogic appeals to Serbian nationalism made it inevitable that Croatia would react by electing an extreme nationalist of its own in 1990—Franjo Tudjman, a former Communist and general. Tudjman, contemptuous of the Kraina Serbs who made up 12 percent of the Croatian population, awoke fears among oversensitive Serbs of a return of the *Ustasha* régime. Milošević insisted that the Serbs had the right to control the lands on which they lived even if the territory was part of Croatia. Concerned that a Croatian declaration of independence would trigger war, Secretary of State James A. Baker III and other American officials tried to talk Tudjman out of secession. But the American pleas seemed to lack conviction, and the Germans lobbied hard in European circles for recognition of Croatia.

In June 1991, Croatia and Slovenia seceded from the Yugoslav federation and declared independence. The Serb-dominated Yugoslav National Army (JNA) allowed the secession of Slovenia after ten days of battle but entered Croatia to help the Kraina Serbs seize a quarter of the territory for themselves. Cyrus Vance, the former secretary of state now serving as a U.N. special envoy, worked out a ceasefire in January 1992, with U.N. peacekeepers arriving a couple of months later to patrol the lines.

The next battleground was Bosnia and Herzegovina (a name usually shortened to just Bosnia), a mixed region whose population was 40 percent Muslim, 32 percent Serb, and 18 percent Croat. With this plurality of Muslims (descendants of Serbs and Croats converted centuries ago by their Turkish overlords), Bosnia had long been known as a land of much intermarriage and of good feelings. President Alija Izetbegović was far from a Muslim extremist, but the others tried to paint him that way. Tudjman told Ambassador Zimmermann, "They're dangerous fundamentalists, and they're using Bosnia as a beachhead to spread their ideology throughout Europe and even to the United States. The civilized nations should join together to repel this threat. Bosnia has never had any real existence. It should be divided between Serbia and Croatia." Izetbegović asked for U.N. peacekeepers for protection. In a cable to Washington, Zimmermann seconded the request "but did not press for it as hard as I should have." Washington rejected the idea, content with the conventional wisdom that the proper time for peacekeepers was after a war, not before.

Refusing to heed the advice of Vance and others, Izetbegović reluctantly led his country to independence, hoping that international recognition would afford Bosnia protection against a resurgent Croatia and a Serbian Yugoslavia. In a February referendum, the Bosnian Muslims and Croats voted in favor of secession, giving the proposal a 64 percent majority. But the Serbs boycotted the vote. Izetbegović declared independence, leaving his government open to the charge by Milošević and Bosnian Serb leader Radovan Karadzić that he was forcing Serbs out of the Yugoslav federation against their will. Karadzić, a blustery psychiatrist with an unruly mane, earned the utter disdain of Ambassador Zimmermann for plotting some of the most horrible massacres of the war. "In his fanaticism, ruthlessness, and contempt for human values," Zimmermann wrote later, "he invites comparison with a monster from another generation, Heinrich Himmler."

With the obvious complicity of Milošević and the Yugoslav army, Karadzić declared a Bosnian Serb republic, and the JNA launched an attack from Serbia to put down the secession of Bosnia in April 1992. Karadzić told the American ambassador, "You have to understand Serbs, Mr. Zimmermann. They have been betrayed for centuries. Today they can not live with other nations. They must have their own separate existence. They are a warrior race, and they can trust only themselves to take by force what is their due." The JNA withdrew officially in two months but left behind enough troops and equipment to create a new Bosnian Serb army. The terrible Bosnian war had begun.

During the Communist era, Tito's stubborn, independent nationalism had angered Stalin and made the Yugoslavs fearful of a Soviet invasion. To counter this, Tito ordered universal military service, intensive guerrilla training, and decentralized command and control within the Serb-dominated Yugoslav National Army (JNA). When the crisis erupted in the 1990s, Bosnia and the rest of Yugoslavia were awash with weaponry and crowded with trained warriors. This made it easy to organize paramilitary bands of peasants and workers and to transform the JNA units of General Ratko Mladić into the Bosnian Serb army.

The Bosnian Serb soldiers and militia fought to create a territorial bridge between Serbia and the Croatian Serb areas so all could unite easily someday into a Greater Serbia. But this bridge was populated by far more than Serbs. The Bosnian population was so mixed that there were large Muslim and Croat minorities even in areas regarded as Serb. In some of these sites, in fact, the Serbs were no more than a plurality, in some a minority. To rid these conquered areas of Muslims and Croats, the Bosnian Serbs began their infamous policy of "ethnic cleansing." A U.N. Commission of Experts, created later to assess war crimes in the Balkans, concluded that the well-planned ethnic cleansing campaign had the blessing and support of Milošević and Serbia.

All sides were guilty of atrocities in the Bosnian war but the Serbs more guilty than others. Most perpetrators were Serbs, most victims Muslims. The bulk of these war crimes—murder, rape, bombardment of civilians, destruction of mosques and churches, confiscation of property—were committed in the name of ethnic cleansing.

Ethnic cleansing, according to the Commission of Experts, followed a pattern. After the Serb paramilitary forces, often augmented by the JNA, seized a town, they destroyed mosques, non-Serb churches, and the homes of Muslims and Croats. Once in control, the paramilitary fighters terrorized the non-Serbs with random killing, looting, and raping. Finally, local Serb politicians formed an administration to run the town, sometimes with the help of the paramilitary forces. The Serbs then turned on the remaining Muslims and Croats, assaulting them, dismissing them from work, confiscating their property, and herding many off to prison camps.

The camps, a vital part of ethnic cleansing, harbored the worst atrocities—rampant murder, torture, and rape. "Not only were prisoners physically abused," the Commission of Experts reported, "but they were also commonly humiliated, degraded, and forced to abuse one another." Some camps of women and girls served as brothels for the soldiers and militia. Women were raped in front of members of their family. Rapists sometimes told Muslim victims that they would now bear Serbian children. Some males were castrated in crude ways. Many prisoners were executed and buried in mass graves near the detention camps.

During the war, the Serbs also laid siege to Sarajevo, once a city of more than a half-million population, the site of the 1984 Winter Olympics. An average of 330 shells a day descended on the city in 1992 and 1993. By November 1993, shelling, sniping, malnutrition, and cold killed almost 10,000, including 1,500 children. The wounded numbered 55,000, including 14,500 children. UNICEF estimated that 73 percent of the city's children lived in homes that had been shelled, 51 percent had seen someone killed, and 40 percent had been attacked by sniper fire. There is little doubt that the civilians of Sarajevo were directly targeted by the besieging Serbs—a war crime under international law.

The Serb soldiers and irregulars moved swiftly, bolstered by the tanks and artillery of the JNA. By the end of 1992, the Serbs controlled 70 percent of Bosnia. The Croats, also at war with the government, held on to 20 percent. The Muslim-dominated Bosnian government administered only 10 percent of the country—Sarajevo and a handful of towns, all under siege, and a swath of land in central Bosnia. The images of dying children, fleeing elders, anguished women, bundled refugees, ravaged towns, devastated mosques, and

swaggering Serbs seared the conscience of the world and aroused demands for a halt to aggression. Despite the misgivings of Boutros-
Ghali, the Security Council ordered peacekeepers into Bosnia to
protect the Sarajevo airport and the convoys of the U.N. High Commissioner for Refugees (UNHCR) carrying food and medicine to besieged towns. The arriving peacekeepers were hailed both inside and
outside Bosnia as saviors come to repel and even turn back aggression. But the peacekeepers would prove a disappointment for they
had authority only to defend themselves and the convoys.

❧❦

For the U.N., a depressing and frustrating pattern ensued. As
world public opinion lost patience with the Serbs, the Security
Council galvanized itself into new actions that excited false hopes.
The first peacekeepers, for example, helped deliver food but did
nothing to stop the aggression that made the food deliveries to the
Bosnian Muslims necessary. "The U.N. mission is feeding them, or
at least trying, while leaving them exposed to unrelenting gunfire,"
wrote Carol J. Williams of the *Los Angeles Times*. "This is little com-
fort for the people of Sarajevo, who risk being cut down by shrapnel
en route to get their share of the shrinking Western dole." Peacekeepers had the authority to shoot their way past Serbs trying to block
a food convoy. But they knew that if they did, convoys might be
harassed at scores of other checkpoints. So peacekeepers sometimes
pleaded and remonstrated with drunken Serb guards for hours or
even days to let a convoy through. Both the Serb aggressors and their
Muslim victims developed a contempt for what seemed like U.N.
impotence.

This contempt, coupled with continual sneering from critics
outside Bosnia, angered Kofi Annan of Ghana, the soft-spoken undersecretary-general in charge of peacekeeping. "I think we have to
be careful not to blame the wrong people for the lack of collective
will," he told a news conference in New York in November 1994.
"Peacekeepers are usually the first on the ground, the last to leave,
and the first to be criticized. Quite frankly, the decisions have to be
made by the capitals and the Security Council and not by the peace-

keepers on the ground. . . . I think where we are presumed to have failed is when we are judged by unrealistic expectations. If we are expected to play the role as enforcers when we don't have the mandate and the resources, then we have failed."

In January 1993, three weeks before the inauguration of Bill Clinton as the American president, former U.S. Secretary of State Cyrus Vance (representing the U.N.) and former British Foreign Secretary David Owen (representing the European Commission) presented their peace plan to the three warring parties. The plan divided a united Bosnia into ten provinces— three dominated by Muslims, three by Serbs, three by Croats, and the tenth (Sarajevo) administered jointly by the three ethnic groups. Under this arrangement, the Serbs would have 43 percent of the territory, the Muslims 36 percent, and the Croats 21 percent.

Vance expected the incoming Clinton administration foreign policy team to welcome the plan. Secretary of State Warren Christopher, after all, had served as Vance's deputy secretary during the Carter administration. Both White House National Security Adviser Anthony Lake and his deputy, Sandy Berger, had come out of the Vance State Department as well. "When Clinton was elected, Vance was smiling like a Cheshire cat," said a U.N. official. "He was pleased as one after another of his protégés were appointed to the top foreign policy jobs. He then waited by the telephone for a call from Christopher. But that call never came."

Vance and Owen had a simple strategy to win acceptance for the plan. They would sign up the Bosnian Croats and the Bosnian government swiftly and then wait for international pressure to force the Bosnian Serbs, who would have to relinquish large chunks of conquered territory, to sign the plan as well. The Croats did accept it immediately. But, "to our astonishment," said a U.N. official close to Vance, "the Muslim government would not sign it and trashed it." The Muslims believed that the Clinton administration would come up with something better. Clinton, during his election campaign, had vowed, "The legitimacy of 'ethnic cleansing' cannot stand." The Bosnians naturally inferred from this rhetoric that he would do all he could as president to roll back the aggression.

In the end, the Clinton administration did not come up with

anything better than the Vance-Owen plan. After a month's deliberations, Secretary Christopher announced that President Clinton "has decided the United States will engage actively and directly in the Vance-Owen negotiations, bringing the weight of American policy to bear." It was a lukewarm endorsement, for it seemed to prize the Vance-Owen negotiations over the plan itself. "It was a polite way of giving us the finger," said the official close to Vance. Yet the Clinton administration offered nothing else. Under American pressure, the Muslims did sign the plan in March, but vital momentum had been lost. Karadzić finally made a show of signing the Vance-Owen plan in May, but the Bosnian Serb electorate repudiated this assent in a referendum. Many U.N. officials believed that the Clinton administration's hesitation in embracing the Vance-Owen plan squandered the last and best chance for an early end to the war. David Owen told a Dutch magazine in December 1933, "If George Bush had won the American elections last year, then the war in Bosnia would have been over long ago." These arguments, however, rested on the untested assumption that the Vance-Owen plan, if all parties accepted it, would have worked in practice.

≈≈

In October 1992, the Security Council imposed a "no-fly zone," banning all military flights in Bosnian airspace. The action, sponsored by the United States and others, came when the American public was agitated about reports of atrocities in Serbian detention camps. The Security Council resolution was obviously no more than a public relations gesture, for the council set up no system of enforcing the zone. Five months later, however, three Serb planes dropped bombs on a village east of Srebrenica. At American insistence and over the objections of the U.N. military commander in the field, the Security Council passed a new resolution in March 1993 authorizing NATO jet fighters to shoot down any plane or helicopter flying over Bosnia without U.N. clearance. The threats emanating from the council were stark. "If they do not heed this," said British Ambassador David Hannay, "the prospects for them are grim indeed."

But NATO planes could not fire upon an offending aircraft

without prior U.N. approval, and Lieutenant General Lars-Eric Wahlgren of Sweden, commander of the peacekeepers, feared that the shooting down of a plane would provoke Serbian retaliations that would endanger the peacekeepers and jeopardize the delivery of humanitarian assistance. "The United Nations is a hostage," said Venezuelan Ambassador Diego Arria. "The U.N. is afraid to do anything because it fears retaliation." NATO jets screamed over Bosnia every day but did little else. By late March 1995, the U.N. reported 4,217 violations by Serbs, Muslim, and Croat helicopters and planes in the two and a half years since the imposition of the no-fly zone. Almost all the violations were by noncombat planes and helicopters ferrying soldiers and civilians from one part of Bosnia to another. The U.N. insisted that it was not worth shooting down these aircraft. Only once did NATO planes engage in an air battle: They shot down four of six Serb jet fighters that had defied the ban in February 1994 and ignored warnings from the NATO fighters. As American, Dutch, and French planes roared overhead one day in Sarajevo, Bosnian journalist Senado Kreso waved a fist at them and shouted over the roar to Williams of the *Los Angeles Times*, "What do they do for us? What are they here for? They don't help anyone."

The establishment of "safe areas" in 1993 was another act of the Security Council that raised false hopes. The plight of Srebrenica, a town almost fifty miles northeast of Sarajevo, had stirred world sympathy. Muslim refugees from ethnic cleansing had doubled the size of the town to seventy thousand, but the Serbs prevented the U.N. from bringing food there. When General Phillipe Morillon, the French commander of the U.N. peacekeepers in Bosnia, dramatically led a convoy to Srebrenica in March 1993, blustering his way past Serbian checkpoints, it was the first U.N. shipment there in three months. The World Health Organization estimated by then that twenty to thirty people died from starvation and illness every day. The people of Srebrenica were so desperate to leave that two women and five children died in the crush as refugees mobbed their way onto the trucks of the departing convoy. To intensify the horror, General Mladić then ordered an assault that carried his Serb soldiers within one mile of Srebrenica's borders.

The prospect of Bosnian Serb warriors overrunning the

wretched people of Srebrenica depressed the ambassadors on the Security Council. But the most powerful of them, including American Ambassador Madeleine Albright, could offer little beyond heartfelt condemnation. They were paralyzed by the failure of their governments to produce a coherent policy on Bosnia and the refusal of their governments to commit the military power that could stop the Serbs. For one hectic moment in April, this vacuum was filled by an unlikely source—Diego Arria, the 54-year-old Venezuelan ambassador. The dapper Arria, a former Caracas mayor and newspaper editor who stepped down corridors with a carved cane and brightened meetings with his pastel shirts and elegant ties, often acted as spokesman for the Third World contingent on the council. He took leadership of the Security Council that weekend by shaming the ambassadors into guaranteeing the safety of Srebrenica. "My country was never under siege," he told Russian Ambassador Yuli Vorontsov one night as the ambassadors grappled with the issue behind closed doors, "but Leningrad was under siege. I was in Leningrad [now Saint Petersburg] some time ago and went to the museum, and I saw how terrible this siege was for the courageous people in Leningrad, and I'm sure their ambassador realizes that Srebrenica is in the same conditions as Leningrad during the Second World War."

At the urging of Arria, the Security Council passed a resolution declaring Srebrenica "a safe area" immune to armed attack and authorizing the dispatch of peacekeepers there. Bolstered by the resolution, General Morillon installed a small group of Canadian peacekeepers in Srebrenica and persuaded the Muslim defenders to lay down their arms and the Serbs to call off their attack. General Mladić obviously did not want to test western resolve by massacring Canadians.

At first the United States and Europe belittled the concept of safe areas as insignificant. In a few months, however, the U.S. and its allies, with no other alternative to offer, embraced the idea. The Security Council passed a resolution in June that declared Sarajevo, Bihać, Tuzla, Zepa, and Gorazde safe areas as well. Ironically, Ambassador Arria abstained this time. He looked on the safe-area status of Srebrenica as an emergency measure. To declare all towns in Muslim hands as safe areas, in Arria's view, tended to make the current territorial divisions of the country permanent. "What we created for an emergency situation has become a model that is completely wrong," he said.

The U.N. was never able to make the safe areas safe. Boutros-Ghali estimated he would need thirty-four thousand more troops to do the job. Knowing that request would be dismissed out of hand by the council's ambassadors, he asked for only seventy-six hundred more peacekeepers. The Security Council authorized that many. But governments hesitated about committing troops to such a dangerous assignment. In nine months Boutros-Ghali could muster no more than an inadequate force of five thousand troops to patrol the safe areas. The Security Council's June resolution threatened the use of airpower to protect the peacekeepers, but it was not clear how this would be used.

In a report to the Security Council in March 1994, the secretary-general concluded that the presence of the peacekeepers "has indeed deterred major attacks on these towns, reduced the level of conflict, lowered casualties and improved basic humanitarian conditions. . . ." But, he went on, "living conditions in the safe areas remain appalling: the areas are inviable socially and economically and suffer high levels of unemployment, overcrowding and crime, as well as the tension of an uncertain future." He deplored the Bosnian government's penchant for using the safe areas as bases for mounting attacks on the Serbs and "thereby provoking Serb retaliation."

It was obvious from the start of the conflict that the United States and Europe would not intervene with their own troops to turn back aggression. But the Bosnian Serbs had one lingering fear—that the West would come to the aid of the Muslims with a terrible onslaught from the air. Military strategists did not believe that airpower alone could drive the Serbs out of their conquered territory. But it might inflict awful punishment upon the aggressors and make many people in the West feel that they had finally throttled evil even if they could not undo its damage.

❦❦

The main pressure for bombing came from the Clinton administration. Secretary of State Warren Christopher had failed in his attempt to persuade the European allies to accept a "lift and strike" policy—lifting the embargo on the sale of arms to Bosnia and holding the Serbs back with air strikes while the Bosnians prepared to reconquer their land. Lifting the embargo struck the Europeans as foolish and dangerous. In their view, the Muslim government had lost the war militarily and had no hope, whether armed or not, of winning it back later. Lifting the embargo would only prolong the war for many years and multiply the devastation and death. European leaders did not look kindly on bombing either, but continual Serbian effrontery made their publics cry for some kind of vengeance.

The pressure from Clinton, however, angered many Europeans. It was easy for the president to advocate bombing. He had no American troops on the ground in Bosnia. But the French and British had several thousand each, and these peacekeepers would be easy targets for the Bosnian Serbs if they wanted to retaliate against an American-led NATO air attack. After listening to American entreaties for bombing, French Foreign Minister Alain Juppe said, "There is a division of tasks which I don't think is acceptable—that of having some flying in planes and dropping bombs, and others, especially the French, on the ground."

The threat of bombing also fostered a conflict between NATO and the U.N., but it was not a clear-cut battle. NATO was a military alliance, and the generals and admirals ached to be cut loose and allowed to inflict damage on the enemy. But the U.N.—bolstered by the diplomats of NATO stalwarts Britain and France—insisted that almost all potential bombing in Bosnia was a political act that had to be approved by the civilian in charge of the U.N. operation. Even though the peacekeepers were charged with defending the safe areas against Serb attack, the U.N. chief, Yasushi Akashi of Japan, insisted that the peacekeepers were still impartial arbiters who needed the trust of both sides. While NATO blustered for permission to bomb, Akashi often met with Bosnian Serb leaders trying to negotiate a peaceful solution to the problem at hand. He believed that patient persuasion would accomplish more with the Bosnian Serbs than painful punishment, and he did not care if the lack of punishment humiliated NATO.

To complicate matters, both the NATO council and the Security Council were divided between the pro-bombers led by the United States and the anti-bombers led by Britain and France. NATO might press the U.N. for air strikes, but two influential members of NATO—Britain and France—did not agree and did their best at the U.N. to encourage Boutros Boutros-Ghali to move gingerly. So while the U.N. sometimes looked like it was defying NATO, it was really doing the bidding of some of the most important European members of NATO. The official positions of both NATO and the U.N. on bombing were rife with ambiguity and contradictions.

In the end, the threat of bombing proved more potent than the bombing itself. After worldwide shock over a mortar attack on the market in Sarajevo that left sixty-eight civilians dead and two hundred wounded on February 5, 1994, NATO and the U.N. finally worked out the procedures for approving both close air support of peacekeepers and air strikes to halt the shelling of civilians in the safe areas. But Akashi, a cautious, sixty-three-year-old Japanese diplomat and U.N. civil servant who had won widespread approval for his deft handling of the delicate Cambodia peacekeeping mission, did not intend to give permission easily. He had succeeded in Cambodia, after all, by deciding to isolate the Khmer Rouge rather than fight them.

When NATO issued an ultimatum demanding the withdrawal of Serbian heavy weapons from the area around Sarajevo, Akashi let the deadline slide by allowing some of the tanks and artillery pieces to remain in place subject to U.N. monitoring. Although the Serbs were not in total compliance, he declared them in "effective compliance" with the ultimatum. The threat of air strikes and Akashi's patient negotiations combined to bring the sniping and shelling of Sarajevo to a halt for much of 1994.

Akashi's legendary patience, however, began to grate on the nerves of those who felt it made NATO look like a toothless tiger. In March, when a French peacekeeping battalion in Bihać requested air support to halt a Serb tank and artillery piece aiming at them, Akashi wasted twenty-nine precious minutes trying in vain to phone Bosnian Serb leader Karadzić and Serbian President Milošević to warn them of the probable NATO attack and request that they not retaliate. When Akashi finally approved—four hours and seven minutes after the original request, one hour after approval was recommended by French General Jean Cot, the U.N. Force commander — it was too late to find the Serb weapons. The Serbs had withdrawn the tank and artillery. Since General Cot and Akashi had approved an attack on the offending weapons and no other, the NATO raid was canceled.

Akashi finally allowed two pinprick bombing attacks on Serb gunners shelling U.N. observers in the enclave of Gorazde in April 1994. When the Serbs defied another NATO ultimatum that they pull their troops and heavy weapons from the Gorazde area, however, Akashi vetoed a NATO proposal to bomb them. It was unnecessary, he said, because he was negotiating a withdrawal. The Serbs finally did withdraw, but they looted and burned several hundred houses with impunity as they left. As far as the Serbs were concerned, they had stared down the NATO ultimatum and escaped unscathed.

U.S. officials were furious at Akashi for his veto. Akashi and other U.N. officials, on the other hand, were fed up with Americans who hectored them but would not commit troops to the battle. Akashi irritated sore American feelings by telling a *New York Times* interviewer, "After Somalia, the U.S. position is somewhat reticent, somewhat afraid, timid and tentative. I understand that President Clinton only wants to send U.S. troops to Bosnia after a peace settlement, but we need more troops now, including U.S. troops, to police a peace that is coming bit by bit and to avoid situations like Gorazde." Two other high-ranking but anonymous U.N. officials in Bosnia—one an officer, the other a civilian—accused the United States of prolonging the war by feeding the Muslim government false hopes that the Clinton administration would come to its aid. The officials were especially exercised by American Ambassador Albright, echoing the *"Ich bin ein Berliner"* speech of President John F. Kennedy in 1961, telling a Sarajevo crowd in Serbo-Croatian, "I am a Sarajevan." These broadsides angered Ambassador Albright. "International civil servants should remember where their salaries are paid—by member states," she said. "They should not even be thinking of criticizing the policies of member states. Frankly, I'm tired of it."

NATO would bomb a few more times during 1994. Planes destroyed an antiquated mobile gun and a T-55 tank in the mountains around Sarajevo in August and September. These were rather Milquetoast reprisals for Serb attacks on peacekeepers. Under its policy of "proportionate" bombing, the U.N. warned the Bosnian Serbs ahead of time of the intended targets so that no one would be hurt. The bombing became more intense at Bihać in November. U.N. officials were annoyed at the Muslims for launching an offensive from Bihać that month. But the officials became more alarmed when the Bosnian Serb counterattack threatened to engulf Bihać, a safe area guaranteed by the U.N. In one wave thirty-nine American, British, French, and Dutch warplanes bombed the runway of a Serbian air base in Croatia but carefully avoided damaging any planes; in another wave, NATO planes destroyed several Serbian antiaircraft and missile sites in Bosnia. But this did not stop the Serbian onslaught; it only provoked the Serbs into furious reaction.

The Serbs took more than four hundred Canadian, French, Russian, Ukrainian, and other peacekeepers hostage. Since peacekeepers were spread throughout Bosnia, often in small groups as observers or humanitarian convoy escorts, it was easy to detain them. In Gorazde, gloating Serb gunmen handcuffed British peacekeepers and beat them with rifle butts. At Banja Luka, the Serbs tied up four U.N. observers and forced them to lie for hours across an airstrip as a human shield against any NATO air attack. The four included a Jordanian officer with a congenital heart disease. A Serb blockade prevented medicine from reaching a Bangladeshi peacekeeper at Bihać in time to prevent his death from a heart attack. NATO sent a third wave of planes into action near Bihać, but Lieutenant General Michael Rose, the British commander of the U.N. troops in Bosnia, called them off at the last moment. He claimed he wanted only a show of force. But it was obvious that neither U.N. officials nor the governments supplying troops wanted to goad the Serbs into killing their hostages. NATO had finally brought airpower to the war in Bosnia, but the Serbs had brushed it aside.

In Washington, U.S. Secretary of Defense William J. Perry saw no point in more air strikes. "The Serbs have demonstrated military superiority on the ground," he said. "Air strikes cannot determine the outcome of the ground combat. They can punish the Serbs, but they cannot determine the outcome of the ground combat." By the end of the year, the Serbs had still not overrun Bihać but only because of a four-month cease-fire for all of Bosnia negotiated by former American President Jimmy Carter.

The bombing scenario was repeated in 1995. When the cease-fire expired in May, the Serbs, provoked by the Muslims, defied the U.N. and NATO by seizing stored heavy weapons and shelling Sarajevo and other safe areas. This brought on NATO air strikes again. The angry Serbs then took more than 300 peacekeepers hostage, halting the bombing.

By late 1994, the United States had accepted the European approach to the war, albeit without much enthusiasm. The U.S. joined Britain, France, Germany, and Russia in what was designated the "contact group." The five governments drew up a new map for Bosnia: 51 percent would go to a federation of Bosnian Muslims and Bosnian Croats, 49 percent to the Bosnian Serbs. The United States now lobbied for a plan that gave the Serbs even more than the Vance-Owen plan would have. As before, the Muslims and Croats accepted, but the Serbs refused, still demanding adjustments in their favor. In their eyes, they were, after all, the victors.

☙ ❧

All that remained of some of the Clinton administration's boldest proposals for dealing with the carnage was the War Crimes Tribunal. The Security Council voted for its establishment in May 1993 but had difficulty naming a prosecutor until it settled fourteen months later on fifty-five-year-old Richard Goldstone, the courageous and meticulous South African justice who exposed the illegal, antiblack campaign of his country's military intelligence officers during the era of white rule. By the end of 1994, Goldstone had indicted 22 Serbs on charges of war crimes and was preparing to try one of them—Dusan Tadić, a former bartender accused of killing 10 Muslims and maiming 150 others while serving as a guard in a prison camp. Germany, which arrested Tadić, promised to extradite the Serb to the tribunal in the Hague. The other indicted Serbs were presumably in Serbia, refusing to present themselves in the Hague.

American Ambassador Albright was the most ardent supporter of the tribunal at the U.N., and, at her urging, the U.S. government became the prime source of documentation for Goldstone and his staff. Even if most defendants could not be brought to trial, she said, an indictment would make them pariahs who could not travel outside Serbian territory. Both British and French diplomats hinted that they would be willing to eliminate the tribunal if that was the price exacted by the Bosnian Serbs for signing a peace agreement. But Ambassador Albright vowed publicly that the United States would never associate itself with a peace agreement that did away with the tribunal. The Serbs had pursued their terrible war with contempt for the rest of the world. There had to be some kind of retribution.

The U.N. mission to Bosnia was hapless and star-crossed but not wholly a failure. In 1994, 2,740,000 Bosnians received relief aid. Many lives were saved, and the war did not spread. As the fiftieth anniversary of the U.N. approached, however, aggression remained unpunished and peace elusive. The mission and the war had also frayed relations between NATO and the U.N., the United States and Europe, the Clinton administration and U.N. bureaucrats. The gravest error made by Boutros-Ghali was to accept the veto on bombing. That made it difficult for the U.N. to rationalize its two roles as peacekeeper and peace enforcer and made it easy for hawks to blame the U.N. for the timidity of the air strikes. Yet, given the nervousness of troop suppliers France and Britain and the refusal of the United States to commit soldiers on the ground, the U.N. accomplished as much as it could of a confused and limited mandate.

Epilogue: *The Fiftieth Anniversary*

Anniversaries are a time for reflection and reappraisal. No one doubted that would happen when the United Nations turned fifty. But, when the celebrations were planned two and three years earlier, everyone had assumed the taking of stock and the proposals for reform would come while all felt upbeat. Few had anticipated a dispirited mood.

At the age of fifty, the U.N. was surely a significant player on the world scene. Yet a malaise permeated its bureaucracy. U.N. officials and diplomats felt misunderstood and scapegoated. Polls showed that the American public still held the U.N. in high regard, but public confidence had slipped from the high levels of the Persian Gulf War. Some key Republicans scorned the U.N. and accused President Bill Clinton of abdicating his leadership in foreign affairs to Secretary-General Boutros Boutros-Ghali. Defense of the U.N. by the administration came slowly. Although legally international territory, U.N. headquarters towered by the East River in New York City, one of the world's media capitals. Its bureaucrats and diplomats could not ignore the brickbats.

Public Opinion Poll: The United States
Should Cooperate Fully with the United Nations

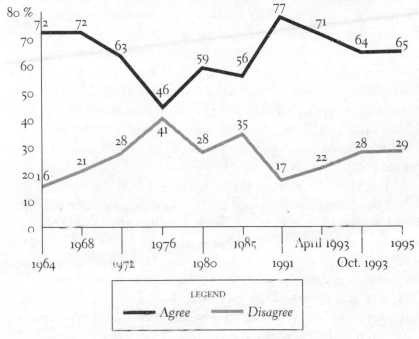

Source: Gallup Organization, Times Mirror Center
for the People and the Press

Sometimes the attacks were ill informed, even ludicrous, though still harmful. Caspar Weinberger, who served as President Ronald Reagan's secretary of defense, told a Council of Foreign Relations symposium in Washington in April 1995, "It's hard to conceal contempt for an organization that can't pass a resolution that condemns ethnic cleansing." By then, the Security Council, of course, had passed more than a half-dozen resolutions condemning ethnic cleansing and even set up an unprecedented international war crimes tribunal to try those involved. Yet no one at the symposium stood up to challenge Weinberger's remark.

American discontent, especially congressional discontent, came out of frustration over the U.N. peacekeeping missions in So-

malia and Bosnia. The Republicans, who took control over both
houses of Congress in the 1994 elections, introduced legislation that
would, in effect, hamstring any president who tried to send American
troops into a peacekeeping mission and also would drastically reduce, if not eliminate, the assessment that the United States paid
each year for peacekeeping—more than 30 percent of the costs. The
conflict seemed to presage a grand debate within the United States
during the next few years about the role of the United Nations. This
might not prove harmful to the U.N. A national debate could re-
dound to its benefit, for the U.N. suffered most from lack of understanding. There was much need in the United States for a serious
debate about the U.N.

The United States was the U.N.'s most important member state.
When the United States reined itself in to play an ineffectual role at
the U.N., the U.N. became ineffectual. When the United States refused to lead, the U.N. did not know where to go. The U.N. did very
little about the carnage in Rwanda because the United States,
burned by the Somalia expedition, shied away from Rwanda. The
U.N. was at a crossroads on its fiftieth birthday, and the American
definition of its own relationship with the U.N. would determine the
direction that the U.N. would take.

Soon after President Clinton took office, Madeleine K. Albright, his ambassador to the U.N., enunciated a policy that she
called "assertive multilateralism." The phrase was not clearly defined
but seemed to denote a process by which the Americans created and
led coalitions at the United Nations to make policies work. The Somalia mission was a good example of this, for it was tailored to American design and controlled by Americans, though it had all the outer
markings of a U.N. project. When the mission fell apart, however,
the Clinton administration did not mind the public blaming the
U.N. rather than Washington for the failure. Since the failed mission
was closely identified with assertive multilateralism, Albright stopped
invoking the phrase, except to say occasionally that it had been mis-

understood. Yet, though used only rarely, assertive multilateralism was not abandoned by the Americans. The forging of a U.N. mission to replace the American intervention in Haiti was a good example of assertive multilateralism at work.

But the critics of Clinton chose to look on assertive multilateralism as an American abrogation of its own interests in favor of the interests of the United Nations. "The real choice," wrote Senate Republican leader Bob Dole of Kansas in 1995, "is whether to allow international organizations to call the shots—as in Somalia or Bosnia—or to make multilateral groupings work for American interests—as in Operation Desert Storm." Dole defined American interests narrowly and found little or none in Somalia, Rwanda, and even Haiti. He would not become involved in such places whether under the U.N. umbrella or not. If the Dole viewpoint prevailed, the United States would play a truncated role at the U.N., crippling the will of the organization. Under the shock of these Republican attacks, Ambassador Albright began a series of speeches around the country in 1995 defending the U.N. as an essential arm of American policy.

The Dole argument posed the image of Americans turning their backs on the rash of murderous conflicts erupting all over the world in the post–Cold War era. Americans and others had done this often before. When the Tutsis slaughtered one hundred thousand to two hundred thousand Hutus in Burundi in 1972—eliminating the modern class of the Hutus in a systematic way—there was little outcry elsewhere in the world. Nor was there any rage over the plight of the black Christians and animists suppressed in a bloody civil war in the Sudan for two generations. In cases like these, however, the horrors managed to elude television cameras. When similar horrors were caught by cameras, Americans tended to demand help for the victims and punishment for the perpetrators. For this reason, Americans might grow uneasy with the Dole argument that it was somehow never in the national interest to do anything about these terrible plights. Yet, though Americans demanded action, they did not want the United States to act alone as the world's policeman. Dealing with the problem through the U.N. surely made better sense.

꧁꧂

Brian Urquhart, the former undersecretary-general who watched over the world organization from his new office at the nearby Ford Foundation, described the early 1990s as a period of "false renaissance" for the U.N. By this he meant that the hopes generated by the Persian Gulf War for a revitalized U.N. presiding over a "new world order" had proven illusory. Yet it also was a time of testing for the U.N. And, while Somalia and Bosnia seemed like peacekeeping failures, Cambodia, Mozambique, Haiti, El Salvador, and others looked like successes. From 1988 to 1995, the number of peacekeeping missions in the field had increased from five to seventeen, the numbers of troops deployed had increased from 9,600 to 73,400, and the cost of peacekeeping had increased from $230 million to $3.6 billion a year. The U.N. needed to learn from this frenetic experience.

The secretary-general tried to do that at the start of 1995. He issued a supplement to the "Agenda for Peace" that he had written three years earlier. The new document, subtitled "Position Paper of the Secretary-General on the Occasion of the Fiftieth Anniversary of the United Nations," represented a somewhat nuanced retreat, in the light of experience and reality, from some of his ideas on peacekeeping. He had once believed that the U.N. could engage in some enforcement operations. Now he all but ruled them out.

Most of the new missions authorized by the Security Council involved conflicts within a single state rather than conflicts between two states. These intrastate conflicts, Boutros-Ghali wrote, "present United Nations peacekeepers with challenges not encountered since the Congo operation of the early 1960s." He said that "they are usually fought not only by regular armies but also by militias and armed civilians with little discipline and with ill-defined chains of command." Their main victims and main targets are civilians. The police, judiciary, and other state institutions have collapsed, he said, "with resulting paralysis of governance, a breakdown of law and order, and general banditry and chaos." Humanitarian agencies find it extremely difficult to take care of the hungry and sick. "The resulting horrors explode on to the world's television screens and create political pressure for the United Nations to deploy troops to facilitate and protect the humanitarian operations," the secretary-general said. The terrible television images pressured governments into hasty and emotional decisions. He cited Somalia and Bosnia as examples.

Boutros-Ghali said that three traditional principles must guide peacekeeping operations: U.N. troops must have the consent of the warring parties before entering a country; U.N. troops must be impartial; U.N. troops must not use force except in self-defense. In Somalia and Bosnia, the secretary-general said, the Security Council assigned the peacekeepers an extra mandate to use force to protect civilians and humanitarian convoys in the case of Bosnia and to speed up national reconciliation in the case of Somalia. In short, the secretary-general said, the troops were asked to serve as peacekeepers and peace enforcers at the same time. "To blur the distinction between the two can undermine the viability of the peacekeeping operation and endanger its personnel," he said.

The secretary-general pleaded for patience in the face of emotional television images when dealing with these crises. "Conflicts . . . usually have deep roots and have defied the peacemaking efforts of others," he said. "Their resolution requires patient diplomacy and the establishment of a political process that permits, over a period of time, the building of confidence and negotiated solutions to long-standing differences. . . . It is necessary to resist the temptation to use military power to speed them up." He said that the Security Council must understand that peacekeeping and the use of military force could not be mixed in the same mission. They were alternatives; the U.N. had to authorize one or the other.

In most cases, however, the U.N., he said, was not strong enough on its own to carry out a military operation to punish aggression or some other breach of the peace. "Neither the Security Council nor the Secretary-General at present has the capacity to deploy, direct, command and control operations for this purpose, except perhaps on a very limited scale," Boutros-Ghali said. He believed that the U.N. should develop such a capacity, but it would be folly to try to do so when the U.N. did not have enough funds or committed troops to carry out all its peacekeeping duties. The U.N. would have to authorize others to do the job the way it once authorized the United States to lead wars against North Korea and Iraq. Boutros-Ghali's latest discourse on peacekeeping annoyed the United States and its European allies for it threw the blame for Bosnia back at them. If they really wanted to repel Serb aggression, it seemed to say, these powerful countries should have organized a force to stop the Serbs instead of sending small numbers of lightly armed U.N. peace-keepers off on a mission impossible. Despite bristles like this, the document would surely command close scrutiny in the ongoing debate over the role of peacekeeping.

❧

The governments of Japan and Germany had hoped that the anniversary year would bring them permanent seats on the Security Council in a major reform of the U.N. After the United States, these two countries were the leading economic powers in the world. For the regular U.N. budget, Japan paid the second-largest assessment in 1995 of any of the 185 member states of the U.N.—12.45 percent. Germany paid the third-largest—just under 9 percent. Together they paid almost as much as the United States, which had an assessment of 25 percent, the highest in the U.N. Japanese diplomats liked to tell American audiences: "There's an old American saying on democracy—no taxation without representation."

Not only did Japan and Germany lack permanent seats. They were members of an international organization whose charter still talked about countries that were "an enemy state." While the U.N. Charter did not name the ten enemy states, everyone knew that Japan and Germany headed the list. The U.N. was created as an organization of the victors of World War II, and the Security Council represented the power structure of that time. As the leading victors, the United States, the Soviet Union (now Russia), and Britain assumed permanent seats on the eleven-member council. Roosevelt added China because he hoped it would replace Japan as the Asian power in the future. Churchill added France because he wanted it to help balance an expansive Soviet Union in Europe. On the twentieth anniversary, the U.N. increased the size of the Security Council from eleven to fifteen members to accommodate new countries from the Third World. But the number of permanent members with veto power was kept at five.

There was general agreement in 1995 that the time had come to eliminate the anachronism of Japan and Germany as enemy states and make them permanent members (though there was argument about allowing them a veto). But the Third World insisted that their most powerful countries deserved permanent seats as well. This provoked bitter wrangling, however, over which ones. Because of population, India, Nigeria, and Brazil seemed logical choices. But rival contenders—Pakistan, Indonesia, South Africa, Egypt, Argentina, and Mexico—did not like the idea of being pushed aside. Nor did Italy, also an "enemy state," like the idea of giving way for Japan and Germany. Italy pointed out that its per capita gross national product was larger than that of Britain, Russia, and China—all permanent members. Italy proposed a three-tier Security Council: the original Big Five, a group of 20 countries that would alternate in ten semipermanent seats, and five to ten nonpermanent seats for the other 160 members to seek in elections every two years. "The longer the discussion goes on," said a senior British diplomat, "the more the blood heats up."

Amid all the wrangling, diplomats fretted about the danger of expanding the Security Council and making it unwieldy. The Clinton administration supported expanding the council to twenty members, by adding Japan and Germany as permanent members with veto power and expanding the two-year nonpermanent seats to thirteen. But the Heritage Foundation, a conservative think tank in Washington, insisted that an expanded Security Council would "dilute American influence" and "be more likely to oppose American values and interests." With a Republican Congress accusing President Clinton of yielding power to the U.N., the fiftieth anniversary was surely not the year to make the Security Council more representative of the rest of the U.N. Faced with all the uncertainty, diplomats said that the decision to expand the Security Council would have to be delayed for a couple of years or so. But there was a widespread belief that reform was inevitable. The Security Council could not reflect the balance of power of 1945 much longer.

❧❧

In 1996 or, if Boutros-Ghali won reelection, in 2001, the Security Council would have to seek a new secretary-general. For years, critics led by Brian Urquhart have argued for some kind of rational system of searching for candidates. Urquhart would end overt campaigning for the post—a practice started by Waldheim, organize a talent search, and for the first time consider possibilities from the Big Five. Urquhart's proposals sometimes sounded like a formula for finding a chief executive officer for a corporation rather than a statesman for a highly charged political post, but he was certainly on the right track. There had to be a more sensible selection process than the insistence in 1991 by the Third World that it was Africa's turn for the post. It was a pernicious idea that so important a job be passed around like some kind of booty.

But even worse last time was the American lack of participation. Once President Bush found his first choice knocked down by the Africa First crowd in 1991, he lost interest in the selection. It is imperative next time that the United States meet early with other members of the Big Five—the most important voters because of their veto—to talk about criteria and candidates. The prestige of the U.N. would be enhanced considerably if the Security Council settled on a renowned figure next time: someone say of the stature of Willy Brandt in the 1970s and 1980s or of Jimmy Carter or Colin Powell in the 1990s. Because of the strained relations between the United States and the United Nations, the new secretary-general also would probably have to perform well on American television.

The job of secretary-general, however, is so unique that it may defy any system of selection. After all, Dag Hammarskjöld was chosen because he seemed like a passive bureaucrat, and Boutros Boutros-Ghali was suspect in the eyes of the Americans because he seemed like a passive bureaucrat, and both turned out to be the most active secretaries-general in history.

❧❧

Defenders of the United Nations often came up with a cliché when asked to justify the world organization. "If the U.N. did not exist," they would say, "it would have to be invented." Or, as Arthur J. Goldberg was quoted in chapter 9, "If the U.N. were junked, we'd have to recreate it tomorrow." That defense was surely true, but it somehow always seemed inadequate, far too self-effacing for the real worth of the U.N. In its first fifty years, the United Nations never fulfilled the hopes of its founders, but it accomplished a good deal nevertheless.

The emergence of the Cold War at the beginning prevented the U.N. from acting as the world's policeman beating down aggression. But the Cold War did not paralyze the U.N. totally. The intense Soviet-American enmity meant that the U.N. had to deal with issues that skirted the Cold War like Israel (at first), Suez, the Congo, and Cyprus. The near paralysis came in the late 1970s and early 1980s when the Third World, with the acquiescence of the Soviet Union, assumed dominance over the U.N. and tried to turn it into a strident, antineocolonialist, ideological talkfest. The end of the Cold War broke that dominance and made the U.N. relevant again. There were some naïve hopes that it could quickly assume the policeman role envisioned by the founders, but this proved beyond its immediate reach. Well-meaning failures like the missions to Bosnia and Somalia forced the organization to undergo crucial redefinition. The new definition would surely include some kind of police role, though less sweeping than once envisioned.

The U.N. did not boast a glorious history; only chauvinist nations boast of glorious histories. But the U.N. created Israel, joined the United States in the war against North Korea, helped put an end to colonial empires at Suez, ended the secession of Katanga, lobbied for peace in Vietnam, supervised the end of the Iraq-Iran war, authorized the Persian Gulf War, and helped keep the peace in Cyprus, Kashmir, El Salvador, Cambodia, South Africa, Mozambique, and a bunch of other trouble spots. It hosted such visionary figures as Dag Hammarskjöld, Adlai Stevenson, and Ralph Bunche. And, though it did not yet know what to do about it, the U.N. learned in the 1990s not to accept that nations can hide behind the sanctity of sovereignty to inflict punishment on their own people.

All in all, it could boast a distinguished and action-packed history. While taking part in some of the most tumultuous events of the century, the United Nations had served the world nobly and well for fifty years.

Sources

1 🍃 The Beginnings:
From Dumbarton Oaks to San Francisco

Robert C. Hildebrand has written a detailed analysis of the Dumbarton Oaks conference in *Dumbarton Oaks* (Chapel Hill: University of North Carolina Press, 1990). Ruth B. Russell's analysis of the San Francisco conference (and other early events) is just as thorough in A *History of the United Nations Charter* (Washington, D.C.: The Brookings Institution, 1978). I have depended on both books for this chapter. Frank Freidel, *Franklin D. Roosevelt: A Rendezvous with Destiny* (Boston: Little, Brown, 1990), covers the Yalta conference (pp. 577–92), as does Russell. The last Hopkins mission to Moscow is covered by Robert E. Sherwood, *Roosevelt and Hopkins* (New York: Grosset & Dunlap, 1950, pp. 885–916). For Harry Truman's attitude toward the U.N. and participation in San Francisco, I depended on both Robert J. Donovan, *Conflict and Crisis: The Presidency of Harry S Truman, 1945–1948* (New York: W. W. Norton, 1977), and David McCullough, *Truman* (New York: Simon &

Schuster, 1992). James Reston discusses press relations at Dumbarton Oaks in *Deadline* (New York: Times Books, 1992, pp. 141–44).

Other sources consulted included Ronald Steel, *Walter Lippmann and the American Century* (New York: Vintage, 1981); Michael Howard, "The United Nations: From War Fighting to Peace Planning" (a paper read at the fiftieth anniversary Dumbarton Oaks conference, 6 May 1994); Henry A. Trofimenko, "Hope That Is Gradually Coming True" (another paper at the fiftieth anniversary conference); Henry Kissinger, *Diplomacy* (New York: Simon & Schuster, 1994); and Brian Urquhart, *Ralph Bunche: An American Life* (New York: W. W. Norton, 1993).

2 ❧ Trygve Lie and Iran: Off to a Bad Start

These early years of the U.N. are covered thoroughly in two memoirs: Trygve Lie, *In the Cause of Peace* (New York: Macmillan, 1954), and Brian Urquhart, *A Life in Peace and War* (New York: W. W. Norton, 1991, pp. 99–112). Don Cook, *Forging the Alliance: NATO, 1945–1950* (London: Secker & Warburg, 1989, pp. 46–64), describes the advent of the Cold War. Robert J. Donovan, *Conflict and Crisis: The Presidency of Harry S Truman, 1945–1948* (New York: W. W. Norton, 1977), has a good account of the Iran crisis on pp. 185–97.

Other sources consulted included Dean Acheson, *Present at the Creation* (New York: W. W. Norton, 1969); David McCullough, *Truman* (New York: Simon & Schuster, 1992); Ronald Steel, *Walter Lippmann and the American Century* (New York: Vintage, 1981); Jeff Broadwater, *Adlai Stevenson* (New York: Twayne, 1994); Brian Urquhart, *Ralph Bunche: An American Life* (New York: W. W. Norton, 1993).

3 ❧ Ralph Bunche and the Infant State of Israel

The indispensable work on the life of Bunche is Brian Urquhart, *Ralph Bunche: An American Life* (New York: W. W. Norton, 1993). For the discussion of the partition of Palestine and the debate in the Truman administration over it, I have depended on Robert J.

Donovan, *Conflict and Crisis: The Presidency of Harry S Truman,* *1945–1948* (New York: W. W. Norton, 1977, pp. 369–87); David McCullough, *Truman* (New York: Simon & Schuster, 1992, pp. 595–620); and Ian J. Bickerton and Carla L. Klausner, *A Concise History of the Arab-Israeli Conflict* (Englewood Cliffs, N.J.: Prentice Hall, 1991, pp. 87–113). Nathan A. Pelcovits discusses the Israeli disappointment in the U.N. in *The Long Armistice: UN Peacekeeping and the Arab-Israeli Conflict, 1948–1960* (Boulder, Colo.: Westview Press, 1993). Kati Marton, *A Death in Jerusalem* (New York: Pantheon, 1994), covers the assassination of Count Bernadotte in detail.

Other sources consulted included Trygve Lie, *In the Cause of Peace* (New York: Macmillan, 1954); Dean Acheson, *Present at the Creation* (New York: W. W. Norton, 1969); Walter LaFeber, *America, Russia, and the Cold War* (New York: McGraw-Hill, 1991); Merle Miller, *Plain Speaking* (New York: Berkley, 1974); Chaim Herzog, *The Arab-Israeli Wars* (New York: Random House, 1982), and Dan Kurzman, *Genesis 1948* (New York: World Publishing, 1970).

4 ❧ The Korean War: No More Manchurias

The responses of the United States and the United Nations to the Korean invasion in the first few weeks and American policies afterward are covered thoroughly by Trygve Lie, *In the Cause of Peace* (New York: Macmillan, 1954); Evan Luard, *A History of the United Nations,* vol. 1 (New York: St. Martin's Press, 1982); David McCullough, *Truman* (New York: Simon & Schuster, 1992); Merle Miller, *Plain Speaking* (New York: Berkley, 1974); and, most important, Robert J. Donovan, *Tumultuous Years: The Presidency of Harry S Truman, 1949–1953* (New York: W. W. Norton, 1982, especially pp. 187–218, 301–12, 340–54). For the conduct of the war, I have relied heavily on Max Hastings, *The Korean War* (New York: Touchstone, 1988).

Other sources consulted included Dean Acheson, *Present at the Creation* (New York: W. W. Norton, 1969); Walter LaFeber, *America, Russia, and the Cold War, 1945–1990* (New York: McGraw-Hill, 1991); Seymour Maxwell Finger, *American Ambassadors at the U.N.*

(New York: U.N. Institute for Training and Research, n.d.); Linda M. Fasulo, *Representing America* (New York: Facts on File, 1984); Don Cook, *Forging the Alliance: NATO, 1945–1950* (London: Secker & Warburg, 1989); Henry Kissinger, *Diplomacy* (New York: Simon & Schuster, 1994); and Anthony Eden, *Full Circle* (Boston: Houghton Mifflin, 1960).

5 🕮 Dag Hammarskjöld

All the poetry and spiritual writings of Hammarskjöld come from his *Markings* (New York: Alfred A. Knopf, 1994). For biographical details and his work as secretary-general, I have depended extensively on Andrew W. Cordier and Wilder Foote, eds., *Public Papers of the Secretaries-General of the United Nations*, vol. 2, *Dag Hammarskjöld, 1953–1956* (New York: Columbia University Press, 1972); Brian Urquhart, *Hammarskjöld* (New York: Alfred A. Knopf, 1972); and Brian Urquhart, *A Life in Peace and War* (New York: W. W. Norton, 1991).

Other sources consulted included Trygve Lie, *In the Cause of Peace* (New York: Macmillan, 1954); John Lindberg, "The Secret Life of Dag Hammarskjöld," *Look* (30 June 1964); Brian Urquhart, *Ralph Bunche: An American Life* (New York: W. W. Norton, 1993); Stephen E. Ambrose, *Eisenhower*, vol. 2, *The President* (New York: Simon & Schuster, 1984); Dwight D. Eisenhower, *The White House Years: Mandate for Change* (New York: Signet, 1965); and Townsend Hoopes, *The Devil and John Foster Dulles* (Boston: Atlantic Monthly Press, 1973).

6 🕮 Suez: The Empires Strike Out

I depended heavily on Keith Kyle, *Suez* (New York: St. Martin's Press, 1991), for details on the overall crisis. Hammarskjöld's role is covered thoroughly in Andrew W. Cordier and Wilder Foote, eds., *Public Papers of the Secretaries-General of the United Nations*, vol 3, *Dag Hammarskjöld, 1956–1957* (New York: Columbia University Press, 1973, pp. 244–411), and Brian Urquhart, *Hammarskjöld* (New York: Alfred A. Knopf, 1972, pp. 159–230). I also made extensive use of

Dwight D. Eisenhower, *The White House Years: Waging Peace 1956–61* (New York: Doubleday, 1965, pp. 20–99, pp. 663–79), and two interviews in the Yale University–United Nations Oral History Project: Guy Millard (20 April 1991) and Christian Pineau (8 April 1991).

Other sources consulted included Brian Urquhart, *Ralph Bunche: An American Life* (New York: W. W. Norton, 1993); Brian Urquhart, *A Life in Peace and War* (New York: W. W. Norton, 1991); Stephen E. Ambrose, *Eisenhower*, vol. 2, *The President* (New York: Simon & Schuster, 1984); Anthony Eden, *Full Circle* (Boston: Houghton Mifflin, 1960); Marc Ferro, *1956: La Crise de Suez* (Paris: La Documentation Française, 1986); Townsend Hoopes, *The Devil and John Foster Dulles* (Boston: Atlantic Monthly Press, 1973); Donald Logan, Yale University–United Nations Oral History Project (22 April 1991); United Nations, *The Blue Helmets: A Review of United Nations Peace-keeping* (New York: Dept. of Public Information, 1990); George Vest, interview by author (Bethesda, MD, 23 November 1994).

7 ⚜ The Battles of Katanga and the Crash of Hammarskjöld

Portions of this chapter appeared in *The Quarterly Journal of Military History* 5, no. 1 (Autumn 1992), as "Crisis in Katanga."

I depended heavily in my account on background in Madeleine G. Kalb, *The Congo Cables* (New York: Macmillan, 1982); Conor Cruise O'Brien, *To Katanga and Back* (New York: Simon & Schuster, 1962); Brian Urquhart, *A Life in Peace and War* (New York: Harper & Row, 1987); and Maj. Gen. H. T. Alexander, *African Tightrope* (London: Pall Mall Press, 1966).

Other sources consulted included Brian Urquhart, *Hammarskjöld* (New York: Alfred A. Knopf, 1972); Per Lind, Yale University–United Nations Oral History Project (7 November 1990); John Lindberg, "The Secret Life of Dag Hammarskjöld," *Look* (30 June 1964); and United Nations, *The Blue Helmets: A Review of United Nations Peace-keeping* (New York: Dept. of Public Information, 1990).

8 ✍ Adlai Stevenson and the
Cuban Missile Crisis: The U.N. as Theater

I have depended heavily on John Bartlow Martin's detailed biography, especially vol. 2, *Adlai Stevenson and the World* (New York: Doubleday, 1977). A great deal has been written on the Cuban missile crisis; I relied mainly on Richard R. Reeves, *President Kennedy: Profile of Power* (New York: Touchstone, 1994, chapters 34–36), and Michael R. Beschloss, *The Crisis Years: Kennedy and Khrushchev, 1960–1963* (New York: Harper Collins, 1991, chapters 15–19). U Thant's point of view came from his memoirs, *View from the U.N.* (New York: Doubleday, 1978, chapter 8). The Harlan Cleveland quotes come from his interview (22 April 1990) in the Yale University–U.N. Oral History Project.

Other sources consulted included Theodore C. Sorensen, *Kennedy* (New York: Harper & Row, 1965); Seymour Maxwell Finger, *American Ambassadors at the U.N.* (New York: U.N. Institute for Training and Research, n.d.); Rudy Abramson, *Spanning the Century: The Life of W. Averell Harriman, 1891–1986* (New York: William Morrow, 1992); Edward Crankshaw and Strobe Talbott, eds., *Khrushchev Remembers* (Boston: Little, Brown, 1970); Michael P. Riccards, "The Dangerous Legacy: John F. Kennedy and the Cuban Missile Crisis," in Paul Harper and Joann P. Krieg, *John F. Kennedy: The Promise Revisited* (New York: Greenwood, 1988); Jeff Broadwater, *Adlai Stevenson and American Politics* (New York: Twayne Publishers, 1994); Walter LaFeber, *America, Russia, and the Cold War, 1945–1990* (New York: McGraw-Hill, 1991); Mary S. McAuliffe, *Cuban Missile Crisis 1962* (Washington: Central Intelligence Agency, 1992); Joseph J. Sisco, interview (18 October 1990) in the Yale University–U.N. Oral History Project; Stewart Alsop and Charles Bartlett, "In Time of Crisis," *Saturday Evening Post* (December 1962); and the files of Louis B. Fleming, the *Los Angeles Times* correspondent who covered the U.N. during this period, which include notes, his unedited dispatches, press releases, and clippings.

9 ✍ U Thant and the Quest for Peace in Vietnam

The views and recollections of U Thant are set down in his memoirs, *View from the U.N.* (New York: Doubleday, 1978). There is a good deal of useful material about U Thant, Cyprus, the Indo-Pakistan War, and the Vietnam Initiative in Brian Urquhart, *Ralph Bunche: An American Life* (New York: W. W. Norton, 1993, chapters 26 and 27), and in Brian Urquhart, *A Life in Peace and War* (New York: W. W. Norton, 1991, chapters 15 and 20). Dean Rusk's vituperative attacks on U Thant come from his memoirs, *As I Saw It* (New York: W. W. Norton, 1990, pp. 462–64). Stevenson's view of the Vietnam controversy is covered in John Bartlow Martin, *Adlai Stevenson and the World* (New York: Doubleday, 1977, pp. 793–863).

Other sources consulted included Rudy Abramson, *Spanning the Century: The Life of W. Averell Harriman, 1891–1986* (New York: William Morrow, 1992); United Nations, *The Blue Helmets* (New York: Dept. of Public Information, 1990); Linda M. Fasulo, *Representing America* (New York: Facts on File, 1985); Walter LaFeber, *America, Russia, and the Cold War, 1945–1990* (New York: McGraw-Hill, 1991); Marcus G. Raskin and Bernard B. Fall, eds., *The Viet-Nam Reader* (New York: Vintage, 1965); William J. Durch, ed., *The Evolution of U.N. Peacekeeping* (New York: St. Martin's Press, 1993); Seymour Maxwell Finger, *American Ambassadors at the U.N.* (New York: U.N. Institute for Training and Research n.d.); Joseph J. Sisco, interview (18 October 1990) in the Yale University–U.N. Oral History Project; and Harlan Cleveland, interview (22 April 1990) in the Yale University–U.N. Oral History Project.

10 ✍ The Six-Day War

To sort out the controversy over U Thant's decision to withdraw UNEF from the Sinai, I have depended mainly on U Thant, *View from the U.N.* (New York: Doubleday, 1978, chapters 12 and 13, and the documents in the appendix, part 4); Meg Greenfield, "A Story of Forty-eight Hours," *Reporter Magazine* (15 June 1967); Brian Urquhart, *Ralph Bunche: An American Life* (New York: W. W. Norton, 1993, chapter 29); Brian Urquhart, *A Life in Peace and War* (New York: W. W. Norton, 1991, chapter 16); Andrew W. Cordier and Wilder Foote, eds., *Public Papers of the Secretaries-General of the United Nations*, vol. 3, *Dag Hammarskjöld*, 1956–1957 (New York: Columbia University Press, 1973); and the files of Louis B. Fleming, the *Los Angeles Times* correspondent who covered the U.N. during this period, which include notes, his unedited dispatches, press releases, and clippings. The U.N. role in the Six-Day War is explored in the U Thant and Urquhart books, the Fleming files, and Seymour Maxwell Finger, *American Ambassadors at the U.N.* (New York: U.N. Institute for Training and Research, n.d.). I depended on The Associated Press, *Lightning out of Israel* (New York, 1967), for both an account of the war and the flavor of the times.

Other sources consulted included Chaim Herzog, *The Arab-Israeli Wars* (New York: Random House, 1982); Ian J. Bickerton and Carla L. Klausner, *A Concise History of the Arab-Israeli Conflict* (Englewood Cliffs, N.J.: Prentice Hall, 1991, chapters 6 and 7); Dean Rusk, *As I Saw It* (New York: W. W. Norton, 1990); Kati Marton, *A Death in Jerusalem* (New York, Pantheon, 1994); Linda M. Fasulo, *Representing America* (New York: Facts on File, 1985); United Nations, *The Blue Helmets* (New York: Dept. of Public Information, 1990); Nathan A. Pelcovits, *The Long Armistice: UN Peacekeeping and the Arab-Israeli Conflict, 1948–1960* (Boulder, Colo.: Westview Press, 1993); Joseph J. Sisco, interview (18 October 1990) in the Yale University–U.N. Oral History Project; and Ralph H. Magnus, ed., *Documents on the Middle East* (Washington, D.C.: American Enterprise Institute, 1969).

11 ✽ Kurt Waldheim: The Big Lie

For the war record of Waldheim, I have depended heavily on Robert Edwin Herzstein, *Waldheim: The Missing Years* (New York: Paragon House, 1989). For the Waldheim years at the U.N., I have depended heavily on Brian Urquhart, *A Life in Peace and War* (New

York: W. W. Norton, 1991, chapters 17–24), and Don Shannon, *Los Angeles Times*, interview by author (Washington, DC, 31 January 1995). Shirley Hazzard, *Countenance of Truth* (New York: Viking, 1990), also was very useful. Kurt Waldheim's memoirs, *In the Eye of the Storm* (Bethesda, Md.: Adler & Adler, 1986), hide the significant details of his World War II years but do cover some of the issues of his ten-year administration as secretary-general. Two Henry Kissinger books helped my understanding of détente and China policy: *Diplomacy* (New York: Simon & Schuster, 1994, chapters 28 and 29), and *White House Years* (Boston: Little, Brown, 1979, chapters 18 and 19).

Other sources consulted included Joseph J. Sisco, interview (18 October 1990) in the Yale University–U.N. Oral History Project; dispatches of the *Los Angeles Times* covering the vote on Communist China and the controversy over Waldheim's past; Jeane Kirkpatrick, interview (13 November 1990) in the Yale University–U.N. Oral History Project; United Nations, *The Blue Helmets* (New York: Dept. of Public Information, 1990), Linda M. Fasulo, *Representing America* (New York: Facts on File, 1985); Benjamin Rivlin and Leon Gordenker, eds., *The Challenging Role of the U.N. Secretary-General* (Westport, Conn.: Praeger, 1993); Bernard Cohen and Luc Rosenzweig, *Waldheim* (New York: Adama Books, 1987); Daniel Patrick Moynihan, *A Dangerous Place* (Boston: Little, Brown, 1978); Seymour Maxwell Finger, *American Ambassadors at the U.N.* (New York: U.N. Institute for Training and Research, n.d.); William J. Durch, ed., *The Evolution of U.N. Peacekeeping* (New York: St. Martin's Press, 1993); Ian J. Bickerton and Carla L. Klausner, *A Concise History of the Arab-Israeli Conflict* (Englewood Cliffs, N.J.: Prentice Hall, 1991); and Richard Bassett, *Waldheim and Austria* (New York: Viking, 1989).

12 ❧ Zionism Is Racism

For details of the General Assembly fight over the "Zionism Is Racism" resolution, I have depended mainly on Daniel Patrick Moynihan, *A Dangerous Place* (Boston: Little, Brown, 1978). The chapters on the Nixon-Ford years and the Carter years in Linda M. Fasulo, *Representing America* (New York: Facts on File, 1985), and the chapters on the Nixon-Kissinger years and the turnaround in American policy in Seymour Maxwell Finger, *American Ambassadors at the U.N.* (New York: U.N. Institute for Training and Research, n.d.), were very useful. I covered the First International Women's Conference in Mexico City, the reign of Idi Amin in Uganda, the genocide of the Hutus in Burundi, and the General Assembly vote revoking the Zionism resolution for the *Los Angeles Times.*

Other sources consulted included Daniel P. Moynihan, "The United States in Opposition," *Commentary* (March 1975); Walter Isaacson, *Kissinger* (New York: Simon & Schuster, 1992); Burton Yale Pines, ed., *A World without a U.N.* (Washington: The Heritage Foundation, 1992); Brian Urquhart, *A Life in Peace and War* (New York: W. W.Norton, 1991); Rosemary Righter, *Utopia Lost: The United Nations and World Order* (New York: The Twentieth Century Fund Press, 1995); Kurt Waldheim, *In the Eye of the Storm* (Bethesda: Adler & Adler, 1986); and the record of the General Assembly proceedings (10 November 1975), A/PV.2400.

13 ⊮ UNESCO: Defenses of Peace in the Minds of Men

For my analysis of the U.N. family of specialized agencies and the Third World influence on them, I found two sources useful: Douglas Williams, *The Specialized Agencies and the United Nations* (London: Hurst & Co., 1990), and Rosemary Righter, *Utopia Lost: The United Nations and World Order* (New York: The Twentieth Century Fund Press, 1995). I have relied a good deal on Howard H. Frederick, *Global Communication & International Relations* (Belmont, Calif.: Wadsworth, 1993, chapter 6), for the background of the debate over the New World Information and Communication Order.

I covered the American withdrawal from UNESCO and its aftermath as Paris correspondent for the *Los Angeles Times.* I discussed the problems of reporting in the developing world in my article "Covering the Third World (or Trying To)," *Columbia Journalism Review* (November–December 1978).

Other sources consulted included Scott Donaldson, *Archibald MacLeish: An American Life* (Boston: Houghton Mifflin, 1992); *Current Biography Yearbook, 1987,* "M'Bow, Amadou-Mahtar"; United Nations Association of the USA, *Schooling for Democracy* (New York, 1993); Don Cook, "UNESCO Board Names New Chief; Spaniard Wins After M'Bow Withdraws," *Los Angeles Times* (18 October 1987); Donald R. Shea and William L. Jarrett, eds., *Mass Communications in the Americas: Focus on the New World Information and Communication Order* (Milwaukee: University of Wisconsin, 1984); Linda M. Fasulo, *Representing America* (New York: Facts on File, 1985); Allan Gerson, *The Kirkpatrick Mission* (New York: The Free Press, 1991); Sean McBride et al., *Many Voices, One World* (Paris: UNESCO, 1990); New Zealand Ministry of Foreign Affairs and Trade, *United Nations Handbook 1994* (Wellington, N.Z.); Michael Traber and Kaarle Nordensteng, *Few Voices, Many Worlds* (London: World Association for Christian Communication, 1992); Kenneth Dadzie, "The U.N. and the Problem of Economic Development," in Adam Roberts and Benedict Kingsbury, eds., *United Nations, Divided World* (Oxford: Clarendon Press, 1993); William Branigin and Keith B. Richburg, "The U.N. Empire," *The Washington Post,* a four-part series (20 September 1992–23 September 1992); Julia Preston, "Massive World Body Resists Shaping Up," *The Washington Post* (3 January 1995); and the Insight Team (Nick Rufford, Ian Burrell, David Leppard), "The Corrupt Heart of the U.N. Bureaucracy," *The Sunday Times* (15 August 1933).

14 ⬥ Javier Pérez de Cuéllar and the End of the Cold War

Cameron R. Hume has presented the most exhaustive case for the accomplishments of Pérez de Cuéllar in *The United Nations, Iran, and Iraq* (Bloomington: Indiana University Press, 1994). Hume sets down in unusual detail the closed-door diplomacy of the Big Five during the Iran-Iraq war and assesses its significance. As usual, Brian Urquhart offers many insights into the Falklands crisis and Pérez de Cuéllar in *A Life in Peace and War* (New York: W. W. Norton, 1991). The chapter on the Falklands in Allan Gerson, *The Kirk-*

patrick Mission (New York: The Free Press, 1991), was very useful. The annual reports of Pérez de Cuéllar are collected in United Nations *Anarchy or Order* (New York, 1991).

I covered Pérez de Cuéllar's last year in office and toured the U.N. peacekeeping mission in El Salvador in September 1992 for the *Los Angeles Times*. I also covered the 1988 Reagan-Gorbachev summit in Moscow.

Other sources consulted included Linda M. Fasulo, *Representing America* (New York: Facts on File, 1985); Don Shannon, interview by author (Washington, DC, February 24, 1995); *Current Biography Yearbook, 1982* s.v. "Pérez de Cuéllar, Javier"; William J. Durch, ed., *The Evolution of U.N. Peacekeeping* (New York: St. Martin's Press, 1993); United Nations, *The Blue Helmets* (New York: Dept. of Public Information, 1990); Henry Kissinger, *Diplomacy* (New York: Simon & Schuster, 1994); United Nations, *El Salvador Agreements: The Path to Peace* (1992); Walter LaFeber, *America, Russia, and the Cold War, 1945–1990* (New York: McGraw-Hill, 1991); Seymour Maxwell Finger, *American Ambassadors at the U.N.* (New York: U.N. Institute for Training and Research, n.d.); Javier Pérez de Cuéllar, "The Role of the U.N. Secretary-General," in Adam Roberts and Benedict Kingsbury, eds., *United Nations, Divided World* (Oxford: Clarendon Press, 1993); Olga Pellicer, "The United Nations in Central America: The Role of the Secretary-General," in Benjamin Rivlin and Leon Gordenker, eds., *The Challenging Role of the U.N. Secretary-General* (Westport, Conn.: Praeger, 1993); and Rosemary Righter, *Utopia Lost: The United Nations and World Order* (New York: The Twentieth Century Fund Press, 1995).

15 ❧ The Persian Gulf War

Micah L. Sifry and Christopher Cerf, *The Gulf War Reader* (New York: Times Books, 1991), proved a very valuable source of documents and viewpoints about the diplomacy of the war. Cameron Hume includes important chapters on the U.N. diplomacy before the Persian Gulf War in his *The United Nations, Iran, and Iraq* (Bloomington: Indiana University Press, 1994). The U.N. Department of Public Information set down all the key U.N. documents in

Resolutions of the United Nations Security Council and Statements by Its President Concerning the Situation between Iraq and Kuwait (revised April 1994). For the conduct of the war itself, I depended on U.S. News & World Report, *Triumph Without Victory* (New York: Times Books, 1993), and Michael R. Gordon and Gen. Bernard E. Trainor, *The Generals' War* (Boston: Little, Brown, 1995).

I began covering the U.N. for the *Los Angeles Times* during the Persian Gulf War and have written extensively for the *Times* about the diplomacy of the war's end and aftermath.

Other sources consulted included "Excerpts from an Interview with Clinton After the Air Strikes," *New York Times* (14 January 1993); Rosemary Righter, *Utopia Lost: The United Nations and World Order* (New York: The Twentieth Century Fund Press, 1995); Benjamin Rivlin and Leon Gordenker, eds., *The Challenging Role of the U.N. Secretary-General* (Westport, Conn.: Praeger, 1993); Richard A. Falk, "Twisting the U.N. Charter to U.S. Ends," in Hamid Mowlana et al., eds., *Triumph of the Image* (Boulder, Colo.: Westview Press, 1992); Javier Pérez de Cuéllar, *Anarchy or Order* (New York: United Nations, 1991); Brian Urquhart, "The U.N. and International Security after the Cold War," and Anthony Parsons, "The U.N. and the National Interests of States," in Adam Roberts and Benedict Kingsbury, eds., *United Nations, Divided World* (Oxford: Clarendon Press, 1993).

16 ⚛ Boutros Boutros-Ghali

This chapter appeared in somewhat different form as "Dateline U.N.: A New Hammarskjöld?" in *Foreign Policy* (spring 1995).

I have covered Boutros-Ghali for the *Los Angeles Times* since his election as secretary-general, traveling with him on trips to Dakar, London, Sarajevo, Mogadishu, and Addis Ababa. Much of the material is based on a series of interviews with him from 1992 onward.

Other sources consulted included Richard Armitage, "Bend the U.N. to Our Will," *New York Times* (24 February 1994); Jeane Kirkpatrick, "Boutros Ghali, Gunslinger of the World, *Los Angeles Times* (11 March 1993); Patrick J. Sloyan, "How the Warlord Outwitted Clinton's Spooks," *The Washington Post* (3 April 1994); George F.

Will, "Wreckage of Feeble Intentions," *The Washington Post* (29 April 1994); and Boutros Boutros-Ghali, interview by David Frost for the David Frost show, WETA, taped in New York (28 April 1993).

17 ✍ The Somalia Debacle

Although Robert B. Oakley was a major player in the Somalian venture, the book he wrote with his aide, John L. Hirsch, *Somalia and Operation Restore Hope* (Washington, D.C.: U.S. Institute of Peace, 1995), attempts a dispassionate narrative of the events from 1992 onward. Balanced with the views of Admiral Jonathan T. Howe and other U.N. officials, it proved very useful for this chapter. I have followed Rick Atkinson's account of the disastrous Ranger raid in Mogadishu, "Firefight in Mogadishu: The Last Mission of Task Force Ranger," *Washington Post* (30 and 31 January 1994). Keith B. Richburg, the foreign correspondent who supplied the best reporting from the scene for more than a year, provided an excellent summary of the problems of the mission in a two-part series, "Peace Under Fire: The United Nations in Somalia," *Washington Post* (5 and 6 December 1993).

I covered Somalia in the late 1960s and early 1970s, traveled with Boutros-Ghali to Mogadishu in 1993, and followed peacekeeping policies and debates closely at the U.N. throughout the duration of the mission to Somalia. I have reviewed all the public documents of the secretary-general and the Security Council relating to Somalia during this period and have had access to some of the confidential correspondence between the secretary-general and American officials, including Secretary of State Warren Christopher. On various occasions, I have talked with Boutros Boutros-Ghali, Robert Oakley, Admiral Jonathan Howe, and Mohamed Sahnoun—either in person or by telephone—about aspects of the Somali mission.

Other sources consulted included Mohamed Sahnoun, *Somalia: The Missed Opportunities* (Washington, D.C.: U.S. Institute of Peace, 1994); Keith B. Richburg, "The US and Somalia: Passing the Torch," *The Humanitarian Monitor* (June 1993); Thomas W. Lippman and Barton Gellman, "A Humanitarian Gesture Turns Deadly," *Washington Post* (10 October 1993); Tom Farer, "From

Warlord to Peacelord?" *Washington Post* (12 September 1993); Matthew M. S. W. Ngulube et al., *Report of the Commission of Inquiry . . . to Investigate Armed Attacks on UNOSOMII Personnel Which Led to Casualties among Them* (United Nations, S/1994/653, 1 June 1994); Sidney Blumenthal, "Why Are We in Somalia?" *The New Yorker* (25 October 1993); Rick Atkinson, "Marines Close Curtain on U.N. in Somalia," *Washington Post* (3 March 1995); William Finnegan, "Letter from Mogadishu: A World of Dust," *The New Yorker* (20 March 1995); *Report to the Congress on U.S. Policy in Somalia* (the White House, 13 October 1993); and United Nations Department of Public Information, *The United Nations and the Situation in Somalia* (New York, 1 May 1994).

18   Alibi: The U.N. in Bosnia

The horrible details of ethnic cleansing are laid out in the final report of the U.N. Commission of Experts, a Security Council document, S/1994/674, including annexes I–V. The commission was headed by Prof. Cherif Bassiouni of De Paul University. For historical background, I depended on two books by Misha Glenny: *The Rebirth of History* (London: Penguin, 1990, chapter 5) and *The Fall of Yugoslavia* (London: Penguin, 1992). Warren Zimmermann's memoir "The Last Ambassador," *Foreign Affairs* (March/April 1995), offers many insights into the beginning of the crisis.

I covered U.N. policy in Bosnia since the war's inception and reviewed all the public documents of the secretary-general and the Security Council relating to Bosnia during this period. I benefited as well from lengthy conversations—most not for attribution—with many of the Security Council ambassadors and the U.N. principals and their advisers. For background about the progress of the war itself, I depended heavily on the dispatches in the *Los Angeles Times*, especially those of Carol J. Williams, who covered the first three years of the war. I also traveled with Boutros Boutros-Ghali to Sarajevo in 1992.

Other sources consulted included Roger Cohen, "Man in the Middle Calls on Confucius," *New York Times* (26 April 1994); U.N. Department of Public Information, *The United Nations and the Situ-*

ation in the Former Yugoslavia (New York, 23 January 1995); U.N., *United Nations Peacekeeping Information Notes* (New York, December 1944); Julia Preston, "Diplomat Holds Key to Bombing," *Washington Post* (26 April 1994); Tyler Marshall et al., "Just What Went Wrong in Bosnia? Almost Everything," *Los Angeles Times* (11 December 1994); and Carol J. Williams, "The Shadow of a Shield," *Los Angeles Times Magazine* (25 July 1993).

Epilogue & The Fiftieth Anniversary

This chapter is based largely on my coverage of the United Nations for the *Los Angeles Times*. I have also depended heavily on certain sections of Boutros Boutros-Ghali's "Supplement to an Agenda for Peace: Position Paper of the Secretary-General on the Occasion of the Fiftieth Anniversary of the United Nations," A/50/60.

Other sources consulted included Brian Urquhart, "Selecting the World's CEO," *Foreign Affairs* (May/June 1995), and Bob Dole, "Shaping America's Global Future," *Foreign Policy* (Spring 1995).

Appendix I
A U.N. *Chronology*

1944

SEPTEMBER 21–OCTOBER 7 Representatives of the United States, the Soviet Union, Britain, and China meet in two phases at Dumbarton Oaks in Washington, setting down the blueprint for the United Nations Organization.

1945

FEBRUARY 11 At Yalta in the Soviet Crimea, American President Franklin D. Roosevelt, British Prime Minister Winston Churchill, and Soviet leader Joseph Stalin iron out differences and reach agreement on procedures in the proposed U.N.

APRIL 25–JUNE 25 Delegates from fifty nations meet in San Francisco to draw up the Charter of the U.N. The charter is signed amid great ceremony in the auditorium of the Veterans Memorial Hall on June 26.

OCTOBER 24 The U.N. is created when the charter is ratified by all five permanent members of the Security Council and a majority of those that signed the charter.

NOVEMBER An organizing conference in London creates UNESCO.

1946

JANUARY 10 The first General Assembly opens in Central Hall, Westminster, London. It has fifty-one members (Poland has been added to the original fifty).

JANUARY 17 The Security Council meets for the first time in Westminster, London.

JANUARY 29 The Security Council selects Trygve Lie of Norway as the first secretary-general.

FEBRUARY 9 Stalin proclaims that "no peaceful international order is possible" between Communists and the capitalist world.

FEBRUARY 22 American diplomat George F. Kennan sends a "long telegram" from Moscow that warns of Soviet ambitions to expand Communism and the need to contain it.

MARCH 5 In a speech at Fulton, Missouri, Winston Churchill says that "an iron curtain has descended" across Europe. This signals the beginning of the Cold War.

MARCH 21 The U.N. moves to New York. The Security Council occupies its first temporary quarters in the United States, the gymnasium on the Bronx campus of Hunter College.

1948

MAY 14 Israel declares itself independent. Arab armies attack in the first Arab-Israeli war.

SEPTEMBER 16 The Stern Gang murders Count Folke Bernadotte of Sweden, the U.N. mediator for Palestine. Ralph Bunche of the United States succeeds him and secures an armistice after negotiations between Israelis and Egyptians on the island of Rhodes in early 1949. He is awarded the Nobel peace prize for this in 1950.

1949

OCTOBER 24 The cornerstone is laid for a permanent U.N. headquarters in New York City on Manhattan alongside the East River.

1950

JUNE 24 North Korea invades South Korea. The Security Council, in the absence of the Soviet Union, authorizes U.N. member states to defend South Korea. American President Harry S Truman orders American troops to South Korea. American Commander Douglas MacArthur is named head of the U.N. command.

1953

JULY 27 The U.N. Command and the Chinese–North Korean Command sign the Korean armistice agreement.

NOVEMBER 10 Lie resigns as secretary-general.

1954

MARCH 31 The Security Council selects Dag Hammarskjöld of Sweden as the second U.N. secretary-general.

1956

NOVEMBER 6 After vetoes by Britain and France prevent action by the Security Council, the General Assembly meets in an emergency session on the Suez Canal crisis. The General Assembly votes to establish the first peacekeeping force, the U.N. Emergency Force (UNEF), to replace British, French, and Israeli troops that have invaded Egypt. The failure of Britain and France to put down President Gamal Abdel Nasser of Egypt after his seizure of the Suez Canal signals the impending end of the colonial empires in Africa.

1960

JUNE 30 The Belgian Congo becomes independent and then erupts into chaos and bloodshed when the army mutinies against its Belgian officers. Belgian troops seize key points, but the Security Council dispatches Blue Helmets to replace Belgian troops, restore law and order, and end the secession of Katanga province. Peacekeepers put down the secession and remain in the Congo for four years.

SEPTEMBER 1960 Seventeen newly independent states, almost all from Africa, become members of the United Nations and attend the opening session of the 1960 General Assembly. This is the session that features Soviet leader Nikita Khrushchev pounding his shoe on a delegate's desk to protest what he regards as the anti-Soviet policies of Hammarskjöld.

1961

SEPTEMBER 18 Dag Hammarskjöld dies in an air crash in Ndola, Northern Rhodesia, while on a mission in the Congo.

NOVEMBER 3 The Security Council selects U Thant of Burma as acting secretary-general in a compromise over Soviet demands that a troika of three secretaries-general be named. U Thant is elected as the third secretary-general of the U.N. a year later.

1963

AUGUST 7 The Security Council votes a voluntary arms embargo against South Africa.

OCTOBER 22 In a national television address, President John F. Kennedy informs Americans that the Soviet Union is preparing offensive missile sites in Cuba. The Cuban missile crisis begins. Three days later, during public debate in the Security Council, American Ambassador Adlai Stevenson tells Soviet Ambassador Valerian Zorin that he is willing to wait "until hell freezes over" for a Soviet admission that missiles are in Cuba.

1964

MARCH 4 The Security Council dispatches peacekeepers to Cyprus.

AUGUST 6 U Thant believes he has the go-ahead from President Johnson and Secretary of State Dean Rusk to approach Ho Chi Minh and attempt to negotiate a peaceful settlement of the Vietnam War. But Washington backs out of any meeting with the North Vietnamese. U Thant feels betrayed, but Rusk later describes U Thant as a liar.

1966

OCTOBER 27 The General Assembly nullifies the South African mandate over South-West Africa.

DECEMBER 16 The Security Council imposes mandatory sanctions on the breakaway British colony of Rhodesia.

1967

MAY 16 Egypt demands the withdrawal of U.N. peacekeepers from Sinai. Despite loud protests from many diplomats and statesmen, U Thant withdraws the peacekeepers, precipitating the Six-Day War between Israel and its Arab neighbors.

NOVEMBER 23 The Security Council adopts Resolution 242, which sets down the general principle that Israel should return occupied territories and receive guarantees of recognition and peace from the Arabs.

1968

JUNE 12 The General Assembly approves the Treaty on Nonproliferation of Nuclear Weapons.

1971

OCTOBER 25 The General Assembly votes to seat Communist China as a member state in place of Taiwan. The Chinese Communists also replace Taiwan as a member of the Big Five on the Security Council.

DECEMBER 22 Kurt Waldheim of Austria is installed as the fourth secretary-general.

1972

JUNE The first U.N. Environmental Conference takes place in Stockholm.

1975

JUNE The first U.N. Women's Conference takes place in Mexico City. The conference ends in controversy as Third World delegates push through a resolution denouncing Zionism.

NOVEMBER 10 The General Assembly passes a resolution declaring that "Zionism is a form of racism and racial discrimination." The vote is seventy-two to thirty-five with thirty-two abstentions.

1977

NOVEMBER 4 The Security Council adopts a mandatory arms embargo against South Africa.

1979

DECEMBER 18 The General Assembly adopts the Convention on the Elimination of Discriminations against Women.

1980

MAY 8 The World Health Organization announces that smallpox has been eradicated.

SEPTEMBER The Iran-Iraq war erupts. The Security Council reaches an agreement on a cease-fire resolution in 1987 as the Cold War recedes and American and Soviet ambassadors iron out differences in closed-door sessions of the council.

1981

DECEMBER 15 Javier Pérez de Cuéllar of Peru takes over as the fifth secretary-general.

1982

APRIL 3 Argentina invades the British Falkland Islands. The U.N. is unable to prevent war.

DECEMBER 10 One hundred seventeen states sign the U.N. Convention on the Law of the Sea.

1984

DECEMBER Pérez de Cuéllar creates the Office for Emergency Operations in Africa to deal with widespread famine.

DECEMBER 31 The United States withdraws from UNESCO, accusing the agency of politicizing its cultural activities.

1986

MARCH 3 The World Jewish Congress releases information that former Secretary-General Waldheim had Nazi ties during World War II.

1987

SEPTEMBER The Treaty on Protection of the Ozone Layer is signed, the first global environment agreement.

1989

APRIL The U.N. sends peacekeepers to Namibia (the former South-West Africa) to monitor elections and the withdrawal of South African troops. Namibia becomes independent four months later.

NOVEMBER 9 The Berlin Wall is broken down, the symbolic end of the Cold War.

1990

AUGUST 2 Troops from Saddam Hussein's Iraq cross the border and seize the emirate of Kuwait. American President George Bush and American Ambassador Thomas R. Pickering galvanize the Security Council into near-unanimous agreement to condemn the invasion and impose sanctions.

SEPTEMBER 30 UNICEF convenes the World Summit for Children.

1991

JANUARY 17 The Bombing of Baghdad begins as the United States leads a coalition in a successful war to oust Iraqi troops from Kuwait.

FEBRUARY 27 The Persian Gulf War ends. The Security Council imposes a harsh peace on Iraq: Iraq must destroy all its programs of building weapons of mass destruction, ending its nuclear, chemical, and biological warfare programs. Sanctions will remain in place until the Security Council is satisfied that Iraq is a peaceful country that no longer harbors aggressive intent against its neighbors.

NOVEMBER 21 The Security Council selects Boutros Boutros-Ghali of Egypt as the sixth secretary-general.

DECEMBER 16 The General Assembly revokes the "Zionism Is Racism" resolution by a vote of 111 to 25, with 13 abstentions.

DECEMBER 31 El Salvador and the rebel FMLN sign peace accords at U.N. headquarters after a ten-year war.

1992

JANUARY 31 The Security Council holds a meeting of heads of state and government for the first time.

FEBRUARY After a cease-fire quiets the war in Croatia, war breaks out in Bosnia-Herzegovina. With the Serbs boycotting the referendum, a majority of Bosnia votes to secede from Yugoslavia. The Yugoslav army comes to the aid of Bosnian Serbs who secede from Bosnia. The Security Council orders U.N. peacekeepers, who already patrol cease-fire lines in Croatia, to protect relief convoys in Bosnia.

JUNE The Earth Summit—the U.N. Conference on Environment and Development—is held in Rio de Janeiro and attended by 104 heads of state and government.

JUNE 17 Boutros-Ghali issues his "Agenda for Peace"—a blueprint for peacekeeping operations.

DECEMBER 3 The Security Council passes a resolution authorizing the United States to lead a coalition of forces to intervene in Somalia and ensure that humanitarian assistance is delivered to the sick and starving.

1993

MAY The U.N. supervises elections in Cambodia, leading to the establishment of a new government after fifteen years of war.

JUNE The World Conference on Human Rights meets in Vienna and passes resolutions that lead to the appointment of a new U.N. High Commissioner for Human Rights.

OCTOBER 3 Eighteen American Rangers die in Somalia in a clash with followers of the warlord Mohamed Farah Aideed. Public outcry leads President Bill Clinton to announce the eventual withdrawal from the U.N. mission in Somalia (which took over from the American troops that invaded Somalia in December). Other countries are reluctant to stay, and the U.N. mission ends in March 1995.

1994

APRIL The U.N. approves the first NATO air strikes in Bosnia. The attacks on Serb positions in Gorazde prove ineffective.

APRIL After the Rwandese president is killed in a mysterious plane crash, majority Hutu tribes kill tens of thousands of Tutsis. With the United States hesitant, the Security Council fails to intervene with any force. French troops finally enter but are too late to prevent the genocide. Rebel Tutsi troops take over the government, and the Security Council authorizes a peacekeeping force of fifty-five hundred.

SEPTEMBER 19 American troops land in Haiti to restore ousted President Jean-Bertrand Aristide. U.N. peacekeepers take over from the Americans early in 1995.

1995

JANUARY Boutros-Ghali issues a supplement to his "Agenda for Peace" that retreats somewhat from some of his original ideas on peacekeeping. He proposes that future missions be much more limited than the intervention in Somalia.

Appendix II
U.N. *Peacekeeping Missions*
(as of April 1995)

1. UNTSO U.N. Truce Supervision Organization (Middle East), June 1948–.

2. UNMOGIP U.N. Military Observer Group in India and Pakistan, January 1949–.

3. UNEF I First U.N. Emergency Force (buffer between Egyptian and Israeli troops), November 1956–June 1967.

4. UNOGIL U.N. Observation Group in Lebanon, June 1958–December 1958.

5. ONUC U.N. Operation in the Congo, July 1960–June 1964.

6. UNSF U.N. Security Force in West New Guinea (West Irian), October 1962–April 1963.

7. UNYOM U.N. Yemen Observation Mission, July 1963–September 1964.

8. UNFICYP U.N. Peacekeeping Force in Cyprus, March 1964–.

9. DOMREP Mission of the Representative of the Secretary-General in the Dominican Republic, May 1965–October 1966.

10. UNIPOM U.N. India-Pakistan Observation Mission, September 1965–March 1966.

11. UNEF II Second U.N. Emergency Force (buffer between Egyptians and Israelis in the Sinai), October 1973–July 1979.

12. UNDOF U.N. Disengagement Observer Force (Golan Heights between Israeli and Syrian troops), June 1974–.

13. UNIFIL U.N. Interim Force in Lebanon, March 1978–.

14. UNGOMAP U.N. Good Offices Mission in Afghanistan and Pakistan, April 1988–March 1990.

15. UNIIMOG U.N. Iran-Iraq Military Observer Group, August 1988–February 1991.

16. UNAVEM I U.N. Angola Verification Mission I, January 1989–June 1991.

17. UNTAG U.N. Transition Assistance Group (Namibia), April 1989–March 1990.

18. ONUCA U.N. Observer Group in Central America, November 1989–January 1992.

19. UNIKOM U.N. Iraq-Kuwait Observation Mission, April 1991–.

20. UNAVEM II U.N. Angola Verification Mission II, June 1991–March 1995.

21. ONUSAL U.N. Observer Mission in El Salvador, July 1991–.

22. MINURSO U.N. Mission for the Referendum in Western Sahara, September 1991–.

23. UNAMIC U.N. Advance Mission in Cambodia, October 1991–March 1992.

24. UNPROFOR U.N. Protection Force (covering Bosnia-Herzegovina, Croatia, and Macedonia; after April 1, 1995, only Bosnia-Herzegovina), March 1992–.

25. UNTAC U.N. Transitional Authority in Cambodia, March 1992–September 1993.

26. UNOSOM I U.N. Operation in Somalia I, April 1992–April 1993.

27. ONUMOZ U.N. Operation in Mozambique, December 1992–December 1994.

28. UNOSOM II U.N. Operation in Somalia II, May 1993–March 1995.

29. UNOMUR U.N. Observer Mission Uganda-Rwanda, June 1993–September 1994.

30. UNOMIG U.N. Observer Mission in Georgia, August 1993–.

31. UNOMIL U.N. Observer Mission in Liberia, September 1993–.

32. UNMIH U.N. Mission in Haiti, September 1993–.

33. UNAMIR U.N. Assistance Mission for Rwanda, October 1993–.

34. UNASOG U.N. Aouzou Strip Observer Group (Chad-Libyan border), May 1994–June 1994.

35. UNMOT United Nations Mission of Observers in Tajikistan, December 1994–.

36. UNAVEM III U.N. Angola Verification Mission III, April 1995–.

37. UNCRO U.N. Confidence Restoration Operation in Croatia, April 1995–.

38. UNPREDEP U.N. Preventive Deployment Force (Macedonia), April 1995–.

United Nations Peacekeeping Operations as of April 1995

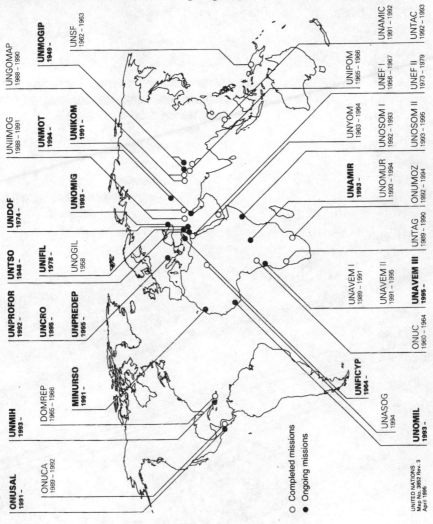

UNITED NATIONS
Map No. 3852 Rev. 3
April 1995

○ Completed missions
● Ongoing missions

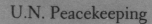

U.N. Peacekeeping

1945   1950   1955   1960   1965   1970

UNTSO
UNMOGIP
UNEF 1
UNOGIL
ONUC
UNSF
UNYOM
UNFICYP
DOMREP
UNIPOM

timeline

The bar chart above shows United Nations peace-keeping operations as of 30 September 1994, in chronological order of deployment.

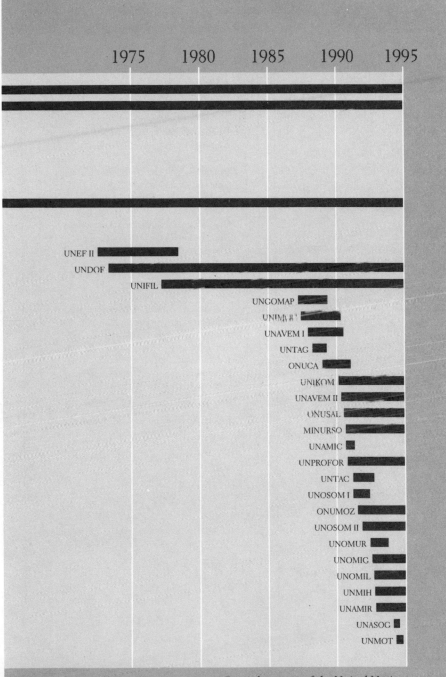

1975 1980 1985 1990 1995

UNEF II
UNDOF
UNIFIL
UNGOMAP
UNIMOG
UNAVEM I
UNTAG
ONUCA
UNIKOM
UNAVEM II
ONUSAL
MINURSO
UNAMIC
UNPROFOR
UNTAC
UNOSOM I
ONUMOZ
UNOSOM II
UNOMUR
UNOMIG
UNOMIL
UNMIH
UNAMIR
UNASOG
UNMOT

Printed courtesy of the United Nations

Appendix III:

| INTERNATIONAL COURT OF JUSTICE | GENERAL ASSEMBLY | ECONOMIC AND SOCIAL COUNCIL |

Main and other sessional committees ~
Standing committees and ad hoc bodies ~
Other subsidiary organs and related bodies ~

UNRWA >
United Nations Relief and Works Agency for Palestine Refugees in the Near East

IAEA >
International Atomic Energy Agency

INSTRAW >
International Research and Training Institute for the Advancement of Women

UNCHS >
United Nations Centre for Human Settlements (HABITAT)

UNCTAD >
United Nations Conference on Trade and Development

UNDCP >
United Nations International Drug Control Programme

UNDP >
United Nations Development Programme

UNEP >
United Nations Environment Programme

UNFPA >
United Nations Population Fund

UNHCR >
Office of the United Nations High Commissioner for Refugees

UNICEF >
United Nations Children's Fund

UNIFEM >
United Nations Development Fund for Women

UNITAR >
United Nations Institute for Training and Research

UNU >
United Nations University

WFC >
World Food Council

WFP >
World Food Programme
ITC >
International Trade Centre UNCTAD/GATT

Functional Commisions ~
Commission for Social Development
Commission on Crime Prevention and Criminal Justice
Commission on Human Rights
Commission on Narcotic Drugs
Commission on Science and Technology for Development
Commission on Sustainable Development
Commission on the Status of Women
Population Commission
Statistical Commission

Regional Commissions ~
Economic Commission for Africa (ECA)
Economic Commission for Europe (ECE)
Economic Commission for Latin America and the Caribbean (ECLAC)
Economic and Social Commission for Asia and the Pacific (ESCAP)
Economic and Social Commission for Western Asia (ESCWA)

Sessional and Standing Committees ~

Expert, Ad Hoc and Related Bodies ~

The U.N. System

SECURITY COUNCIL	SECRETARIAT	TRUSTEESHIP COUNCIL

ILO +
International Labour Organisation

FAO +
Food and Agriculture Organization of the
United Nations

UNESCO +
United Nations Educational, Scientific and
Cultural Organization

WHO +
World Health Organization

IMF +
International Monetary Fund

ICAO +
International Civil Aviation Organization

UPU +
Universal Postal Union

ITU +
International Telecommunications Union

WMO +
World Meteorological Organization

IMO +
International Maritime Organization

WIPO +
World Intellectual Property Organization

IFAD +
International Fund for Agricultural
Development

UNIDO +
United Nations Industrial Development
Organization

GATT +
General Agreement on Tariffs and Trade
(Scheduled to become the World Trade
Organization–WTO- in January 1995)

World Bank Group
IBRD +
International Bank for Reconstruction and
Development (World Bank)

IDA +
International Development Association

IFC +
International Finance Corporation

MIGA +
Multilateral Investment Guarantee Agency

Peacekeeping Operations ~

Military Staff Committee ~
Standing Committees and Ad Hoc
Bodies ~

> United Nations programmes and organs
  (representative list only)

+ Specialized agencies and other
  autonomous organizations within the
  system

~ Other commissions, committees and ad
  hoc and related bodies

Printed courtesy of the United Nations

Index